CW01081028

THE METHOD OF FREEDOM
An Errico Malatesta Reader

THE METHOD OF FREEDOM

An Errico Malatesta Reader

Edited by
Davide Turcato

Original translations by
Paul Sharkey

The Method of Freedom: An Errico Malatesta Reader
© 2014 Edited by Davide Turcato. Original translations by Paul Sharkey.

This edition © 2014 AK Press (Oakland, Edinburgh, Baltimore).
ISBN: 978-1-84935-144-7 | eBook ISBN: 978-1-84935-155-3
Library of Congress Control Number: 2013945487

AK Press
674-A 23rd Street
Oakland, CA 94612
USA
www.akpress.org
akpress@akpress.org

AK Press
PO Box 12766
Edinburgh EH8 9YE
Scotland
www.akuk.com
ak@akedin.demon.co.uk

The above addresses would be delighted to provide you with the latest AK Press distribution catalog, which features the several thousand books, pamphlets, zines, audio and video products, and stylish apparel published and/or distributed by AK Press. Alternatively, visit our websites for the complete catalog, latest news, and secure ordering.

Cover design by John Yates (stealworks.com).
The production of this book was made possible in part by a generous donation from the Anarchist Archives Project.
Printed in the USA on acid-free paper.

CONTENTS

Introduction, Davide Turcato 1

I. "Whoever is Poor is a Slave": The Internationalist Period and the Exile in South America, 1871–89

1. Neapolitan Workers' Federation 9
2. Letter to the *Bulletin de la Fédération Jurassienne* 11
3. Dear Comrades at *Ilota* 13
4. The Republic of the Boys and that of the Bearded Men 17
5. The Economic Question 23
6. Program and Organization of the International Working Men's Association 33

II. "Let's Go to the People": *L'Associazione* and the London Years of 1889–97

7. About a Strike 69
8. Propaganda By Deeds 79
9. Another Strike 85
10. A Revolt is No Revolution 89
11. Our Plans 95
12. Matters Revolutionary 101
13. Anarchy 109
14. The Products of Soil and Industry 149
15. A Bit of Theory 155
16. Tactical Matters 161
17. The First of May 165
18. Let Us Go to the People 169
19. The Duties of the Present Hour 175
20. The General Strike and the Revolution 181
21. Anarchy and Violence 187
22. Doing Good by Force 193
23. Should Anarchists Be Admitted to the Coming International Congress? 195
24. Errors and Remedies 199

III. "A Long and Patient Work...": The Anarchist Socialism of *L'Agitazione*, 1897–98

25. The Socialists and the Elections: A Letter from E. Malatesta 209
26. From a Matter of Tactics to a Matter of Principle 213
27. A Few Words to Bring the Controversy to an End 219
28. Let Us be of Good Cheer! 225

29. The Duty of Resistance 229
30. Organization 233
31. Anarchism's Evolution 247
32. The Decline of the Revolutionary Spirit and the Need for Resistance 255
33. Anarchism in the Workers' Movement 259
34. Our Tactics 263

IV. "Toward Anarchy": Malatesta in America, 1899–1900

35. Against the Monarchy 269
36. Signor Malatesta Explains 277
37. An Anarchist Programme 279
38. The Anarchists' Task 295
39. Toward Anarchy 299

V. "The Armed Strike": The Long London Exile of 1900–13

40. The Monza Tragedy 307
41. The Armed Strike 315
42. In Relation to Strikes 319
43. The Workers' New International 327
44. Bourgeois Seepage Into Socialist Doctrine 331
45. Anarchism and Syndicalism 337
46. Anarchists and the Situation 343
47. Capitalists and Thieves 349
48. The War and the Anarchists 353

VI. "Is Revolution Possible?": *Volontà*, the Red Week, and the War, 1913–18

49. Liberty and Fatalism, Determinism and Will 363
50. Science and Social Reform 369
51. Is Revolution Possible? 375
52. The General Strike and the Insurrection in Italy 377
53. Anarchists Have Forgotten their Principles 379
54. Pro-Government Anarchists 385

VII. "United Proletarian Front": The Red Biennium, *Umanità Nova* and Fascism, 1919–23

55. The Dictatorship of the Proletariat and Anarchy 391
56. Thank You, but Enough Already 395
57. Untited Proletarian Front 397
58. This is Your Stuff! 399
59. The Two Routes: Reform or Revolution? Freedom or Dictatorship? 401
60. The Revolutionary "Haste" 411

61. Class Struggle or Class Hatred?: "People" and "Proletariat" 415
62. Revolution in Practice 419
63. Further Thoughts on Revolution in Practice 425
64. Interests and Ideals 431
65. Anarchists' Line within the Trade Union Movement 435

VIII. "Achievable and Achieving Anarchism": *Pensiero e Volontà* and Last Writings, 1924–32

66. "Idealism" and "Materialism" 445
67. Ideal and Reality 449
68. On "Anarchist Revisionism" 453
69. Individualism and Anarchism 459
70. Syndicalism and Anarchism 463
71. Gradualism 469
72. Let's Demolish—And Then? 475
73. A Project of Anarchist Organisation 481
74. Some Thoughts on the Post-Revolutionary Property System 493
75. The Anarchists in the Present Time 501
76. Against the Constituent Assembly as against the Dictatorship 507
77. Peter Kropotkin: Recollections and Criticisms By One of His Old Friends 511
78. Apropros of "Revisionism" 523

EDITOR'S INTRODUCTION

The most distinctive and universal anarchist principle is the principle of coherence between ends and means: human emancipation cannot be achieved by authoritarian means. However, the same principle could also be read in the opposite direction, though this is less frequently done: our ends should not be disconnected from our action; our ideals should not be so lofty as to make no difference to what we do here and now. The anarchist whose deeds and words have best illustrated both sides of that principle—the "idealist" and the "pragmatist" one—is Errico Malatesta.

Malatesta was born on 4 December 1853 in Santa Maria Capua Vetere. Southern Italy was then still ruled by the Bourbons, whose fall Malatesta witnessed as a child. As a young student in Naples, he adhered to republicanism, the party of revolution in Italian *Risorgimento*. However, under the impression of the Paris Commune in 1871 he turned to socialism, the rising gospel of social redemption, which, in Italy, was born anarchist. The next year Malatesta had his first encounter with Bakunin at the St. Imier congress, where the founding of the federalist International marked the birth of the anarchist movement. For the following six decades Malatesta's name would be linked to the history of that movement. He lived most of his adult life abroad as an exile and a workman, in countries of strong Italian migration and anarchist presence: France, Belgium, Switzerland, and Egypt in 1878–82; Argentina in 1885–89; the United States in 1899–1900; and England, more specifically in London, in 1889–97, 1900–13, and 1914–19. Yet for half a century he was a protagonist of all onsets of social struggle in Italy: the Benevento uprising of 1877, one of the first instances of propaganda by the deed and one of most popular and symbolic events in the history of the anarchist movement; the bread riots of 1898, which brought him to jail and then to forced residence, from whence he escaped in 1899; the insurrectionary Red Week in 1914, when the Romagna and the Marches remained for days in the hands of anarchists, republicans, and socialists; and the red biennium of 1919–20, when the factory occupation seemed to bring Italy on the verge of revolution. Malatesta died in Rome on 22 July 1932, under the heel of the fascist regime, in a state of undeclared house arrest.

Thus Malatesta was portrayed by his London fellow-exile Peter Kropotkin at the turn of the twentieth century: "Malatesta was a student of medicine, who had left the medical profession and also his fortune for the sake of the revolution; full of fire and intelligence, a pure idealist, who all his life—and he is now approaching the age of fifty—has never thought whether he would have a piece of bread for his supper and a bed for the night. Without even so much as a room that he could call his own, he would sell sherbet in the streets of London to get his living, and in the evening write brilliant articles for the Italian papers. Imprisoned in France, released, expelled, re-condemned in Italy, confined in an island, escaped, and again in Italy in disguise; always in the hottest of the struggle, whether it be in Italy or elsewhere,—he has persevered in this life for thirty years in succession. And when we meet him again, released from a prison or escaped from an island, we find him just as we saw him last; always renewing the struggle, with the same love of men, the same absence of hatred toward his adversaries and jailers, the same hearty smile for a friend, the same caress for a child."

Malatesta equally contributed to the anarchist movement with his action and his thought, which he could not conceive as separate. His pamphlets *Fra Contadini* (Between Peasants), *L'Anarchia* (Anarchy), and *Al Caffè* (At the Café) are among the greatest anarchist "best-sellers" of all times, with countless reprints and translations. However, his thought found expression above all in the myriads of articles scattered in the anarchist press around the world and in the numerous periodicals he edited: the two runs of *La Questione Sociale,* published in Florence in 1883–84 and in Buenos Aires in 1885; *L'Associazione,* which marked the beginning of Malatesta's first London exile, in 1889–90; *L'Agitazione,* published in Ancona in 1897–98, until the bread riots broke out; *La Questione Sociale* of Paterson, edited in 1899–1900 while he was in America; *La Rivoluzione Sociale,* appeared in London in 1902–03, during Malatesta's second London exile; *Volontà,* also published in Ancona, in 1913–14, until the Red Week; the anarchist daily *Umanità Nova,* in 1920–22; and *Pensiero e Volontà,* edited in Rome in 1924–26, well after the advent of fascism. Some of these are among the most significant periodicals in the history of anarchist thought.

In his writing, Malatesta has the rare ability of being both deep and clear. This is best illustrated by an example. In the *Anarchy* pamphlet, which we reprint in this volume, Malatesta defines anarchy in a single sentence: "Anarchy, in common with socialism, has as its basis, its point of departure, its essential environment, *equality of conditions*; its beacon is *solidarity* and *freedom* is its method." In its reference to the standard values of the French Revolution, *égalité, fraternité,* and *liberté,* the definition may seem a cliché. Yet, behind its deceptive simplicity, it expresses a whole, original conception of anarchism, which rests on the role assigned to each of those standard values. Equality of conditions means common ownership of the means of production, for there cannot be equality of conditions when a class monopolizes the means of production. Thus, a socialist society is being described here. Yet socialism is not an end-point; it is just a point of departure of an open-ended process. The beacon of that process is solidarity. By assigning the driver's seat of social evolution to an intentionally pursued value Malatesta is expressing a voluntarist view, in contrast to the marxist emphasis on the development of productive forces. And by assigning that seat to solidarity he is rejecting individualism. Finally, by advocating freedom as a method Malatesta is re-asserting free initiative in contrast to authoritarian socialism. Malatesta is offering no blueprint of the future society, yet his definition is strongly characterized in terms of the process: he is describing an experimentalist, pluralist, socialist open society.

Moreover, in defining anarchy in terms of a sentiment and a method—solidarity and freedom—that anarchists already practice here and now, Malatesta is positing continuity between the present society and the future one. And since that sentiment and that method are conscious choices of each individual, Malatesta's is a gradualist view of anarchy: the more people will embrace that sentiment and that value, the more broadly anarchy will be realized. In fact, immediately after the above definition, Malatesta explains that anarchy "is not perfection, it is not the absolute ideal which like the horizon recedes as fast as we approach it; but it is the way open to all progress and all improvements for the benefit of everybody."

We see here how coherence between ends and means works both ways for Malatesta. When ends are so abstract as to have no link with our present action, everybody can safely agree on those ends. Rather, Malatesta writes, "it is the method which above all distinguishes between the parties and determines their historical importance." Apart from the method, he adds, "they all talk of wanting the wellbeing of humanity." Therefore, "one must consider anarchy above all as a method." The distinctive method that anarchists have to offer is the method of freedom.

Malatesta explicitly introduced concepts like anarchist gradualism only in his late writings. However, their seeds can be detected much earlier. A deep coherence pervades Malatesta's entire action and thought, at the same time that both action and thought evolved under the impulse of experience. We have aimed to capture both Malatesta's coherence and pragmatism in this collection, which differs from previous ones in many respects. Since anthologies of Malatesta's writings, such as Vernon Richards's excellent *Life and Ideas,* usually have a thematic structure, they tend to give a flat and somewhat frozen image of Malatesta's ideas. Instead, for a man who was active in the anarchist movement for sixty years, the temporal dimension is crucial. We have added that missing dimension by giving our collection a chronological structure. Our aim is not, or not only, to present the "best" of Malatesta, but to document his entire trajectory. In this way we illustrate how different tactics were advocated at different times and make mature ideas better understood by putting them in perspective. This involves including early writings, which the late Malatesta might no longer have fully subscribed to, and documenting not only the "high" moments, but also the more obscure transition phases, such as the years 1894 and 1899, which constitute fundamental turning points in Malatesta's theory and tactics. We have also aimed to represent Malatesta's full range of writings, from pamphlets to long theoretical articles, to occasional but illuminating arguments. All writings are presented in their entirety.

A prominent criterion in editing Malatesta's texts has been documentary accuracy. Articles originally published in English have been reprinted without changes, aside from the correction of obvious typos. Likewise, when we have used previously published translations of Malatesta's articles, we have compared them with the sources and amended them only where mistranslations or omissions made the original meaning unrecoverable. Otherwise, we have refrained from making stylistic changes, even when the translations would have likely benefited from them.

The greatest asset of this collection is that it is the first one to be based on Malatesta's complete works, which are in the process of being published and whose temporal partition is closely mirrored here. Traditionally, anthologies are based on Malatesta's latest, or best known, or most readily available periodicals. Instead, we have tapped into Malatesta's entire production and included key articles that have never appeared before in English or have been long forgotten. Nearly two thirds of the seventy-eight texts included here have been newly translated and printed for the first time in English, while many of the remaining articles have never been reprinted after their first and only appearance in the anarchist and socialist English-language press of Malatesta's time.

We like to think of this collection as a contribution to establishing the cultural dignity of the anarchist tradition, which anarchists themselves have sometimes unwittingly concurred to downplay by misdirecting their iconoclasm to their predecessors. That tradition has in Malatesta one of its best representatives, whose clarity of thought remains hard to surpass.

Davide Turcato

Malatesta during his internationalist years

I.

"Whoever is Poor is a Slave": The Internationalist Period and the Exile in South America, 1871–89

Until the mid 1880s Malatesta's activity unfolded under the banner of the International, first as an actual organization, then as a project he tried to revive. For young republicans like Malatesta, socialism meant the discovery of the "social question": formal equality and freedom were a mockery in the presence of material inequality and submission to capitalists. As Marx had emphasized, economic matters were at the root of all political, religious, and other social matters. "Whoever is poor is a slave" was one the young internationalists' catch phrases. Malatesta's own periodical, tellingly titled *La Questione Sociale*, sported that phrase in its masthead. Long after the International's demise, Malatesta's hopes to re-establish it were still alive. His program of 1884 bore witness to this effort and summed up his internationalist beliefs. Then, in 1885 Malatesta fled to Argentina to escape a conviction for criminal association. This marked the end of Malatesta's internationalist period. However, the experience of the First International, informed by that reliance on workers, collective action, and organization that constituted the common denominator of socialists of all persuasions, would imprint forever his anarchism.

1. NEAPOLITAN WORKERS' FEDERATION[1]

No rights without duties. No duties without rights.[2]

The Neapolitan Workers' Federation recognizes and proclaims the following principles:

1. All beings human in nature are equal and, since they all share the same rights and duties, there are *no rights without duties, no duties without rights.*

2. Since labor is a human necessity, there is a duty upon all to labor and everyone is entitled to enjoyment of the entire product of his labor.

3. For that very reason, the instruments of labor and raw materials belong to the whole of humanity and everyone is entitled to make use of them in pursuit of his own activities.[3]

4. Every individual born is entitled to be reared, fed, and educated technically, comprehensively and equally by the collective to which he has ties, and that collective is under a duty to guarantee and uphold his freedom of choice in whatever area of expertise.

5. Union, association and federation between individuals and collectives should be voluntary and achieved from the bottom up.

6. To us, the implementation of this represents the authentic Emancipation of the Proletariat, that being the great—the only goal—towards which all of our efforts should be directed; these, ipso facto, being directed, not at the establishment of fresh privileges, but at the establishment of a universal equality of rights and duties.

---

1 Originally published as an undated flyer around the end of 1871. The present translation is from the reprint in Max Nettlau, *Bakunin e l'Internazionale in Italia: dal 1864 al 1872* (Geneva, 1928).

2 This motto was part of the preamble to the provisional rules of the International and was one of two sentences that Marx had inserted there as a concession to the moral language of members that followed the Italian republican Giuseppe Mazzini.

3 This point and the previous one, together, formulate collectivism, the belief in the common ownership of the means of production and the individual enjoyment of the products of one's labor.

7. Since the cause of labor recognizes no borders, has no fatherland other than the world, and cannot succeed without the unanimous agreement of all the world's workers, the *Neapolitan Workers' Federation,* founded upon the precepts of freedom and autonomy, stands with all those nuclei and Workers' Societies across the world that set themselves the same purpose as that for which it was established.[4]

The Federal Secretary:
Errico Malatesta, student.

[The signatures of nine Federation members, including Carlo Cafiero, follow.]

4 As Max Nettlau notes, this point expresses membership in the International in a necessarily vague form because the International had been banned by the authorities in Naples. The points from the second to the fifth reflect Bakunin's ideas, while the others summarize items from the preamble to the provisional rules of the International.

2.
LETTER TO THE *BULLETIN DE LA FÉDÉRATION JURASSIENNE*[1]

Comrades,

In light of a number of inaccuracies and omissions in the official minutes of the Berne Congress, certain newspapers have drawn from the report presented by us on the situation and principles of the International in Italy some conclusions that do not quite match with the facts.[2] We therefore ask you to carry the following statement in your newspaper:

1. We never said anything that might lead one to suppose that in Italy the International was split into two branches subscribing to two different schools of thought. The vast majority of Italian socialists have rallied around the Italian Federation's anarchist, collectivist, revolutionary program, and the few who have, thus far, as a consequence of intrigues and lies, remained outside, are now all beginning to enter our organization. We are not referring here to a tiny group that, being prompted by personal views and reactionary purposes, is out to conduct what it terms "gradual and peaceful" propaganda: these people have already been judged by the Italian socialists and represent no one but themselves.

2. The Italian Federation holds that the *act of insurrection*, designed to assert socialist principles through deeds, is the most effective method of propaganda and the only one that, without deceiving and corrupting the masses, can delve into the deepest strata of society and draw the cream of humanity into the struggle, backed by the International.[3]

3. The Italian Federation looks upon collective ownership of

---

1 Translated from *Bulletin de la Fédération Jurassienne* (Sonvillier) 5, no. 49 (3 December 1876).

2 Malatesta and Cafiero, co-authors of this letter, had been among the delegates of the Italian Federation to the congress of the federalist branch of the International held in Berne at the end of October 1876. The letter summarizes some of the key views held by the Italian Federation at the time.

3 Malatesta and Cafiero are expressing here the tactics that would later come to be known as "propaganda by the deed," of which the Benevento uprising of the next year would be a notable example.

the products of labor as the necessary complement to the collectivist program, *the contribution by all towards the meeting of each and everyone's needs* being the only rule of production and consumption compatible with the principle of solidarity.[4] The federal congress in Florence has eloquently expressed the Italian International's view on this issue, as well as on the preceding one.

Greetings and solidarity.
The Italian federal delegates to the
Berne Congress:
Errico Malatesta
Carlo Cafiero

4 This is one of the earliest statements in which the replacement of collectivism with communism—"the collective ownership of the products of labor"—is advocated. In the months preceding the Berne congress the issue had been discussed by Malatesta, Cafiero, and others during conversations in Naples. They had come to the conclusion that the traditional bakuninist formula of collectivism had to be abandoned in favor of communism. This change of perspective had been approved by the congress of the Italian Federation, held near Florence a few days before the Berne congress, and then expressed at Berne by Malatesta and Cafiero.

3.
DEAR COMRADES AT *ILOTA*[1]

I have watched the efforts you have been making to step up the socialist party's organizing and I congratulate you upon them. Organization represents the very life and strength of a party and without it we would not even be able to effectively spread our program, let alone try to implement it.

But it strikes me that in offering a broad outline of the sort of organization we want, you have made a serious mistake that might generate either failure today or the certainty of our breaking up in the future.

Out of an excessive love of unity and concord, you would like to see us organized regardless of differences of opinion regarding aims and means, the only bond between us being the shared aspiration for some vague, indeterminate socialism.

If a party—especially a party of action—is to thrive, it needs to be aware of the goal it intends to reach and especially the means by which it intends to reach it. Otherwise, it is inescapably doomed to remain powerless and to peter out amidst internal differences.

I am certainly not referring to those secondary differences of opinion that are not indicative of definitive parting of the ways. For instance, there is the view that oral propaganda may be more effective than the printed word, or that the pamphlet is preferable to the newspaper, urban insurrection over armed bands, attacks upon property over attacks upon the person, the Irishman's dagger over the Russian's mine, or vice versa, without there being anything to inhibit membership of the same organization. These are matters to be resolved in different ways depending on circumstances and means that are not mutually exclusive and upon which, in the worst

1 Translated from "Cari Compagni dell'*Ilota*," *Ilota* (Pistoia) 1, no. 9 (1 April 1883). The background to this letter was the defection from anarchism of Andrea Costa, one of the chief members of the Italian Federation, who in 1879 had started advocating the extension of socialist tactics to parliamentary ones. Costa had a significant following, especially in the Romagna region, and in November 1882 he had been elected to parliament. His tactics had sparked heated debates in part of the socialist press, and *Ilota* was one of the periodicals that considered those tactics legitimate. In a recent series of articles, the *Ilota* had thus called for the union and joint organization of all socialist forces, despite the tactical differences.

scenario, a revolutionary can defer to majority opinion for the sake of the need for agreement.

But when it comes to programs that are, or are believed to be, incompatible, how can you ever amalgamate them and bring together folk who from the word "go" must bicker and fight with one another?

How, for instance, do you propose to organize me alongside a legalitarian, when I believe that driving the people towards the ballot box and getting them to hope that parliament can bring us reforms likely to make our task easier, already means betraying the cause of socialism? A legalitarian, at best, looks upon universal suffrage as a gain that can be a great boost to the socialist party; whereas I believe it is the best means the bourgeoisie has for oppressing and blithely exploiting the people. He sees universal suffrage as a first step in the direction of emancipation; I see it as the secret to getting the slave to fasten his own chains and a guarantee against revolt, getting the slave to believe he is the master.

So how would you see us united? While he will be campaigning to secure such voting rights and, when he gets them, to persuade the people to exercise them, I will be striving to prevent voting rights being *granted* or, if they are, to ensure that the ballot-boxes are empty and held in contempt.

I do not wish to dwell upon the reasons of either side here. No matter which of us is right, it makes no difference to the fact that, until such time as one side wins the other over, we cannot seriously hope to see them being useful members of the same organization. This is not the first time I have advanced this notion.

When the volte-face, which is now known by the slick euphemism "Costa's *evolution,*" came about, Costa did all he could to hide the changes he was making to our shared program and strove to preserve the party's unity—despite the shattered unity around the program—by insisting that we were all basically in agreement. We alerted people to the danger, underlined the differences, and tried to save the revolutionary party, even at the price of seeing its ranks thinned.

We were overruled, and instead of there being, as there should be, two co-existing parties that would spur each other on, what we had instead was, primarily, disorganization, impotence, personality clashes, coolness, and a muddling of things and ideas. And wherever the party remained more or less united, as it did in Romagna, it was because of bamboozlement and deceptions and a change that was designed to arrive at an extreme lullaby socialism, and was swallowed by our comrades at an undetectable snail's pace, without their even being conscious of where they were being led. Luckily, we've seen signs that make us hopeful that, soon, the stalwart socialists of Romagna, who are and have always been revolutionaries, will come to their senses, see where they have been tricked, and feel all of the outrage and wonder that they would have felt years ago, had they been told then that "you are to have a representative who will sit in His Majesty's parliament on behalf of the *Romagna democratic coalition*, a colleague and friend to the bourgeoisie's representatives."

Now that enlightenment has finally arrived, do we want to travel once again the very trail that did the Italian socialist party so much damage, and call for a sinking of the deep-seated differences between us and build a unity founded upon a deceitful outward agreement?

That might suit someone eager for a seat in the benches of Montecitorio,[2] who therefore needs to do his best to muster a large body of voters, but it will not suit us who are out to make the revolution.

Without letting ourselves be deceived by beloved traditions ruined beyond recovery by treachery, in practice today there is less real difference between us and the action-oriented republicans—with whom we can travel at least the first stage along the road (namely, armed insurrection against the monarchy)—than there is between us and those who lull the socialists and harness socialism into serving the interests of whichever faction of the bourgeoisie finds it expedient to dress itself in red.

And Costa showed that he was perfectly well aware of the situation when he was shunned by the socialists in Naples and sought a recommendation from Bovio, happily sitting at a republican banquet alongside the Honourable Mr. Aporti.[3]

Let Costa do what he will: we shall not lift a finger to slow his political downfall since we regard him as doomed to sink to the bottom of the slippery slope.

But let us organize ourselves.

Yes, let us marshal all of our party's resources, but let us remember that, as far as we revolutionaries, we insurrectionists are concerned, those who uphold parliamentarianism are not welcome in our party.

---

2 Montecitorio is the seat of the Italian Chamber of Deputies.

3 Giovanni Bovio was a philosopher and republican politician, and Pirro Aporti was a senator of the extreme left.

It will, assuredly, be painful parting company with old comrades. It will affect me as much as anyone else, since among my adversaries there are dear friends who were, for a long time, my companions in prison, in exile, in poverty, and who will, I hope, be my companions on the barricades and share in our victory.

But whenever the talk turns to the interests of the revolution, all considerations of personality must be silenced. We reach out a hand to all who believe, in good faith, that they serve the revolution's interests and we cling to the hope that we may see them follow their hearts. But our party should be *our* party and our organization should be *our* organization. And that organization should be the International Working Men's Association, whose program, hatched over a long time, rings out today as COMMUNISM, ANARCHY and REVOLUTION.

So, comrades, let us close the ranks of that association, which its deserters, having tried in vain to kill it off, are busy proclaiming dead, because the association's existence is a standing rebuke to their behavior, and because the remorse of abandoning it may be pricking their conscience.

Yours, Enrico Malatesta[4]

4 Though Malatesta's first name was Errico, many called him Enrico. Accordingly, articles and published letters often contained the latter spelling in his signature.

4. THE REPUBLIC OF THE BOYS AND THAT OF THE BEARDED MEN[1]

About fifteen years ago, this writer was a youngster studying rhetoric and Roman history, Greek, Latin, and Giobertian philosophy.[2]

Despite the best efforts of my teachers, schooling did not managed to stifle my nature and, in the stultifying, corruptive modern high school setting, I managed to keep my mind wholesome and my heart unblemished.

By nature affectionate and impassioned, I dreamed of an ideal world in which all would love one another and be happy. Whenever I wearied of daydreams, I succumbed to reality, took a look around me, and saw: here, someone shivering from cold and hunger and meekly seeking alms in the shape of a crust of bread; there, some children crying; and over yonder, some men mouthing curses; and my heart froze in horror.

Later, I was more vigilant and realized that a tremendous injustice—a nonsensical system—was grinding humanity down and condemning it to pain; labor was degraded and almost regarded as dishonorable, the working man dying of hunger so there was food for his idle master's orgies. As my heart was swollen with rage, I was reminded of the Gracchi and Spartacus and I could feel the spirit of the tribune and the rebel inside me.

And as I had often heard it said that the republic is the very negation of what was worrying me, and that in the republic all men are equals; since wherever and whenever the echo of a rebellion of the wretches and slaves reached me from, it was intermingled with the word "republic"; and since we in school were left in ignorance of the modern world so that we might be rendered dolts by the truncated, phoney history of ancient Rome, and would never have been able to

1 Translated from "La repubblica dei giovanetti e quella degli uomini colla barba," *La Questione Sociale* (Florence) 1, no. 3 (5 January 1884).

2 The philosopher and politician Vincenzo Gioberti was the author of *Primato morale e civile degli Italiani,* published in 1843, where he argued for Italy's superiority over the other European nations.

find a mode of social coexistence outside of the Roman formulae, I called myself a republican and, it seemed to me, that made up for all of the desires and wrath swirling in my head.

I was not clear as to what this republic would be like , but I reckoned I knew and that was enough for me: in my eyes, the republic was the kingdom of equality, love, and happiness; it was the loving dream of my imagination become reality.

Oh, how my heart beat in my youthful breast! I imagined myself now as some modern day Brutus, plunging a blade into the breast of a latter-day Caesar; or at the head of a band of rebels; or atop a barricade, scattering the tyrant's acolytes; or I imagined myself on a rostrum, thundering against the people's enemies. I measured my height and stroked my lips to see if any whiskers had sprouted; oh, how I yearned to be grown up and to leave high school and commit myself entirely to the republican cause!

That day finally arrived and I entered the outside world filled with selfless intentions, filled with hopes and dreams.

The republic had been so much the stuff of my dreams that I could not help but scurry to wherever I had been told there was a republican venture, aspiration or yearning; and it was as a republican that I had my first sight of the king's jails.

But then I had second thoughts. I studied the history that I had previously learned from inane, lying textbooks and saw how the republic had always turned out to be a government like any other—or even worse than the rest—and that under the republic, as under the monarchy, there is wretchedness and injustice and the people are mown down when they try to shrug off the yoke.

I looked around the contemporary world and saw that countries where there is a republic are no better off than those under a monarchy. There is a republic in America, and, for all her expanses of free land, for all her super-abundant production, there are people starving to death. They have a republic, but despite the freedom and equality written into the constitution, the poor man has no human dignity, and the cavalry uses its clubs or sabres to disperse workers clamoring for bread and jobs. They have their republic, but the native peoples are reduced to desperate straits and hunted down like wild animals... What am I saying? In America, as in Rome and in Greece before her, we have seen that the republic is compatible with slavery!

There's a republic in Switzerland, yet there is poverty, the Protestant and Catholic clergy rule the roost, and one cannot live in a city without a residence permit, and the free citizens of Switzerland trade their votes for a few glasses of beer!

There's a republic in France (it had recently been established, then) and it started its existence with the slaughter of 50,000 Parisians. It remains deferential towards the clergy and it sends its troops in whenever the workers raise their heads, to force submission to the bosses and quiet acceptance of their wretchedness.

So I said to myself, the republic is not what I dreamt it was; the high-school student's vague aspiration was to one thing, but the reality was different, very different. My oldest comrades, the ones I thought of as my teachers, had indeed said that the republics in existence were not real republics and that, in Italy, the republic would deliver justice, equality, liberty, well-being; but I knew that the same things had been said in France prior to the triumph of the republic, and I also knew that similar things had been said and promised by every single party needing the people's support in order to ascend to power... and I wanted to see things clearly.

The nature of a society, I reckoned, cannot depend on names and incidental forms, but rather must depend on the relationship of each member with the other members and with the society as a whole. Neither could the effect of a change in society be determined solely by the wishes and intentions of the party that advocates it, since a party that accepts and subscribes to certain positions suffers the consequences, or it gets caught up in hatching rebellions that come to nothing until that party makes up its mind to change its position.

I began to probe the very essence of modern society, the nature of social relations, the derivation of public powers, the operation of political and economic factors and everything prompted me to conclude that there is essentially no difference between monarchy and republic. So I was no longer surprised that republics bear such a strong resemblance to monarchies.

As man's primary need and the essential prerequisite of existence is that he is able to eat, it is only natural that the character of a society is determined primarily by the manner in which man secures the means of survival, how wealth is produced and distributed... Economic factors dominate every aspect of the life of society.

Under a monarchy, all means of production are in the hands of a few individuals, and the masses, who have nothing but their labor force, have to seek work from those who own those means, and must abide by their conditions. The distribution of goods is based on the reciprocal but unequal need that bosses and workers have of each other and on the competition between the famished. And since the bosses enjoy the benefit of an established position and can fall back upon their savings, whereas the worker needs to work on a daily basis in order to eat, and since, also, there are generally more workers than the bosses need, the working man's wages do not normally exceed what is strictly necessary for the most primitive and vegetative survival. And so, at the end of the day, under a monarchy we find a tiny ruling class that is corrupt and corrupting, and on the other side, the impoverished and brutalized masses.

Would a republic be any different? Certainly not, since the republic preserves the foundation of the present organization—private property—and cannot escape the consequences of that ownership model.

But, as the more advanced republicans object, under the republic it is the people that command by means of universal suffrage: let us make our republic and the people, should they see fit, will amend the ownership arrangements. But universal suffrage can be found under the monarchy, too, and the people use it to endorse their subject status; how on earth could the people acquire the consciousness and capability they lack today just by sending the king packing and swapping one status for another? But the republic has been made time and time again in many countries, and universal suffrage has not been any more productive than it is under the monarchy. Why would it be any different this time?

What does it matter if some right is granted to the people, when the people are not equipped with the means to exercise it? As I have already stated, economic factors dominate everything: a people dying of hunger will always be stupid and slavish, and, if they vote, will vote for their masters.

We need to move beyond republican thinking and instead of accepting the present economic position as our starting point, we need to make a fresh start by radically altering it, and effectively doing away with private ownership. Then we will assure our survival, will all be equal in terms of wealth, and may well be able to begin to understand one another.

All of these things passed through my mind and before my eyes, and what happens to all men of feeling who investigate the laws of human coexistence without preconceptions happened to me: I was horrified by the republic, which is a form of government whose sole use is that—like every other government—it sanctions and champions established privileges… And I turned into a socialist.

Selfless youngsters, who share this dream of a republic that will deliver peace and well being: Think again! The real republic, the republic of the rulers, is not the one I dreamed of at school. Once the republic has been made, if you remain pure and honest like you are today, you will be going to jail or will be mown down just the same as you would be today. At that point you will feel betrayed, but that will not be true: you will have reaped just what you sowed.

5.
THE ECONOMIC QUESTION[1]

The greatest discovery of this century was made by the International when it proclaimed that *the economic question is fundamental* in Sociology, and that other matters—political, religious, etc.,—are merely its reflections, perhaps even the shadows it casts.

Indeed, in the past, lacking this key, all political problems (in the broadest sense, encompassing everything related to the existence of society) were insoluble, indeed, unfathomable.

In Greece, for instance, in order to deliver the greatest well-being to the people, they sought the best government, or "the government of the most." But in the end, it turned out that *government is always government by the few* and not by the best either *but by scoundrels*—whether monarchist, aristocratic, or democratic, it was still despotic or, to use a modern term, *the business of the haves*.

Rome came closer to the truth, when it looked for the phoenix of social well-being in *equality of circumstance for all citizens of the State*. The agrarian laws that were proclaimed twenty-seven centuries ago from atop the Campidoglio, plus the social and slave wars show that there was some vague inkling of the truth: that *economic circumstances are the real yardstick of the civil and political status* of a man or a class. But having an inkling is one thing and understanding and announcing it is quite another; the first being a glimmer and the other a light. The vagueness of the idea was mirrored in the vagueness of the set of demands that went by the name of "primitive Christianity"; and the weak sunbeams were soon swallowed up by the darkness of the Middle Ages.

There, too, the struggles for political power flared up: the *economic question* resurfaced timidly in the Communes, but fed into petty internecine strife and was not the banner of widespread social upheaval. Democracies, aristocracies, tyrannies—here again we have the terms designed to solve the enigma. And centuries more of experience, right up until our own day, up until the French revolution, up until 1860, up until almost today, have borne out the principle that:

1 Translated from "Questione economica," *La Questione Sociale* (Florence) 1, no. 13 (29 June 1884).

all established governments, founded as they are upon inequalities of circumstances, are despotic and monopolise the national wealth; that the political question cannot be resolved, nor any other *issue of interest to society,* unless there is a *resolution of the economic question.*

This truth is the big advance on the present century and the compendium, the quintessence of theoretical and practical socialism, the key to the resolution of all the problems that tax our brains and torment our hearts; it has burst forth from three sources simultaneously: from the workers' painful experiences of the freest forms of government; from study of the relations between Capital and Labor, which is to say, Economics; and finally from the brand new *positive* approach of the Social Sciences. Therefore it represents the hinge of Science and modern history; it had brought a far-reaching revolution of ideas, and lays the groundwork for a no less grandiose one in the realm of facts.

Let us get used to *expressing* all social problems that may crop up as the *economic question* and reducing them to this formula:

Economic inequality is the source of all moral, intellectual, political, etc. inequalities.

In other words, let us try to *talk with precision,* for, as Condorcet says, Science is a well-made language, and we shall be on the right road.

We offer a few examples:

The Emancipation of Woman

Woman's emancipation is a topic that has been debated over and over again to the point of exhaustion, seriously and for a laugh, with varying degrees of success, albeit with no outcome, not even a theoretical one. Some argue that woman is born *inferior* to man, like the slave to the master; others want to see her become his equal. Physiology, history, anthropology, etc. have been invoked by one and all, and nothing has come of it all.

If, instead, it had been said that, "The matter is an entirely economic one. With feudalism gone, with there being no more dowries and estates; with withdrawal into a convent no longer an option; with property so jeopardized that *in order to survive everyone has to rely upon his own resources*—that is, upon his labors, if he is a worker, or his industry, if he is a capitalist—by what right is a woman to be told: you are barred from labor and from industry, you are barred from life and are a burnt offering to some old prejudice, or rather to some *law governing the allocation of functions within the family* that is better suited to other times, other institutions, other circumstances?" If it had been put like that, and if the conclusion drawn from that was that *woman today should go out to work, choosing, as any man does, whatever work she had the greatest aptitude for,* would a genuine solution to the problem not have been arrived at? Would that solution not hit the nail on the head? Does *the women's problem not lead back to the men's problem,* that is, to the question of labor—which should be incumbent upon us all and should be shared by everyone—which is to say, to the *economic question*?

Let us stress, however, that today the *economic question* can be resolved only theoretically; *work by all and for all* is still an aspiration of Science and Humanity; in practice we have *competition,* which is to say, *civil war* between workers, man versus woman, adult versus child, and capitalist versus all. *One man's meat is another man's poison; your death is my life.* Hence, the resistance to the *economic emancipation* of womankind; hence the *current* impossibility of any such emancipation. *The emancipation of woman, as of man, can only come about in a new social order.*

Religious Matters

We come now to an equally important matter: the religious question. Contrary to what it might appear, this too is an *economic question,* and it is precisely because of its not having been examined from that angle that the apostles of Freethought have failed thus far. Their theories have made no inroads among the masses, and despite the wrangles between State and Church—which they could and should have turned to their advantage—and the modern Sciences' *general consent* in favor of Freethought, they have not managed to *snatch* a single soul away from the Satan in the Vatican, nor wrested as much as one yard of ground from the rule of Pope and cardinals. The religious question is, as we have stated, an economic one. In actual fact, a religion has two component parts: theory and organization. The philosophical and moral truths that make up a religion's theory are not up for debate; they may be the *truth* or they may well be *errors,* but since the *truth,* like any human matter, is forever bettering itself, that which is *true* at one point in time, or that which is suited to the thinking and expression of a given time, no longer suits in a different one. The Roman Church itself has had to adopt a different language between one century and another and, like it or not, an encyclical today is written differently from a Bull from the first or second Christian eras. So it is not the theory that makes up the Church, but the organization.

The organization of the Church, and of every church from every age, is a perfect fit for that of Governments. We have the same hierarchy, the same *top-to-bottom* descending order—at the top, the power, the wealth, the enormous stipends; down below, debasement, passive obedience, meager lives and meager stipends. The difference between Church and State lies solely in the *way they extract from the people what is needed to feed and sustain their hierarchy*. They both extract it from the people, one by means of *lesser coercion* than the other; one by means of superstition, the other through the use of force. In other words, Government and Church, meaning the ruling and dominant classes, have adopted the following rationale: The people, they have said to themselves, can be divested of their possessions in two ways; either through threats or through persuasion, or rather, through the threat of earthly punishments or the terror of other-worldly punishments. These two means cannot be used by the same power at the same time. So the Church said to the State: Let us divide the task; you can enjoy the *dominion of force, leaving the safer, quieter dominion of fraud to me*; as for you, O people, *render unto Caesar that which is Caesar's, and to Christ that which is Christ's*, and never weary of giving. Besides, the Church has always told the State: I shall unfailingly uphold your rights through my preaching and my excommunications, my encyclicals, in short, my *moral arsenal*; and, if need be, you will put my enemies—Albigensians, Arnalds of Brescia, Giordano Brunos, and such like—to the stake. Ours is a redoubtable partnership.

They have said this and they have delivered. The Church has usurped half of the world, the other half has been seized by the State. An anecdote recounted by Washington Irving in his biography of George Washington comes to mind: Irving speaks of certain native American tribes torn between the English (who they described as their "fathers") and the French (who nominated themselves their "brothers"). One day these poor natives sent the message to representatives of the two powers that went something like this: It is all very well your being *fathers and brothers*; but the moment either of you tries to take half of our land, what is left to us who are doomed to live surrounded by "fathers" and "brothers"? Which is where the People stand today where Church and State are concerned. Of course, once Church and State had seized everything, they finished up squabbling between themselves about who should have the lion's share. The Church argued that the State was indebted to it for the obedience of the populace, and this was the truth. The State argued that the Church was obliged to it for its tolerance and for its occasional *armed favors,* and this was very true. Here again the knot linking Church and State could not be unravelled, it involved *tithes, patronage, cardinals' caps,* etc., until they both realized that, just like the stomach and the limbs, they needed each other, and so they patched things up, so as to carry on their old tricks at the people's expense.

And note too that the soil is not the only thing that they have pretty much carved up between them. *The Church has a system of levies very much like the State's.* From birth to death, it is forever pestering you for pennies; pennies being a figure of speech, for in fact its levies are pretty substantial. It is hard to believe what the Church levies voluntarily from the faithful under a hundred different names—*Mass charges, alms, funeral charges, death duties, parish funds, St Peter's pence, etc.* The Church is made up of the faithful, their offerings and vows. On the proceeds of all these *voluntary levies,* which we pay to the Clergy, they live a life of idleness and keep their... housekeepers. They charge us millions even for the making of saints; and the lifestyles of Monsignors and Cardinals are known to all. The Church has this going for it: that it manages to *milk the poorest people*; in its view, there is not a pauper, bankrupt, or beggar exempt from contributing. It *usurps the pauper's alms*; and marries the utmost arrogance to the basest degradation; it is a brazen mendicant, the most irksome and repugnant sort of human being.

In short, Church policy can be summed up by the Archbishop of Seus's famous dictum: *The Clergy's contribution is prayer,* so it makes a living out of praying. The Church is the *class of those who have ducked out of their labor obligations in order to devote themselves to God*; as if the believers' God, having sentenced all to labor, has made an exception for this one class.

The religious question therefore also boils down to the *issue of labor,* or the *economic question.* The labors of the priest are on a par with those of the usurer, the stock-broker, the collector of State taxes; the priest being nothing but a collector of ecclesiastical taxes. In any case, any man can serve as his own priest. The class comprised of those who *dodge work using the pretext of prayer,* is the one that needs abolishing: let the workers who labor so mightily give some thought to this: that, for want of the time to pray, they are in danger of going to hell.

Education

Education is talked about. The Palermo Congress did well to declare: *he who does not have enough to live on, is in no position to go to school.*[2] Then again, the *struggle for survival* means that every new student, every educated worker, harms the rest. Reserved for the would-be ruling class, education has to be a monopoly; how else, other than a little difference in cleverness, without politics, laws, and official Science, etc., being shrouded in secrecy, can millions of workers be held at bay?

We shall be instructed, and that instruction will reflect our callings and we shall help one another to understand and investigate once the *economic question* has been answered. We are always around.

Right to Combine

Strikes, or the right to *combine.* The question is this: how is it that workers, who are the majority, cannot bring the bosses to obedience, using their own weapons against them, and thus grappling with them on the economic terrain? From Mill comes the answer:

"A property-owner, landlord, manufacturing boss, and merchant can, generally speaking, survive for a year or two on monies he has saved up, without employing a single worker. Most of the workers could not survive a week, very few of them a month, and hardly any of them a year without work. In the long run, the employer can no more do without the worker than the worker without the employer, but the employer's is not so pressing a need." Besides, the bosses use the weapons at their disposal in order to break or corrupt the working man. Workers' unions are faced by employers' unions; and the victory goes to the deepest pockets. Mill himself says that "when it comes to sorting out major issues, small assets do not do the job" and it requires large ones if the socio-economic question is to be resolved.

2 A Universal Workers' Congress had taken place in Palermo in 1882, on the occasion of the sixth centennial of the Sicilian Vespers movement.

Political liberty and universal suffrage

Freedom of the press, of assembly, of association, and all the political freedoms in the world—Universal Suffrage included—cannot do the trick. The facts show as much: but what is the reason for this? Those with no understanding of social issues shrug their shoulders and say that the fault lies in those who do not know how to make use of them. No, the fault lies with them as they persist in gazing at the moon in the bottom of the well. *Freedom between less than equals is the consecration of the whim of the one at the top.* As long as it suits his purpose, the latter will exercise freedom, only to renege upon it as soon as it serves the purposes of his adversaries. Universal Suffrage is a snare; it may be the People that do the electing, but the person elected is the boss, the Sovereign. *No matter what class they may be drawn from, the deputies make up a discrete class, which is the class of those who live off the backs of the People.* Their interests fly in the face of those of the people from whom they receive their mandates. Hence the talk of disloyalty, betrayal, etc. Empty verbiage: to date, every deputy has turned traitor, and every one of them will! *Inequality of economic circumstances*—that is the worm in the bud of every freedom.

Government

We come now to dwell somewhat upon Government.

Be it absolute, constitutional, or republican, it is always an East India Company; one class commands, the other obeys; one enjoys a life of leisure on the exertions of other people, and the other is whipped from pillar to post, without so much as a crust of bread to call their own. Here too, behind the semblance of a *political question*, under the veil of unusual verses, there is nothing, and nothing lurks but the *economic question* of working versus not working, eating versus starving to death.

Government consists in *levying taxes from the people and sharing the proceeds around the members of the ruling class.*

We know that every tax hits the poor man; the land tax is paid by the tenant, the farmer, the consumer; indirect taxes are paid by the consumer. And the poorer one is, the more one pays; thus the poor man uses more salt and pays the same levy on poor quality wine as the rich man pays on better quality wines, etc. In short—all the economists concede as much—*the poorer one gets, the heavier the tax take*. Furthermore, being deputies, civil servants, etc., the ruling class enjoys certain privileges such as, say, reduced rail fares, free use of the trams, etc.; whereas the poor man pays more than anyone else.

Now, if one adds up the levies that the State demands year after year, the Public Purse, the assets stripped from private owners, the pious works it administers, its Private account, and the Banks it operates or runs, the sums would number in the billions. And then we are surprised by people starving to death!

This is what it demands; let us have a look at how it shares it! Let us take a look around us: who lives like Croesus or like Sardanapalus? A few bankers, deputies, a few officials. Otherwise we can only lament the general pauperism.

A Minister is in fact a deputy on a glorious stipend, who can call upon a few million in unforeseen and extra-ordinary expenses, who can give out or take away jobs, who can negotiate with the Stock Exchange and win, who creams off a percentage from every big State contract, and finally, upon stepping down from his post, becomes a wealthy property-owner.

The deputy in the Chamber is a potential Minister, a key figure in the conclusion of big deals. Take the railway contracts, say: the Company will make billions at the nation's expense, but every deputy has his own *share portfolio*; so, by voting for the Contracts, he *lines his pockets*, meaning that he *turns that Nation to his personal profit*. So, no matter how scandalous they may be, the Contracts will be passed; just the way the Tobacco Regulations, the laws on the National Bank passed and so on and so on! Every one of these laws, we note, saw billions siphoned off.

And the deputy has a foothold in the Civil Service, can expedite matters and advance his own profession at the expense of others (one need only think of the deputies who are lawyers), and, as in the case of provincial and town councillors, can come up with a way of *making a living despite not lifting a finger*. Puzzling! Yet this is the fact of the matter.

Then again, *in his constituency*, the deputy is a king in octodecimo; he can appoint and dismiss prefects, allocate posts, fix the city budget, buy up public and private assets, build himself a castle. All hail the new feudal lord!

We have pretty much stated what civil servants are: the clientele of ministers and deputies and of the State generally. They are many and they noisily chant homilies and hymns to the King and Homeland. They are the State's *political electoral army*.

The army and the police and the bench are the *hand* of Government and of the ruling class, ready to lash out and command obedience from any who might rebel.

The fact that, in order to cling on, the Government needs so much support and all this expense is really very telling. But that is the way things are: Governments *cost a packet* and for every *one* pocketed by the Minister, or Banker or Deputy, the poor tax-payer coughs up a *thousand* because he has to pay the tax-collector, the civil servant, the copper and the executioner, and all the rest as well.

Lest we go on too long, let us conclude with this quotation from Proudhon: "Analysis and the facts," he said, "demonstrate: that the tax of assessment, the tax upon monopoly, instead of being paid by those who possess, is paid almost entirely by those who do not possess; that the tax of *quotite*, separating the producer from the consumer, falls solely upon the latter ... finally, that the army, the courts, the police, the schools, the hospitals, the almshouses, the houses of refuge and correction, public functions, religion itself, all that society creates for the protection, emancipation, and relief of the proletaire, paid for in the first place and sustained by the proletaire, is then turned against the proletaire or wasted as far as he is concerned; so that the proletariat, which at first labored only for the class that devours it—that of the capitalist—must labor also for the class that flogs it—that of the nonproducers."[3]

This is where our analysis of the functions of Government, which is to say the *political system* through the prism of the *economic question*, takes us.

Government by all, an administration-government, a government free of extortion, ambushes, injustices, privileges, with some made wealthy and others impoverished, a non-governing government, or the mere *distribution and performance of work and distribution of goods*, such an *un-government* is only feasible once the economic problem has been resolved through collective ownership of the land and workers joining forces. The political problem too can be traced back to the economic one.

---

3 The passage is taken from *System of Economical Contradictions: or the Philosophy of Misery*, chapter 7, section 1. We have used Benjamin Tucker's translation of 1888.

Punishment and War

Now we can speak of punishment—another problem that defies resolution without a *turn of the key*, economic reasoning.

Crime is either rebelliousness on the part of the oppressed against the oppressor, or the child of poverty, or is sired by poverty by way of ignorance. Owen has explained this very well: *the solution to the economic problem is also the solution to the problem of crime.*

The issue of *war* can also be broken down like this: equality of circumstances between the classes leads to equality of circumstances between peoples, and that equality of peoples leads to an end to wars. Today these are waged, as Leopardi had it, in pursuit of *sugar or cinnamon;* for a trading pre-eminence, for industrial exploitation; as witness Tunisia, Egypt, and Morocco.

The Republicans, Costa, and Us

We could keep this up for some time. All problems confronting Science and modern Life are connected in the same fashion: the *economic question.* A real Gordian knot that we need to cut through with the sword of...[4]

Meanwhile, the word is that the *political question* and the *economic question* march hand in hand, and that there are *governments that can also "foster the spread of socialist ideas."*

So say the republicans; so writes Costa in *L'Avanti!*

The republicans need to admit that they have no understanding whatever of current social problems and that they still cling to the old litany of *God, Homeland, Liberty, and Family.* But Costa purports to be still a socialist yet reneges upon Socialism's greatest conquest, its most precious discovery, its first and last word?!!

Artfully done though it may be, the *travestying of the socialist programme* is no less complete in *Costa*'s programme. We need to look to our real principles and the sacred source of socialism; that is where we need to return and be baptized again if we are serious about recovering from the leprosy of *politicism* that dampens our ardor and saps our strength.

---

4 The sentence is probably left incomplete to avoid censorship or legal proceedings.

6. PROGRAM AND ORGANIZATION OF THE INTERNATIONAL WORKING MEN'S ASSOCIATION[1]

To the Internationalists[2]

Dear comrades,
We have tried to sum up our association's fundamental principles, the ideals of which it dreams, and the paths by which it means to reach them.

We think we have faithfully interpreted your ideas and your intentions. In any event, we hope that this brief, hurried exposition of ours will be such as to spark a lively exchange among you regarding the still controversial matters that must be the object of the deliberations of forthcoming congresses.

Should you wish to pass on to us your observations, we shall take these into account in a second, more comprehensive, more methodical edition, which we should like to be a collective effort with each of us bringing his expertise and experience to it.

Depend upon our devotion to the common cause.

The editors of the newspaper
La Questione Sociale

---

1 Translated from *Programma e Organizzazione della Associazione Internazionale dei Lavoratori* (Florence, 1884). The title page specifies that the pamphlet was issued by the editorial staff of the periodical *La Questione Sociale*. By the time this pamphlet was published, the International had practically ceased to exist, though there were local federations that still claimed affiliation to it. Even the London congress of 1881, which is considered the last congress of the federalist International, was rather an attempt to revive it. The present pamphlet should be seen in the same light. It was a proposal summarizing the views of Malatesta and his group, rather than a document collectively issued by an actual organization. When, in 1930, Malatesta's friend and comrade Luigi Fabbri asked his authorization to reprint the pamphlet, Malatesta accepted, on condition that it would be published as a "historical document," with a new preface he would write. "I would regret" he explained "if it was published as my work, without my preface, because in many respects I have changed my ideas and I would no longer want to take responsibility for everything that is said therein." Unfortunately, that preface never saw the light of day.

2 This preface is preceded by an ironic disclaimer addressed to the board of censors, which we have omitted.

INTERNATIONAL WORKING MEN'S ASSOCIATION

Charter (London, 28 September 1864)[3]

Considering:

That the emancipation of the workers must be conquered by the workers themselves;

That the struggle for the emancipation of the workers means not a struggle for new privileges, but for equal rights and duties for all;

That the economical subjection of the man of labour to the owner of the raw materials and the means of labour lies at the bottom of servitude in all its forms: political, moral, and material;

That the economical emancipation of the workers is therefore the great end to which every political movement ought to be subordinate;

That all efforts aiming at that great end have hitherto failed from the want of union and solidarity between the workers of the manifold divisions of labour and different countries;

That the emancipation of labour is neither a local, nor a national, but a worldwide problem, embracing all civilized nations and depending for its solution on their concurrence, practical and theoretical;

That the present revival of labour in the most industrious countries, while it raises a new hope, gives solemn warning against a relapse into the old errors, and calls for the immediate combination of the still-disconnected movements;

For these reasons

The *International Working Men's Association* has been founded. This Association and all societies and individuals adhering to it acknowledge *truth, justice, and morality* as the basis of their conduct towards all men, without regard to colour, creed, or nationality, and consider their duty to claim the human and citizen's

3 This is the text of the preamble to the provisional rules adopted at the founding conference of the International. The preamble, drafted by Marx, constituted the fundamental declaration of principles that, after the split, both branches of the International would equally follow. Though it is not Malatesta's text, we have preserved it for completeness, since Malatesta makes reference to it later. Where differences arise, we have adjusted the text to reflect Malatesta's version.

rights not only for the members of the Association but for all those who fulfill their duties.

No rights without duties, no duties without rights.

Preliminaries

The International Working Men's Association, was formed in 1864 in order to "afford a central medium of communication and co-operation between Workingmen's Societies exisiting in different countries and aiming at the same end; viz., the protection, advancement, and complete emancipation of the working classes," and from the outset, acknowledged no program but the general one set out in the charter cited above.[4]

It was a vague, incomplete program that identified rather than resolved problems, that did not fix the Association's position vis à vis the Society from which it arose, and was silent on the matter of methods of struggle and means of action. It laid down the principles, but did not set out their consequences, which the bulk of its members may well never even have anticipated.

At first glance, it might have seemed that this Association was merely a larger-scale repetition of the Workers' Societies that, for many years, had been looking to cooperation, lawful resistance or laws protective of labor for the emancipation of the worker, without rebelling against the politico-social constitutions of their several countries and without straying beyond the confines of the bourgeois world. And indeed that appeared so much to be the case that, in the International's beginnings, while the French government was trying to draw it into its orbit and make it an instrument of influence and corruption in the ranks of the impoverished classes, the International also received plaudits and encouragement from many influential members of the Republican party. But, later, once its program began to be expounded and to entail practical consequences, these were among its bitterest enemies and most ferocious persecutors.

Compared to many organizations and political parties of the time, the International seemed, to casual observers, rather harmless and even anti-revolutionary. Since then, those organizations and parties have either vanished without a trace or proven themselves patently bourgeois and reactionary, while the International has increasingly

4 The phrase about the International's aim is taken from the first of the International's provisional rules.

been enriching its program with all of the findings of social science and has hoisted its redemptive colors ever higher. It has taken the lead of Revolution and become a foretaste of the new civilization that must sprout from the ruins of this old bourgeois world.

What is the secret behind the International's success? What lies behind the vast powers of expansion and assimilation that, in a few years, have turned the International into the terror of the privileged and the hope of proletarians?

The International was born spontaneously from the womb of the people, and even as it answered the most heartfelt needs and the most ancient instincts of the oppressed masses, it was, from the outset, founded upon exclusively humane principles, upon a realistic philosophy that probes the true nature of human society and espouses ideals consonant with nature's laws of existence and growth. It carried within, in germ, the whole of the philosophical and social revolution encapsulated in its program today.

Acknowledging that the *worker's economic dependency upon the owner of raw materials and of the instruments of labor is the prime cause of all servitude*, the International, right from inception, took as the foundation of its program sociology's most important truth, the very foundation of socialism, which is that the economic question overshadows every politico-social issue, and that the economic emancipation of workers is the only way that justice and the common good can triumph.

Affirming that the emancipation of the workers should not tend to establish fresh privileges but rather to abolish all class rule and establish equal rights and duties for all, the International recognized that the real and complete emancipation of the working class is not achievable unless the whole of humanity is set free, and so it mirrored the feelings of solidarity that had developed in men's hearts down through the ages, despite a thousand obstacles. And by virtue of its universalism, as well as its declaration that all are entitled to be treated in accordance with the principles of truth, justice, and morality, without distinctions as to creed, color, and nationality, it extended such solidarity to all peoples.

Affirming that the emancipation of the workers must be the workers' own doing, the International showed that it understood that no ruling class has ever surrendered its privileges, no matter how much a proper understanding of its own interests might prompt it to do so—it never develops any such understanding by itself—and foresaw all the revolutionary needs that complicate resolution of the social question.

So—thanks to a few true precepts and to the instincts of the laboring classes, so widely represented in its ranks—within a short time, the initially timorous International has turned into the fearsome *anti-parliamentary-revolutionary-anti-religious-anarchist-communist* International, which intends to stand in the front rank of progress and is bent on destroying the whole social edifice of today, from the foundations up, so as to raise an architecture of peace, freedom and well-being upon the ruins.

In this pamphlet we shall not be rehearsing the stages through which the International passed prior to its espousal of the plainly socialist, revolutionary character that is its distinguishing feature today, for such scrutiny would take us far beyond what we have in mind to do; we shall try merely to set out, in brief, the conclusions at which the International has arrived thus far.

Program

Discounting any metaphysical notion, any other-worldly purpose, any mission imposed upon man by a chimerical God; focusing upon the purpose of human life here on earth, the latter cannot, as we see it, be anything other than happiness, which consists of the full and optimum development of our faculties; of achievement of the greatest well-being with the least quantum of pain possible. Society (itself the consequence of the search and need for well-being) can have no purpose other than satisfying the affective instincts growing inside our brains and the increase in and assurance of our happiness, of which it is, in any event, an essential pre-requisite.

It requires only a superficial glance at humanity's current circumstances to see how society, as presently constituted, is ill equipped to accomplish its purpose. Humanity is divided into two large parts, the larger of which seems fated to labor, obey, and endure the greatest woes so as to afford the other a life of idleness and of meddling in other people's wishes and dignity. Poverty, ignorance, corruption, prostitution, disease, criminality, an uncertain future, untimely death, wars, outrages, hatreds—these are but a few of the features that characterize the current face of the human consortium.

What lies behind such a ghastly circumstance? What remedies would the International seek to apply to it?

There is nothing that is outside of nature, nothing that cannot be made to conform to natural laws. Man is the highest organized state thus far attained by matter, the loftiest creature in the animal hierarchy, but that does not stop him being an aggregation of material atoms—still an animal—and, as such, subject to all the laws of chemistry and biology. Shaped by slow evolution under the dominion of natural laws, in the midst of the thousand vagaries of the struggle to survive against his environment in general and the other animals in particular, it is thanks to the spectrum of natural laws that we can fathom his past and his future. It is on the basis of the very same spectrum that we can glance ahead into his future and discover the conditions wherein he may achieve a higher degree of civilization and the well-being to which he aspires.

Scarcely had he arrived in this world than man, had to fight for his very survival; he fought other men as well as the rest of nature, and it was a brutal kill-or-be-killed battle. Later, man realized that the help of another man was of a thousand times more service to him than that man's death, and no longer was battle intended so much to exterminate one's adversary as to bring him to heel; to reduce him to a slave and beast of burden. This new, wiser, more humane character in man's struggle against his fellow man was the factor that determined the high degree of civilization attained by man. It is, however, the reason why such civilization is founded upon the subjugation and impoverishment of the majority of men and is fated to sup upon human blood and tears—until such time as the strife between men is effectively ended and that civilization has as its foundation genuine, complete solidarity of the human race in the struggle to bend nature to its needs.

Man's struggle to subjugate his fellow man has had two chief consequences: property and authority. Property arose when, at daggers drawn with all the rest, each man seized whatever portion of wealth he could; those who were not strong enough or favored enough to claim their part of the loot were set to work on another's behalf, and, lacking the materials and instruments of labor, they had to endure the conditions imposed by whoever held those materials and those instruments. The entitlements he had awarded himself were passed on to his offspring or his friends and he helped divide humankind into two castes: one caste of haves, born with an entitlement to live without working; the other of proletarians whose lot from birth is wretchedness; subjection; exhausting, unrewarded toil; and it is only the odd one, in very rare instances and exceptional circumstances, who manages to ascend to a more humane life and, sometimes, to property. Authority began with man's brutal oppression of woman, child and weaker fellow man, and culminated in the establishment of governments, whereby, through regulation, social privileges and social injustices—first and foremost, property rights—are enshrined and championed.

Property and authority—wedded to religious beliefs, grown out of the ignorance and fearful imagination of primitive man back when he was first teetering on the brink of conscious thought—have the source of their durability in the interests of the privileged and in the brutalization caused by impoverishment. Wedded to the sentiments of hatred and the racial, national, religious, commercial, familial rivalries, spawned by the antagonistic interests and innuendoes of priests and tyrants, property and authority can be found in every aspect of social life and are the root causes of all the woes we have been deploring.

As we have already stated, if these woes are to be banished, we must alter the principle by which human relationships are presently regulated; the principle of strife must be replaced by the principle of solidarity.

Many have tried and try still, all in vain, to banish or lessen those woes with political changes and moralizing, but along came socialism to provide the explanation for their lack of success and to point the way to effective remedies.

Just as, in nature, organic forms derive their origins and basic sustenance from inorganic matter, so, in the social world (which is nothing but the continuing development of natural forms), political institutions and moral sentiments derive their raison d'être from economic conditions.

If he is to survive, man needs sustenance above all else. The manner in which he successfully finds food, the greater or lesser roughness of the struggle that he is obliged to wage, the greater or lesser ease of his victory, its greater or lesser comprehensiveness, his more or less suitable sustenance, and every other material condition of existence, dominate man's physiological existence and thus his entire moral and social existence.

And just as work is the requisite means for acquiring sustenance, and just as work requires materials and tools, so, if a society is to be transformed, working conditions above all have to be transformed along with the logistics of raw materials and the instruments of labor.

In a society where the means of production are in the hands of a few, those deprived of them are necessarily obliged to abide by the conditions laid down by the few who have the power to provide or withhold work, and are in a position to bestow or deprive them of a livelihood.

What is the point of writing freedom, equality, and popular sovereignty into statutes when a fetter much tougher than any convict's—hunger—hitches the *free and sovereign* people to the chariot of the few who are blessed with the means of having their wishes carried out, the property-owners? True freedom is not the right but the opportunity, the strength to do what one will —and freedom, in the absence of the wherewithal for exercising it, is an atrocious irony.

What is the point of preaching brotherhood and love of one's neighbor when the proletarian has to fight for a crust of bread and is obliged, each and every day, to compete for it with his neighbor?

What is the point of preaching science when poverty dulls wits, and the chimerical hope of paradise is the only thing making this earthly hell bearable?

If all are to enjoy freedom and know happiness, if solidarity is to stand in place of strife, the primary necessity is for private ownership to be done away with; and that is the essential task that the International has set itself.

Once all of nature's bounty belongs to everybody and once each of us has the right and the wherewithal to apply his efforts to raw materials, then solidarity will have a chance of success in this world, and man will be released from the three terrifying nightmares grinding him down: economic subjection, authority, and religion.

Authority, which is to say political power, will be rendered useless and impossible since, with sheer brute force being now powerless to impose itself in any lasting way, there will be no way any more for a few men to bend the masses to their will.

Religion will vanish since science has now banished metaphysical phantoms once and for all, and religion will no longer have the ignorance and woes of the masses upon which to fuel its continued existence.

***

Thus property lies at the heart of the social question and it need only be abolished for the way to be opened to all human progress. However, political authority stands guard over property—and in order to reach the property-owner, one has to walk over the body of the gendarme who defends him.

So political power and property need to be tackled and destroyed simultaneously. Doing away with property without abolishing government is impossible, and if the government were to be brought down without property's being touched, it would swiftly be resuscitated under its old designation or some newer one.

And such a simultaneous abolition should be effected swiftly, by way of revolution. Staged abolition is not feasible, since property, in accordance with the principle that the stronger always grows stronger still, tends, as a result of competition or abetted by the spread of machinery, to become concentrated in the hands of an ever decreasing circle and to grow ever more oppressive; and, no matter how altered, political power, established by and for property-owners, never abdicates its essential mission, namely, to act in defense of property.

***

With the government overthrown and the property expropriated by means of revolution, how and by whom will the new society be organized?

Not by means of universal suffrage, for the greater number of the people, still being ignorant, still under the moral sway of the priest and property owner, would not, could not conceive of a society of free equals. And because universal suffrage, which is in theory the subjection of the minority to the majority, in practice, by the very nature of the mechanism itself, produces an outcome that, even when it has not been tampered with, does not represent the interests nor the wishes of the voters.

Not by means, either, of the dictatorship of a single or of several persons, because one or more individuals may well organize a brand new dominion, though not a society catering for the interests and enthusiasms of multi-faceted human nature; because privileged power is by its very essence a corrupter and would spew out the finest men; because, when it comes to revolution, starting by enforcing obedience to brand new rulers is not the right approach for an enslaved people; and, finally, because the better part of the people would neither seek nor countenance dictatorship of any sort.

So all that remains is the unfettered action of all the thoughtful heads among the people, the spontaneous initiative of all men of good will, the active intervention of the parties that have made the revolution. That is the Internationals' favored approach.

***

Informed by these principles, let us briefly examine the main problems the International must grapple with in its reforming endeavors, and set its solutions alongside the current state of affairs.

Religion. — *Qua* belief in an immaterial being, creator and ruler of all things, religion ought to wither away along with every cult through which men's ignorance and priests' cunning have manifested themselves. The International looks to science to ensure such withering away once its propagation is freed of obstructions in the form of the poverty of the masses and the interests of governments. It will observe the most utter respect for freedom of conscience, but will do everything it can to ensure that the poison of religion is not injected into the minds of children; it will bring about the destruction of anything that might uphold the habit of worship in the people; it will wage a war to the death on the Church and priest who may attempt, through their guile, to hold the people under the yoke of religion; and above all, it will highlight the contradiction between the people's true interests and those of the peddlers of religion.

Morality. — Human morality and the International's morality have nothing to do with the religious and bourgeois morality that teaches rulership to some and subjection to others, and a narrow, anti-social selfishness to one and all. True morality is the science of what is good for humanity, what most benefits each and every one of us; and it advances and changes as social science progresses.

If, as we shall attempt to show, the revolution is the *sine qua non* of humanity's well-being, the first principle today, the premier moral duty is to cooperate whole-heartedly with the advent of the social revolution.

In the wake of the revolution, it shall be a moral duty incumbent upon all to display love and respect for one's fellow men, to protect the weak and the children, to work, to consider the interests of society in every individual action—in short, everything that science and experience has or may demonstrate useful to men.

Society and Sovereignty. — Society, which has thus far been the forcible submission of men to a common regimen, organized in service of the interests of the ruling classes, ought to be the unsolicited outcome of the needs and gratifications that we all derive from being associated with one another, and should have, as its goal, greater well-being and increased freedom for all human beings.

Sovereignty, credited these days either to anointment by God or to a majority among the people and, through them, their chosen representatives, and which, in practice, belongs always to whoever has secured themselves a privileged position, by force and property, is by nature vested in every individual and is inalienable. Like any common tyrant, the majority may have might on its side, but it certainly has no more right than any single individual.

Therefore it is only through the unanimous agreement of us all, through a harmony of interests and sentiments, and, at worst, through freely arranged compacts and by virtue of the law of nature, under which solidarity is the essential precondition for freedom, that the sovereignty of the individual can be reconciled with social peace.

GOVERNMENT. — Is the collection of persons, delegated or otherwise, who hold the sum of social forces in their hands and impose their will upon each and every one, on the pretence of making provision for public services and overall security.

In a harmonious society founded upon solidarity and the greatest possible satisfaction of everybody's needs, in a society where the smooth running of public affairs is a condition of the smooth running of the private affairs of each of us, and where there are no lordlings to protect and no masses to be held in check, there is no reason for government to exist. Those governmental functions genuinely necessary or useful and that the government wields to the almost-exclusive advantage of the ruling classes, can be wielded directly by society for the benefit of all, since the government can only wield them if it can draw the necessary strength and capacities from within society.

Social organization should not be imposed by one or more men who hog power and wield it in the name of God or of the people, but ought to be an expression of the wishes of all (rather than of the majority), the outcome of the expansion and reconciliation of human interests and sentiments, starting from the equal entitlement of all to raw materials and the instruments of labor. No more authority, therefore, but rather spontaneous organizing from the bottom up, altering with every shift in interests and whim happening within the society;

no more delegation of powers, but rather delegation of functions; no more government, but, rather, ANARCHY.

WOMAN. — The subservience of woman to man ranks among the greatest injustices we have inherited from past ages; it is offensive to the spirit of fraternity and human fellowship and contrary to the true interests of man himself, since he is not going to be able to achieve a higher civilization nor enjoy any assurance of progress and social peace as long as one half of the human race is to be deemed inferior—and enslaved—and, at that, the very half to which it falls, on physiological grounds, to be the primary educator of upcoming generations.

For women, the International demands the very same freedom and guarantees of unhindered development as it does for men—in short, the completest social equality, and when it talks of the rights of *man*, that word is meant to apply to all *human beings*, regardless of sex.

If differences between the faculties of man and woman persist even after equality of circumstance has been achieved, they will give rise to differing functions and never to differing rights.

HOMELAND AND HUMANITY. — The dividing up of humanity into such a wide variety of *homelands* is also a by-product of the state of strife in which the human race has been living and still does. The International, which wants all men duty bound to think of themselves as brothers and to be held together by the close bonds of moral and material solidarity and to enjoy the world in common as their shared inheritance, yearns to amalgamate all homelands into one shared homeland, the world; and to banish from men's hearts the sentiment of patriotism, this being the exclusive or at any rate preferential love for the land or the people where and into whom one was born, the claim to an entitlement in *one's* homeland to more rights that those born elsewhere and which boils down to indifference, rivalry, and hatred vis à vis other peoples and thus to contention and war.

Initially, the homeland was restricted to the tribe and the city. With the establishment of modern states, with the concentration of powers, with the demolition of communal independence, the homeland has swollen to vast territorial units, fashioned more or less on a whim depending on geography, language, and governments. Thus bloated, the homeland is more artificial, but certainly no more justifiable than the communal homeland.

Those wishing to reconcile the notion of homeland with the comprehensively human outlook that has begun to prevail in science, say that the homeland is the link between the individual and humanity and is needed for the division of labor among men. Rather, patriotism is a serious impediment to brotherhood among men and flies in the face of a rational division of labor being applied across the full range of soil and climate conditions around the globe. Work in the world must be divided up according to the nature of the soil and climate, the ease of communications and outlooks of men, and such divisions do not coincide with the political and national divisions that homelands represent. The division of labor should vary in accordance with fresh discoveries, new roads, new production processes, new consumer needs, whereas the homeland remains or should remain relatively stuck between the hills and seas marking its boundaries. Division of labor renders one country mutually dependent upon another and patriotism claims that each individual country can survive by itself and for itself, since, in the event of war, it needs to be able to survive without looking to the foreigner. Division of labor requires complete reciprocation, and patriotism, of necessity, arouses rivalry, since either the division into homelands stays as a merely geographical term with no added politico-social implications, or men will always be striving to secure greater benefits for the countries where they enjoy greater rights or towards which they feel greater affection.

The homeland not only does not bring the individual closer to humanity, it detaches him from it; it is not the spontaneous agglomeration generated by real, pertinent affections and needs, but is an aggregation spawned by conditions that no longer obtain, that is foisted upon man from his very birth; it is the past oppressing the present and the future.

The International wants to see all men amalgamated into one huge, organic whole—humanity—so it deplores and tries to render impossible strife between peoples. An Internationalist, compelled by circumstances to take part in such strife, *is not guided by the interests of his native land, but by the interests of the whole of humanity and sides with this or that camp depending on the extent to which he reckons that the cause of revolution, emancipation, and human progress will be advanced or disadvantaged by its victory.*

Backward Races. — The so-called *civilized* peoples either abandon the *barbarous* or *savage* peoples to their own devices or make their lives miserable.

In the view of the International, however, it should be incumbent upon the most advanced peoples, *once these have lifted themselves out of poverty*, to bring civilization to the backward races, demonstrating *through their actions* that they are the latter's friends and *making them taste* the benefits of work, affluence, and freedom. And such a duty is also self-interest since, due to the barbarous circumstances of so many strains of humanity, a bottomless well of latent talents, which may well be different from our own and which might enrich our common inheritance, is left untapped; much of the earth's surface remains effectively sterile, and civilization is forever threatened by a terrifying invasion that might drag it back into barbarism.

Property.— As we have already said, private ownership is to be done away with, as its abolition and that of all alleged rights deriving from it (rights of inheritance, etc.) are the pre-requisite for the triumph of solidarity in human relations. Let us now say a few words about the organizational arrangements that are to take the place of the private-ownership system.

The International has long been *collectivist*; that is, it wanted the land, raw materials, the instruments of labor, in short, everything man uses in the pursuit of his activities and production, to be collective property, with everyone entitled to the use of them in his work, and for the entire product of labor— except for a quotient set aside for general costs—to belong to the worker, be he alone or in partnership.

Hence the formula *to each according to his labors*, or, which amounts to the same thing, *to the worker the entire product of his labors; —let him that works eat and him that does not work not eat*, except for those unable to work, in which case the incapacitated would have a right to receive from society the means to satisfy their every need.

But collectivism is open to many serious objections.

It is, in economic terms, wholly based upon the principle of the value of products being gauged by the amount of labor they require. Now that sort of definition of value cannot possibly be determined once one tries to take account not only of the time element or of some other outward attribute of labor, but also the overall mechanical and intellectual effort it demands. Furthermore, just as various patches of dirt are more productive or less productive, and the instruments of labor not all equally good, so each person would try to find the best soil or instruments by trying to reduce the worth of those worked by other people, just as he would try to talk up the value of his own products and downplay those of the others as much as he could. And so the distribution of tools and exchange of products would wind up being conducted in accordance with the law of supply and demand, which would imply a relapse into out-and-out competition, a reversion to the bourgeois world.

But above all else, collectivism is flawed in its moral foundation. Like bourgeois-ism, it is founded upon the principle of strife, except that it tries to restore equality between strivers at the starting point. Where there is striving, there must necessarily be winners and losers, and whoever scores the first victory gains certain advantages that almost always guarantee him further successes. Collectivism is impotent when it comes to bringing about that revolution, that thoroughgoing moral transformation in man, following which the individual will not do and will not be willing to do something that might harm others, and therefore it is untenable. It is incompatible with *anarchy*; it would require some regulating, moderating authority, which might well then become oppressive and exploitative, and it would lead initially to corporate ownership and then, later, back to private ownership.

For these reasons the International has decided, virtually unanimously, to embrace a broader, more consistent solution, the only one that allows for the comprehensive expansion of the solidarity principle: COMMUNISM. *Everything belongs to everyone, everything is exploited for the benefit of all; each of us ought to do on behalf of society all that his resources allow him to do, and each is entitled to insist that society meet all of his needs, insofar as the sum of production and social forces allow.*

But if it is to be feasible, communism requires a huge moral improvement in the members of society, plus a highly developed and deep-seated sense of solidarity that the thrust of revolution may well not be enough to bring forth, especially if, in the early days, the material conditions that encourage its development (to wit, such an abundance of production that each person may have his needs met in full without detriment to others, plus a working arrangement such as ensures that this is not burdensome) may not be in place.

Such contradictions can be remedied through the immediate implementation of communism only in those areas and to the extent that circumstances allow, while collectivism is applied to the rest, but only *on a transitional basis*. In the early stages, amended by the enthusiasm of a people bent upon a new way of life and driven by the mighty thrust of revolution, collectivism is not going to have time to make its damaging effects felt. However, lest it then relapse into bourgeois-ism, it is going to have to make a rapid evolution in the direction of communism. And it is here that action by a consciously communist party, action by the International, will be of crucial importance.

The International is going to have to lobby for communism everywhere, highlighting the advantages delivered wherever it may have been introduced and trying to bring under common ownership as many things as it may, and, above all, to call for communism's immediate and wholesale implementation (in addition to those areas where it already applies, such as water, ordinary streets, lighting, public cleansing, etc.) in respect of housing, education, care of the sick, the rearing of children, and in staple foodstuffs, and then extend it gradually into every sphere of production.

Work. — Work, as it is the primary necessity of human society, is also men's first duty. It is to be regulated in accordance with the needs that are to be satisfied and the resources available and is to be made as comfortable and as attractive as possible and shared in such a way as to introduce as much harmony as possible between social usefulness and personal inclinations and preferences—to the extent where such work may no longer be the satisfaction of the physiological need to be active and exercise the organs. All useful labor is equally noble and entitles the laborer to have his needs met. Brainwork, the greatest delight of man and the thing that elevates him so much higher than his natural surroundings, ought not to be the privilege of a caste. Everyone has brawn as well as brain, and all should labor with brain and brawn alike; and society must see to it that everyone has the opportunity to develop and exercise all their faculties.

Once manual labor is no longer like a chain, to which the masses are bound, and no longer oppressed and scorned, care will be taken to simplify its processes, not, as is presently the case, in the interests of capitalist production, but in the interests of the laborer himself. The usage of all tools can be broken down to a few basic principles, and a small number of approaches, whereby a man will easily learn to turn his hand to a variety of trades; machines and scientific processes will do away with or improve unhealthy, repugnant, and onerous trades; and so, given the vast spectrum of human outlooks and preferences, it is to be hoped that each area of production will be willingly pursued by whoever has a natural predisposition towards it.

Still, let us suppose that there will be some tasks not susceptible to efforts to introduce improvements and to which nobody will feel that they are "called." Well, if those jobs are genuinely useful and the benefits they bring make up for the onerousness in the doing of them, and if there is no one prepared to take them on, on the basis of either predisposition or self-sacrifice, then everybody will take them on; everyone can take his turn at them, by means either of some sort of conscript labor, or however it may be decided, but those jobs will be done by us all.

Once work is properly organized and performed in the interests of all, once the spirit of solidarity has grown and the idler been exposed to public disapproval, there will be none who refuse to work, except for the odd case attributable to pathology, which will up to medical science to try to cure or mitigate.

In the period of transition leading up to the new arrangements, revolution will be afoot and we must cope as best we can.

Production, Consumption, and Exchange. — These three terms encapsulate the whole economic life of society and at present, under the private ownership system, are regulated by the *competition* and *profit* principle, which is to say, by the interest of the individual pitted against all his fellows. As a result, production is in disarray; there is a glut in one area and scarcity in another; land lies untilled; mines unworked; natural or human resources are frittered away or left unproductive, maybe because the owner has no spare capital and cannot survive the competition or because he chooses a different use for his capital; sophistication of goods; continual crises that leave the workers swinging between over-work and a murderous idleness; no regard is shown for the interests of the worker and consumer, except insofar as these profit the capitalist; and increasingly serious strife between the worker and the boss.

When it comes to consumption, there is a dearth of that which the greater part of humanity most vitally needs, even when there is a glut of products.

In exchange, there is a vast number of useless intermediaries, fraud, monopolies, speculation, etc.

At all times and first and foremost, there is squandering of effort, tremendous suffering, no regard for the collective interest and even the notion of the private interest is ill served.

Such is the monstrousness of the current economic arrangement that abundance itself becomes a cause of suffering and any improvements in production methods, any new application of machinery generates an upsurge in misery. Indeed, every new machine deprives a certain number of people work and thus of bread, and a glut in a given commodity makes the labors of some of those who get their livelihood by producing it pointless. If, say, America produces a glut of wheat and it is imported into Europe, that wheat—strange to say!—adds to the famishing of European peasants, in that it makes their labors redundant to the landowners.

In the society advocated by the International, however, everything is regulated in accordance with man's needs. *Production* will be governed by consumer demand; and every advance in farming and industry would serve either to boost the amount of products for the good of all or to render work more amenable and to reduce the number of hours spent on it daily. *Consumption* will be free for everyone, the only restriction being, should it apply, shortages in the supply of products; those natural or man-made items not available in sufficient quantities to cater for all, would be utilized, with common consent, by the sick or others whose needs for them might be greater, or, at worst, allocated by ballot or by rotation. *Exchange* will be the operation whereby goods abounding in some countries are shipped to others where they are in short supply, and insofar as this is possible, the measure of well-being enjoyed around the globe will be standardized.

Children.—According to the International, children should be placed under the guardianship of all, and reared and educated by society as its shared issue so that they can be assured of the greatest possible well-being and physical, intellectual, and moral development, and made the most useful and happiest adults possible.

As long as the child is of too tender an age for him to be able to live usefully in common with others, his education should be entrusted to his mother, as long as she can be relied upon sufficiently. After that, the child should be removed, not from the affections and contact, but from the exclusive influence of his parents and educated by society in conjunction with other children.

In any event, preference must be given to whichever method experience may have shown best serves the children themselves and society as a whole.

Family.—With woman released from her subjection to man, which was the original root of the family; with the religious prejudices that have misrepresented the true nature of sexual relations, now banished; with private ownership and its concomitant right of succession that currently forms the real basis of the family, done away with; with children, the protection of whom is the sole justification for the family as such, entrusted to the care of society, there is no further reason for the present family as a union legitimized by society and made more or less indissoluble, to exist. Sexual relations should be wholly free and governed solely by love and fellow-feeling. The International calls for the abolition of all bonds that currently hamper freedom in love, be these enshrined in law or merely enforced by custom and social convention, so-called.

It will then be left to posterity to determine if exclusive and lifelong sexual relations are inherent in human nature and individually and collectively useful, or rather, as many and varied as moral and intellectual relations.

Nothing can better determine what best suits the natures of man and woman than freedom itself.

Instruction and Education.—According to the International, instruction should be delivered, under society's responsibility, to all without distinction and so all of the wherewithal for study and pursuit of the sciences—e.g. libraries, museums, offices and experimental and research laboratories, lectures, etc.—should be made publicly accessible. Instruction should be comprehensive, which is to say, designed to harmoniously develop every faculty of mind and body; it should be both theoretical and practical, i.e. should teach knowledge and understanding as well as practicalities, and should be positive, which is to say, founded upon verified fact.

Education, of which instruction is the technical aspect, should derive not only from the school but from the entire social environment and should be designed above all to develop the sentiment of love and respect for people, to ensure the success of whichever habits and tastes best serve the general good and elevate the intellectual, moral, and material assets of the individual to the highest possible level.

Crimes and Punishments.—Crimes are largely social in origin; most offenders are such because they are impoverished and ignorant, or because they have been *mis*-educated, or, generally speaking, because they cannot find an opportunity within society to deploy their resources and satisfy their needs other than by trespass against the rights of others. Furthermore, lots of actions held criminal today are so only because they offend against the privileges of those who have made or do make the laws, or because they run counter to established prejudices.

Once society is so arranged that the freedom and well-being of one is complemented by the freedom and well-being of another, once work itself turns into an outlet for the bodily need for exercise and activity, once one is loved and respected from birth and schooled in love and respect for others, there will be no more criminality deriving from society. And even those offences that sprout from more or less unexplored causes of cosmic or physiological derivation, will, as the sciences make progress and climatic conditions improve and a rational cure is administered to those showing any signs of mischievous tendencies, fade away, just as all or nearly all common sicknesses will vanish. But let us admit, however, that there will always be some who, for whatever reason, have a tendency to do evil, to trespass against the persons of others, who will to live without working, etc. In the light of science, such people cannot be held responsible because, in reality, they are merely sick, and society has no right to punish them; it does, though, have the right to defend itself from them and the duty to cure them. So it will, sometimes forcibly, ensure that those sick persons are denied the opportunity to do harm and will look to the curing of them as a matter of urgency.

***

To sum up: the International is out to replace: God with SCIENCE; the State with the spontaneous organization of humanity upon the foundations of universal solidarity, which is to say, ANARCHY; the homeland with the UNITY OF THE HUMAN CONSORTIUM; private ownership with COMMUNISM; the Family with LOVE; Strife between men with the BATTLE AGAINST NATURE ON BEHALF OF THE HAPPINESS OF ALL HUMAN BEINGS. And in order to bring this ideal about, it reckons there is no option but the COMPLETE AND SIMULTANEOUS ABOLITION OF PRIVATE PROPERTY AND POLITICAL POWER, by means of **REVOLUTION** mounted against the Government and against the PROPERTIED.

The prime, essential objective, in the short term, is therefore: revolution. And since all words have been shrouded with misrepresentations and since there are those who, while purporting to be revolutionaries, have no desire ever to see the revolution made and who guile the people with empty hopes and ineffectual palliatives, we need to be clear in our explanations. The revolution that the International prepares and will make is an armed, violent revolution, what might be termed a recourse to material force for the purpose of destroying an order that is upheld by material force, and the replacement thereof by a brand new order whose very right to exist is forcibly denied. Its weapons are bands and barricades, rifles and dynamite, steel and fire, deployed for the destruction of armies, navies, fortresses, prisons, and anything that stands in the way of socialism's triumph and compels the poor to put up with their sorry conditions.

For men of sensibility who have dedicated their entire lives to the good of humanity, it is painful to have to wade through blood before they can reach the promised land. Painful, especially when we know that man is the product of physiological heredity and of his cosmic and social environment, and that as a result, property owners as such, and the police and all who will be targets of the blows of the revolution are themselves irresponsible victims of the society that they found as a splendid finished product. And painful because those soldiers engaged during the opening skirmish are virtually all proletarians forcibly wrenched away from their labors and their loved ones and, among them, there are many comrades of ours who shudder at having to don their despised uniforms. It is painful, but it is necessary.

The privileged will never willingly surrender their privileges, even though surrendering them might be useful and necessary for them, too. The whole of history is there as proof of this: progress in the direction of equality and freedom has never been achieved without revolution; the strong have never made a concession to the weak that was not wrenched from them by the menacing coalition of the weaklings. On the night of 4 August 1789, the French nobles, seemingly voluntarily but actually deceptively, sacrificed their seigneurial rights. This was feasible only because of the precedent of the great feats of 14 July, when the people had dismantled the Bastille and because revolt was rumbling in Paris and in the provinces, and the nobles, quaking, had a sense of its terrifying energy.

No, the privileged will never yield, and the present stubbornness of governments and the bourgeoisie is there to prove it. The ferocious repression that has been their answer to every attempt from the proletariat, the reactionary fever by which the bourgeoisie is possessed now that socialism has emerged as a threat, plainly demonstrate that it is no less stupid and no less brutal than any privileged caste or class history has to show us.

The use of force, of physical force, is a necessity.

Governments have their hirelings, soldiers, cannons, prisons and vast resources with which to cow and corrupt; property-owners control the livelihoods of an entire population, have accessories in the priests who stultify the masses and school them in subjection, and are championed by governments whose moral and material might is entirely organized for their benefit.

How can we hope to defeat them without recourse to strong, radical measures?

It is pointless placing one's hopes in universal suffrage, insofar as modern states, especially republican ones, claim to be founded upon the will of the people. Experience and logic dictate that extending the vote to a famished, ignorant people, is nothing but another weapon in the arsenal of the ruling classes, one that works wonderfully well as a guarantee against rebellion, by peddling to the slave the belief that he is the master.

In the face of this position, sentimentality is out of place. A choice must be made: we either accept the established order of poverty and ignorance for the vast majority, with its prostitution, crime, imprisonment, war, and periodical uprisings drowned in blood; or we embrace revolution that might cause great but fruitful hurts, which are a pledge of happiness to come; either we endure an order that, in a single day, claims more victims than the ghastliest of revolutions claims in its entire course; or embrace a disorder that will usher in the reign of peace for man.

Guided by love for all men, knowing that the blame lies with institutions rather than personalities, the International is nevertheless mindful that the revolution is warfare and that, in war, the overriding consideration is victory. Not driven by hatred, not with vengeance in its heart, but impelled by awareness of its purpose, the International wants inexorable revolution; not a stone must be left upon a stone of the injustices, crime, and prejudices by which the world is oppressed—and anyone or anything standing in the way of the great work of demolition must fall... or else the revolution will fall!

A revolution that falters is a revolution lost; and the only means of minimizing the bloodshed and destruction, without giving up success, is to *strike hard and strike swiftly*.

Besides, whether the revolutionary principle is accepted or not, revolutions have always occurred, and we shall have more as long as society is rooted in slavery and wretchedness for the greater number. And before the centralization of property and the expansion of machinery can reduce the masses to a utterly brutish condition and render them incapable of the very thought of rebelling, a great social war will take place: everything portends it, and one would need to be as blind as a bourgeois not to see it. So the actual position boils down to this: either some conscious, organized party writes armed revolution into its program and targets the complete emancipation of oppressed humanity, conjuring up a civilization wherein violence is rendered forever pointless and impossible; or the revolution will be mounted by the angry masses with no clear consciousness of ends and means and directed more at persons than things. From that will assuredly come a hundred times as much bloodshed than is necessary; it will destroy the blessings of science and civilization, which the masses cannot appreciate because today, these being monopolized by the bourgeoisie, they are the instruments of their wretchedness—and, in the wake of ghastly massacres, it will throw up new and more brutal forms of oppressiveness, most likely flanked by the clerical backlash that is even now beginning to threaten. Given the enormous amount of hatred and resentment that the bourgeoisie has managed to rack up against itself, given the condition of ignorance and abjection in which it has held the masses, only a consciously and resolutely revolutionary party can inject humanity into the revolution and make it a bringer of civilization.

Practical Action

Having established the goal that the International has set itself, namely, universal solidarity through freely, *anarchically* organized communism; and having established the necessity for a revolution characterized by forcible expropriation of property owners by means of the masses' directly assuming possession of all natural and man-made wealth; and through the abolition of all political authority, which is to say, of any formally acknowledged authority, we can summarise the practical action that the International brings to bear or means to bring to bear before, during, and after the insurrection.

The International today aims primarily to spread its principles, so that these become as widely known and understood by the people as possible, and so that the most intelligent and vigorous segments of the people may constitute that party, that army that will not only have to neutralize the material might that stands guard over the current institutions, but will have the task of ensuring that the revolution is authentically socialist and carried out to the advantage of all, rather than of some new classes or parties. They will have to be so attuned to the purpose in mind and the necessary means as is required to organise victory and guard against the backlash that might well ensue, due either to violence from without or disaffection within.

In quiet times, the main mission of the International includes drawing the masses' attention to the wretched, undeserved circumstances of the workers; alerting them to the unfairness of such a state of affairs and the reasons for it; showing them that only common ownership can offer them a remedy and that as long as private property endures there can be no hope of any serious, lasting improvement, that, instead, poverty must inevitably become ever more widespread and all who, due to exceptional circumstances, may find themselves better off, are under the continual threat of tumbling into the common abyss; instilling into the people the lively impression that everything that exists belongs to all, especially to the workers and that the property-owners are thieves and oppressors who live off other people's labors; getting it across that, be it monarchist or be it republican, the only function of government is to protect the privileged against the claims of the oppressed, and it is only strong because people support it and furnish its soldiers, mercenaries, and money; whipping up hatred of the oppressors, whether they oppress by means of property or bayonets; inspiring love towards all men and the craving for a free and happy existence; drawing into its ranks all those who have best absorbed its propaganda and stand ready to commit themselves to the emancipation of their brethren by braving persecution, imprisonment, and death, wherever necessary; organizing the laboring masses into trades associations based on the principle of resistance and of attacking the bosses; giving priority at all times to feeding the spirit of revolt.

But the International does not look exclusively to the laboring classes. As a class, the bourgeoisie is the enemy of the proletariat and rabidly attached to all the privileges and all the injustices enshrined in the established institutions; but there is a faction of it which, despite the poisonous influences of its education and its privileged circumstances, has preserved its kind heart and alert intelligence.

And the International looks to this fraction of the bourgeoisie, which is to be found mostly among the student youth and small proprietors, industrialists, and businessmen, who are knocked about by competition and hurtling towards expropriation and bankruptcy. The International says to them: Socialism does not belong to a single class only; the largest and surest number of its advocates can be found in the ranks of the workers, because these suffer most from the current arrangement, because, more than anyone else, they are in need of emancipation and can only achieve that through the emancipation of all, and because they are used to toil, which is the pre-eminent factor in civilization and morality. But socialism is still an essentially human thing, and under its banner there is room for all men of feeling who seek well-being and freedom for all and who could not stomach the suffering of others, as well as for intelligent folk who have recognized the trend in historical evolution and appreciate the huge, immense benefits that the whole of humanity would derive once, rather than expending the better part of his energies on war, rebellions and repression, every human being works in concert in pursuit of well-being for all.

Within the ranks of the International there is room for all who are out to fight on behalf of the future, the outriders of the brand new civilization. No matter what class they may come from, nor the race to which they belong, nor the party or religion they once followed, all are brothers within the International, once a clean break has been made with the past and with the present and the fight for human redemption resolved upon.

***

Today as on the day after the revolution, the International rigorously shuns all compromise and all *opportunism*.

A party that is not out to massage petty personal ambitions and particular interests by being the victor of the hour, but wants to make an effective impact on human progress, even though it leads an everyday existence and avails of every opportunity that presents itself, must never lose sight of the ultimate objective and must gauge its every action on that basis.

All means are good and no way should remain untried, no force remain idle when we are dealing with a mission as grand as the one that the International Association has taken upon itself. But clearly such means have to further the end, and the pathways tried should lead towards the aim at which one wishes to arrive.

The immediate object of the International is a simultaneous uprising against the political authorities (with an eye to their abolition) and against property-owners (with an eye to taking wealth under common ownership), and so it must select in advance those means useful in the preparation of the insurrection and apt to ensure its anti-authoritarian and anti-property tenor.

EVERYTHING THAT HASTENS AND EASES THE SOCIALIST INSURRECTION IS FINE; EVERYTHING THAT POSTPONES IT OR MAKES IT MORE DIFFICULT OR TINKERS WITH ITS ANARCHIST-SOCIALIST CHARACTER IS BAD; this is the criterion by which the International is guided in its actions.

The agitations that help highlight the economic basis to the social question, that create a gulf between proletarians and the propertied, between bosses and workers, that affirm the righteousness and necessity of expropriation and violent revolution, enjoy the International's sympathy and support. Those agitations, however, that skirt the question and turn an essentially economic issue into a political one, as well as those that would have us believe that the economic question can be resolved without touching political institutions; all agitations that encourage hope in improvement and emancipation through compacts and peaceful reforms, face the open and determined hostility of the International.

Strikes, resistance societies, labor organizations; books, newspapers, talks, study circles; blows dealt to the authorities and the bosses—all of these the International approves and endorses.

Demands for and hopes vested in peaceful reforms, attempts at reconciling proletarians and bourgeois, election contests, parliamentary activity—these are things that the International looks upon as harmful, because they lull the people by empty illusions, are a distraction to the activities of the revolutionary party and serve merely to offer a comfortable haven to faint-hearts and traitors.

All of the bourgeois parties are the same to the International, and the latter confronts them all.

And so, by struggling against all the economic, political, religious, judicial, and pseudo-scientifically moral institutions of bourgeois society; using the spoken and printed word to spread the message; encouraging workers to band together and resist the bosses; drawing attention to their program through agitations, attempted uprisings, and trials; by making use of both the government's forced tolerance and its persecutions; issuing appeals to the oppressed masses and welcoming with open arms any deserters from the ranks of the bourgeoisie who come to fight the battle for justice and civilization alongside the people—by all these means the International gets on with its organizing and prepares the forces with which it will mount its final attack upon bourgeois institutions, gauges the enemy's strength, and creates the climate that will make victory possible.

***

There is no way that we can foresee how the revolution will come about. It may be made directly by the organized forces of the International taking to the streets, or taking to the hills; or it may be sired by an uprising of a people irked by misery and frustration galore; it may come on the occasion of an attempt to institute a republic or some attempted restoration; or from a strike that spreads and triggers clashes; or because of some wars or dynastic crisis... Be that as it may, whether the International—with its own resources and those of other socialist organizations—confronts the enemy on the field of battle with some likelihood of success, or whether some circumstances or other leave it duty-bound to take to the streets right away, at that point less than ever must the International lose sight of its own program; less than ever should it agree to the compromises and horse-trading that would translate into its efforts being exploited by bourgeois revolutionary parties.

Tacit or open alliance with bourgeois parties unhappy with the established order may have its use when it comes to the material effort required to smash the army and police that stands guard over the common foe, and then only if there is a serious likelihood of not being subsequently overwhelmed by erstwhile allies. But once victory has been secured and the political authorities and their soldiery have been shoved aside, the parties who we have been fighting alongside, whether they are republicans or clericals, will be as much our enemies—indeed more so since they will represent a current threat—as the late government. And the International will wage war on them to ensure that they do not oppose expropriation and do not set themselves up as a new government, whether they should seek to do so openly or resort to the elections lie.

Even while the fighting is happening on the barricades, the International will have been encouraging the people to take over the masters' houses and throw open the food and manufactured goods depots to the public, with an eye to getting the masses to engage with the revolution right from the start, as well as making its socialist character plain beyond question. But once the all-consuming worries of battle are behind them—either because they have gained the victory or through their shifting of the theater of the struggle elsewhere—the chief concern of Internationalists, as well as of socialists in the broader sense, will have to be giving encouragement to the masses to assume direct, immediate possession—without the need for votes, decrees, or debate—of lands, housing, machinery; and every other instrument of labor; the mines, shipping, the railways, and every means of transportation; foodstuffs and manufactured goods—in short, of anything there is that might prove useful to man.

The communes, which is to say, all who reside in the same housing cluster, plus the crafts and trades bodies, that is, the gamut of those engaged in the same work, will be the two hubs around which the revolution will revolve, the two factors that will carry out the expropriation and from which the re-organization of production, consumption, and exchange will radiate. They will be the first representatives, the first tangible elements of the *human society*, that will only become a living reality when, as the revolution spreads through an ever broader trade-to-trade and commune-to-commune agreement, a unity of interests and a unity of organization is achieved, covering the entire human race.

The International—whose membership will be mightily increased by the eruption of revolution and will carry on growing as the storm of revolution makes headway among the masses and awakens their latent or dulled faculties—will resist, by means of propaganda and force, the establishment of governments and formal authorities intent upon using the people's might to foist their own wishes upon the people. Besides, it will deploy every iota of its influence to encourage and inspire all manner of ventures and activities.

Those assets that must become the whole of humanity's common inheritance shall be directly under the control of those who are located within their reach—under the control of the commune, if they are consumer goods; under the control of the corporations, which operate them, in the case of instruments of production.

The peasants, who shall be encouraged to organize themselves into farmers' corporations, shall take possession of the land. Banding together into corporations, workers plying the same trade are to take possession of the machinery, tools, and premises involved in their trade; thus, seamen will take over shipping, railroad workers the railways and so on. In addition, housing accommodation shall be occupied by the commune's residents, and consumer goods gathered into public depots—their distribution organized quickly by the most willing and aptest volunteers.

All deeds and all material indicators of private ownership must be destroyed; the public debt record, destroyed; the land registry, mortgage deeds, notarial records, contracts, etc., all destroyed. All conventional bonds are to be annulled or destroyed, and the same goes for the currency and its replacements.

In the countryside, hedges, walls, and all boundary markers will be done away with, as long as they are of no use and only serve to indicate, delimit, and protect owners' rights.

The machinery and tools of each trade will, insofar as this is feasible, be removed from their present sites and gathered into large workshops, the purpose being to erase all sign or indication of private ownership and to make a start, from day one, on organizing work along collective lines.

All this through the unfettered and spontaneous actions of all men of goodwill, and of all the groups and all the committees that take on a task and carry it out through their own efforts and those of whomsoever they may attract to their side.

Similarly, through the good offices of freely self-organizing committees and groups, operating without a mandate or any official authorization, steps will be taken to ensure that all the corporations step up production, especially of basic necessities; exchange, roads, training, a postal service, care of the sick and of dependents will be organized; and work will begin on the compilation of statistics that will provide the working basis for organization of the society of the future, since, reckoning on the basis of consumer requirements, accumulated assets, and production resources, the swift satisfaction of everyone's needs can be ensured without wastefulness, imbalance, or crisis.

To be sure, many mistakes will be made and progress will often be tentative. There may well be instances of abuse, bullying, and unfairness, but since there is no established authority to endorse the mistakes and defend the unfairness and deploy society's powers against innovations and progress, the mistakes will be corrected and the unfairness stamped out thanks to the parties that will have been the makers of the revolution and will be loath to see its outcome misdirected, and thanks to the masses that, having tasted its benefits from day one, will think of the revolution as being their very own and defend it to the bitter end.

A variety of organizational arrangements will be tried out: in one place there will be collectivism, in another it will be communism, in some more backward locations property may very well be split between the commune residents, but at all times and above all else, the social dimension will be a matter of concern to all, and everybody will be entitled to an opportunity to bring to bear upon collective life an influence in proportion with their capacity. If revolutionaries can thwart the formation of a government, if they manage to crush, possibly through the use of material violence, any attempt to resurrect private property, we can rest assured that, surrounded by thousands of experiments, wrangles and attrition, progress, at a greater or lesser speed, towards anarchist communism will be made; that being the only arrangement under which society will be able to achieve the peace and well-being it craves.

In the midst of all this turmoil, this upheaval from which a new world is to emerge, the International will have to actively invite, elicit, and monitor. Unless they are not up to their mission, it will be Internationalists who will set the boldest examples; it will be they, in their armed bands, who invade the recalcitrant areas, bringing revolution to them and encouraging or, sometimes, carrying out the expropriation. They will be the ones to take on the task of pushing the revolution as far as it will go, preventing the means of production and communication from being monopolized by those who operate them and giving encouragement to the ever-wider federation of communes and corporations; they will be the ones to watch out lest any party monopolize power or attempt a backlash.

It will be chiefly up to the Internationalists to help spread the revolution quickly through the civilized world. Taking as their springboard the first country to rebel, they will send equipment, men, and weapons to other countries, striving to ensure that the masses feel the contagion of example and to ensure that governments, rather than contemplating invasion of countries in the throes of revolution, will not know what to do to escape the encroaching revolution.

The sacred battalion of the revolution, the International will remain in the breach, always in the front ranks of the fighters as long as there is a single injustice or a single person whose unhappiness can be blamed on a fellow man.

Organization

The International is a free union of fighters with a common cause.

– Its name invokes workers, and by "worker" is meant anybody plying a useful trade who does not exploit another person's labors. However, the International welcomes all who sincerely offer to contribute their efforts, be they victims of oppression yearning for redemption or deserters from the ruling class defecting to the people. Thus it has been said that in the International's eyes *anyone who toils at the destruction of bourgeois order is a worker*, and in a sense, there is some truth in that; but it should not be forgotten that socialism, though it is the cause of all men, is chiefly the cause of the wage-earners who suffer most under the existing order; and that the revolution, while harnessing all contributions, looks to proletarians alone for its guarantees, in that these cannot be emancipated except through the achievement of social equality.

– The International is made up of many local or trades societies, which generally assume the name *sections*, but which it might please their members to refer to as *circles, groups, corporations*, etc.

– The various sections in a given locality normally band together into *local federations*; the *sections* and *federations* from the same region usually band together into *regional federations* and so on. Every section is at liberty to make connections and arrangements with whichever sections it deems best, regardless of geography.

– Liaison between the various sections and federations is maintained by means of *federal commissions* made up of representatives elected by each section or federation. Such delegates wield no powers; they are duty-bound to enact the wishes of their mandatories, to whom they must answer for the carrying out of the mandate issued to them. They are elected for a fixed term, normally a short one, and are liable to be recalled at any point.

– From time to time, suitable delegates from the various sections meet in provincial, national, or general congresses or, in the case of sections made up of members plying the same trade, in corporative congresses. Those congresses, meetings of which will normally coincide with the expiration of the mandate of the relevant federal commissions in that department, evaluate the stewardship of the outgoing commission, appoint the incoming commission, discuss new ideas produced by or coming into the Association, thereby contributing to the ongoing elaboration of the overall program, and resolve on all interests held in common by the collectives represented. The resolutions, not being conducted under imperative mandates, are in no way binding until such time as they have been approved by the assemblies of the sections, and then are binding only upon those sections that endorse them, other than in the case of some special compacts and conventions.

– Any person or society subscribing to and defending the principles of the Association can be accepted into its ranks on the responsibility of whichever section or federation does the welcoming. Persons seeking admission to the Association will apply to the section or to one of the sections in their locality. The society shall forward the application to the nearest federal commission, which will pass the proposal to the sections and federations in its jurisdiction, or, in accordance with special regulations, shall provisionally decide on the application, referring the matter for a final determination to the congress.

– Any subscriber to the principles of the association living in towns where there is as yet no section in existence, can be admitted to a section in a different town or communicate their support to the nearest federal commission and give a moral undertaking to foster the establishment of a regular section in their town.

– Where the International has no presence in a region, those subscribing to its ideas should seize the initiative and launch a branch, which will then have to apply for admission and recognition, under the rules, through the federal commissions and congresses.

– The commissions handle correspondence and provide for all of the organization's needs, by means of the dues payable by members and sections.

– No authority exists within the International. Other than in regard to any particular obligations assumed by persons and sections in coming together and federating with one another, they remain utterly autonomous vis à vis the International, and are at liberty to pursue their own activities on behalf of the cause as they deem fit, as long as they *abide strictly by the program, do not falter in their duty of solidarity in the struggle against the bosses and governments, and do not knowingly do injury to the work of the entire association or some branch thereof.*

– The program, which is always under discussion and always open to whatever further debate or changes may be required to keep it up to date with science and the needs of the revolution, remains binding upon all members, at least in its essentials and all those parts, which, if tinkered with, would entail a different current line of practice. New ideas raised for discussion regarding the Association's principles and performance, when in contradiction with accepted principles and practice and that may entail significant modification, are not to affect practice unless they have first successfully carried the day within the Association and been embraced, on the decision of all sections, as an integral part of the general program. Any who may decide that there is no need for them to sacrifice their own particular viewpoint or to wait until they win in later discussions, should quit the Association.

– The flag adopted by the International is red, framed in black.

***

The strife-torn conditions in which the International exists imply that, often, its organization cannot be regular, that sometimes it lacks all or some of its federal bodies, that correspondence is sometimes interrupted and that congresses sometimes cannot be held because of the police or whatever. This does not mean that the International has ceased to exist. If there is no international federal commission, then the national commissions correspond with one another directly; if the national commissions are missing, the provincial ones handle the correspondence, and so on; or if they are all absent, each member carries on with his work as best he can, together with those comrades with whom he can meet, or on his own, until such time as changed circumstances make an attempt at re-organization possible.

In order to set a limit to the duration and damage done by such periods of dis-organization, as well as to intensify the flow of ideas and fellow-feeling around the association, all sections and all members should try to connect and correspond as much as they can with comrades elsewhere, within the bounds, naturally, of the requisite economy of effort and prudence.

Malatesta at the time of an 1891 underground stay in Italy / Source: Schweizerisches Bundesarchiv, Berne, E21, 1000/131, no. 9157

"Let's Go to the People": *L'Associazione* and the London Years of 1889–97

When Malatesta returned to Europe from South America in 1889, at thirty-five years of age, he had already the experience of a veteran, but still the energy of a young man. With his short lived but momentous periodical *L'Associazione* he began laying new foundations for his anarchism. Prompted by the drawn-out anarchist controversy between collectivists and communists, Malatesta took a pluralist stance and argued that the controversy was unjustified, for anarchism was to be regarded primarily as a method. He began reconsidering the relation between conscious minorities and masses, on the basis of a more realistic outlook on the people than the early internationalists' naïve reliance on the people's revolutionary instincts. Nobody knew when the times were ripe for revolution, so anarchists had to profit from every opportunity, every popular movement, whether or not it it had an explicit anarchist content. However, in order to do that effectively, anarchists had to "go to the people," share their life, and move forward with them. Above all, economic struggles and strikes were the highroad to revolution. Malatesta's realistic re-appraisal of anarchism was the groundwork for the entire later evolution of his ideas.

7.
ABOUT A STRIKE[1]

One issue that rightly preoccupies revolutionaries is how the revolution will come about.

The established society cannot last, they say, but still it does reflect huge interests, is backed by a heap of time-honored prejudices, and, above all, is defended by a mighty military organization that will fall apart just as soon as the spell of discipline is broken, but in the meantime is a redoubtable guard dog and means of repression. Where are we going to find the strength and the unity of action required to win? Plots and conspiracies are fine when it comes to mounting a specific action needing only a handful of people, but they are generally unable to determine a popular upheaval sufficiently widespread to stand a chance of winning. Spontaneous movements are nearly always too small and too localized, they erupt too recklessly and are all too easily smothered to give any hope of turning them easily into a general uprising.

Reasoning along these lines, the conclusion almost always reached is that the best occasions for attempting a social revolution is provided by some political movement mounted by the bourgeoisie, or a war.

Though we are always ready to take the opportunity that wars and political upheavals may offer us for expropriation and social revolution, we do not believe that those are the most likely, nor the most desirable of circumstances.

A war can trigger a revolution, at least in the defeated country. But war arouses the evil seed of patriotic feelings, inspiring hatred of the country that won, and the revolution to which this might give rise—being largely prompted by the wish for revenge and confronted with the necessity of resisting invasion—has a tendency to go no further than a political to-do. There is even a danger that the people, irked by the depredations and bullying of foreign soldiery, might forget about the fight against the bourgeois and fraternize with the latter in a war against the invader.

---

1 Translated from "A proposito di uno sciopero," *L'Associazione* (Nice) 1, no. 1 (6 September [*recte* October] 1889). Only seven issues of this periodical were published, the first three out of Nice, the remaining out of London.

A political upheaval carries the same sort of dangers, albeit on a smaller scale; the people blithely accept as friends all who are fighting against the government, and the socialists, who naturally would be trying to turn the turmoil into social revolution, would stand accused of placing victory in jeopardy and serving the government's interests.

Such events are becoming increasingly unlikely. The bourgeoisie has grown somewhat inured to uprisings ever since the emergence of the socialist party that threatens to dash victory from its hand, and the people, enlightened by experience and propaganda, are no longer so eager to let themselves be slaughtered for the glory and profit of their bosses. Then again, the bourgeoisie has no real incentive to make revolution—in the western European countries and in the Americas at any rate. In those countries, it is the bourgeoisie that actually governs. The fact that part of it finds itself in dire straits and facing bankruptcy and poverty does not depend on the political institutions and cannot be altered by a mere change of government. It is, rather, the outcome of the very capitalist system to which the bourgeoisie owes its existence. And, no matter how inevitable and imminent war may appear for a thousand economic and political reasons, it is always put off and becomes more and more unlikely to happen as the advances of international socialism make rulers frightened to plunge into the darkness that follows a great European war.

Anyway, wars and political upheavals are not dependant on us, and our propaganda, by its very nature, tends to make them increasingly harder and unlikely. It would therefore be very bad tactics on our part if we were to base our plans and hopes on events that we cannot and wish not to trigger.

In fact, we believe that the prejudice of waiting for opportunities that we cannot bring about ourselves is largely to blame for the sort of inertia and fatalism to which some among us sometimes succumb. Of course, he who cannot do anything or thinks he cannot do anything, is inclined to let things take their course and to leave it to the course of nature to sort matters out. And that very same prejudice may well be to blame for the fact that lots of sound socialists, whose warm love for the people and ardent revolutionary spirits we could not deny, believe they are obliged to lay down their weapons and wait for something to fall from the sky. Unable to bear such idleness, they throw themselves, just for something to do, into the electoral contest and then, bit by bit, abandon the revolutionary route altogether and discover that they have, against their wills, turned into vulgar politicos. How often what looks like—and may well have turned out to be—treachery has started out as zeal and impatience that have lost their way!

Luckily there are other avenues by which revolution can come about, and among these it seems to us that labor agitation in strike form is the most important one.

The great strikes that have occurred over recent years in a number of European countries were already pointing revolutionaries towards that somewhat neglected method; but, of them all, the colossal strike by dock workers in London a short while ago has proved especially instructive.[2]

***

Here are the facts:

Following a short but busy propaganda campaign, the casual laborers of London docks, numbering in the region of 50,000, organized themselves into a union and quickly came out on strike. Casuals are jobbing workers who report to the gates of the yards each morning and, if there is work for them, are employed for the day or indeed for just several hours at a stretch. These are poor laborers living in cramped and fetid slums, feeding themselves or rather keeping their hunger at bay with waste food and tainted spirits, and dressing in rags. Living day to day, their work always uncertain, exposed to competition from all the starvelings pouring in from every part of England and the rest of the world, well used to vying with one another for a bit of work, scorned by workers from the better-off trades, they certainly satisfied every condition necessary to be regarded as unsuited to organization and a conscious revolt against the exploiters. Yet it took only two years of propaganda carried out by a handful of willing men capable of addressing them in intelligible terms for these men to prove that they are well able to join forces, stand straight, and command the attention of

2 Malatesta is referring to what has come to be known as the Great Dock Strike, which took place in London from 14 August to 16 September 1889. This is generally acknowledged as the start of British "new unionism," which differed from the older craft unionism for its effort to achieve a broad base of unskilled and semi-skilled workers and its focus on industrial action. There is evidence that Malatesta, recently returned from South America, was in London at the time, before moving to Nice to edit *L'Associazione*. Therefore he was a direct witness of the strike.

the entire civilized world. Which just goes to show that the people are actually more advanced than some would believe, and that a slow but dogged elaboration is under way among the masses of the people, all unbeknownst to the philosophers, preparing them for the great day that will alter the face of the world.

The strikers were demanding six pence an hour (rather than five) for a day's work; and eight pence an hour for labor before 8 o'clock in the morning and after 6 o'clock in the evening; the abolition of the arrangement whereby work was sub-contracted to second-level exploiters who, in turn, often sub-contracted further; a minimum of four-hours work for those hired on, and a few other regulatory changes.

The strike of the casual workers had scarcely been declared when all the other unions connected with the loading and unloading of cargo ships—stevedores, coal porters, lightermen, carters, etc.—also stopped work, some of them not even seeking any improvements but just out of solidarity with the casuals. They rejected all compromise and any concessions until the casuals got what they wanted.

Carried away by example, other unions unrelated to the docks simultaneously tabled their own demands and went on strike.

And London, that great capital of monopolies, witnessed as many as 180 thousand people on strike, and impressive demonstrations by men with gaunt faces, dressed in rags, whose severe glowering struck terror into the souls of the bourgeoisie.

But there was more:

Workers employed in the gas plants offered to come out on strike. London would have been left in darkness come nightfall and the homes of the bourgeois would have been exposed to grave danger. The same offer was made by the tram-drivers, the steelworkers, and the woodworkers.

In short, there was quite an upsurge in enthusiasm, a rapture of solidarity, a reawakening of dignity that looked like bringing about a general strike; with production, transport and public services brought to a halt in a city of some 5 million inhabitants!

Other cities in England felt the impact of the example set, and more or less large strikes were erupting here and there. At home and abroad, the proletariat realized that the London workers were fighting in the common cause, and extraordinary assistance flooded in from everywhere.

The strikers were to be admired for the steadfastness with which they endured the harshest privations, and for the fortitude with which they rejected any suggestion of compromise, for the intelligence they displayed in anticipating what would be needed for the struggle, and for the spirit of solidarity and sacrifice that prevailed in their ranks.

They strove to feed a population, women and children included, of upwards of half a million people; to raise subscriptions and collections across the city; to keep up with vast correspondence by letter and telegram; to organize meetings, demonstrations, and talks; to keep an eye out, put pen to paper, and stay alert lest the bosses successfully trick English or foreign poor into blacklegging; to monitor all the docks' entrances to see if there were people going to work and how many. All of this, stunningly well done by unsolicited volunteers.

There was one noteworthy incident: a shipload of ice arrived and a rumor was rife that this ice was meant for the hospitals. The strikers raced in such numbers to help unload it without a care for whether they would be paid for the job or not. The sick—and especially the patients in the hospitals—were not to suffer on account of the strike.

No doubt about it; such folk deserve to and are capable of looking after their affairs for themselves and, if free, would be guided in their labors by this care for the general good—something entirely absent from the bourgeois system of production!

Those workers possessed a wide-ranging, often instinctive, cognisance of their rights and their usefulness to society, and had the combative mentality required to make a revolution; they felt a vague yearning for more radical measures that might end their suffering once and for all, and erase from production all the bosses and go-betweens who, though they produce not a thing, claim the greater part of what is produced, and turn work, which should be an obligation—something to glory in and derive satisfaction from—into a hell of pain and a badge of inferiority.

The city was in uproar, provisions had largely been exhausted, many factories had been closed down due to coal shortages or lack of raw materials, and with the growth in discomfort, irritation was on the rise. On the street corners, talk was beginning to turn to raiding the wealthier districts.

A blast of social revolution was blowing down the streets of the great city.

Unfortunately the masses are still imbued with the authority principle and believe that they cannot and should not to do anything without orders from above. And so it was that the strikers were swayed by a committee of men who certainly deserve praise for the part that they had played in the laying of the groundwork for the strike or for previous services, but who were plainly not suited to the position into which they had been hoisted by circumstances. Faced with a brand new situation that had moved beyond anything they had aspired to and for which they had no heart, they could not grapple with the responsibilities incumbent upon them and drive things forward, and they did not have the modesty and intelligence to stand aside and let the masses act. They began by hobbling the strike with an anti-general strike demonstration, and carried on doing all in their power to keep the peace and keep the strike within the parameters of the law. Later, after the moment of opportunity had passed, and weariness had begun to undermine the enthusiasm, they pressed for what they had previously rejected and issued a call for a general strike, only to retract it due to fresh fears and pressures.

The city's mayor and high clergy, who had been standing idly by, caring nothing for the workers' suffering, poured back into the city once they saw that things were dragging out too long and that business was in difficulty and facing ruination. Overcome as they were by tender feelings for the dearly beloved good folk, they offered to mediate... And after five weeks of heroic effort, the whole thing ended in a compromise, in the wake of which the workers returned to work with the promise that their demands would be met beginning on 4 November.

***

Behold how easily a revolution may come about and, alas! How easily the opportunity can be allowed to slip away.

If only in London the general strike had been encouraged and allowed to proceed, the situation would have become very problematic for the bourgeoisie, and revolution would have quickly occurred to the people as the simplest solution. Factories closed; railways, trams, buses, carriages and cabs brought to a standstill; public services cut off; food supplies suspended; nights spent without gaslight; hundreds of thousands of workers on the streets—what a situation for a group of men, had they but had a little grey matter and a modicum of gumption!

If only a little plain and clear-cut propaganda on behalf of violent expropriation but been mounted beforehand; if some gangs of valiants had set about seizing and handing out foodstuffs, clothing, and the other useful items with which the warehouses were so packed and of which proletarians were in such dire need; if only other groups or isolated individuals had forced or tricked their way into the banks and other government offices in order to set them alight, and others had entered the homes of the gentry and billeted the people's wives and children there; and if others had only given their just deserts to the most grasping bourgeois and others put out of action government leaders and any who, in time of crisis, might take their places, the police commanders, the generals and all the upper echelons of the army, taken by surprise in their beds or as they set foot outside their homes: in short, if only there had been a few thousand determined revolutionaries in London, which is so huge, then today the vast metropolis—and with it, England, Scotland, and Ireland—would be facing into revolution.

And such things, so very problematic and almost impossible to pull off— should they be put in readiness and prepared by some central committee—turn instead into the easiest thing in the world if revolutionaries, agreed on their aims and methods, act together with their comrades to push things in the direction they think best when the opportunity comes along, rather than waiting for anybody's opinions or orders.

There are more than enough people of courage, men of determination, in every city and town. If nothing else, the high crime rate would suggest as much; it is very often nothing but the unruly eruption of penned-up energies that can find no useful outlet in the present state of affairs. What is missing is the propaganda: when someone has a clear picture in his mind of the goal to be achieved and the means leading to it, he will act unsolicited and in the confidence that he is doing good and will feel no fear and no craven hesitancy.

***

Let us own up to having made mistakes:

Back in the days when anarchist ideas were starting to gain ground within the International, two schools of thought regarding the strike were extant among the proletariat. Some, who did not subscribe to any broad ideals of wholesale emancipation and social change, reckoned that the strike was the best means available to the working man in bettering his circumstances and they reckoned that this, plus the cooperative, ought to be the last word as far as the workers' movement goes.

The others, the authoritarian socialists, grasped and spelled out plainly that the strike was an economic nonsense and that it was powerless to bring any lasting improvement, let alone emancipate the proletariat; but they conceded that it is a fine weapon of propaganda and agitation, made frequent use of it and advocated the general strike as a means of starving the bourgeoisie out and forcing them to surrender. The only thing was that, by virtue of their being authoritarians, they imagined that a general strike could be organized in advance to break out on a specified date scheduled on the agenda of some central committee, once the majority of workers had joined the ranks of the International, and bourgeois exploitation brought to a pretty much peaceful end.

We anarchists, sandwiched between the bourgeois prejudices of one faction and the authoritarian utopianism of the other, were ourselves perhaps somewhat imbued with the old Jacobin mentality that paid small heed to the actions of the masses and thought the latter might be emancipated using the very same methods employed to enslave them, and we were quick to criticize the strike as an economic weapon and failed to give it its due as an index of moral rebellion. Gradually we surrendered the entire labor movement into the hands of reactionaries and moderates.

We, who mean to engage with any insurrection, no matter how small, we who will feel ashamed if, once the barricades begin to go up somewhere, we do not do all in our power to echo the upheaval or rush to fill the breech, have witnessed tens of thousands of men turning their shields against capital, seen the struggle grow more embittered and taking revolutionary turns… and we have stood idly by, leaving the field open to that class of self-styled revolutionaries who show up primarily to preach restraint and tranquillity and turn everything into an opportunity for them to put forward a candidate.

It is high time we re-examined ourselves. We are certainly not swearing off other means of action at our disposal or that might suit us—but above all else, let us get back among the people.

The masses are led to big demands by way of small requests and small revolts: let us blend with them and spur them forwards. Right across Europe, minds are at present inclined to big strikes by agricultural or industrial workers, strikes that involve vast areas and unions galore. Well, then, let us spark and let us organize as many strikes as we can; let us see to it that the strike becomes a contagion and that, once one erupts, it spreads to ten or a hundred different trades in ten or a hundred towns.

But let every strike carry its revolutionary message: let every strike summon up men of vigor to chastize the bosses and, above all, to commit trespasses against property and thus show the strikers how much easier it is to take than to ask.

A revolution that grows out of a huge proliferation of strikes would have the merit of finding the question already posed in economic terms and would more securely lead to the comprehensive emancipation of humanity.

The tactics we propose will bring us into direct and unbroken contact with the masses, will provide us with a bridgehead for importing and spreading our propaganda everywhere, and will allow us to set those examples and carry out that *propaganda by deeds,* which we are forever preaching but so rarely practise, not because of any lack of determination or courage, but for want of opportunity.

So let us be off in search of such opportunities.

8.
PROPAGANDA BY DEEDS[1]

One Way of Marking Socialism's Anniversaries

A comrade writes us: "It is our custom to mark our anniversaries with gatherings, talks, the putting up of posters and displaying of banners. Indeed we have stood trial and passed many a long month in prison for precisely these things. Meanwhile, as a rule, our gatherings and lectures are usually attended only by comrades who are already believers, our manifestoes are scarcely read and soon torn down, and our banners are poorly understood if at all. So I wonder , given the results produced by these things, whether they are worth the trouble of exposing the bravest of us to the danger of being taken out of circulation for a long time at intervals.

"Something occurs to me. Would it not be a good idea for groups of comrades, on such anniversaries and of course choosing the place, time, and manner likely to have the greatest impact, to burst into the wealthiest grocery, clothing, footwear stores, etc., and hand out their contents to poor folk passing by or loitering there? And, out in the countryside, could small teams of daring folk not unexpectedly swamp the landowners' warehouses, invite the peasants to follow suit and grab and carry home some wheat, oil, wine, tools, and everything to be found there?

"And if, in the doing of these things, our principles will be spoken of and manifestoes distributed to explain the action, tell of past struggles, and hint at the battles and victories in the near future, then the event of which we are celebrating the anniversary will indeed be etched into people's minds and will serve as propaganda and example.

"True, we shall often have dangers and commitments to grapple with; but that is no reason not to try. If we can compromise ourselves over matters of paltry or questionable usefulness, why could we not when it is a matter of securing big and certain outcomes? Besides, if a modicum of prudence and skill can be added to the enthusiasm, it is

1 Translated from "La propaganda a fatti," *L'Associazione* (Nice) 1, no. 2 (16 October 1889).

much easier to get away with matters that easily gain the complicity of the crowd, instead of those that leave the crowd uninvolved and indifferent. And getting away with something, when one can, is always a good thing, because then one can move on to something else."

***

We whole-heartedly endorse our correspondent's suggestion and commend it to all other comrades so that each of them may do whatever he can to implement it.

In fact, the sort of action the comrade proposes strikes us as so fruitful and so easy that we should like to see it carried out not just on anniversaries but at any time, everywhere.

***

Action of this sort offers the double advantage of a direct assault on property and of being feasible for all, and applicable, in however varied a form, always and everywhere.

Private ownership is the foundation upon which the entire edifice of exploitation, oppression, infamy, corruption, hate, vice, criminality, and warfare making up much vaunted modern civilisation rests. Above all else, we must destroy private ownership.

***

The property prejudice with which priests, moralists, lawmakers, and politicians have striven down the ages to imbue men right from the cradle, lives on those who suffer its murderous consequences.

In strikes, for example, we very often find ourselves faced with men of vigor who thrash or slay bosses and foremen; we have seen, for instance in Montceau-les-Mines, in France, working men dispatched to prison by the dozens for having tossed bombs into the homes of engineers and administrators; and we have seen, as we have in Belgium, mobs of rebellious miners manhandling the bourgeois, setting fire to the mines, and for days at a time being masters of large districts including wealthy cities—but we have never seen such strikers seizing goods and homes and proving that they have understood that the bosses are useless bloodsuckers and that everything that is has been created by them and belongs to them.[2]

2 The episodes at Montceau-les-Mines, a company-town near Lyons, occurred in 1882, when the town's mines were hard hit by a recession. An organization known

The sort of working man who defies the boss and uses a knife to repay him for the lengthy martyrdom he inflicts upon his wage slaves is not so rare. But the one that blithely makes off with the boss's belongings, with the calm and contented conscience of one who knows that he is merely exercising his rights is very, very rare. Impelled by need, the working man carries off whatever he can, but does so in shame, in the belief that he is doing wrong; and what should be an act of revolt in pursuit of demands remains common thievery and degrades one's character and dignity.

This business of ownership is one of the greatest prejudices and we have to bend all of our efforts to destroying it.

War, out and out war on property!

The people must get it into their head that the approaching revolution is going to be the revolution of the wretched, of the starvelings and that, wherever possible, it should have a foretaste of its benefits. Therein lies the success of the revolution, the assurance of the future, the salvation of humanity.

***

How much there is that could be done with just a little good will, a little get-up-and-go, a little imagination!

An employer is handing out wages to his workers: one strong man would be enough to wrestle his strongbox away from him and to toss all the cash it contains to his comrades.

A landlord shows up to collect his rents: what would it take to send him tumbling down the stairs, albeit unbeknownst to the poor widow or the ailing pauper, from the mouths of whose children the vulture was about to snatch the bread?

Carts belonging to some landlord or speculator arrive to collect the harvest that has cost the poor farmer such a lot of sweat: it would take only a few people who had come to a prior arrangement between themselves to seize those carts and divide their loads between the neediest families.

A tax collector makes his rounds, from house to house: how much effort would it require to dump him at the bend in some lonely street?

---

as the Black Band sent warning letters to managers and government officials, then began resorting to direct action. Twenty-three men were arrested and brought to trial. In Belgium, large strikes for better salaries and universal suffrage occurred in 1886 among the miners of the Borinage area, Liège, and Charleroi. The agitations were bloodily repressed by the army, under general Van der Smissen's command.

A landlord has evicted his share-cropper or his tenant for failure to pay his dividend or rent: might it not be good practice to present his heirs with a terrifying example of the vengeance of the oppressed?

There are, in our country districts especially, bulls and rams being fattened for our masters' tables; why not butcher one when the opportunity presents itself and invite the scurvy, anaemic peasants to help themselves to a bit of the meat they so sorely need? And if, on the first occasion, these wretches do not dare show up, why not bring the wholesome food to their very hovels? The *carabinieri* simply cannot be everywhere... and then again, they too are flesh and blood, and if they realize that people mean business, they know how to keep off.

But why be drawn into further examples? Once embarked upon the path of conscious independent action, anyone, if he has the will, will be able to set himself a task and find the comrades he may need.

***

Time now to own up to more mistakes.

Once upon a time we raised bands of armed men.

The band, in the classical sense of the word, and this is the sense in which we practised it, is a war party; it takes strong-arm methods, chosen weapons and specially trained personnel. It is very hard to do, but vital that that preparation is shrouded in strict secrecy; the personnel have to be chosen from wherever they may be and removed from their setting and natural center of activity; an extensive organization operating along authoritarian lines is needed; and expert leaders of some prestige are required. Then, once all the difficulties have been surmounted, the band takes to the field, to find the ground not prepared and is scattered and defeated before the people even get to learn what it is that the band wanted!

Meanwhile, the bulk of the support, unable to take part in the band, looks on impassively, useless as far as the attempted revolt is concerned.

It really is a truism that new things require new methods.

We want a popular revolution, made through the handiwork of all the willing, with no leaders imposed; so we need to embrace methods accessible to all and to accommodate every attitude and support.

In place of the classical band—formal, solemn, no longer reflecting the conditions and the party's aspirations, and made ever more difficult by changing topographical, military, and political conditions in the area—which comes together once and then goes ten or twenty years without being put to the test, let us have the unfettered, spontaneous, and unrelenting action of individuals and groups.

There is another sort of band that can still be put together anywhere, be it in the village or in the city, and requires no assets or only those assets that it procures for itself: this is the, so to speak, free-wheeling, temporary band that comes together in order to carry out a specific act and disbands as soon as it has been done, even before the authorities have had wind of it or been able to take steps.

We should practice that sort of band arrangement wherever individual action is inadequate or ineffective, pending the day when we can take to the streets with the masses of the people to deliver the coup de grace.

***

We have been stymied for a long time by an obsession with doing things on a grand scale.

We have wasted years constantly hatching ventures, which then never came to fruition, or, worse yet, waiting for others to hatch them.

Let us at last set about the real, practical, useful work : let us do whatever we can, but let us do it.

Some things that are in themselves insignificant, if repeated over and over and in lots of places are of more use than important things that are done once every ten years.

We shall never weary of stating it: the great revolution, the mass uprising will come as the result of relentless propaganda and an exceptional number of individual and collective revolts.

9.
ANOTHER STRIKE[1]

For the past several weeks the dock porters of Rotterdam (Holland) had set about starting their strike. On 26 September, the strike spread and the number of strikers climbed to four or five thousand; on 10 October they all returned to work, having secured a 10 cents an hour rise in pay.

The police actively sided with the bosses and were violent and brutal.

On the 27th they sabre-charged and dispersed the strikers, wounding several of them. The reporter from the English *Daily News* says that the ones who should have been kept under surveillance and restraint were the police officers rather than the strikers, who bore the insults and sabre blows with resignation. No English workman, the reporter adds, would ever have put up with such treatment!

It is only natural: act like a lamb and be eaten by the wolf. In the London dockers' strike the police refrained from all provocation, and the bourgeois, or at any rate the more intelligent among them, instead of calling for a violent crackdown, did their best to play up to the workers and keep them calm and amenable.

***

Back to the incidents in Rotterdam. Several social democrats (authoritarian socialists) arrived from Amsterdam and the Hague and, in concert with local colleagues, busied themselves urging calm and action within the law as usual.

On the other hand, the strikers turned down the offer made by the socialists to "lead" the strike and made it their business to distance themselves from any suggestion of socialism. At one meeting, they drove out one workman who had begun indulging in socialist talk, and unanimously cheered the House of Orange (the ruling dynasty in Holland).

All of this is painful—no mistake about it—and at first glance triggers a sense of profound pity and something bordering on fury,

---

1 Translated from "Un altro sciopero," *L'Associazione* (Nice) 1, no. 2 (16 October 1889).

like the spectacle of a crowd cheering its death and wishing its life was over. Victims of poverty, these blind men manhandled one who talked to them about doing away with poverty and, with their shoulders still bruised from the flat of the Orange soldiers' blades, cried out "Long live the House of Orange!"

Yet, on reflection, there is nothing there to make one wonder nor to dishearten.

And indeed, is it not small wonder that these strikers gave a hostile and suspicious welcome to individuals upon whom they had never before set eyes nor met but who were now stepping forward to offer themselves as ready-made "leaders" of the strike, which is to say, to claim the credit and the glory for it?

Is it any wonder that they rejected the socialists when the latter, without doing anything that others had not also done, were bringing to the dispute nothing but a word, which—given that determination to stay within the law—served only to add to the authorities' suspicion and violence and make any concession on the part of the bosses that much harder to come by?

Before one can wield any influence over the masses, one has to live among them, work alongside them, suffer and struggle alongside them. When the opportunity to act comes around, there is no need to offer oneself as a leader; instead, one should dive into the melee, preaching by example and paying the price in person. And, rather than stopping at abstract affirmations of theory, one should put himself in the masses' shoes, lower himself to their same starting point, and urge them on from there.

***

History teaches us that revolutions nearly always started with moderate demands—something akin to protests against abuses rather than outright revolts against the essence of institutions—and often with shows of respect and devotion towards the powers-that-be.

But where there is a ferment of ideas, and if one steps outside of the dead sea of legality and resorts to force, and the turmoil lasts long enough to grow, it always ends up toppling all the idols against which, initially, even the most timid attack could not be dared.

Revolt has a logic of its own; and every strike can—if it can hold out and spread—end up as a brazen and open assault on the principle of mastery, just the same as open insurrection against the monarchy can be the outcome of any attack on a town hall or on a *carabinieri* post, even if mounted to cries of "Long live the king! Long live the queen!"

Governments know this: let us learn it and capitalize upon it too.

In newspapers and books and everything addressed to the general public, as in debates between socialists, there is the essential need to specify one's thinking and to proclaim the entirety of our program loud and clear, without regard to persons or occasion. In one-to-one propaganda, however, and in the midst of a rioting populace, if one wants to make some headway, one has to be able to adapt to the intelligence, circumstances, practices, and prejudices of the individuals or masses so as to steer them by the best route towards socialist beliefs and socialist action.

There is a reluctance to get personal: fine, let us not name names when it helps to get things done.

What does it matter if the people cry out "Long live the king!" as long as it revolts against the king's men?

What does it matter if the people do not want to hear any talk of socialism, as long as they turn away from the bosses and seize their stuff?

Was the applause for the king with which the people of Paris, with unwitting irony, hailed every victory over royalty in any way an impediment to Louis Capet's having his head lopped off?

Let us take the people as they are and let's move forward with them. Casting them aside simply because they have no abstract grasp of our formulas and our rationale would be both idiocy and treason.

***

But let us be clear on this: this is no excuse for dumping our program and forgetting to call things by their proper names.

We can, we must, in certain circumstances, avoid mentioning socialism and anarchy, but only as long as our practice is socialism and anarchy. We may well not speak out against the government, but only as long as we are actually attacking the government; we can steer clear of talk directed against property, but only as long as our practice is expropriation.

10.
A REVOLT IS NO REVOLUTION[1]

This was the headline under which *La Rivendicazione* in Forlì carried, in its 5 October edition, an article over the signature of N. Sandri, regarding which a few critical comments may be in order.

Revolution, the author writes, taken in the precise sense of *thoroughgoing and lasting upheaval* affecting any established institution, is rather more than some revolt or cobbled-together riot on the part of the people. Such riots, he goes on to say, nearly always backfire on those who mount them, and public affairs fall back into the hands of folk who bide their time as long as the fighting lasts and then make of the fighters' dead bodies a footstool for themselves to rise on.[2] Then, out of the blue, he goes on to say that "any partial revolt is a revolution aborted"; that *real, humanitarian revolution* has made great strides, that the proletarian stands on the brink of seeing his legitimate wishes realized and that he must not "through nervousness or hysteria jeopardize the stability of what has been built up through so much effort and sweat and almost completed."

For a start, we need to agree on some terms when it comes to the meaning of the word revolution. *Thoroughgoing and lasting change* is all well and good, but we have to add, achieved by breaching the law, meaning by means of *insurrection*. It seems to us that the notion of revolution needs to be understood as an insurrection and, in any case, that is precisely how it is construed in everybody's political vocabulary.

Occasionally one hears references to peaceful revolution or violent revolution, indicative of the sort of elasticity of meaning always attached to words which concisely articulate widely varying actions and relationship, such as phenomena in the socio-political realm. But mention of revolution on its own is understood by all to refer to a

---

1 Translated from "La sommossa non è rivoluzione," *L'Associazione* (Nice) 1, no. 3 (27 October 1889).

2 This last metaphor is a paraphrase of a verse from Vincenzo Monti's tragedy *Aristodemus*, where the character of the ambitious is portrayed: "The man who is ambitious must be cruel / Between his views of greatness and himself, / Place ev'n his father's and his brother's heads,— / Beneath his feet he'll trample them; and make / Of both, a footstool for himself to rise on."

popular uprising intent upon forcibly overthrowing the existing order and replacing it with a different one that denies and is dismissive of the legality that went before it.

Let us not get muddled here. No matter how thoroughgoing and lasting, any change procured by lawful and peaceful means would be described as a reform and not as a revolution. And it is precisely according to whether they believe in the possibility of achieving a given purpose by lawful means or reckon it necessary to resort to insurrection that parties, regardless of their ideals, are divided into the reformist and the revolutionary.

We are for revolution, first because we think it useful and necessary and then because we can see its coming as inexorable and would regard it as puerile and harmful to go off looking for impossible alternatives; but since, above and beyond our being revolutionaries we are socialists and anarchists, we are out, and this the chief aim of our propaganda, to ensure that in the coming revolution, the people, far from trusting in good or bad spokesmen, take the resolution of the social question into its own hands, take immediate possession of property, demolish government in any guise, and sort out its affairs for itself. If in this revolution, as in political ones, people have to bear the cost of the war and then await its reward from a new government, then, to be sure, all the blood that an uprising costs will have been shed in vain and, in the current circumstances, that upheaval would merely postpone the social revolution for a generation or two.

But although this might not be clear from the article in question nor from the overall conduct of the newspaper, our belief is that even *Rivendicazione* purports to be revolutionary and wants to see the people, without delegation of powers, itself carrying out the thoroughgoing social change that anarchist socialists advocate.[3] So the question boils down to an argument over whether revolts, partial riots, hasten or postpone the great revolutionary eruption that should end the bourgeois world.

The writer of the *Rivendicazione* article says that "every partial revolt is a revolution aborted". Our belief, rather, is that revolts play a huge part in bringing the revolution about and laying its groundwork, and that it is always revolts that are the deciding factor.

---

3 Though nominally revolutionary, *La Rivendicazione* was open to electoral tactics and rejected the sharp separation between revolutionary and parliamentary tactics that Malatesta had urged since the 1880s.

It is deeds that trigger ideas, which in turn react with deeds and so on. But for turmoil and popular rioting, generated by necessity, but for the outrages and crimes of every sort that undermine the very foundations of social coexistence and shout a terrifying reminder in the revellers' ears, minds would never have been prompted to inquire into the causes of public malaise and to search for a cure and socialism would never have been born. Once it was, and once the propaganda increasingly opening eyes to needs started up and fixed a specific target for the hopes and agitations of sufferers, riots and increasingly conscious revolts have begun that give a fresh impetus to propaganda—and so on until revolution.

How could it be otherwise?

How ever could those millions of men—brutalized by exhausting toil; rendered anaemic by inadequate and unwholesome food; educated down through the ages in respect for priest, boss, and ruler; forever absorbed in the quest for their daily bread; superstitious; ignorant; fearful—one fine day perform an about face and emerge from their hovels, turn their backs on their entire past of patient submission, tear down the social institutions oppressing them and turn the world into a society made up of equals and brothers—had not a long string of extraordinary events forced their brains to think? If a thousand partial battles had not nurtured the spirit of rebellion in them, plus an appreciation of their own strength, a feeling of solidarity towards their fellow oppressed, hatred for the oppressor, and had not a thousand revolts taught them the art of people's warfare and had they not found in the yearned for victory a reason to ask themselves: what shall we do tomorrow?

Or was this down to all the newspapers and pamphlets they were unable to read and the speeches that never reached their ears?

Propaganda and the idea are undoubtedly the mighty catalyst that will set the inert masses in motion and raise slaves to the status of men, but this only appears among them and only affects them in the form of actions.

Socialism has made enormous strides, to be sure: certainly, as Sandri states, the bourgeois who laughed at socialist ideas fifty-odd years ago quakes before them these days. But does he think that the partial revolts of which he is so unfairly dismissive had not some hand in this? Babeuf's conspiracy, the Lyon uprising; the June days; the communes of '71; the uprising in Spain; the troubles in Italy; the nihilists in Russia; the regicides in Germany, Italy, and Spain; the Chicago anarchists; and the thousands of outrages thanks to which nearly every country in the world has its socialist martyrs of whom to boast? And what of the countless revolts that show that the idea is getting somewhere and that the people are starting to wake up? Or does all that count for nothing in the progress of socialism and the fear instilled into the bourgeois?

The history of past revolutions provides quite splendid proof of what we contend. Every one of them was preceded, triggered, and determined by a number of revolts that had already prepared minds for the fray. The great French revolution would never have happened had the countryside, thoroughly worked upon by propagandists, not started torching the chateaux and hanging the *seigneurs* and had the people of Paris, provoked into riot, not committed the sublime folly of attacking the fortress of the Bastille with its picks; Italy would be a geographical term still, like Poland, had not Italian patriots left their bones strewn around the peninsula in a hundred heroic partial revolts.[4]

And the contemporary history of socialism, which we have all witnessed and been part of... Is that not a reminder to us that out of a riot in Montmartre grew the Paris Commune and out of the Commune came a whole splendid ferment of ideas, an entire period of frantic socialist activity? Does that not show us how every bold deed, every venture mounted in Europe, has its corresponding fresh impulse given to propaganda and a new stratum of the populace won over to the revolution?

On the other hand you agree that "the building work has come to an end," meaning the preparations and evolution are now finished and the revolution ripe. Do we need a moment or two now before making up our minds to begin it? And how should we go about that if not by means of revolts?

To be sure, whilst every revolt makes propaganda, it is only the few that have the good fortune to come in timely enough fashion to trigger a revolution. But who is to say what the right timing is? Balilla threw a stone and the Austrians were driven out of Genoa because the people rose up; Caporali threw a stone and they called

4 It is worth mentioning that the argument that "ideas spring from deeds and not the other way around" had already been made by Carlo Pisacane, a foremost figure of Italian *Risorgimento* and a forerunner of libertarian socialism, in his *Political Testament*, written in 1857 on the eve of the attempted uprising of Sapri, where Pisacane met his death.

him a madman and worse, because Naples did not stir.[5] Had the Parisians been repelled by the Bastille's walls and massacred by the Royal Guard, 14 July would be a reminder to us of a mere revolt. Had the Bourbon ships sent Garibaldi and his thousand to a watery grave off Marsala, the victors of Calatafimi would be mourned today the way the vanquished of Sapri are.

So let us allow history to play out its course.

Nobody is asking to rise in revolt to anybody who does not want to or reckons he has better things to be doing: but if there are hardy souls eager to act, do not stand in their way. Do not pour water on the flames, now that the time has come to inflame minds and make ready for the great battle ahead.

***

In setting out our views alongside those of *Rivendicazione,* we have opted to ignore the truly inappropriate innuendo with which Sandri chose to adorn his article. This was lest we introduce into our argument a factor that was certainly unlikely to contribute towards the calm and level-headedness that ought to distinguish any discussion conducted with an eye to uncovering or spreading the truth. We shall do so now, not for our own sake, since the matter does not affect us, but rather to point the thing out to our friends in Romagna that, not being of the same mind as us and not supportive of our tactics, they nonetheless look sincerely to serious debate and mutual respect.[6]

"Be wary," Sandri tells the proletarians, "of makeshift spokesmen who daze you with roars or with the whining voices of monotonous Jeremiahs, *voices and roars probably fortified by wine drawn from the cellars at police headquarters and from the sacristy*."

What sort of talk is that? At whom is it directed?

We honestly do not know if, in these times, there is a statesman to be found who reckons that provoking revolts is the stuff of good government. It might have been the case once upon a time, in certain

5 Balilla is the nickname of the boy who, on 5 December 1746, sparked the insurrection that drove the Austrians out of Genoa, by throwing a stone at a group of soldiers. He went on to become one of the most popular figures of *Risorgimento.* Emilio Caporali was a young worker who attacked Prime Minister Francesco Crispi with a stone in Naples, on 13 September 1889. Malatesta commented on the episode in the first issue of *L'Associazione,* in the article "Bravo Caporali."

6 The city of Forlì, where *La Rivendicazione* was published, is in the Romagna region.

strange circumstances; but it cannot happen now, as there would be too many dangers in the people's taking the thing seriously; in any case, spontaneous revolts are more frequent than any that even the minister keenest on police procedures could hope for.

Anyway, if the folks at *Rivendicazione* or anybody else have serious grounds for being suspicious of anyone, let them spell it out clearly and plainly, and name names and they will be doing the cause a service and us a service as well. If not, let them stop spreading distrust and casting aspersions, the above not being the only example; let us hope that these things are only there in order to fill some column inches.

That way nobody gets wronged, since it is common knowledge that there has scarcely ever been a revolutionary whose adversaries, especially his most moderate adversaries, have not accused of being a spy. The only practical outcome of this is that it sparks angry retorts, generates a damaging sensationalism and, above all, creates an opening for the real spies who will certainly not forget to keep their heads down.

Mazzini, Bakunin, Hoedel, the Chicago Martyrs were all called spies; the Communards were labelled Bonapartists by the Versaillese and we ourselves were called spies, or as good as, when we raised the banner of revolt against Mazzinian dogmatism. Thus, Terzaghi, who really was a spy, was able to tell innocents, with every appearance of veracity: they call me a spy because I am more of a revolutionary than they are.[7]

In conclusion: if you know of any spies in our midst, let us know, as we will do with you, no matter how relations between us might stand otherwise. Meanwhile, uphold your ideas just we uphold ours and fight us decently just as we will fight you decently whenever we think serves the cause: act according to the promptings of your conscience, just we are prompted by ours—but do not stoop to the sin of innuendo and insult to which you take such loud exception when others take against you.

7 Carlo Terzaghi was an Internationalist turned spy. Only days before this article was published, Malatesta had denounced, from the columns of *L'Associazione*, Terzaghi's latest attempt to infiltrate once again the anarchist ranks under a false name.

11.
OUR PLANS

Union between communists and collectivists[1]

Some friends of ours have passed comment on the proposal we have put, and which has been generally well received, that a party be formed embracing all revolutionary anarchist socialists, regardless of the matter of the economic arrangement any faction may advocate for the society of the future.[2] Said comments show, on the one hand, a degree of repugnance on the part of some communists to the notion of coming together with collectivists, and, on the other, a fear lest we are out to revive an organization such as those past ones that collapsed because they were a spent force and no longer suited to the times.

Allow us to explain ourselves briefly with regard to the two aspects of this matter; we promise to revisit the matter, if need be.

As we see it, the co-existence within the one party of anarchist-communists and anarchist-collectivists is the logical and necessary consequence of the anarchist idea and method. Doubts would never have arisen about this but for the emergence of a certain brand of "collectivists" who are neither anarchists nor revolutionaries and who to all intents ensure that socialism adds up to nothing more than the pointless and corruptive struggle to win seats in representative bodies; in Italy and France where the vast majority of anarchists are communists, they have ensured that the meaning that all of us in Italy invested in the word "collectivism" prior to '76 and to which most Spanish anarchists still subscribe, has been forgotten about.[3]

1 Translated from "I nostri propositi. I. L'Unione tra comunisti e collettivisti," *L'Associazione* (London) 1, no. 4 (30 November 1889). The controversy over communism versus collectivism as the best form of the future anarchist society had divided the anarchist movement for years, especially in Spain.

2 The proposal to which Malatesta refers was contained in the circular *Appello*, published in Italian in Nice in September 1889 and translated into Spanish by the Barcelona anarchist periodicals *La Revolución Social* of 29 September and *El Productor* of 2 October.

3 1876 was the year when the Italian Internationalists, including Malatesta, claimed the inadequacy of collectivism and declared themselves in favor of communism, thus setting the controversy in motion.

We could scarcely see eye to eye with the sort of collectivists that are today out to ensconce themselves among the lawmakers and promote political reforms and so-called social legislation within the parameters of the law and who, come the revolution, would be out to establish a "workers' state." If, on the other hand and as a friend of ours assumes, collectivism means the entire wealth of society, money included, being equally divided between people so that each person might then carry on buying and selling the way they do today, that would be such a nonsense that, assuming that any could be found, it would have only a few, superficial supporters who would certainly not represent any boon to or a hope for the revolution and it would be a waste of our time to bother ourselves much about them.

But the truth is that the old collectivism of the pre-1876 International is not dead and in all likelihood it is not going to die out until the practicalities of the free life have definitively proved it wrong, and the evolution that will ensue upon the downfall of bourgeois rule will have induced all to embrace a superior mode of social coexistence, entirely founded upon the sentiment of solidarity and greater common advantage. Such collectivism is still subscribed to, as we have said, by the vast majority of the Spanish and, though knocked about by the logic of communism, it stands its ground and whilst there are, on the one hand, many defectors to the communist camp, on the other it is still making new recruits, and not just in Spain.

That collectivism—the one we ourselves subscribed to back in the days of Bakunin's propaganda and right up until 1876—means (we would remind any who may have forgotten this) violent expropriation effected directly by the people; the taking into common ownership of whatever there is, and then, reached by means of anarchy, which is to say, spontaneous evolution, the arrangement of a society wherein every person, having access from birth to all of the means of development civilization has to offer man and after receiving a comprehensive, integral physical and intellectual education, is guaranteed the raw materials and instruments of labor needed to be able to work freely with whichever partners he may choose and enjoy the full product of his labors.

We communists do not accept this program, and in forthcoming issues we shall spell out the reasons why as amply as we can since, whereas we mean to bring unity where division should not be found, we nevertheless are bound to publicize our ideals undiluted; but that is no reason for us to ignore the great affinity that exists between us and anarchist-collectivists and think that we are separated by an abyss when there are a thousand ties uniting us and making us brothers.

Let us take a look at what the differences and similarities are.

We both vigorously reject any alliance with bourgeois parties, any truck with elections and other legalitarian mumbo-jumbo. We are both out to make the revolution and we seek to do it by inciting the people to hatred and insurrection against the state and against property. We both seek expropriation by violence and the taking into common ownership not merely of raw materials and those instruments of labor not employed by the owner himself, but also of existing stocks of products and the destruction of all registers and every material accoutrement of private ownership. We both reject the intrusion of any sort of constituent body, or any delegated body and are resolved to resort to force and, if need be, to more extreme measures in order to ensure that no new government, however disguised, grows out of the revolution. For the organization of the new society, we both look to the deployment of humanity's innate resources, to the free reconciliation of the interests and feelings of all. We both want everyone to be free to do as they think best, provided only that they afford the same freedom to others.

Our differences therefore reside not in what we mean to do now and on the day of the revolution, not in what we mean and are bound to do by force and which properly constitutes the program of a revolutionary party; but, rather, of what we anticipate should happen next, in respect of the manner in which we should prefer to produce and consume and in the goal towards which we reckon the new phase of civilization, on the threshold of which we stand, should lead us.

But are such differences, founded as they are mainly on theoretical opinions and forecasts, sufficient grounds to separate us and set us yapping at one another, perhaps on the very eve of the insurrection and when we are talking about folk who do and will continue to fight alongside us against the very same enemies and for the very same demands?

And from the point of view of communist propaganda too, is it right to alienate those who are better disposed than anybody else to embrace our ideas, in that they share our enthusiasms, our feelings and, for the most part, the very same scientific beliefs as us?

It is our belief that the collectivist arrangement would not live up to the notions of justice and solidarity that drive, not just us but the collectivists themselves; we believe that it could not be operated other than by means of a complicated machinery that would be a reproduction of the state under a different name; we believe that it would, sooner or later, but inevitably, turn into communism or lapse back into bourgeois-ism. But, since a reversion to privilege and wage-slavery would be a moral impossibility on account of the moral revolution that would, of necessity, accompany the economic revolution, and specifically on account of anarchy, which is to say the absence of government, which is beyond question for us both, it strikes us that we have nothing to fear from an experiment, which we could not in any case prevent and which, let it be said, might in certain circumstances and in certain countries, help us surmount teething problems.

If anarchy means spontaneous evolution, if being anarchists means not believing that anyone is infallible and holding that only through freedom will humanity discover the solution to the problems that beset it and arrive at a general harmony and well-being, by what right and for what reason might we turn solutions we prefer and advocate into dogmas and impose them? And then again, using what means?

Were we an authoritarian party, which is to say, if we were out to become the government that might be conceivable. After taking power by means of revolution, we might introduce communism by decree and, if we were strong enough for it, there would be communism, though it would no longer stand for a harmonious society of free equals, but for a new form of slavery, which, in order to survive, would need an army, a police force, and the whole machinery the state has at its disposal for the purposes of corrupting, repressing, and enslaving.

Being anarchists, we are not going to have any means of ensuring the success of the solutions we propose other than propaganda and example, safe in the knowledge that they really will win through if they actually are the best.

So let us not look for enemies where there are naught but friends and let us not split the forces of the revolution, which will have only too sore a need for the support of all sincere anarchists in placing obstacles in the way of the bamboozlers and reactionaries and in ensuring that socialism triumphs.

One can have the most widely varying ideals when it comes to the re-making of society, but the method will always be the one that determines the goal achieved, since it is common knowledge that in sociology as in topography, one does not go wherever one *wishes*, but wherever the path one is on may lead.

For the formation of a party, it is necessary and sufficient that there should be a shared method. And the method, which is to say, the practical conduct that anarchist socialists mean to abide by, is shared by all, communists and collectivists alike.

That the authoritarians, the *electioneers*, and often the republicans are or are fond of styling themselves collectivists, is a matter of no importance to us and should engender neither confusion nor hybrid alliances within our ranks, since we are not saying that we are uniting with mere collectivists, but make it an essential precondition that they be *anarchists and revolutionaries* to boot.

It seems to us that the program we have put forward is such as to exclude absolutely every politicker, be he bourgeois or socialist. If there are some among our friends who find this inadequate, let them suggest whatever amendments or additions they see fit. We shall publish them and debate them and then it will be up to each of us to judge and to act upon his convictions.

12. MATTERS REVOLUTIONARY[1]

We have had the following letter from comrade Malatesta:

Dear comrades,

A French-language paper has chosen to dwell upon what I said at the anti-parliamentary conference held in London on 3 August in the hall of the Autonomie Club, and reports me as saying pretty much the opposite of what I actually did say.

Would you allow me to re-state the truth? It might well also provide an opening for a discussion between comrades regarding matters of the utmost interest to the anarchist party.

Here, then, are the thoughts I put to the comrades gathered at the Autonomie—albeit at rather greater length than I was able to express them in the little time afforded to each speaker.

The main topic that the conference had set itself was how to go about ensuring international solidarity in respect of revolutionary activity.

Which boils down to the much-debated question of organization: a matter which has a bearing equally upon international action and national or local activity.

Within the anarchist camp, there are comrades who reject all thought of organization for fear that it lead to the creation of an authority and hobble free initiative. To be sure, all or nearly all of the revolutionary organizations formed in the past have been more or less tainted by authoritarianism; but are we to deduce from that that all organization is, of necessity, authoritarian? Certainly not. An organization is authoritarian where there are some among its membership who are out to wield authority and another faction prepared to defer to it; an organization made up of thoughtful anarchists is, of necessity, libertarian.

I would go further: the very inability to conceive of an authority-free organization is proof that the anarchist idea has yet to sink properly into our heads. Indeed, what is an anarchist society but

1 Translated from "Questions révolutionnaires," *La Révolte* (Paris) 4, no. 4 (4–10 October 1890).

organization without authority? And if it feasible in the future society when it comes to meeting every human need, why would it not be feasible today between those who understand and have a feeling for Anarchy when it comes to meeting the needs of the fight against the Bourgeoisie?

Authoritarian organization is a menace and damaging to the revolution: it places the entire movement at the mercy of particular thinking, or indeed of the shortcomings and treachery of a handful of leaders; it leaves us wide open to the blows of governments and, worst of all, it schools revolutionaries in abdicating their initiative to the hands of a few, and the people to look to some sort of providence for its salvation.

But non-organization, on the other hand, spells powerlessness and death; it accustoms people to lack of solidarity and hateful rivalry of each against all, and its upshot is inactivity.

Free initiative is certainly progress's great asset; but for it to operate, there still has to be some cognisance of its force. Folk toil and take risks and make sacrifices when they believe that there is some end-product to these things, when they know that what they are doing will be understood, abetted, and followed up by their comrades.

Heroes who act on an idea without a care for what others may say or do, are very few and far between; we need not depend on them. And though their action is never entirely fruitless, still its impact, should it remain isolated, is out of all proportion to the effort expended.

The loner is the most powerless of creatures; and the further we travel down the civilisation, the more overwhelming becomes the part played by cooperation and solidarity in life.

Moreover, all this really comes down to nothing but a quibble.

Should they happen to be men of action, those who preach against organization of any sort will do just what the rest of us will: they will combine their several efforts so as to achieve a thing and strive to widen their circle of friends and come to arrangements and more or less stable relations with the individuals and groups that serve their purpose.

True, they rack their brains to come up with names to take the place of organization, but in actual fact they quite sheepishly engage in organization or attempts at organization. Just like Mr Jourdain who used to churn out prose quite unwittingly.[2]

2 Jourdain is the character of Molière's *The Bourgeois Gentleman,* who aims to rise above his middle-class origins and be accepted as an aristocrat. In his fatuous

If it were only a quibble over words, this would leave us wholly cold and we should readily allow them to call it by whichever name they deem best. But the fact is that by preaching that Anarchy does not countenance organization, they are doing an injury to the idea in the minds of sensible folk, causing precious time to be wasted on idle controversies and keeping many a comrade in a dither that prevents them from doing a thing.

Besides, as it happens, folk who might have all of the makings of an anarchist but who think we are doomed to impotence (as indeed we would be if we really were to abjure the benefits of association), prefer—making the best of a bad situation—to sign on with the social democrats and other politickers.

And besides, non-organization culminates in an authority which, being unmonitored and unaccountable, is no less of a real authority for all that. Indeed, vigorous types, men of action do not shrink from banding together and organizing so as to amass the strength that springs from cooperation; so all the propaganda directed against organization merely succeeds in making organization the privilege of the few. The bulk of the party, floundering in dis-organization, is naturally led by those who, being united, are strong and who, even though they may not wish it, impose their thinking and their will thanks to their single-mindedness and by the coordination they inject into their propaganda and into their actions.

We want to see free initiative in organization as in every other domain; let each person organize himself as he sees fit, with those who suit him, in accordance with whatever his purpose necessitates and according to affinities of temperament, leanings, and interests; but just as long as there is the least possible number of isolated individuals and squandered energies.

We are certainly not about to give up on organization, which is life and force; on the contrary, we shall strive to develop it so as to become as strong as we may. But, being anarchists and given that we are not out to use it as an instrument of domination, we want all our comrades to strive too to acquire as much strength as they can by tightening the ties that bind them together. And the strength of us all will be the strength of the Revolution and will be the lever with which we shall overturn the bourgeois world.

---

vanity, he is surprised and delighted to learn that he has been speaking prose all his life without knowing it.

There is a fear of leaders—and rightly so—but the genuine, the only way of dispensing with leaders is knowing what one wants and how to get it. So the preventive against leaders is the spread of anarchist principles and methods. An anarchist organization has no leaders because it is founded, not upon belief in an individual, but upon a comprehensive understanding of the program on the part of every member of the organization.

And if, even among the anarchists, there are those who blindly follow certain persons, that is a blight attributable to the authoritarian education by which humankind is still oppressed after so many centuries. Such people will find leaders no matter what they may do or where they may be; if they are to be rid of leaders the darkness must first be banished from their minds. There are no two ways about that.

***

Since the foundation stone and chief bond of an anarchist organization should be the program understood and embraced by all, it might be useful to say something about that program in terms of its comprehensiveness, so as to see what manner of men we might consider as belonging to our party and with whom we must strive to come to agreement and organize.

Plainly, we can work only with fellow anarchists. There are too many differences over aims and methodologies between us and the non-anarchist socialists for agreement to be feasible, especially right now when the latter, swept along by the logic of their methodology, are edging ever closer to the bourgeoisie and virtually forgetting that they are socialists.

But among the anarchists there are factions that differ over their notions about the society of the future. Why should we not all be on the same side provided that we all see eye to eye over how the Revolution is to be prepared and carried out?

We, for instance, are communists; but there are also the anarchist collectivists, who are quite rare in other countries but who are, in Spain, many, well-organized, and very active workers on behalf of the common cause. Needless to say, they are not to be confused with the French "collectivists" who may well be communists but who are primarily authoritarians and parliamentarists, which is to say, anti-anarchists.

Now, like us, these collectivist anarchists dismiss all hope vested in or expediency in parliament and they are for revolution by force. Like us, they seek the expropriation of property-owners by force and the taking in hand and into common ownership of all private and public wealth, by means of direct action by the people. Like us, they want to see governments of any description destroyed, and society reorganized through direct action of the people and without delegation of authority. Like us, they mean to use force to prevent any new form of authority's tampering with the results of the Revolution.

So why would we not collaborate with one another in our common endeavour?

Between us and them, there are differences galore over matters having to do with how production and distribution should be organized in the society of the future. We communists reckon that the only solution that can resolve all possible difficulties and conflicts in an egalitarian society, while satisfying cravings for justice and fraternity, is a social organization founded upon the solidarity principle: *From each according to his abilities, to each according to his needs,* meaning that *everything belongs to everybody*.

The collectivists, on the other hand, believe that society will be reorganized in accordance with the fairness principle: *from each according to his abilities, to each according to his handiwork,* meaning that *each owns the product of his work*—a solution we find both unfair and narrow-minded and which is, worst of all (according to communists), unrealizable in practice or at least incapable of surviving without either quickly evolving in the direction of communism or collapsing back into bourgeois practice.

But all of this relates to the post-revolutionary period, and cannot be a dividing line in the struggle we have to wage today. And even after the Revolution such divergence of opinion should produce only a brotherly competition in the bestowal of the greatest social good. Were we an authoritarian party, that is, if it was our aspiration to establish a government and impose our view, then, of course we could only march in step with those who are out to lay down the same decrees, the same laws as us. But since, according to us, it is the people itself and every single person who goes to make the people that should fashion its organization and its accommodation with other factions; it being the spontaneous evolution and unfettered inter-play of needs and enthusiasms and everyone's observation and experimentation that should fashion the shape or shapes of social life, we anarchists, of whatever hue, will need only to preach by example by putting our ideas and solutions to the test of experience.

In social struggles as in scientific research, the method precedes and determines the outcomes. And parties form around what they mean to do rather than around wishes or anticipations.

As a result, it seems to me that all anarchist socialists who espouse the same methods of struggle can be counted as and make up the same party, regardless of matters of reorganization.

***

Let me close with a few remarks about revolutionary tactics.

We must immerse ourselves in the life of the people as fully as we can; encourage and egg on all stirrings that carry a seed of material or moral revolt and get the people used to handling their affairs for themselves and relying on only their own resources; but without ever losing sight of the fact that revolution, by means of the expropriation and taking of property into common ownership, plus the demolition of authority, represents the only salvation for the proletariat and for Mankind, in which case a thing is good or bad depending on whether it brings forward or postpones, eases or creates difficulties for that revolution.

As we see it, it is a matter of avoiding two reefs: on the one hand, the indifference towards everyday life and struggles that distance us from the people, making us unfathomable outsiders to them—and, on the other, letting ourselves be consumed by those struggles, affording them greater importance than they possess and eventually forgetting about the revolution.

Let us apply this to the question of strikes.

As we are slightly prone to doing, we have stumbled from one exaggeration to another one.

Once upon a time, being convinced that the strike was powerless not only to emancipate but also to bring any lasting improvement to the workers' lot, we were too dismissive of the moral side of things and, with the exception of a few regions, had left that mighty weapon of propaganda and agitation almost entirely to the authoritarian socialists and the lullaby-singers.

Having recovered from such indifference in the wake of the recent great strikes and above all the London docks strike, which gave one to believe that if the men leading it had had a clear-cut revolutionary outlook and had not been afraid of the responsibility, the dock workers might have been induced to march on the wealthier districts and carry out the revolution. Now there are signs of a tendency to swing too far in the opposite direction, that is, towards unrealistic expectations of strikes, with the strike being almost conflated with revolution.[3]

This is a very dangerous trend since it conjures up chimerical hopes and the practice is—not so corruptive to be sure, but equally as disappointing and soporific—as parliamentarism itself.

The general strike is preached and this is all to the good; but, as I see it, imagining or announcing that the general strike is the revolution is plain wrong. It would only be a splendid opportunity for making the Revolution, but nothing more. It might be transformed into revolution, but only if the revolutionaries wielded enough influence, enough strength and enough enterprise to drag the workers down the road to expropriation and armed attack, before the effects of hunger, the impact of massacre or concessions from the bosses come along to erode the strikers' morale and bring them to a state of mind (so readily produced among the masses) where they are ready to submit, no matter what the cost, and where anybody calling for all-out struggle comes to be looked upon as an enemy or an agent provocateur.

Moreover, given the current economic and moral circumstances of the worldwide proletariat, I regard an authentic general strike as unachievable; and I hold that the revolution will be carried out well before that strike can be mounted. But big strikes are already afoot and, with the right activity and agreement, even bigger ones could be triggered. This might well be the form in which, in industrialized countries at least, the social revolution will arrive. So we need to be on the lookout so as to cash in on any opportunities that might arise.

No longer should the strike be the warfare of folded arms.

Far from their being made redundant by strikes, rifles and all the means of attack and defence placed at our disposal by science are still instruments of emancipation and will find in strikes a splendid opportunity for advantageous use.

---

3 We already have hereafter part of the arguments that Malatesta would oppose to syndicalism after the turn of the century.

13.
ANARCHY[1]

Anarchy is a word which comes from the Greek, and signifies, strictly speaking, *without government*: the state of a people without any constituted authority, that is, without government.

Before such an organization had begun to be considered possible and desirable by a whole class of thinkers, so as to be taken as the aim of a party (which party has now become one of the most important factors in modern social warfare), the word anarchy was taken universally in the sense of disorder and confusion, and it is still adopted in that sense by the ignorant and by adversaries interested in distorting the truth.

We shall not enter into philological discussions, for the question is not philological but historical. The common meaning of the word does not misconceive its true etymological signification, but is derived from this meaning, owing to the prejudice that government must be a necessity of the organisation of social life, and that consequently a society without government must be given up to disorder,

---

1 Parts 1–9, *Freedom* (London), nos. 58–65 (September 1891–April 1892) and 67 (June 1892). Originally published as *L'Anarchia* (London: Biblioteca dell'Associazione, 1891). An earlier, shorter version of this work appeared in three parts in *La Questione Sociale* (Florence) 1, nos. 8–10 (4, 11, and 18 May 1884). Together with *Fra contadini* (*Between Peasants*) and *Al caffè* (*At the Café*), this is one of Malatesta's best-known pamphlets and one of the most popular works in the history of anarchist literature. At the same time that it is a clear exposition of general anarchist principles, it bears the distinct imprint of Malatesta's own brand of anarchism. *Freedom*'s serial edition was reprinted in pamphlet form in 1892 and reissued many times in the following decades. Freedom Press published an eighth edition in 1949. In the United States, the same translation was published in San Francisco by A. Isaak in the "Free Society Library" in 1900, and in Buffalo, undated, by the "Friends of Malatesta" around 1971. New translations have later appeared. At present, the most widely available is the one made by Vernon Richards for Freedom Press in 1974, which has been frequently reprinted since. We republish this work in its entirety from its first English edition because, in addition to being a fairly complete and accurate translation, it has value as a historical document. Not only it was the only English translation made during Malatesta's lifetime, but it was also published in the city where he lived, and by an editing group with whom he was in close contact. The translation has been checked against the Italian original, and occasional translation errors or omissions have been amended. In the latter case, the interpolations have been indicated in footnotes.

and oscillate between the unbridled dominion of some and the blind vengeance of others.

The existence of this prejudice and its influence on the meaning which the public has given the word is easily explained.

Man, like all living beings, adapts and habituates himself to the conditions in which he lives, and transmits by inheritance his acquired habits. Thus being born and having lived in bondage, being the descendant of a long line of slaves, man, when he began to think, believed that slavery was an essential condition of life, and liberty seemed to him an impossible thing. In like manner, the workman, forced for centuries, and thus habituated, to depend upon the good will of his employer for work, that is, for bread, and accustomed to see his own life at the disposal of those who possess the land and capital, has ended in believing that it is his master who gives him to eat, and demands ingenuously how it would be possible to live, if there were no master over him?

In the same way, a man who had had his limbs bound from his birth, but had nevertheless found out how to hobble about, might attribute to the very bands that bound him his ability to move, while, on the contrary, they would be diminishing and paralysing the muscular energy of his limbs.

If then we add to the natural effect of habit the education given him by his master, the parson, teacher, etc., who are all interested in teaching that the employer and the government are necessary; if also we add the judge and the bailiff to force those who think differently—and might try to propagate their opinions—to keep silence, we shall understand how the prejudice as to the utility and necessity of masters and governments has become established. Suppose a doctor brings forward a complete theory, with a thousand ably invented illustrations, to persuade that man with bound limbs whom we were describing, that, if his limb were freed, he could not walk, could not even live. The man would defend his bands furiously, and consider any one his enemy who tried to tear them off.

Thus, since it is believed that government is necessary, and that without government there must be disorder and confusion, it is natural and logical to suppose that anarchy, which signifies without government, must also mean absence of order.

Nor is this fact without parallel in the history of words. In those epochs and countries where people have considered government by one man (monarchy) necessary, the word republic (that is, the government of many) has been used precisely like Anarchy, to imply disorder and confusion. Traces of this signification of the word are still to be found in the popular language of almost all countries.

When this opinion is changed, and the public convinced that government is not necessary, but extremely harmful, the word anarchy, precisely because it signifies without government, will become equal to saying Natural order, harmony of the needs and interests of all, complete liberty with complete solidarity.

Therefore, those are wrong who say that Anarchists have chosen their name badly, because it is erroneously understood by the masses and leads to a false interpretation. The error does not come from the word, but from the thing. The difficulty which Anarchists meet with in spreading their views does not depend upon the name they have given themselves, but upon the fact that their conceptions strike at all the inveterate prejudices that people have about the function of government, or the *State,* as it is called.

Before proceeding further, it will be well to explain this last word (the State) which, in our opinion, is the real cause of much misunderstanding.

Anarchists, and we among them, have made use, and still generally make use of the word State, meaning thereby all that collection of institutions, political, legislative, judicial, military, financial, etc., by means of which the management of their own affairs, the guidance of their personal conduct and the care of ensuring their own safety are taken from the people and confided to certain individuals. And these, whether by usurpation or delegation, are invested with the right to make laws over and for all, and to constrain the public to respect them, making use of the collective force of the community to this end.

In this case the word State means government, or, if you like, it is the impersonal expression, abstracted from the state of things, of which government is the personification. Then such expressions as Abolition of the State, or Society without the State, agree perfectly with the conception which Anarchists wish to express of the destruction of every political institution based on authority, and of the constitution of a free and equal society, based upon harmony of interests, and the voluntary contribution of all to the satisfaction of social needs.

However, the word State has many other significations, and among these some which lend themselves to misconstruction, particularly when used among men whose sad social position has not afforded them leisure to become accustomed to the delicate distinctions of scientific language, or, still worse, when adopted treacherously by adversaries, who are interested in confounding the sense, or do not wish to comprehend. Thus the word State is often used to indicate any given society, or collection of human beings, united on a given territory and constituting what is called a social unit, independently of the way in which the members of the said body are grouped, or of the relations existing between them. State is used also simply as a synonym for society. Owing to these significations of the word, our adversaries believe, or rather profess to believe, that Anarchists wish to abolish every social relation and all collective work, and to reduce man to a condition of isolation, that is, to a state worse than savagery.

By State again is meant only the supreme administration of a country, the central power, distinct from provincial or communal power, and therefore others think that Anarchists wish merely for a territorial decentralization, leaving the principle of government intact, and thus confounding Anarchy with cantonal or communal government.

Finally, state signifies condition, mode of living, the order of social life, etc., and therefore we say, for example, that it is necessary to change the economic state of the working classes, or that the Anarchical state is the only state founded on the principles of solidarity, and other similar phrases. So that if we say also in another sense that we wish to abolish the State, we may at once appear absurd or contradictory.

For these reasons, we believe it would be better to use the expression *abolition of the State* as little as possible, and to substitute for it another clearer and more concrete—*abolition of government*.

In any case, the latter will be the expression used in the course of this little work.

We have said that Anarchy is society without government. But is the suppression of government possible, desirable, or wise? Let us see.

What is the government? There is a disease of the human mind called the metaphysical tendency, causing man, after he has by a logical process abstracted the quality from an object, to be subject to a kind of hallucination which makes him take the abstraction for the real thing. This metaphysical tendency, in spite of the blows of positive science, has still strong root in the minds of the majority of our contemporary fellow men. It has such influence that many consider government an actual entity, with certain given attributes of reason, justice, equity, independently of the people who compose the government.

For those who think in this way, government, or the State, is the abstract social power, and it represents, always in the abstract, the general interest. It is the expression of the right of all, and considered as limited by the rights of each. This way of understanding government is supported by those interested, to whom it is an urgent necessity that the principle of authority should be maintained, and should always survive the faults and errors of the persons who succeed to the exercise of power.

For us, the government is the aggregate of the governors, and the governors—kings, presidents, ministers, members of parliament, and what not—are those who have the power to make laws, to regulate the relations between men, and to force obedience to these laws. They are those who decide upon and claim the taxes, enforce military service, judge and punish transgressors of the laws. They subject men to regulations, and supervise and sanction private contracts. They monopolise certain branches of production and public services, or, if they wish, all production and public service. They promote or hinder the exchange of goods. They make war or peace with the governments of other countries. They concede or withhold free-trade and many things else. In short, the governors are those who have the power, in a greater or lesser degree, to make use of the collective force of society, that is, of the physical, intellectual, and economic force of all, to oblige each to do the said governors' wish. And this power constitutes, in our opinion, the very principle of government, the principle of authority.

But what reason is there for the existence of government?

Why abdicate one's own liberty, one's own initiative in favor of other individuals? Why give them the power to be the masters, with or contrary to the wish of each, to dispose of the forces of all in their own way? Are the governors such very exceptionally gifted men as to enable them, with some show of reason, to represent the masses, and act in the interests of all men better than all men would be able to do for themselves? Are they so infallible and incorruptible that one can confide to them, with any semblance of prudence, the fate of each and all, trusting to their knowledge and their goodness?

And even if there existed men of infinite goodness and knowledge, even if we assume what has never been verified in history, and what we believe it would be impossible to verify, namely, that the government might devolve upon the ablest and best, would the possession of governmental power add anything to their beneficent influence? Would it not rather paralyse or destroy it? For those who govern find it necessary to occupy themselves with things which they do not understand, and, above all, to waste the greater part of their energy in keeping themselves in power, striving to satisfy their friends, holding the discontented in check, and mastering the rebellious.

Again, be the governors good or bad, wise or ignorant, who is it that appoints them to their office? Do they impose themselves by right of war, conquest, or revolution? Then, what guarantees have the public that their rulers have the general good at heart? In this case it is simply a question of usurpation, and if the subjects are discontented nothing is left to them but to throw off the yoke, by an appeal to arms. Are the governors chosen from a certain class or party? Then certainly the ideas and interests of that class or party will triumph, and the wishes and interests of the others will be sacrificed. Are they elected by universal suffrage? Now numbers are the sole criterion, and numbers are certainly no proof of reason, justice or capacity. Under universal suffrage the elected are those who know best how to take in the masses. The minority, which may happen to be half minus one, is sacrificed. And that without considering that there is another thing to take into account.

Experience has shown it is impossible to hit upon an electoral system which really ensures election by the actual majority.

Many and various are the theories by which men have sought to justify the existence of government. All, however, are founded, confessedly or not, on the assumption that the individuals of a society have contrary interests, and that an external superior power is necessary to oblige some to respect the interests of others, by prescribing and imposing a rule of conduct, according to which the interests at strife may be harmonised as much as possible, and according to which each obtains the maximum of satisfaction with the minimum of sacrifice. If, say the theorists of the authoritarian school, the interests, tendencies, and desires of an individual are in opposition to those of another individual, or mayhap all society, who will have the right and the power to oblige the one to respect the interests of the other or others? Who will be able to prevent the individual citizen from offending the general will? The liberty of each, say they, has for its limit the liberty of others; but who will establish those limits, and who will cause them to be respected? The natural antagonism of interests and passions creates the necessity for government, and justifies authority. Authority intervenes as moderator of the social strife, and defines the limits of the rights and duties of each.

This is the theory; but the theory to be sound ought to be based upon facts and explain them. We know well how in social economy theories are too often invented to justify facts, that is, to defend privilege and cause it to be accepted tranquilly by those who are its victims. Let us here look at the facts themselves.

In all the course of history, as at the present epoch, government is either the brutal, violent, arbitrary domination of the few over the many, or it is an instrument ordained to secure domination and privilege to those who, by force, or cunning, or inheritance, have taken to themselves all the means of life, and first and foremost the soil, whereby they hold the people in servitude, making them work for their advantage.

Governments oppress mankind in two ways, either directly by brute force, that is physical violence, or indirectly by depriving them of the means of subsistence and thus reducing them to helplessness at discretion. Political power originated in the first method; economic privilege arose from the second. Governments can also oppress man by acting on his emotional nature, and in this way constitute religious authority. But as spirit cannot exist independently, so bodies constituted for the propagation of lies have no ground for existence, except insofar as they are the consequences of political and economic privileges, and are a means of defending and consolidating them.

In primitive society, when the world was not so densely populated as now, and social relations were less complicated, when any circumstance prevented the formation of habits and customs of solidarity, or destroyed those which already existed, and established the domination of man over man, the two powers, the political and the economical, were united in the same hands—and often also in those of one single individual. Those who had by force conquered and impoverished the others, constrained them to become their servants, and perform all things for them according to their caprice. The victors were at once proprietors, legislators, kings, judges, and executioners.

But with the increase of population, with the growth of needs, with the complication of social relationships, the prolonged continuance of such despotism became impossible. For their own security the rulers, often much against their will, were obliged to depend upon a privileged class, that is, a certain number of co-interested individuals, and were also obliged to let each of these individuals provide for his own sustenance. Nevertheless they reserved to themselves the supreme or ultimate control. In other words, the rulers reserved to themselves the right to exploit all at their own convenience, and so to satisfy their kingly vanity. Thus private wealth was developed under the shadow of the ruling power, for its protection and—often unconsciously—as its accomplice. Thus the class of proprietors arose. And they, concentrating little by little the means of wealth in their own hands, all the means of production, the very fountains of life—agriculture, industry, and exchange—ended by becoming a power in themselves. This power, by the superiority of its means of action, and the great mass of interests it embraces, always ends by more or less openly subjugating the political power, that is, the government, which it makes its policeman.

This phenomenon has been reproduced often in history. Every time that, by invasion or any military enterprise whatever, physical brute force has taken the upper hand in society, the conquerors have shown the tendency to concentrate government and property in their own hands. In every case, however, as the government cannot attend to the production of wealth, and overlook and direct everything, it finds it needful to conciliate a powerful class, and private property is again established. With it comes the division of the two sorts of power, that of the persons who control the collective force of society, and that of the proprietors, upon whom these governors become essentially dependent, because the proprietors command the sources of the said collective force.

But never has this state of things been so accentuated as in modern times. The development of production, the immense extension of commerce, the extensive power that money has acquired, and all the economic results flowing from the discovery of America, the invention of machinery, etc., have secured such supremacy to the capitalist class that it is no longer content to trust to the support of the government, and has come to wish that the government shall emanate from itself. A government which owed its origin to the right of conquest (*divine right* as the kings and their priests called it) though subjected by existing circumstances to the capitalist class, went on maintaining a proud and contemptuous attitude towards its now wealthy former slaves, and had pretensions to independence of domination. That government was indeed the defender, the property owners' *gendarme*, but the kind of *gendarmes* who think they are somebody, and behave in an arrogant manner towards the people they have to escort and defend, when they don't rob or kill at the next street corner; and the capitalist class got rid of it, or is in the process of so doing by means fair or foul, and replacing it by a government of its own choosing;[2] a government composed of members from its own class, continually under its control and specially organised to defend its class against the possible revenge of the disinherited. Hence the origin of the modern parliamentary system.

To-day the government is composed of proprietors, or people of their class so entirely under their influence that the richest of them do not find it necessary to take an active part in it themselves. Rothschild, for instance, does not need to be either M.P. or minister, it is enough for him to keep M.P.'s and ministers dependent upon himself.

In many countries, the proletariat participates nominally, more or less, in the election of the government. This is a concession which the *bourgeois* (i.e., proprietory) class have made, either to avail themselves of popular support in the strife against royal or aristocratic power, or to divert the attention of the people from their own emancipation by giving them an apparent share in political power. However, whether the "bourgeoisie" foresaw it or not, when first they conceded to the people the right to vote, the fact is that the right has proved in reality a mockery, serving only to consolidate the power of the "bourgeois," while giving to the most energetic only of the proletariat the illusory hope of arriving at power.

So also with universal suffrage—we might say, especially with universal suffrage—the government has remained the servant and police of the bourgeois class. How could it be otherwise? If the government should reach the point of becoming hostile, if the hope of democracy should ever be more than a delusion deceiving the people, the proprietory class, menaced in its interests, would at once rebel,

2 In this paragraph, the sentences from "A government which owed its origin ..." to "... a government of its own choosing" were missing from the original English version.

and would use all the force and influence which come from the possession of wealth, to reduce the government to the simple function of acting as policeman.

In all times and in all places, whatever may be the name that the government takes, whatever has been its origin, or its organization, its essential function is always that of oppressing and exploiting the masses, and of defending the oppressors and exploiters. Its principal characteristic and indispensable instruments are the bailiff and the tax collector, the soldier and the prison. And to these are necessarily added the lying professions of priests and teachers, as the case may be, supported and protected by the government, to render the spirit of the people servile and make them docile under the yoke.

Certainly, in addition to this primary business, to this essential department of governmental action other departments have been added in the course of time. We even admit that never, or hardly ever, has a government been able to exist in a country that was at all civilized without adding to its oppressing and exploiting functions others useful and indispensable to social life. But this fact makes it none the less true that government is in its nature oppressive and a means of exploitation, and that its origin and position doom it to be the defence and hot-bed of a dominant class, thus confirming and increasing the evils of domination.

The government assumes the business of protecting, more or less vigilantly, the life of citizens against direct and brutal attacks; acknowledges and legalizes a certain number of rights and primitive usages and customs, without which it is impossible to live in society. It organizes and directs certain public services, as the post, preservation and construction of roads, care of the public health, benevolent institutions, workhouses and such like, and it pleases it to pose as the protector and benefactor of the poor and weak. But it is sufficient to notice how and why it fulfils these functions to prove our point. The fact is that everything the government undertakes is always inspired with the spirit of domination, and ordained to defend, enlarge, and perpetuate the privileges of property, and those classes of which government is the representative and defender.

A government cannot rule for any length of time without hiding its true nature behind the pretence of general utility. It cannot respect the lives of the privileged without assuming the air of wishing to respect the lives of all. It cannot cause the privileges of some to be tolerated without appearing as the custodian of the rights of everybody. "The law" (and, of course, those that have made the law, that is, the government) "has utilised," says Kropotkin, "the social sentiments of man, working into them those precepts of morality, which man has accepted, together with arrangements useful to the minority—the exploiters—and opposed to the interests of those who might have rebelled, had it not been for this show of a moral ground."[3]

A government cannot wish the destruction of the community, for then it and the dominant class could not claim their exploitation-gained wealth; nor could the government leave the community to manage its own affairs, for then the people would soon discover that it (the government) was necessary for no other end than to defend the proprietory class who impoverish them, and would hasten to rid themselves of both government and proprietory class.

To-day in the face of the persistent and menacing demands of the proletariat, governments show a tendency to interfere in the relations between employers and work people. Thus they try to arrest the labour movement, and to impede with delusive reforms the attempts of the poor to take to themselves that which is due to them, namely an equal share of the good things of life which others enjoy.

We must also remember that on the one hand the "bourgeois," that is, the proprietory class, make war among themselves, and destroy one another continually, and on the other hand that the government, although composed of the "bourgeois" and, acting as their servant and protector, is still, like every other servant or protector, continually striving to emancipate itself and to domineer over its charge. Thus this see-saw game, this swaying between conceding and withdrawing, this seeking allies among the people against the classes, and among the classes against the masses, forms the science of the governors, and blinds the ingenuous and phlegmatic, who are always expecting that salvation is coming to them from on high.

With all this, the government does not change its nature. If it acts as regulator or guarantor of the rights and duties of each, it perverts

---

3 This quotation is from chapter five of "Anarchist Morality." The chapter was first published in French in *La Révolte* (Paris) 3, no. 40 (21–27 June 1890) and in English translation in *Freedom* of February 1892. The passage in question reads thus: "law has merely utilised the social feelings of man, to slip in, among the moral precepts he accepts, various mandates, useful to an exploiting minority, to which his nature refuses obedience. Law has perverted the feeling of justice, instead of developing it."

the sentiment of justice. It justifies wrong and punishes every act which offends or menaces the privileges of the governors and proprietors. It declares just, *legal*, the most atrocious exploitation of the miserable, which means a slow and continuous material and moral murder, perpetrated by those who have on those who have not. Again, if it administrates public services, it always considers the interests of the governors and proprietors, not occupying itself with the interests of the working masses, except in so far as is necessary to make the masses willing to endure their share of taxation. If it instructs, it fetters and curtails the truth, and tends to prepare the mind and heart of the young to become either implacable tyrants or docile slaves, according to the class to which they belong. In the hands of the government everything becomes a means of exploitation, everything serves as a police measure, useful to hold the people in check. And it must be thus. If the life of mankind consists in strife between man and man, naturally there must be conquerors and conquered, and the government, which is the prize of the strife, or is a means of securing to the victors the results of their victory, and perpetuating those results, will certainly never fall to those who have lost, whether the battle be on the grounds of physical or intellectual strength, or in the field of economics. And those who have fought to conquer, that is, to secure to themselves better conditions than others can have, to conquer privilege and dominion added to power, and have attained the victory, will certainly not use it to defend the rights of the vanquished, and to place limits to their own power and to that of their friends and partizans.

The government—or the State, if you will—as judge, moderator of social strife, impartial administrator of the public interests, is a lie. It is an illusion, a utopia, never realised and never realizable. If in truth, the interests of men must always be contrary to one another, if indeed, the strife between mankind was a necessary law of human society, and the liberty of the individual must be limited by the liberty of other individuals, then each one would always seek to make his interests triumph over those of others. Each would strive to enlarge his own liberty at the cost of the liberty of others, and there would be government. Not simply because it was more or less useful to the totality of the members of society to have a government, but because the conquerors would wish to secure to themselves the fruits of victory. They would wish effectually to subject the vanquished, and relieve themselves of the trouble of being always on the defensive, and they would appoint men, specially adapted to the business, to act police. Were this indeed actually the case, then humanity would be destined to perish amidst periodical contests between tyrannical dominators and the rebellion of the conquered.

But fortunately the future of humanity is a happier one, because the law which governs it is milder.

This law is the law of *solidarity*.

I.

Man has two necessary fundamental characteristics, *the instinct of his own preservation*, without which no being could exist, and *the instinct of the preservation of his species*, without which no species could have been formed or have continued to exist. He is naturally driven to defend his own existence and well-being and that of his offspring against every danger.

In nature living beings find two ways of securing their existence, and rendering it pleasanter. The one is in individual strife with the elements, and with other individuals of the same or different species; the other is *mutual support*, or *co-operation*, which might also be described as association for strife against all natural factors, destructive to the existence, or to the development and well-being of the associated.

We do not need to investigate in these pages—and we cannot for lack of space—what respective proportions in the evolution of the organic world these two principles of strife and co-operation take.

It will suffice to note how co-operation among men (whether forced or voluntary) has become the sole means of progress, of improvement or of securing safety; and how strife—relic of an earlier stage of existence—has become thoroughly unsuitable as a means of securing the well-being of individuals, and produces instead injury to all, both the conquerors and the conquered.

The accumulated and transmitted experience of successive generations has taught man that by uniting with other men his preservation is better secured and his well-being increased. Thus out of this same strife for existence, carried on against surrounding nature, and against individuals of their own species, the social instinct has been developed among men, and has completely transformed the conditions of their life. Through co-operation man has been enabled to evolve out of animalism, has risen to great power, and elevated himself to such a degree above the other animals, that metaphysical philosophers have believed it necessary to invent for him an immaterial and immortal soul.

Many concurrent causes have contributed to the formation of this social instinct, that starting from the animal basis of the instinct for the preservation of the species (which is the social instinct limited to the natural family),[4] has now become so extended and so intense that it constitutes the essential element of man's moral nature.

Man, however he evolved from inferior animal types, was a physically weak being, unarmed for the fight against carnivorous beasts. But he was possessed of a brain capable of great development, and a vocal organ, able to express the various cerebral vibrations, by means of diverse sounds, and hands adapted to give the desired form to matter. He must have very soon felt the need and advantages of association with his fellows. Indeed it may even be said that he could only rise out of animalism when he became social, and had acquired the use of language, which is at the same time a consequence and a potent factor of sociability.

The relatively scanty number of the human species rendered the strife for existence between man and man, even beyond the limits of association, less sharp, less continuous, and less necessary. At the same time, it must have greatly favored the development of sympathetic sentiments, and have left time for the discovery and appreciation of the utility of mutual support. In short, social life became the necessary condition of man's existence, in consequence of his capacity to modify his external surroundings and adapt them to his own wants, by the exercise of his primeval powers in co-operation with a greater or less number of associates. His desires have multiplied with the means of satisfying them, and have become needs. And division of labor has arisen from man's methodical use of nature for his own advantage. Therefore, as now evolved, man could not live apart from his fellows without falling back into a state of animalism. Through the refinement of sensibility, with the multiplication of social relationships, and through habit impressed on the species by hereditary transmission for thousands of centuries, this need of social life, this interchange of thought and of affection between man and man has become a mode of being necessary for our organism. It has been transformed into sympathy, friendship, and love, and subsists

4 The part in parentheses was missing from the original English version.

independently of the material advantages that association procures. So much is this the case, that man will often face suffering of every kind, and even death, for the satisfaction of these sentiments.

The fact is that a totally different character has been given to the strife for existence between man and man, and between the inferior animals, by the enormous advantages that association gives to man; by the fact that his physical powers are altogether disproportionate to his intellectual superiority over the beasts, so long as he remains isolated; by his possibility of associating with an ever increasing number of individuals, and entering into more and more intricate and complex relationships, until he reaches association with all humanity; and, finally, perhaps more than all, by his ability to produce, working in co-operation with others, more than he needs to live upon. It is evident that these causes, together with the sentiments of affection derived from them, must give a quite peculiar character to the struggle for existence among human beings.

Although it is now known—and the researches of modern naturalists bring us every day new proofs—that co-operation has played, and still plays, a most important part in the development of the organic world, nevertheless, the difference between the human struggle for existence and that of the inferior animals is enormous. It is in fact proportionate to the distance separating man from the other animals. And this is none the less true because of that Darwinian theory, which the bourgeois class have ridden to death, little suspecting the extent to which mutual co-operation has assisted in the development of the lower animals.

The lower animals fight either individually, or, more often, in little permanent or transitory groups against all nature, the other individuals of their own species included. Some of the more social animals, such as ants, bees, etc., associate together in the same anthill, or beehive, but are at war with, or indifferent towards, other communities of their own species. Human strife with nature, on the contrary, tends always to broaden association among men, to unite their interests, and to develop each individual's sentiments of affection towards all others, so that united they may conquer and dominate the dangers of external nature by and for humanity.

All strife directed towards obtaining advantages independently of other men, and in opposition to them, contradicts the social nature of modern man, and tends to lead it back to a more animal condition.

Solidarity, that is, harmony of interests and sentiments, the sharing of each in the good of all, and of all in the good of each, is the state in which alone man can be true to his own nature, and attain to the highest development and happiness. It is the aim towards which human development tends. It is the one great principle, capable of reconciling all present antagonisms in society, otherwise irreconcilable. It causes the liberty of each to find not its limits, but its complement, the necessary condition of its continual existence—in the liberty of all.

"No man," says Michael Bakounine, "can recognise his own human worth, nor in consequence realise his full development, if he does not recognize the worth of his fellow men, and in co-operation with them, realise his own development through them. No man can emancipate himself unless at the same time he emancipates those around him. My freedom is the freedom of all, for I am not really free—free not only in thought, but in deed—if my freedom and my right do not find their confirmation and sanction in the liberty and right of all men my equals.

"It matters much to me what all other men are, for however independent I may seem, or may believe myself to be, by virtue of my social position, whether as Pope, Tsar, Emperor, or Prime Minister, I am all the while the product of those who are the least among men. If these are ignorant, miserable, or enslaved, my existence is limited by their ignorance, misery, or slavery. I, though an intelligent and enlightened man, am made stupid by their stupidity; though brave, am enslaved by their slavery; though rich, tremble before their poverty; though privileged, grow pale at the thought of possible justice for them. I, who wish to be free, cannot be so, because around me are men who do not yet desire freedom, and, not desiring it, become, as opposed to me, the instruments of my oppression."[5]

Solidarity then is the condition in which man can attain the highest degree of security and of well-being. Therefore, egoism itself, that is, the exclusive consideration of individual interests, impels man and human society towards solidarity. Or rather egoism and altruism (consideration of the interests of others) are united in this one sentiment, as the interest of the individual is one with the interests of society.

5 For an English version of the full text from which this excerpt is taken, see "Solidarity in Liberty: The Workers Path to Freedom," in *Bakunin's Writings*, edited by Guy A. Aldred (Indore: Modern Publishers, [1947]).

However, man could not pass at once from animalism to humanity; from brutal strife between man and man to the collective strife of all mankind, united in one brotherhood of mutual aid against external nature.

Guided by the advantages that association and the consequent division of labor offer, man evolved towards solidarity, but his evolution encountered an obstacle which led him, and still leads him, away from his aim. He discovered that he could realise the advantages of co-operation, at least up to a certain point, and for the material and primitive wants that then comprised all his needs, by making other men subject to himself, instead of associating in equality with them. Thus the ferocious and anti-social instincts, inherited from his bestial ancestry, again obtained the upper hand. He forced the weaker to work for him, preferring to domineer over rather than to associate fraternally with his fellows. Perhaps also in most cases it was by exploiting the conquered in war that man learnt for the first time the benefits of association and the help that can be obtained from mutual support.

Thus it has come about that the establishment of the utility of co-operation, which ought to lead to the triumph of solidarity in all human concerns, has turned to the advantage of private property and of government; in other words, to the exploitation of the labor of the many, for the sake of the privileged few.

There has always been association and co-operation, without which human life would be impossible; but it has been co-operation imposed and regulated by the few in their own particular interest.

From this fact arises a great contradiction with which the history of mankind is filled. On the one hand, we find the tendency to associate and fraternise for the purpose of conquering and adapting the external world to human needs, and for the satisfaction of the human affections; while, on the other hand we see the tendency to divide into as many separate and hostile factions as there are different conditions of life. These factions are determined, for instance, by geographical and ethnological conditions, by differences in economic position, by privileges acquired by some and sought to be secured by others, or by suffering endured, with the ever recurring desire to rebel.

The principle of each for himself, that is, of war of all against all, has come in the course of time to complicate, lead astray, and paralyse the war of all combined against nature for the common advantage of the human race, which could only be completely successful by acting on the principle of all for each, and each for all.

Great have been the evils which humanity has suffered by this intermingling of domination and exploitation with human association. But in spite of the atrocious oppression to which the masses submit, of the misery, vices, crime, and degradation which oppression and slavery produce, among the slaves and their masters, and in spite of the hatreds, the exterminating wars, and the antagonisms of artificially created interests, nevertheless, the social instinct has survived and even developed. Co-operation, having been always the necessary condition for successful combat against external nature, has therefore been the permanent cause of men's coming together, and consequently of the development of their sympathetic sentiments. Even the oppression of the masses has itself caused the oppressed to fraternise among themselves. Indeed it has been solely owing to this feeling of solidarity, more or less conscious and more or less widespread among the oppressed, that they have been able to endure the oppression, and that man has resisted the causes of death in his midst.

In the present the immense development of production, the growth of human needs which cannot be satisfied except by the united efforts of a large number of men in all countries, the extended means of communication, habits of travel, science, literature, commerce, even war itself—all these have drawn and are still drawing humanity into a compact body, every section of which, closely knit together, can find its satisfaction and liberty only in the development and health of all other sections composing the whole.

The inhabitant of Naples is as much interested in the amelioration of the hygienic condition of the peoples on the banks of the Ganges, from whence the cholera is brought to him, as in the improvement of the sewerage of his own town.[6] The well-being, liberty, or fortune of the mountaineer, lost among the precipices of the Apennines, does not depend alone on the state of well-being or of misery, in which the inhabitants of his own village live, or even on the general condition of the Italian people, but also on the condition of

6 In this reference there is a direct link to Malatesta's own life experience. In 1884, when an outbreak of cholera occurred in Naples, Malatesta and other anarchists rushed there to assist and cure the population hit by the disease.

the workers in America, or Australia, on the discovery of a Swedish scientist, on the moral and material conditions of the Chinese, on war or peace in Africa; in short, it depends on all the great and small circumstances which affect the human being in any spot whatever of the world.

In the present condition of society, the vast solidarity, which unites all men, is in a great degree unconscious, since it arises spontaneously from the friction of particular interests, while men occupy themselves little or not at all with general interests. And this is the most evident proof that solidarity is the natural law of human life, which imposes itself, so to speak, in spite of all obstacles, and even those artificially created by society as at present constituted.

On the other hand, the oppressed masses, never wholly resigned to oppression and misery, who to-day more than ever show themselves ardent for justice, liberty, and well-being, are beginning to understand that they cannot emancipate themselves except by uniting, through solidarity with all the oppressed and exploited over the whole world. And they understand also that the indispensable condition of their emancipation is the possession of the means of production, of the soil and of the instruments of labor, and further the abolition of private property. Science and the observation of social phenomena show that this abolition would be of immense advantage in the end, even to the privileged classes, if only they could bring themselves to renounce the spirit of domination, and concur with all their fellow men in laboring for the common good.

***

Now should the oppressed masses some day refuse to work for their oppressors, should they take possession of the soil and the instruments of labor, and apply them for their own use and advantage, and that of all who work, should they no longer submit to the domination, either of brute force or economic privilege; should the spirit of human fellowship and the sentiment of human solidarity, strengthened by common interests, grow among the people, and put an end to strife between nations; then what ground would there be for the existence of a government?

Private property abolished, government—which is its defender—must disappear. Should it survive, it would continually tend to reconstruct, under one form or another, a privileged and oppressive class.

And the abolition of government does not, and cannot, signify the doing away with human association.

Far otherwise, for that co-operation which today is enforced, and directed to the advantage of the few, would be free and voluntary, directed to the advantage of all. Therefore it would become more intense and efficacious.

The social instinct and the sentiment of solidarity would develop to the highest degree; and every individual would do all in his power for the good of others, as much for the satisfaction of his own well understood interests as for the gratification of his sympathetic sentiments.

By the free association of all, a social organisation would arise through the spontaneous grouping of men according to their needs and sympathies, from the low to the high, from the simple to the complex, starting from the more immediate to arrive at the more distant and general interests. This organisation would have for its aim the greatest good and fullest liberty to all; it would embrace all humanity in one common brotherhood, and would be modified and improved as circumstances were modified and changed, according to the teachings of experience.

This society of *free men*, this society of *friends* would be *Anarchy*.

II.

We have hitherto considered government as it is, and as it necessarily must be in a society founded upon privilege, upon the exploitation and oppression of man by man, upon antagonism of interests and social strife, in a word, upon private property.

We have seen how this state of strife, far from being a necessary condition of human life, is contrary to the interests of the individual and of the species. We have observed how co-operation, solidarity (of interest) is the law of human progress, and we have concluded that, with the abolition of private property and the cessation of all domination of man over man, there would be no reason for government to exist—therefore it ought to be abolished.

But, it may be objected, if the principle on which social organisation is now founded were to be changed, and solidarity substituted for strife, common property for private property, the government also would change its nature. Instead of being the protector and representative of the interests of one class, it would become, if there were no longer any classes, representative of all society. Its mission would be to secure and regulate social co-operation in the interests of all, and to fulfil public services of general utility. It would defend society against possible attempts to re-establish privilege, and prevent or repress all attacks, by whomsoever set on foot, against the life, well-being, or liberty of each.

There are in society certain matters too important, requiring too much constant, regular attention, for them to be left to the voluntary management of individuals, without danger of everything getting into disorder.

If there were no government, who would organize the supply and distribution of provisions? Who regulate matters pertaining to public hygiene, the postal, telegraph, and railway services, etc.? Who would direct public instruction? Who undertake those great works of exploration, improvements on a large scale, scientific enterprises, etc., which transform the face of the earth and augment a hundredfold the power of man?

Who would care for the preservation and increase of capital, that it might be transmitted to posterity, enriched and improved?

Who would prevent the destruction of the forests, or the irrational exploitation, and therefore impoverishment of the soil?

Who would there be to prevent and repress crimes, that is, anti-social acts?

What of those who, disregarding the law of solidarity, would not work? Or of those who might spread infectious disease in a country by refusing to submit to the regulation of hygiene by science? Or what again could be done with those who, whether insane or no, might set fire to the harvest, injure children, or abuse and take advantage of the weak?

To destroy private property and abolish existing government without reconstituting a government that would organise collective life and secure social solidarity, would not be to abolish privilege and bring peace and prosperity upon earth. It would be to destroy every social bond, to leave humanity to fall back into barbarism, to begin again the reign of "each for himself," which would re-establish the triumph firstly of brute force, and secondly of economic privilege.

***

Such are the objections brought forward by authoritarians, even by those who are Socialists, that is, who wish to abolish private property and class government founded upon the system of private property.

We reply:

In the first place, it is not true that with a change of social conditions the nature of the government and its functions would also change. Organs and functions are inseparable terms. Take from an organ its function, and either the organ will die, or the function will reinstate itself. Place an army in a country where there is no reason or fear of foreign war, and this army will provoke war, or, if it do not succeed in doing that, it will disband. A police force, where there are no crimes to discover, and delinquents to arrest, will provoke or invent crimes, or will cease to exist.

For centuries, there existed in France an institution, the *louveterie,* now included in the administration of the forests, for the extermination of the wolves and other noxious beasts. No one will be surprised to learn that, just on account of this institution, wolves still exist in France, and that, in rigorous seasons, they do great damage. The public take little heed of the wolves, because there are the appointed officials, whose duty it is to think about them. And the officials do hunt them, but in an *intelligent* manner, sparing their caves, and allowing time for reproduction, that they may not run the risk of entirely destroying such an *interesting* species. The French peasants have indeed little confidence in these official wolf-hunters, and regard them rather as the wolf-preservers. And, of course, what would these officials do if there were no longer any wolves to exterminate?

A government, that is, a number of persons deputed to make the laws, and entitled to make use the collective forces of society to make every individual to respect these laws, already constitutes a class privileged and separated from the rest of the community. Such a class, like every elected body, will seek instinctively to. enlarge its powers; to place itself above the control of the people; to impose its tendencies, and to make its own interests predominate. Placed in a privileged position, the government always finds itself in antagonism to the masses, of whose force it disposes.

Furthermore, a government, with the best intention, could never satisfy everybody, even if it succeeded in satisfying some. It must therefore always be defending itself against the discontented, and for that reason must ally itself with the satisfied section of the community for necessary support. And in this manner will arise again the old story of a privileged class, which cannot help but be developed in conjunction with the government. This class, if it could not again acquire possession of the soil, would certainly monopolise the most favored spots, and would not be in the end less oppressive, or less an instrument of exploitation than the capitalist class.

The governors, accustomed to command, would never wish to mix with the common crowd. If they could not retain the power in their own hands, they would at least secure to themselves privileged positions for the time when they would be out of office. They would use all the means they have in their power to get their own friends elected as their successors, who would in their turn be supported and protected by their predecessors. And thus the government would pass and repass into the same hands, and the *democracy*, that is, the government presumably of the whole people, would end, as it always has done, in becoming an *oligarchy*, or the government of a few, the government of a class.

And this all-powerful, oppressive, all-absorbing oligarchy would have always in its care, that is, at its disposition, every bit of social capital, all public services, from the production and distribution of provisions to the manufacture of matches, from the control of the university to the music hall.

***

But let us even suppose that the government did not necessarily constitute a privileged class, and could exist without forming around itself a new privileged class. Let us imagine that it could remain truly representative, the servant—if you will—of all society. What purpose would it then serve? In what particular and in what manner would it augment the power, intelligence, spirit of solidarity, care of the general welfare, present and to come, that at any given moment existed in a given society?

It is always the old story of the man with bound limbs, who, having managed to live in spite of his bands, believes that he lives by means of them. We are accustomed to live under a government, which makes use of all that energy, that intelligence, and that will which it can direct to its own ends; but which hinders, paralyses and suppresses those that are useless or hostile to it. And we imagine that all that is done in society is done by virtue of the government, and that without the government there would be neither energy, intelligence, nor good will in society. So it comes (as we have already said) that the proprietor who has possessed himself of the soil, has it cultivated for his own particular profit, leaving the laborer the bare necessities of life for which he can and will continue to labor. While the enslaved laborer thinks that he could not live without his master, as though it were *he* who created the earth and the forces of nature.

What can government of itself add to the moral and material forces which exist in a society? Unless it be like the God of the Bible, who created the universe out of nothing?

As nothing is created in the so-called material world, so in this more complicated form of the material world, which is the social world, nothing can be created. And therefore governors can dispose of no other force than that which is already in society. And indeed not by any means of all of that, as much force is necessarily paralysed and destroyed by governmental methods of action, while more again is wasted in the friction with rebellious elements, inevitably great in such an artificial mechanism. Whenever governors originate anything of themselves, it is as men, and not as governors, that they do so. And of that amount of force, both material and moral, which does remain at the disposition of the government, only an infinitesimally small part achieves an end really useful to society. The remainder is either consumed in actively repressing rebellious opposition, or is otherwise diverted from the aim of general utility, and turned to the profit of the few, and to the injury of the majority of men.

So much has been made of the part that individual initiative and social action play respectively in the life and progress of human society, and such is the confusion of metaphysical language, that those who affirm that individual initiative is the source and agency of all action seem to be asserting something quite preposterous. In reality it is a truism which becomes apparent directly we begin to explain the actual facts represented by these words.

The real being is the man, the individual; society or the collectivity, and the State or government which professes to represent it, if not hollow abstractions, can be nothing else than aggregates of individuals. And it is within the individual organism that all thoughts and all human action necessarily have their origin. Originally individual, they become collective thoughts and actions, when shared in common by many individuals. Social action, then, is not the negation, nor the complement of individual initiative, but it is the sum total of the initiatives, thoughts and actions of all the individuals composing society: a result which, other things equal, is more or less great according as the individual forces tend towards the same aim, or are divergent and opposed. If, on the other hand, as the authoritarians make out, by social action is meant governmental action, then it is again the result of individual forces, but only of those individuals who either form part of the government or by virtue of their position are enabled to influence the conduct of the government.

Thus, in the contest of centuries between liberty and authority, or, in other words, between social equality and social castes, the question at issue has not really been the relations between society and the individual, nor the increase of individual independence at the cost of social control, or *vice versa*. Rather it has had to do with preventing any one individual from oppressing the others; with giving to everyone the same rights and the same means of action. It has had to do with substituting the initiative of all, which must naturally result in the advantage of all, for the initiative of the few, which necessarily results in the suppression of all the others. It is always, in short, the question of putting an end to the domination and exploitation of man by man in such a way that all are interested in the common welfare, and that the individual force of each, instead of oppressing, combating or suppressing others, will find the possibility of complete development, and every one will seek to associate with others for the greater advantage of all.

From what we have said, it follows that the existence of a government, even upon the hypothesis that the ideal government of authoritarian Socialists were possible, far from producing an increase of productive force, would immensely diminish it, because the government would restrict initiative to the few. It would give these few the right to do all things, without being able, of course, to endow them with the knowledge or understanding of all things.

In fact, if you divest legislation and all the operations of government of what is intended to protect the privileged, and what represents the wishes of the privileged classes alone, nothing remains but the aggregate of individual governors. "The State," says Sismondi, "is always a conservative power that authorises, regulates and organises the conquests of progress (and history testifies that it applies them to the profit of its own and the other privileged classes) but never does inaugurate them. New ideas always originate from beneath, are conceived in the foundations of society, and then, when divulged, they become opinion and grow. But they must always meet on their path, and combat the constituted powers of tradition, custom, privilege and error."[7]

***

In order to understand how society could exist without a government, it is sufficient to turn our attention for a short space to what actually goes on in our present society. We shall see that in reality the most important social functions are fulfilled even now-a-days outside the intervention of government. Also that government only interferes to exploit the masses, or defend the privileged, or, lastly, to sanction, most unnecessarily, all that has been done without its aid, often in spite of and in opposition to it. Men work, exchange, study, travel, follow as they choose the current rules of morality, or hygiene; they profit by the progress of science and art, have numberless mutual interests without ever feeling the need of any one to direct them how to conduct themselves in regard to these matters. On the contrary, it is just those things in which there is no governmental interference that prosper best, and that give rise to the least contention, being unconsciously adapted to the wish of all in the way found most useful and agreeable.

Nor is government more necessary in the case of large undertakings, or for those public services which require the constant co-operation of many people of different conditions and countries. Thousands of these undertakings are even now the work of voluntarily formed associations. And these are, by the acknowledgment of every one, the undertakings which succeed the best. Nor do we refer to the association of capitalists, organised by means of exploitation, although even they show capabilities and powers of free association, which may extend *ad libitum* until it embraces all the peoples of all

7 Jean-Charles-Léonard Simonde de Sismondi was a Swiss economist and historian of the first half of the nineteenth century. In fact, he attributed a positive role to a "conservative power," expression of an aristocratic spirit, as an essential component of good government and a counterweight to democratic impulses. In volume eleven of his monumental sixteen-volume *Histoire des rèpubliques italiennes du moyen âge*, he writes: "Il faut surtout qu'on retrouve, dans une république, les représentans du temps passé, comme ceux du temps présent, qu'on y voie un pouvoir conservateur comme un pouvoir rénovateur" (it is especially important that the representatives of both the past and the present be found in a republic, that both a conservative and an innovative power be present).

lands, and includes the widest and most varying interests. But we speak rather of those associations inspired by the love of humanity, or by the passion for knowledge, or even simply by the desire for amusement and love of applause, as these better represent such grouping as will exist in a society where, private property and internal strife between men being abolished, each will find his interests synonymous with the interests of every one else, and his greatest satisfaction in doing good and pleasing others. Scientific societies and congresses, international life-boat and Red Cross associations, etc., laborers' unions, peace societies, volunteers who hasten to the rescue at times of great public calamity are all examples, among thousands, of that power of the spirit of association, which always shows itself when a need arises, or an enthusiasm takes hold, and the means do not fail. That voluntary associations do not cover the world, and do not embrace every branch of material and moral activity is the fault of the obstacles placed in their way by governments, of the antagonisms created by the possession of private property, and of the impotence and degradation to which the monopolising of wealth on the part of the few reduces the majority of mankind.

The government takes charge, for instance, of the postal and telegraphic services. But in what way does it really assist them? When the people are in such a condition as to be able to enjoy, and feel the need of such services, they will think about organising them, and the man with the necessary technical knowledge will not require a certificate from government to enable him to set to work. The more general and urgent the need, the more volunteers will offer to satisfy it. Would the people have the ability necessary to provide and distribute provisions? Oh! never fear, they will not die of hunger, waiting for a government to pass laws on the subject. Wherever a government exists, it must wait until the people have first organised everything, and then come with its laws to sanction and exploit that which has been already done. It is evident that private interest is the great motive for all activity. That being so, when the interest of every one becomes the interest of each (and it necessarily will become so as soon as private property is abolished) then all will be active. And if now they work in the interest of the few, so much the more and so much the better will they work to satisfy the interests of all. It is hard to understand how any one can believe that public services indispensable to social life can be better secured by order of a government than through the workers themselves who by their own choice or by agreement made with others carry them out under the immediate control of all interested.

Certainly in every collective undertaking on a large scale there is need for division of labor, for technical direction, administration, etc. But the authoritarians are merely playing with words, when they deduce a reason for the existence of government, from the very real necessity for organisation of labor. The government, we must repeat, is the aggregate of the individuals who have had given them or have taken the right or the means to make laws, and force the people to obey them. The administrators, engineers, etc., on the other hand, are men who receive or assume the charge of doing a certain work, and who do it. Government signifies delegation of power, that is, abdication of the initiative and sovereignty of every one into the hands of the few. Administration signifies delegation of work, that is, a charge given and accepted, the free exchange of services founded on free agreement.

A governor is a privileged person, because he has the right to command others, and to avail himself of the force of others to make his own ideas and desires triumph. An administrator or technical director is a worker like others, in a society, of course, where all have equal opportunities of development, and all are, or can be, at the same time intellectual and manual workers; when there are no other differences between men than those derived from diversity of talents, and all work and all social functions give an equal right to the enjoyment of social advantages. The functions of government are, in short, not to be confounded with administrative functions, as they are essentially different. That they are to-day so often confused is entirely on account of the existence of economic and political privilege.

But let us hasten to pass on to those functions for which government is thought indispensable by all who are not Anarchists. These are the internal and external defence of society, *i.e.*, War, Police and Justice.

Government being abolished, and social wealth at the disposal of every one, all antagonism between various nations would soon cease, and there would consequently be no more cause for war. Moreover, in the present state of the world, in any country where the spirit of rebellion is growing, even if it do not find an echo throughout the land, it will be certain of so much sympathy that the government will not dare to send all its troops to a foreign war for fear the revolution should break out at home. But even supposing that the rulers of countries not yet emancipated would wish and could attempt to reduce a free people to servitude, would these require a government to enable them to defend themselves? To make war we need men who have the necessary geographical and technical knowledge, and, above all, people willing to fight. A government has no means of augmenting the ability of the former, or the willingness or courage of the latter. And the experience of history teaches that a people really desirous of defending their own country are invincible. In Italy everyone knows how thrones tremble and regular armies of hired soldiers vanish before troops of volunteers, *i.e.*, armies Anarchically formed.[8]

***

And as to the police and justice, many imagine that if it were not for the police and the judges, everybody would be free to kill, violate or injure others as the humour took him; that Anarchists, if they are true to their principles, would like to see this strange kind of liberty respected; "liberty" that violates or destroys the life and freedom of others unrestrained. Such people believe that we, having overthrown the government and private property, shall then tranquilly allow the re-establishment of both, out of respect for the "liberty" of those who may feel the need of having a government and private property. A strange mode indeed of construing our ideas! In truth, one may better answer such notions with a shrug of the shoulders than by taking the trouble to confute them.

The liberty we wish for, for ourselves and others, is not an absolute, abstract, metaphysical liberty, which in practice can only amount to the oppression of the weak. But we wish for a tangible liberty, the possible liberty, which is the conscious communion of interests, *i.e.*, voluntary solidarity. We proclaim the maxim: *Do as you will*; and in this our program is almost entirely contained, because, as may be easily understood, we hold that in a society without government or property, each one *will wish that which he should.*

But if, in consequence of a false education, received in the present society, or of physical disease, or whatever other cause, an individual should wish to injure others, you may be sure we should adopt all the means in our power to prevent him. As we know that

8 Giuseppe Garibaldi's "red shirts" are an example of such troops of volunteers.

a man's character is the consequence of his physical organism and of the cosmic and social influences surrounding him, we certainly shall not confound the sacred right of self-defence, with the absurdly assumed right to punish. Also, we shall not regard the delinquent, *i.e.*, the man who commits anti-social acts, as the rebel he seems in the eyes of the judges nowadays. We shall regard him as a sick brother in need of cure. We therefore shall not act towards him in the spirit of hatred, when repressing him, but shall confine ourselves solely to self-protection. We shall not seek to revenge ourselves, but rather to rescue the unfortunate one by every means that science suggests. In theory Anarchists may go astray like others, losing sight of the reality under a semblance of logic; but it is quite certain that the emancipated people will not let their dearly bought liberty and welfare be attacked with impunity. If the necessity arose, they would provide for their own defence against the anti-social tendencies of certain amongst them. But how do those whose business it now is to make the laws protect society? Or those others who live by seeking for and inventing new infringements of law? Even now, when the masses of the people really disapprove of anything and think it injurious, they always find a way to prevent it very much more effectually than all the professional legislators, constables or judges. During insurrections the people, though very mistakenly, have enforced the respect for private property, and they have secured this respect far better than an army of policemen could have done.

Customs always follow the needs and sentiments of the majority, and they are always the more respected, the less they are subject to the sanction of law. This is because every one sees and comprehends their utility, and because the interested parties, not deluding themselves with the idea that government will protect them, are themselves concerned in seeing the custom respected. The economical use of water is of very great importance to a caravan crossing the deserts of Africa. Under these circumstances, water is a sacred thing, and no sane man dreams of wasting it. Conspirators are obliged to act secretly, so secrecy is preserved among them, and obloquy rests on whosoever violates it. Gambling debts are not guaranteed by law, but among gamblers it is considered dishonorable not to pay them, and the delinquent feels himself dishonored by not fulfilling his obligations.

Is it on account of the police that more people are not murdered? The greater part of the Italian people never see the police except at long intervals. Millions of men go over the mountains and through the country, far from the protecting eye of authority, where they might be attacked without the slightest fear of their assailants being traced, but they run no greater risk than those who live in the best guarded spots. Statistics show that the number of crimes does not vary in proportion to the increase of repressive measures, whilst they vary rapidly with the fluctuations of economic conditions and with the state of public opinion.

Punitive laws, however, only concern unusual, exceptional acts. Every-day life goes on beyond the limits of the criminal code, and is regulated almost unconsciously by the tacit and voluntary assent of all, by means of a number of usages and customs much more important to social life than the dictates of law. And they are also much better observed, although completely divested of any sanction beyond the natural odium which falls upon those who violate them, and such injury as this odium brings with it.

When disputes arise, would not voluntarily accepted arbitration or the pressure of public opinion be far more likely to bring about a just settlement of the difficulties in question than an irresponsible magistrate, who has the right to pass judgment upon everybody and every thing, and who is necessarily incompetent and therefore unjust?

As every form of government only serves to protect the privileged classes, so do police and judges only aim at repressing those crimes, often not considered criminal by the masses, which offend only the privileges of the rulers or property-owners. For the real defence of society, the defence of the welfare and liberty of all, there can be nothing more pernicious than the formation of this class of functionaries, who exist on the pretence of defending all, and therefore habitually regard every man as game to be hunted down, often striking at the command of a superior officer, without themselves even knowing why, like hired assassins and mercenaries.

***

All that you have said may be true, say some; Anarchy may be a perfect form of social life; but we have no desire to take a leap in the dark. Therefore, tell us how your society will be organised. Then follows a long string of questions, which would be very interesting if it were our business to study the problems that might arise in an emancipated society, but of which it is useless and absurd to imagine that we could now offer a definite solution. According to what method will children be taught? How will production and distribution be organised? Will there still be large cities? or will people spread equally over all the surface of the earth? Will all the inhabitants of Siberia winter at Nice? Will every one dine on partridges and drink champagne? Who will be the miners and sailors? Who will clear the drains? Will the sick be nursed at home or in hospitals? Who will arrange the railway time-table? What will happen if the engine-driver falls ill while the train is on its way? And so on, without end, as though we could prophesy all the knowledge and experience of the future time, or could, in the name of Anarchy, prescribe for the coming man what time he should go to bed, and on what days he should cut his nails!

Indeed if our readers expect from us an answer to these questions, or even to those among them really serious and important, which can be anything more than our own private opinion at this present hour, we must have succeeded badly in our endeavour to explain what Anarchy is.

We are no more prophets than other men, and should we pretend to give an official solution to all the problems that will arise in the life of the future society, we should have indeed a curious idea of the abolition of government. We should then be describing a government, dictating, like the clergy, a universal code for the present and all future time. Seeing that we have neither police nor prisons to enforce our doctrine, humanity might laugh with impunity at us and our pretensions.

Nevertheless, we consider seriously all the problems of social life which now suggest themselves, on account of their scientific interest, and because, hoping to see Anarchy realised, we wish to help towards the organisation of the new society. We have therefore our own ideas on these subjects, ideas which are to our minds likely to be permanent or transitory, according to the respective cases. And did space permit, we might add somewhat more on these points. But the fact that we to-day think in a certain way on a given question is no proof that such will be the mode of procedure in the future. Who can foresee the activities which may develop in humanity when it is emancipated from misery and oppression? When all have the means of instruction and self-development? When the strife between men, with the hatred and rancour it breeds, will be no longer a necessary condition of existence? Who can foresee the progress of science, the new sources of production, means of communication, etc.?

The one essential is that a society be constituted in which the exploitation and domination of man by man are impossible. That the society, in other words, be such that the means of existence and development of labor be free and open to every one, and all be able to co-operate, according to their wishes and their knowledge, in the organisation of social life. Under such conditions everything will necessarily be performed in compliance with the needs of all, according to the knowledge and possibilities of the moment. And every thing will improve with the increase of knowledge and power.

***

In fact, a program which would touch the basis of the new social constitution could not do more, after all, than indicate a method. And method, more than anything else, defines parties and determines their importance in history. Method apart, every one says he wishes for the good of mankind, and many do truly wish for it. As parties disappear, every organised action directed to a definite end disappears likewise. It is therefore necessary to consider Anarchy as, above all, a method.

There are two methods by which the different parties, not Anarchistic, expect, or say they expect, to bring about the greatest good of each and all. These are the authoritarian or State Socialist and the liberal methods.[9] The former entrusts the direction of social life to a few, and it would result in the exploitation and oppression of the masses by that few. The second party trusts to the free initiative of individuals, and proclaims, if not the abolition, the reduction of government. However, as it respects private property, and is founded on the principle of each for himself, and therefore on competition, its liberty is only the liberty of the strong, the license of those who have, to oppress and exploit the weak who have nothing. Far from producing harmony, it would tend always to augment the distance between the rich and the poor, and end also through exploitation and domination in authority. This second method, Liberalism, is in theory a kind of Anarchy without Socialism. It is therefore no better than a lie, because liberty is not possible without equality, and true

9 In this paragraph, the Italian "*liberale*" and "*liberalismo*" were respectively translated as "individualist" and "individualism." We find these terms confusing, and therefore we have replaced them with the more literal translations "liberal" and "liberalism."

Anarchy cannot be without Solidarity, without Socialism. The criticism which Liberals pass on government is merely the wish to deprive it of certain functions, to virtually hand them over to the capitalist. But it cannot attack those repressive functions which form the essence of government, for without an armed force the proprietary system could not be upheld. Nay, even more, under Liberalism, the repressive power of government must always increase, in proportion to the increase, by means of free competition, of the want of equality and harmony.

Anarchists present a new method; the free initiative of all and free agreement, when, after the revolutionary abolition of private property, every one will have equal power to dispose of social wealth. This method, not admitting the re-establishment of private property, must lead, by means of free association, to the complete triumph of the principles of solidarity.

Thus we see that all the problems put forward to combat the Anarchistic idea are on the contrary arguments in favor of Anarchy; because it alone indicates the way in which, by experience, those solutions which correspond to the dicta of science, and to the needs and wishes of all, can best be found.

How will children be educated? We do not know. What then? The parents, teachers and all, who are interested in the progress of the rising generation, will meet, discuss, agree and differ, and then divide according to their various opinions, putting into practice the methods which they respectively hold to be best. That method which, when tried, produces the best results will triumph in the end.

And so for all the problems that may arise.

***

According to what we have so far said, it is evident that Anarchy, as the Anarchists conceive it, and as alone it can be comprehended, is based on Socialism. Furthermore, were it not for that school of Socialists who artificially divide the natural unity of the social question, considering only some detached points, and were it not also for the equivocations with which they strive to hinder the social revolution, we might say right away that Anarchy is synonymous with Socialism. Because both signify the abolition of exploitation and of the domination of man over man, whether maintained by the force of arms or by the monopolisation of the means of life.

Anarchy, like Socialism, has for its basis and necessary point of departure *equality of conditions*. Its aim is *solidarity*, and its method *liberty*. It is not perfection, nor is it the absolute ideal, which, like the horizon, always recedes as we advance towards it. But it is the open road to all progress and to all improvement, made in the interest of all humanity.

***

There are authoritarians who grant that Anarchy is the mode of social life which alone opens the way to the attainment of the highest possible good for mankind, because it alone can put an end to every class interested in keeping the masses oppressed and miserable. They also grant that Anarchy is possible, because it does nothing more than release humanity from an obstacle—government—against which it has always had to fight its painful way towards progress. Nevertheless, these authoritarians, reinforced by many warm lovers of liberty and justice in theory, retire into their last entrenchments, because they are afraid of liberty, and cannot be persuaded that mankind could live and prosper without teachers and pastors; still, hard pressed by the truth, they pitifully demand to have the reign of liberty put off for a while, indeed for as long as possible.

Such is the substance of the arguments that meet us at this stage.

A society without a government, which would act by free, voluntary co-operation, trusting entirely to the spontaneous action of those interested, and founded altogether on solidarity and sympathy, is certainly, they say, a very beautiful ideal, but, like all ideals, it is a castle in the air. We find ourselves placed in a human society, which has always been divided into oppressors and oppressed; and if the former are full of the spirit of domination, and have all the vices of tyrants, the latter are corrupted by servility, and have those still worse vices, which are the result of enslavement. The sentiment of solidarity is far from being dominant in man at the present day, and if it is true that the different classes of men are becoming more and more unanimous among themselves, it is none the less true that that which is most conspicuous and impresses itself most on human character to-day is the struggle for existence. It is a fact that each fights daily against everyone else, and competition presses upon all, workmen and masters, causing every man to become as a wolf towards every other man. How can these men, educated in a society based upon antagonism between individuals as well as classes, be transformed in a moment and become capable of living in a society in which each shall do as he likes, and as he should, without external coercion, caring for the good of others, simply by the impulse of their own nature? And with what heart or what common sense can you trust to a revolution on the part of an ignorant, turbulent mass, weakened by misery, stupefied by priestcraft, who are to-day blindly sanguinary and tomorrow will let themselves be humbugged by any knave, who dares to call himself their master? Would it not be more prudent to advance gradually towards the Anarchistic ideal, passing through republican, democratic and socialistic stages? Will not an educative government, composed of the best men, be necessary to prepare the advancing generations for their future destiny?

These objections also ought not to appear valid if we have succeeded in making our readers understand what we have already said, and in convincing them of it. But in any case, even at the risk of repetition, it may be as well to answer them.

We find ourselves continually met by the false notion that government is in itself a new force, sprung up one knows not whence, which of itself adds something to the sum of the force and capability of those of whom it is composed and of those who obey it. While, on the contrary, all that is done is done by individual men. The government, as a government, adds nothing save the tendency to monopolise for the advantage of certain parties or classes, and to repress all initiative from beyond its own circle.

To abolish authority or government does not mean to destroy the individual or collective forces, which are at work in society, nor the influence men exert over one another. That would be to reduce humanity to an aggregate of inert and separate atoms; an impossibility which, if it could be performed, would be the destruction of any society, the death blow to mankind. To abolish authority means to abolish the monopoly of force and of influence. It means to abolish that state of things by which social force, *i. e.*, the collective force of all in a society, is made the instrument of the thought, will and interests of a small number of individuals. These, by means of the collective force, suppress the liberty of every one else, to the advantage of their own ideas. In other words, it means to destroy a mode of organisation by means of which the future is exploited, between one revolution and another, to the profit of those who have been the victors of the moment.

Michael Bakounine, in an article published in 1872, asserts that the great means of action of the International were the propagating of their ideas, and the organisation of the spontaneous action of its members in regard to the masses. He then adds:

"To whoever might pretend that action so organised would be an outrage on the liberty of the masses, or an attempt to create a new authoritative power, we would reply that he is a sophist and a fool. So much the worse for those who ignore the natural, social law of human solidarity, to the extent of imagining that an absolute mutual independence of individuals and of masses is a possible or even desirable thing. To desire it would be to wish for the destruction of society, for all social life is nothing else than this mutual and incessant dependence among individuals and masses. All individuals, even the most gifted and strongest, indeed most of all the most gifted and strongest, are at every moment of their lives, at the same time, producers and products. Equal liberty for every individual is only the resultant, continually reproduced, of this mass of material, intellectual and moral influence exercised on him by all the individuals around him, belonging to the society in which he was born, has developed and dies. To wish to escape this influence in the name of a transcendental liberty, divine, absolutely egoistic and sufficient to itself, is the tendency to annihilation. To refrain from influencing others would mean to refrain from all social action, indeed to abstain from all expression of one's thoughts and sentiments, and simply to become non-existent. This independence, so much extolled by idealists and metaphysicians, individual liberty conceived in this sense would amount to self-annihilation.

"In nature, as in human society, which is also a part of this same nature, all that exists lives only by complying with the supreme conditions of interaction, which is more or less positive and potent with regard to the lives of other beings, according to the nature of the individual. And when we vindicate the liberty of the masses, we do not pretend to abolish anything of the natural influences that individuals or groups of individuals exert upon one another. What we wish for is the abolition of artificial influences, which are privileged, legal and official."[10]

---

10 The excerpt is from a text with the original French title "Protestation de l'Alliance" or "Appel de l'Alliance," which Bakunin wrote in July 1871. For an English version, see the third section of "The Program of the Alliance," in *Bakunin on Anarchy*, edited by Sam Dolgoff (New York: Vintage Books, 1972).

Certainly, in the present state of mankind, oppressed by misery, stupefied by superstition and sunk in degradation, the human lot depends upon a relatively small number of individuals. Of course all men will not be able to rise in a moment to the height of perceiving their duty, or even the enjoyment of so regulating their own action that others also will derive the greatest possible benefit from it. But because now-a-days the thoughtful and guiding forces at work in society are few, that is no reason for paralysing them still more, and for the subjection of many individuals to the direction of a few. It is no reason for constituting society in such a manner that the most active forces, the highest capacities are, in the end, found outside the government, and almost deprived of influence on social life. All this now happens owing to the inertia that secured positions foster, to heredity, to protectionism, to party spirit and to all the mechanism of government. For those in government office, taken out of their former social position, primarily concerned in retaining power, lose all power to act spontaneously, and become only an obstacle to the free action of others.

With the abolition of this negative potency constituting government, society will become that which it can be, with the given forces and capabilities of the moment. If there are educated men desirous of spreading education, they will organise the schools, and will strive to make the use and enjoyment to be derived from education felt. And if there are no such men, or only a few of them, a government cannot create them. All it can do, as in fact it does now-a-days, is to take these few away from practical, fruitful work in the sphere of education, and put them to direct from above what has to be imposed by the help of a police system. So they make out of intelligent and impassionate teachers mere politicians, who become useless parasites, entirely absorbed in imposing their own whims, and in maintaining themselves in power.

If there are doctors and teachers of hygiene, they will organise themselves for the service of health. And if there are none, a government cannot create them; all that it can do is to discredit them in the eyes of the people—who are inclined to entertain suspicions, sometimes only too well founded, with regard to every thing which is imposed upon them—and cause them to be massacred as poisoners when they visit people struck by cholera.[11]

11 The last phrase, about doctors being massacred, was missing from the original English version. Indeed, when the first cholera pandemic swept Europe in the

If there are engineers and mechanics, they will organise the railways, etc; and if there are none, a government cannot create them.

The revolution, by abolishing government and private property, will not create force which does not exist, but it will leave a free field for the exercise of all available force and of all existent capacity. While it will destroy every class interested in keeping the masses degraded, it will act in such a way that every one will be free to work and make his influence felt, in proportion to his own capacity, and in conformity with his sentiments and interests. And it is only thus that the elevation of the masses is possible, for it is only with liberty that one can learn to be free, as it is only by working that one can learn to work. A government, even had it no other disadvantages, must always have that of habituating the governed to subjection, and must also tend to become more oppressive and more necessary[, in proportion as its subjects are more obedient and docile]. [12]

Besides, if one wants a government which has to educate the masses and put them on the road to anarchy, one must also indicate what will be the background, and the way of forming the government.[13]

Suppose government were the direction of affairs by the best people. Who are the best? And how shall we recognize their superiority? The majority are generally attached to old prejudices, and have ideas and instincts already outgrown by the more favored minority. But of the various minorities, who all believe themselves in the right, as no doubt many of them are in part, which shall be chosen to rule? And by whom? And by what criterion, seeing that the future alone can prove which party among them is the most superior? If you choose a hundred partizans of dictatorship, you will discover that each one of the hundred believes himself capable, if not of being sole dictator, at least of assisting very materially in the dictatorial government. The dictators would be those who, by one means or another, succeeded in imposing themselves on society. And, in course of time, all their energy would inevitably be employed in defending themselves against the attacks of their adversaries, totally oblivious of their desire, if ever they had had it, to be merely an educative power.

Should government be, on the other hand, elected by universal suffrage, and so be the emanation, more or less sincere, of the wish of

1830s, poisoning hysteria often spread among the populations, causing popular revolts in which physicians and government officials were killed.

12 The phrase in brackets is not present in the Italian original version.

13 This paragraph was missing from the original English version.

the majority? But if you consider these worthy electors as incapable of providing for their own interests, how can they ever be capable of themselves choosing directors to guide them wisely? How solve this problem of social alchemy: To elect a government of geniuses by the votes of a mass of fools? And what will be the lot of the minority, who are the most intelligent, most active and most advanced in society?

***

To solve the social problem to the advantage of all, there is only one way. To expel the government by revolutionary means, to expropriate the holders of social wealth, putting everything at the disposition of all, and to leave all existing force, capacity and good-will among men free to provide for the needs of all.

We fight for Anarchy and for Socialism because we believe that Anarchy and Socialism ought to be brought into operation as soon as possible. Which means that the revolution must drive away the government, abolish private property, and entrust all public service, which will then embrace all social life, to the spontaneous, free, unofficial and unauthorised operation of all those interested and all willing volunteers.

There will certainly be difficulties and inconveniences; but the people will be resolute, and they alone can solve all difficulties anarchically, that is, by direct action of those interested and by free agreement.

We cannot say whether Anarchy and Socialism will triumph after the next revolutionary attempt, but this is certain, that if any of the so-called transition programs triumph, it will be because we have been temporarily beaten, and never because we have thought it wise to leave in existence any one part of that evil system under which humanity groans.

Whatever happens, we shall have some influence on events, by our numbers, our energy, our intelligence and our steadfastness. Also, even if we are now conquered, our work will not have been in vain; for the more decided we shall have been in aiming at the realisation of all our demands, the less there will be of government and of private property in the new society. And we shall have done a great work, for human progress is measured by the degree in which government and private property are diminished.

If to-day we fall without lowering our colours, our cause is certain of victory tomorrow.

14. THE PRODUCTS OF SOIL AND INDUSTRY[1]

(An Anarchist Concern)

No longer in a position to deny the righteousness of socialist aspirations, the bourgeois say that the woes by which men are afflicted are attributable to a harsh necessity of nature, which has nothing to do with the way society is organized. Poverty can never be eradicated, they say, because poverty derives from an actual dearth of produce rather than faulty distribution; in any event, what is required is a boost to the amount of production, rather than any attempt to overthrow society as presently constituted, with an eye to replacing it with a different society based on different foundations.

And even as they talk about shortfalls in output, they have the land they have taken over worked according to the most irrational methods, without availing of the means being made available with every passing day by science for the purpose of boosting production, and, indeed, they leave enormous tracts of perfectly fertile soil fallow; and deploy machinery on the small scale that suits their private profit, and condemn legions of workers to perish from hunger and joblessness, workers who require only free access to the means of production in order to generate tremendous wealth.

On the other hand, socialists, especially the anarchists, not paying enough attention to the difference between what could be produced and what actually is produced in today's society, have retorted that there is no shortage of produce and that the entire social question is simply a distribution issue. And, taking things to extremes, along come some comrades, basing their calculations upon statistics

1 Translated from "Los productos de la tierra y de la industria," *El Productor* (Barcelona) 5, no. 278 (24 December 1891). The article was published during an extensive speaking tour that Malatesta undertook in Spain, together with the Barcelona anarchist Pedro Esteve, between November 1891 and January 1892. The tour was interrupted as a consequence of the repression that ensued following the anarchist uprising in the Andalusian town of Jerez on 8 January 1892. The claim that Malatesta had a role in the uprising is unsubstantiated.

more or less well construed, to argue that, even under the current bourgeois system of production, twice as much foodstuffs are being produced as are needed and four times as many industrial products as science tells us people need to eat and wear, which is to say, for all of our needs to be met.[2]

Nonsensical though it might seem to the disinterested observer, this claim was accepted without scrutiny and well nigh dogmatically—such is man's tendency to believe blindly in whatever pleases or suits him—and it is forever being repeated without inquiry into its veracity.

It is high time for an objective, critical scrutiny of it, free from all prejudice, in short, for an impartial evaluation; because if it were a mistake to claim such abundance of produce, as it seems to us, that belief would pose a very great threat to the revolution's success. Indeed, if revolutionaries believe that produce galore is available, and that vast quantities of food are already held in our warehouses, plus enough other consumer goods to meet the needs of the entire human race for several years to come, then it is only natural that they should not regard the matter of production and of the organization of work as pressing, nor would they regard the proper administration of existing goods as a matter of importance; and so the initial phase of revolution would be frittered away on a lot of palaver and waste, with work and the registering of the real assets available being left until later. Is it not true that there are revolutionaries who contend that all that matters in the revolution is destruction and that there will be more than enough time later for arranging production? Well if, in actual fact, it turns out that stocks of produce are very low and the only thing in plentiful supply is the means of production, then unless those means of production are promptly turned to use and output wisely husbanded, within a few months of the revolution scarcity

2 Malatesta is referring here to two pamphlets, *Les Produits de la Terre* and *Les Produits de l'Industrie*, respectively published in 1885 and 1887, to which his article's title makes explicit reference. The pamphlets had become especially popular among anarchist communists, as providing empirical evidence that taking from the "inexhaustible stockpile," and therefore communism, would be immediately practicable after the revolution. It should be noted that the Spanish controversy between anarchist collectivists and anarchists communists was not just about the future society, but also had tactical ramifications, with the collectivists advocating collective struggle and union involvement and the communists favoring autonomous action by small groups. Despite being a communist, Malatesta's tactical ideas were closer to those of the Spanish collectivists, and in fact, Pedro Esteve and *El Productor* belonged to this current.

and impoverishment due to falling output would make themselves felt, and the people, oblivious of the true reason for the shortage, would lose any taste for revolution and their disgust may well drive them to the extreme of letting themselves be placed under the yoke again by the first adventurer to promise them bread.

We do not at the moment have to hand the means of backing our opinion up with figures to prove that stocks of produce in existence are very low and that, if everybody was to have his needs met in terms of consumption, they would last for only a few months; but we can back it up right here and now with a few reasoned considerations, putting off a more prolonged scrutiny of the matter until such time as we have the tools for the job. Anyway, we are making no claim now to offer definite and finished results, but can instead offer comrades a brief to be studied and we will be satisfied if we manage to get across its transcendental importance as far as the success of our ideals in concerned.

Let us all look into this matter and ferret out the truth, let us actively publicize it, because only through truth can mankind make progress, and only through truth can the revolution succeed.

They say that every year much more is produced than might be needed, even if everyone were to have all his needs met; meaning that as the vast majority of the human race cannot have even its more vital needs met, every year's output must far exceed what is consumed. But where are all the goods, of which vast quantities must have built up over a few years? And how come the haves and the capitalists of every sort, being the ones who control the means of production, ordain the production of that which they could neither sell nor give away?

Being under the control of capitalists, all current production is governed, not by the broader interest, but by its profitability as far as the capitalists are concerned. So the capitalists drive production, deploying machinery and scientific advances to the extent that abundant supply and cheapness of product can boost their earnings; but once such abundance and cheapness seem to pose a threat to their profits, production is halted.

Actually, because of the complete randomness of production and inter-capitalist competition, it is sometimes the case that some capitalists produce far in excess of what is consumed and what they can market, but then, once the products have piled up in warehouses over a period of time, crisis strikes and workers find themselves jobless and breadless until such time as the previously stockpiled products have been sold off.

The fact is that sometimes those very same capitalists destroy a portion of the harvest in order to keep the prices for the rest high, or some harvest are left to rot in new territories for want of transport; but if that happens one year, come the following year the landowner sees to it that he does not pay wages unnecessarily and cancels production.

The owner is never going to produce more than he can sell at a profit. Once America and Australia began shipping wheat to Europe, lots of European landowners, especially in England, seeing no further profit in its production, switched their arable land over to pasture or left them fallow. And even now, so that landowners in Europe can carry on making profits from their land, there is nothing for it but for them to be protected by means of tariffs; and plainly, once American landowners can no longer market their wheat in Europe, they will cut back on production of it; and the amount of wheat produced in a year will normally not exceed consumer demand.

So we cannot understand how all this over-production they talk to us about has come to pass. Some contend that the surplus production is used up by the rich, but that just goes to prove that no such surplus exists. The rich are a tiny minority and their consumption cannot be that significant when set alongside the overall consumption; and anyway no one believes that the purpose of the revolution is to cut back on the consumption by the rich for now so as to align it with the consumption level of the poor; instead, our purpose is to boost everybody's consumption to the highest possible level.

Right now, we in Europe have an example of a real lack of produce: the scarcity in Russia. A single poor harvest has been enough to inflict a terrifying shortage upon the people, even relative to the normal circumstances of the Russian workers, namely, a state of continual dearth. And Russia is Europe's bread-basket! True, the avarice displayed by the monopolists who seized the grain for shipment to Russia or for later re-sale within Russia at exorbitant prices was a big factor in worsening the people's conditions. But obviously monopoly would be an impossibility and pointless had there really been surplus food.

Not that that is any argument in favor of bourgeois society. It is very clear to see that the poverty issue is a matter of social organization, and that the private ownership arrangement upon which the whole of contemporary social life rests, is the reason for so many human beings perishing from hunger and all manner of suffering. From which it follows that, broadly speaking, in that society, the wealth already produced does not go to waste, but the means of production lie idle and men are prevented from producing and satisfying the natural demand completely. Which is rather worse.

Advances in machinery and technology have rendered man's productive capability all but boundless; and agronomic science has demonstrated with telling proof the possibility of extracting stunning quantities of produce from the land, from a small strip of land. It has been shown that, no matter what the climate and location around the world, any plant can be grown through artificially replicating the appropriate climate and soil conditions, producing up to four crops per year; and that, by rational farming methods and the use of the appropriate chemical fertiliser, countries such as France, which at present can barely sustain three dozen million inhabitants, might produce plenty of food for a hundred million, and through work that has been shortened, rendered hygienic, and agreeable too. But this will never come to pass as long as there is private ownership, because the capitalists have no interest in its coming to pass.

We need to get it across to the people, then, that they suffer because of the bourgeois' seizure of all the means of production and their preventing of any more production than suits them; we have to get the people to understand that if they are to be emancipated, they have no option other than a general expropriation for the good of all, with society's wealth harnessed for the whole of humanity and their looking to their own interests. But the people need to be made to understand that taking over the means of production is not enough, and that they need to put these to work as a matter of urgency; and, for that to happen, on the very day the bourgeoisie surrenders, the people simply must get back promptly to work and search for every opportunity to increase and accelerate production, especially agricultural production.

That by itself can guarantee the revolution's victory.

15.
A BIT OF THEORY[1]

Rebellion is rumbling on all sides. Here, it is the expression of an idea; there, the result of need; more often it is the consequence of a network of needs and ideas which reciprocally give rise to and re-enforce one another. It devotes its attention to the causes of social ills or it follows a side issue, it is conscious or instinctive, it is humane or brutal, generous or narrow and selfish, but it is steadily growing and spreading.

This is history in the making, and it is useless to waste one's time complaining of the course it takes, because this course has been laid out by all the evolution that went before.

But history is made by men, and since we do not wish to be mere passive and indifferent spectators of the historic tragedy, since we wish to co-operate with all our strength in bringing about the circumstances which seem to us the most favourable to our cause, we must have some standard to guide us in judging the events that occur, and especially in choosing the position that we will occupy in the struggle.

The end justifies the means. This maxim has been greatly slandered. As a matter of fact, it is the universal guide to conduct.

One might better express it thus: each end carries with it its own means. The morality or immorality lies in the end sought; there is no option as to the means.

Once one has decided upon the end in view, whether by choice or by necessity, the great problem of life is to find the means which, according to the circumstances, will lead most surely and economically to the desired end. The way in which this problem is solved determines, as far as human will can determine, whether a man or a party reaches the goal or not, is useful to the cause or—without meaning to—serves the opposite side. To have found the right means is the whole secret of the great men and great parties that have left their mark in history.

The object of the Jesuits is, for the mystics, the glory of God, and for the others the power of the Company of Jesus. They must,

1 *Freedom* (London) 37, no. 411 (October 1923), translated by F.A.B. Originally published as "Un peu de théorie," *L'En Dehors* (Paris), August 1892.

therefore, endeavour to degrade the masses, terrorise them, and keep them in submission. The object of the Jacobins and all authoritarian parties, who believe themselves to be in possession of absolute truth, is to force their ideas upon the common herd and to bind humanity upon the Procrustean bed of their beliefs.

With us it is otherwise; entirely different is our goal and very different, therefore, must be our means.

We are not fighting to put ourselves in the place of the exploiters and oppressors of to-day, nor are we fighting for the triumph of an abstract idea. We are not like that Italian patriot who said, "What matters it if all the Italians die of hunger, provided Italy be great and glorious." Neither do we resemble that comrade who admitted that he would not care if three-fourths of the human beings were massacred, provided Humanity was free and happy.

We wish men to be happy—all men, without exception. We wish every human being to be free to develop and live as happily as possible. And we believe that this freedom, this happiness, cannot be given to men by any man or any party; but that all men must, by their own efforts, discover the conditions of happiness and win them. We believe that only the most thorough application of the principle of solidarity can put an end to struggle, oppression, and exploitation; and that solidarity can come only as a result of a voluntary agreement, an intentional and spontaneous harmonizing of interests.

For us, therefore, everything that aims to destroy economic or political oppression, everything that helps to raise the moral and intellectual level of humanity, to make men conscious of their rights and their power and to get them to look after their interests themselves, everything that arouses hatred of oppression and promotes human brotherhood, brings us nearer to our goal and, therefore, is desirable—subject only to a quantitative calculation as to how to secure, with the resources available, the maximum useful result.

And, *per contra,* anything is undesirable, because opposed to our aim, which seeks to preserve the present state of things, or to sacrifice a man, against his will, to the triumph of a principle.

What we desire is the triumph of love and freedom. But does that mean that we refrain from using violent means? Not at all. The means we employ are those that circumstances make possible or necessary. It is true that we would prefer not to hurt a hair of anybody's head; we would like to wipe away all tears and not to cause any to be shed. But the fact is that we have to make our fight in the world as it is, or else be condemned to be nothing but fruitless dreamers.

The day will come, we firmly believe, when it will be possible to work for men's happiness without doing any harm either to oneself or to others. To-day this is not possible. Even the purest and gentlest of martyrs, one who, for the triumph of the right, would let himself be dragged to the scaffold without resistance, blessing his persecutors like the Christ of the legend, even such a one would still be doing much harm. Apart from the harm that he would be doing to himself—which, after all, counts for something—he would cause all those who love him to shed bitter tears.

The main problem always, therefore, in all the acts of our life, is to choose the lesser evil, to try to accomplish the largest possible total of good with the least possible harm.

Humanity drags painfully along under the weight of political and economic oppression. It is stupefied, degraded, killed—and not always slowly—by poverty, slavery, ignorance, and their consequences. For the maintenance of this state of things there exist powerful military and police oganisations which meet any serious attempt at a change with prison, hanging, and massacre. There is no peaceful, legal way of getting out of this situation—and that is perfectly natural because the laws are made by the privileged class in order to protect their privileges. Against the physical force that blocks our way there is no appeal except to psysical force—there can be no revolution except a violent one.

There is no doubt that the revolution will cause much misfortune, much suffering. But it might cause a hundred times more and it would still be a blessing compared to what we endure to-day.

It is a well-known fact that in a single battle more people are killed than in the bloodiest of revolutions. It is a well-known fact that millions of children of tender age die every year for lack of care, that millions of workers die prematurely of the disease of poverty, that the immense majority of people lead stunted, joyless, and hopeless lives, that even the richest and most powerful are much less happy than they might be in a society of equals, and that this state of things has lasted from time immemorial. Without a revolution it would last indefinitely, whereas one single revolution which went right to the causes of the evil could put humanity for all time on the road to happiness.

So let the revolution come! Every day that it delays means an enormous mass of suffering inflicted on mankind. Let us work so that it shall come quickly and shall be the kind of revolution we must have in order to put an end to all oppression and exploitation.

It is through love of mankind that we are revolutionists; it is not our fault if history drives us to this painful necessity.

Therefore, for us and for all those who look at things as we do, each piece of propaganda or of direct action, whether by word or deed, whether done by a group or by an individual, is good when it helps to bring the revolution nearer and make it easier, when it helps to gain for the revolution the conscious co-operation of the masses and to give it that character of universal liberation without which we might, indeed, have a revolution, but not the revolution that we desire. And it is specially in connection with a revolution that we must keep in mind the principle of using the most economical means, because here the cost is figured up in human lives.

We know too well the terrible material and moral conditions in which the working class lives not to be able to understand the acts of hatred, vengeance, and even ferocity which may occur. We understand how there can be some of the oppressed who, having always been treated by the bourgeoisie with the most shameful cruelty, having always seen that anything is permitted to those who have the power, may say to themselves some fine day when they have the power, "Now we will do what the bourgeois used to do." We understand how it can happen in the fever of battle that some people, naturally kind-hearted but not prepared by long moral training—very difficult under present conditions—may lose sight of the goal to be reached and may regard violence as an end in itself and let themselves be swept along to savage excesses.[2]

But it is one thing to understand and excuse, and another thing to recommend. Those are not the kind of deeds that we can accept, encourage, and imitate. We must, indeed, be resolute and energetic, but we must try never to go beyond what is absolutely necessary. We

---

2 These words clearly refer to the deeds of François Koenigstein, known as Ravachol, a French anarchist who had carried out a series of dynamite attacks in the preceding months, as a result of which he was guillotined on 11 July 1892. Malatesta's article provoked a response in the same periodical from Émile Henry, who argued that nobody had the right to judge the deeds of a fellow anarchist. Henry himself died under the guillotine two years later, after throwing a bomb at the Café Terminus in Paris.

must be like the surgeon, who cuts when he must but avoids causing needless suffering. In a word, we should be guided by love for mankind, for all mankind.

We consider this love for mankind as the moral basis, the very seed of our social programme; we believe that only by conceiving of the revolution as the great human jubilee, as the liberation and fraternizing of all men, to whatever class or party they may have belonged—only in this way can our ideal be made real.

Brutal revolt will undoubtedly occur, and it may, indeed, help to give the last great blow which shall overthrow the present system; but if it is not steadied by revolutionists acting for an ideal, it will devour itself.

Hate does not create love: with hatred one cannot rebuild the world. And a revolution inspired by hate either would fail completely or else would lead to fresh oppression, which might, indeed, be called "anarchist," as the present Governments are called "liberal," but which would none the less be oppression and would not fail to bring about all the conditions that oppression inevitably produces.

16.
TACTICAL MATTERS[1]

The point is the making of propaganda; getting our ideas across to the masses; pushing the workers into handling their affairs for themselves, weaning them away from politics and persuading them that only by means of expropriation and the abolition of political power can they emancipate themselves—the co-operators are no worse than anybody else when it comes to working among them at this task.

The point is that we are not content with the aristocratic delights of knowing or thinking that we know the truth. We want the revolution made by the people and for the people. We think that a revolution made by a party without the participation of the masses, even were it possible today, would lead only to the ascendancy of that party, which would not be an anarchist revolution at all.

---

1 Translated from "Questions de tactique," *La Révolte* (Paris) 6, no. 3 (1–7 October 1892). The background to this article is a protracted controversy that had taken place in the columns of *La Révolte* from August to September 1892 between Malatesta and the Italian anti-organizationist Amilcare Pomati. This was part of a broader, heated debate on organization in which Malatesta and his friend Saverio Merlino engaged in the early 1890s. The main issue at stake—as already discussed in the previous article "Matters Revolutionary"—was whether anarchists should organize in any permanent, structured form. Anti-organizationists opposed the idea, and rejected organization in institutional forms such as parties, programs, and congresses. Thus, Pomati had argued that, "in the presence of a popular event or commotion, anarchists will always agree on the course of action to be taken, without any need for previous agreements." The contrast had far-reaching ramifications, which involved such issues as participation in labor organizations. The anti-organizationists' preoccupation was that anarchists would compromise and ultimately lose their anarchist identity in trade unions, becoming progressively involved in questions of palliative improvements that diverted them from their real focus. In general, anti-organizationists were critical not only of attempts at anarchist organizations, but also of tactical alliances with non-anarchist parties and of anarchist efforts to take a leading role in organized collective movements. On the basis of such premises, Pomati had claimed that Merlino and Malatesta's "evolution towards the legalitarian parties was becoming every day more pronounced." The present article was preceded by the following editor's note: "Being eager to have done with the polemic between Pomati and Malatesta, relative to personal issues and which was threatening to turn nasty, we had picked out this portion of Malatesta's response, asking that he expand upon it for us in his exposition of principles that we had promised he could discuss. We now publish that section and reply to it." We have omitted the editor's response to Malatesta's article.

So, insofar as it is possible today, we want to win the masses over to our ideas, and to that end, we must at all times be among the masses, fighting and suffering with them and for them.

When it was said by some comrade or other in *La Tribuna dell'Operaio* that we have to get into the workers' associations and, in places where none exists, create some so as to spread our ideas *afterwards*, he was merely articulating a common-sense truth—a virtual banality. If we are out to band together the workers who are not anarchists, in order to target them with our propaganda, plainly we cannot expect that they have become anarchists *before* banding them together. Pomati finds that he has never witnessed anarchists *going to such lengths*. I say, however, that for the past twenty years, ever since the days of the International, we have never thought nor spoken otherwise. And whilst there were times when we found ourselves remote from the masses and when we left the field free to the legalitarians, there were lots of reasons for that, especially persecution at the hands of government, which from time to time put us out of action, but it was never because of any deliberate decision on our part. Quite the opposite: we have always considered such periods as defeats for which revenge was due.

Let us understand one another properly. Inside anarchist groups, where we marshal our supporters and come to agreement on how to make our efforts more effective, we want only anarchists, we even want ourselves to hobnob only with anarchists whose thinking and sentiments are in harmony with our own, and to remain groups only for as long as such harmony obtains. But outside of our groups, when it comes to the making of propaganda and cashing in on popular upheavals, we strive to reach out in all directions and employ every useful means in order to rally the masses, school them in revolt, and afford ourselves the opportunity of preaching socialism and anarchy. I mean all means that do not run counter to the goal we have set ourselves—it goes without saying. For instance, we could not meddle in the business of political or religious factions, except to confront them and try to break them up; but we can and we should always try to organize the masses to resist capital and government. And wherever nothing else is achievable, wherever toil has them trapped in isolation and brutishness, we will be doing well, for want of an alternative, if we resort even to dancing and musical societies as a way of initiating the young into social life and finding ourselves an audience. We cannot confirm the delusions of those who reckon that they might be able to achieve emancipation through cooperatives or strikes; but we should be in among them if we mean to turn the setbacks suffered by co-operators to our advantage, or combat their tendency towards bourgeois-ification and if we mean to help nurture the seed of revolt to be found within every strike.

We contend that agreement, association, and organization represent one of the laws governing life and the key to strength—today as well as after the revolution. To which end we mean to organize ourselves as best we can with those of like mind. But we also want to see the masses organized, as widely as possible, as should anyone who sees in the revolution a purpose other than his personal or party ascendancy.

After all, tomorrow can only grow out of today—and if one seeks success tomorrow, the factors of success need to be prepared today.

Now I could not care less if the legalitarians say, when we preach organization, that we are not anarchists. They are acting like bourgeois who, having said, and perhaps even believed, that anarchists are savages and brutes, cry out, when confronted by a genuine anarchist (which is to say, a man of courage and common sense): "But this fellow is no anarchist!" Two or three years ago the Italian legalitarians, aping the Germans, saw fit to say that the anarchists were only bourgeois free-traders respectful of private ownership, competition in business, etc. When we replied that anarchists are the bitterest and most rational foes of bourgeois individualism, and are the only true socialists, the answer was that then we were not anarchists. Where does one go from there?

Besides, the thoughts I am expressing are not mine alone. They are the thoughts of the vast majority of anarchists. (Pomati admits as much since he expresses regret for their "lamentable impact" in Italy, above all, and in Spain) and, unless I am mistaken, they speak for the tendency that predominates even among the editors of *La Révolte*. And it took all the wrath of the personalities of which certain "enemies of personalism" are possessed to lay at the door of a handful of individuals something that constitutes one of the major strands within the anarchist movement.

Ah, but we might just as easily tell them: Heal thyselves of individuals.

Yours and for anarchy,
E. MALATESTA

17. THE FIRST OF MAY[1]

For the third time the thinking proletariat of all countries affirms by means of an international demonstration, true solidarity among the workers, hatred of exploitation, and the will, which from day to day grows more determined, to bring the existing system of things to an end.

Governments and the classes tremble, and they have good reason. Not because on this day the revolution will break out—for that is an event which may happen on any day in the year—but because when the oppressed people begin to feel the weight and the shame of oppression, when they feel themselves brothers, when they forget all the historic hatreds fomented by the governing classes, when they clasp hands across frontiers and feel solidarity in the struggle for a common emancipation, then is the day of deliverance close at hand.

What matters it that men and parties give various reason now-a-days as to their immediate ends, and according to the profit that they hope to derive from them? The main fact remains that the workers announce that they are all united, and are of one accord in the struggle against masters. This fact remains, and will remain, as one of the most important events of the century, and as one of the signs heralding the Great Revolution—a revolution which will bring to birth a new civilisation founded on the welfare of all, and the solidarity of labour: It is a fact, the importance of which is only equalled in the present day by that other proletarian announcement of international association among the workers.

And the movement is the most significant as being the direct work of the masses, and quite apart from and even in opposition to the action of parties.

When the State Socialists in the Paris Congress of 1889, called the 1st of May a day of *international strike*, it was merely one of those platonic definitions that are made at congresses just to state a principle, and which are forgotten as soon as the congress is over. Perhaps they thought further that such a decision might help to give importance to their party, and to be useful to certain men as an electoral top; for

1 *The Commonweal* (London) 1, new series, no. 1 (1 May 1893).

unhappily these people seem to have hearts that can only beat with enthusiasm for election purposes. In any case it remains certain that from the moment they perceived that the idea had made headway, and that the demonstrations became imposing and threatened to draw them into revolutionary paths, they endeavoured to check the movement and take away from it the significance with which popular instinct had endowed it. To prove this, one need but recollect the efforts that have been made to shift the demonstration from the first *day* of May to the first *Sunday* in May. Since it is not the rule to work at all on Sunday, to speak of suspension of labour on that day is simply a farce and a fraud. It is no longer a strike, no longer a means of asserting the solidarity of the workers and their power of resisting the orders of the employers. It remains nothing but a *fête* or holiday—a little marching about, a few speeches, a few indifferent resolutions, passed with applause from larger or smaller meetings—that is all! And in order still more effectually to kill the movement which they unthinkingly started, they have got so far as to want to ask the Government to declare the 1st of May an official holiday!

The consequence of all these lulling tactics is that the masses who at first threw themselves into the movement with enthusiasm are beginning to lose confidence in it, and are coming to regard the 1st of May as a mere annual parade, only different from other traditional parades as being duller and more of a bore.

It is for revolutionists to save this movement, which might at some time or other give occasion for most important consequences, and which in any case is always a powerful means of propaganda which it would be folly to give up.

Among Anarchists and Revolutionists there are some who take no interest in the movement, some who even object to it because the first impulse, in Europe at least, was given by the parliamentary Socialists who used the demonstrations as a means of obtaining public powers, the legal eight hours day, international legislation with regard to labour, and other reforms which we know to be mere baits, serving only to deceive the people, and divert them from putting in substantial claims, or else to appease them when they menace the Government and the proprietary classes.

These objectors are wrong in our opinion. Popular movements begin how they *can*; nearly always they spring from some idea already transcended by contemporary thought. It is absurd to hope that in the present condition of the proletariat the great mass are capable before they stir of conceiving and accepting a programme formulated by a small number to whom circumstances have given exceptional means of development, a programme which can only come to be consciously accepted by the great number through the action of moral and material conditions which the movement itself must supply. If we wait to plunge into the fray until the people mount the Anarchist Communist colours, we shall run great risk of remaining eternal dreamers; we shall see the tide of history flow at our feet while scarcely contributing anything toward determining its course, leaving a free field meanwhile to our adversaries who are the enemies, conscious or unconscious, of the true interests of the people.

Our flag we must mount ourselves, and we ought to carry it high wherever there are people who suffer, particularly wherever there are people who show that they are tired of suffering, and are struggling in any way good or bad against oppression and exploitation.

Workers who suffer, but who understand little or nothing of theories, workers who are hungry and cold, who see their children pine and die of starvation, who see their wives and sisters take to prostitution, workers who know themselves to be marching straight to the workhouse or the hospital—these have no time to wait, and are naturally disposed to prefer any immediate amelioration no matter what—even a transitory or an illusory one, since illusion so long as it lasts passes for reality. Yes, rather this than wait for a radical transformation of society which shall destroy forever the *causes* of wretchedness and of man's injustice to man.

This is easy to understand and to justify, and it explains why the constitutional parties who exploit this tendency by speaking always of pretended reforms as "practicable" and "possible," and of partial but *immediate* improvements generally succeed better than we do in their propaganda among the masses.

But where the workers make a mistake (and it is for us to set them right) is in supposing that reforms and improvements are more easy to get than the abolition of the wage system and the complete emancipation of the worker.

In a society based upon an antagonism of interests, where one class retains all social wealth and is organised in political power in order to defend its own privileges, poverty and the subjection of the disinherited masses always tend to reach the highest maximum compatible with the bare existence of man and with the interests of the ruling class. And this tendency meets with no obstacle except in the resistance of the oppressed: oppression and exploitation never stop till that point is reached at which the workers show themselves determined to endure no more of it.

If small concessions are obtained instead of great ones, it is not because they are easier to get, but because the people content themselves with them.

It has always been by means of force or of fear that anything has been won from the oppressors; it has always been force or fear that has hindered the oppressors from taking back what they have granted.

The eight hours' day and other reforms—be their worth what it may—can only be obtained when men show themselves resolved to take them by force, and will bring no improvement to the lot of the workers unless these are determined no longer to suffer what they are suffering to-day.

Wisdom then, and even *opportunism*, requires that we do not waste time and energy on soothing reforms, but struggle for the complete emancipation of all—an emancipation which can only become a reality through the putting of wealth in common, and by the abolition of governments.

This is what Anarchists have to explain to the people, but in order to do so they must not disdainfully hold aloof, but join the masses and struggle along with them, pushing them forward by reasoning and example.

Besides, in countries where the disinherited have tried for a strike on May 1st they have forgotten the "8 hours," and the rest, and the 1st May has had all the significance of a revolutionary date, on which the workers of the whole world count their forces and promise one another to be unanimous in the approaching days of decisive battle.

On the other hand, governments work hard to remove all illusion which anyone may cherish, as to the intervention of public powers in favour of the workers; for instead of concessions, all that has been obtained up to the present time have been wholesale arrests, charges of cavalry, and discharge of firearms!—murder and mutilation!

Then LONG LIVE the 1st May!

It is not, as we have said, the revolution day, but it remains all the same a good opportunity for the propagation of our ideas, and for turning men's minds towards the social revolution.

18. LET US GO TO THE PEOPLE[1]

Let us own up right away: anarchists have not shown themselves equal to the circumstances.

Setting to one side the Carrara uprising, which was proof of their courage and commitment to the cause, but also of the shortcomings in their organization, anarchists would scarcely have rated a mention in relation to the popular unrest in Sicily and elsewhere around Italy.

After all the ranting about revolution, the revolution was upon us and we found ourselves bewildered and remained all but inert.

It may be a painful admission, but to say nothing and cover it up would be tantamount to a betrayal of the cause and to sticking with the errors that have brought us to this pass.

It is time for a re-think!

As we see it, the main reason for our shortcomings is the isolation into which we have primarily fallen.

For a gamut of reasons it would take us too long to go into here, following the break-up of the International, anarchists lost touch with the masses and were gradually whittled down to tiny groups solely preoccupied with endless discussions and, alas! tearing one another to shreds or, at best, waging a little warfare against the legalitarian socialists.

---

1 Translated from "Andiamo fra il popolo," *L'Art. 248* (Ancona) 1, no. 5 (4 February 1894). In 1893, the Fasci movement had spread over Sicily—"*fasci*" being the plural for "*fascio*" (bundle), a term that symbolized the strength of union and bore no relation but etymological with the later Fascist movement. It was a movement of peasants, miners, and workers that started with economic demands but escalated into a revolt, with strikes, attacks on city halls, destruction of custom-houses, and refusal to pay taxes. Dozens of workers were massacred by the armed forces. On 4 January 1894, the state of siege was declared in Sicily and a harsh repression ensued. In response, demonstrations took place in various Italian cities, peaking with an uprising that occurred in the anarchist stronghold of Carrara, where the state of siege was eventually declared, too. Malatesta had strongly supported the Fasci movement all along, and, at the beginning of 1894, he left his London exile to clandestinely enter Italy. The present article, written while Malatesta was still in Italy, draws a balance of the agitations on behalf of the Italian anarchist movement. The periodical where the article appeared was ironically named after the penal code article concerning the "association of malefactors," which was standardly used against anarchists.

On a number of occasions, an effort was made to rectify this situation, with varying degrees of success. But just when it looked as if we might resume serious, broad-based endeavors, up popped a few comrades who, due to a wrong-headed intransigence, made a virtue of isolation and—aided and abetted by the laziness and timidity of so many others, who found such "theory" a handy excuse for doing nothing and taking no risks—successfully steered us back into impotence.

Thanks to the handiwork of those comrades—many of whom (we are pleased to acknowledge) are driven by the best of intentions—propaganda work and organizing have been rendered impossible.

You want to join a workers' association? Be damned! That association has a president, statutes, and does not swear by the anarchist message. Any good anarchist should avoid it like the plague.

You want to establish a workers' association to get them used to solidarity in the fight against the bosses? Treachery! A good anarchist should only ever enter into association with anarchist believers, meaning that he should always keep to the company of the same comrades, and if he must found associations, all he can do is bestow different names upon a group made up of the same people every time.

You are out to organize and support strikes? Bamboozlement, palliatives!

Trying your hand at demonstrations and popular campaigns? Tomfoolery!

In short, the only thing one is allowed to do by way of propaganda is the odd talk, unattended by the public unless it is drawn in by the speaker's exceptional gifts of oratory; some printed matter, always read by the same circle of folk; and man-to-man propaganda, if you can find somebody prepared to hear you out. That, plus a lot of palaver about revolution—a revolution that, preached in this way, ends up like the Catholics' paradise, a promise for the hereafter, one that lulls you into a blessed inertia as long as you believe, and leaves you sceptical and selfish, once the faith evaporates.

And in the meantime the people around us stir and follow other persuasions; and the legalitarian socialists get the better of us and often meet with success, even in countries such as Italy, where socialism was first proclaimed and popularized by us and where we boast far from inglorious traditions of struggle and sacrifice borne with consistency and pride.

This is a lethal tactic, tantamount to suicide. The revolution is not made behind closed doors. Isolated individuals and groups can carry out a little propaganda; audacious *coups de main,* bombings and such like, if done astutely (which is not always the case) can draw public attention to the woes of the workers and to our ideas, may earn us the cachet of people's avengers, and may rid us of some mighty hindrance, but the revolution comes only once the people have taken to the streets. And if we want to make it we have to win over the crowd, as much of a crowd as we can.

Besides these isolationist tactics run counter to our principles and to the purpose we set ourselves.

Revolution, of the sort we have in mind, should be the start of active, direct, genuine participation by the masses, which is to say, by everybody, in the organizing and running of the life of society. If, by some freak, the revolution could be made by ourselves alone, it would not be an anarchist revolution, since we would then be the masters and the people being disorganized and thus powerless and thoughtless, would await their instructions from us. In which case the whole of anarchy will be reduced to a hollow declaration of principles, whereas, in practice, there would still be a tiny faction making use of the blind strength of the unthinking masses, harnessed in order to impose the faction's own ideas—and that is the very essence of authority.

Just imagine that tomorrow, by means of some *coup de main,* we were able to rout the government by ourselves, without involving the masses and that we were able to retain control of the situation. The masses, who would have played no part in the struggle and would not have sampled the potency of their strength would applaud the winners and remain inert as they wait for *us* to bestow upon them all of the well-being we promise them.

What would we do then? Either we would take on a de facto dictatorship, which would amount to our conceding that our anti-governmentalist ideas are impracticable and our confessing that, as anarchists, we have failed; or we would make *through cowardice the great refusal,*[2] we would back off declaring our abomination for command and leave it to our adversaries to take over the reins.

2 This is a passage from Dante Alighieri's *Divine Comedy* (Inferno, III, 60) about Celestine V, who resigned the papacy in 1294.

That is what happened, for very different reasons, to the Spanish anarchists back in the rising of 1873.[3] Due to freak circumstances, they found themselves masters of the situation in several towns, like Sanlúcar de Barrameda and Córdoba. The people made no move of their own and waited for someone to tell them what to do; the anarchists declined to take charge because that conflicted with their principles... whereupon in came, first the republican backlash and then the monarchist reaction, which reinstated the old regime, this time aggravated by massive persecution, arrests, and massacres.

Let us go to people: that is our only salvation. But let us not go to them with the smug arrogance of people who claim to hold the infallible truth and, from their alleged infallibility, look down their noses at those who do not subscribe to their ideas. Let us go out and become brothers with the workers, struggle with them, and sacrifice ourselves alongside them. If we are to earn the right and opportunity to demand of the people the sort of commitment and spirit of sacrifice required in the great days of decisive battle ahead, we need to have proved ourselves in the people's eyes, and shown that we are second to none when it comes to courage and self-sacrifice in its small, day-to-day struggles. Let us enter all the workers' associations, establish as many as we can, weave ever larger federations, support and organize strikes, and spread everywhere and by every means the spirit of cooperation and solidarity between workers, the spirit of resistance and struggle.

And let us beware of becoming disgusted just because the workers often do not understand or embrace all of our ideals and retain an attachment to the old ways and old prejudices.

In the making of the revolution, we cannot and refuse to wait for the masses to become full-fledged anarchist socialists. We know that, for as long as the current economic and political arrangement of society lasts, the vast majority of the population is doomed to ignorance and brutishness and has a capacity only for fairly blind rebellions. We need to dismantle that arrangement, making the revolution as best we can, with whatever resources we can muster in real life.

---

3 The reference is to the federalist movement known as "cantonalism," which broke out after the proclamation of the first republic. After president Pi y Margall pledged to lead the country toward a decentralized administration, many large cities in the south of Spain took their independence for granted and declared themselves free cantons. Though the International as an organization had passed a resolution that condemned all political activity, anarchists became involved in certain independent activities.

Much less can we wait for the workers to turn into anarchists before we set about organizing them. How could they, if left to their own devices, wrestling with the sense of powerlessness that comes from their isolation?

As anarchists we should organize among ourselves, among folk who are perfectly persuaded and perfectly in agreement; and, around us, in broad, open associations, we should organize as many of the workers as we can, accepting them for what they are and striving to nudge them into whatever progress we can.

As workers, we should always be primarily beside our companions in weariness and wretchedness.

Let us remember that the people of Paris started out demanding bread of the king in the midst of applause and tender-hearted tears and, within two years, having—as was only to be expected—been treated to his lead rather than bread, they lopped off his head. And only recently the people of Sicily were on the verge of making a revolution, despite applauding the king and all his kin.

Those anarchists who opposed and sneered at the "fasci" movement just because it was not organized the way we might have preferred—in that the fasci were often called after "Mary the Immaculate", or because they had a bust of Marx rather than of Bakunin on display in their halls, etc.—have proven that they had neither revolutionary sense nor spirit.

We have no mercy—far from it!—for those who taint everything with the parliamentary poison and boil everything down to a question of candidacy and who (acting in good faith or in bad, it matters not which) would like to turn the masses into a floating flock. But does preaching dispersion and leaving all of the proletariat's organized forces in their hands not amount to playing along with such would-be deputies and, worse still, playing the game of the bourgeoisie and government?

Let us take stock. These are solemn times. We have come to one of those watershed moments in human history when an entirely new era is ushered in. The success and orientation of the coming revolution depend on us, who have inscribed upon our banners the redemptive and inseparable words "socialism" and "anarchy."

19. THE DUTIES OF THE PRESENT HOUR[1]

Reaction is let loose upon us from all sides. The *bourgeoisie,* infuriated by the fear of losing her privileges, will use all means of repression to suppress not only the Anarchist and Socialist, but every progressive movement.

It is quite certain that they will not be able to prevent these outrages which served as the pretext of this present reaction; on the contrary, the measures which bar all other outlets to the active temper of some seem expressly calculated to provoke and multiply them.

But, unfortunately, it is not quite certain that they may not succeed in hampering our propaganda by rendering the circulation of our press very difficult, by imprisoning a great number of our comrades, and by leaving no other means of revolutionary activity open to us than secret meetings, which may be very useful for the actual execution of actions determined on, but which cannot make an idea enter into the mass of the proletariat.

We would be wrong to console ourselves with the old illusion that persecutions are *always* useful to the development of the ideas which are persecuted. This is wrong, as almost all generalizations are. Persecutions may help or hinder the triumph of a cause, according to the relation existing between the power of persecution and the power of resistance of the persecuted; and past history contains examples of persecutions which stopped and destroyed a movement as well as of others which brought about a revolution.

Hence we must face, without weakness or illusion, the situation into which the *bourgeoisie* has placed us to-day and study the means

1 *Liberty* (London) 1, no. 8 (August 1894). This little-known and almost forgotten article marks in fact a turning point in Malatesta's ideas. Written only six months after the preceding article, it expresses the same urge to "go to the people." Yet, while the earlier article's theme is still the indeterminacy of collective action, expressed by references to the French revolution as we already find in the 1889 articles for *L'Associazione,* the present work's novel references to economic and legal resistance foreshadow concepts that are fully developed in the 1897–8 articles for *L'Agitazione.*

to resist the storm and to derive from it the greatest possible profit for our cause.

There are comrades who expect the triumph of our ideas from the multiplication of acts of individual violence. Well, we may differ in our opinions on the moral value and the practical effect of individual acts in general, and of each act in particular, and there are in fact on this subject among Anarchists various divergent and even directly opposed currents of opinion; but one thing is certain, namely, that with a number of bombs and a number of blows of the knife, a society like bourgeois society cannot be overthrown, being based, as it is, on an enormous mass of private interests and prejudices, and sustained, more than it is by the force of arms, by the inertia of the masses and their habits of submission.

Other things are necessary to bring about a revolution, and specially the Anarchist revolution. It is necessary that the people be conscious of their rights and their strength; it is necessary that they be ready to fight and ready to take the conduct of their affairs into their own hands. It must be the constant preoccupation of the revolutionists, the point towards which all their activity must aim, to bring about this state of mind among the masses. The brilliant acts of a few individuals may help in this work, but cannot replace it; and in reality, they are only useful if they are the result of a collective movement of spirit of the masses and if being accomplished under such circumstances that the masses understand them, sympathise with, and profit by them.

Woe to us, woe to our cause if we remain in inactivity, waiting from time to time for men like Caserio and Vaillant, Pallas and Berkman to sacrifice their lives for the cause and be admired for their bravery! Who expects the emancipation of mankind to come, not from the persistent and harmonious co-operation of all men of progress, but from the accidental or providential happening of some acts of heroism, is not better advised than one who expects it from the intervention of an ingenious legislator or of a victorious general.

After all, in any case, but a very limited number of individuals do really commit acts of this kind. And the others? What are we doing, we, the great majority of Anarchists, who throw no bombs and kill no tyrants? Must we content ourselves with praising the dead and wait with equanimity of conscience for others to come forward to get killed? It is important that we should agree as to the line of conduct fitted for the bulk of Anarchists: which would not prevent individuals of exceptional energy and devotion bringing to the struggle their personal audacity and sacrifice.

What have we to do in the present situation?

Before all, in my opinion, we must as much as possible resist the laws; I might almost say we must ignore them.

The degree of freedom, as well as the degree of exploitation under which we live, is not at all, or only in a small measure, dependent upon the letter of the law: it depends before all upon the resistance offered to the laws. One can be relatively free, notwithstanding the existence of draconian laws, provided custom is opposed to the government making use of them; while, on the other side, in spite of all guarantees granted by laws, one may be at the mercy of all the violence of the police, if they feel, that they can, without being punished, make short work of the liberty of the citizens.

In Italy, the government used to dissolve, from time to time, such associations as they considered dangerous to the monarchical institutions. Protests, and cries of indignation were raised and, what is most important, the dissolved societies were forthwith reconstituted: and the government could not but let this pass, and is aims to suppress the right of association of its opponents were continually frustrated. After having several times used this method against the International Workingmen's Association (which, in Italy, was from the beginning Anarchist) and not succeeding in making it disappear, the government hit upon prosecuting its members as persons affiliated to an association of criminals. But it was impossible to prosecute all. From time to time arrests were made, sentences passed; the accused openly vindicated their ideas and the right to associate for their propagation; the sections of the International continued their work, and in the end, whilst a number of individuals suffered personally—and those who fight against the existing order of things must expect to suffer—the aims of the government were frustrated and the propaganda profited by it ever so much. But then Anarchists began to say that to form associations meant giving an opportunity for prosecution of associations of criminals to the government; they caused the dissolution of the existing association, combated all efforts to reorganize it... and, in this way, voluntarily renounced the right of association. This did not, of course, prevent a single condemnation; on the contrary, at present Anarchists are accused of forming criminal associations if perchance they meet each other in a café—they may even not know one another—simply because they are Anarchists.

The results of the new laws which are being forged against us will depend to a large degree, upon our own attitude. If we offer energetic resistance, they will at once appear to public opinion as a shameless violation of all human right and will be condemned to speedy extinction or to remain a dead letter. If, on the contrary, we accommodate ourselves to them, they will rank with contemporary political customs, which will, later on, have the disastrous result of giving fresh importance to the struggle for political liberties (of speaking, writing, meeting, combining, and associating) and be the cause more or less of losing sight of the social question.

We are to be prevented from expressing our ideas: let us do so none the less and that more than ever. They want to proscribe the very name of Anarchist: let us shout aloud that we are Anarchists. The right of association is to be denied us: let us associate as we can, and proclaim that we are associated, and mean to be. This kind of action, I am quite aware, is not without difficulty in the state things are in at present, and can only be pursued within the limits and in the way which commonsense will dictate to everybody according to the different circumstances they live under. But let us always remember that the oppression of governments has no other limits than the resistance offered to it.

Those Socialists who imagine to escape the reaction by severing their cause from that of the Anarchists, not only give proof of a narrowness of view which is incompatible with aims of radical reorganisation of the social system, but they betray stupidly their proper interest. If we should be crushed, their turn would come very soon.

But before all we must go among the people: this is the way of salvation for our cause.

Whilst our ideas oblige us to put all our hopes in the masses, because we do not believe in the possibility of imposing the good by force and we do not want to be commanded, we have despised and neglected all manifestations of popular life; we contented ourselves with simply preaching abstract theories or with acts of individual revolt, and we have become isolated. Hence the want of success of what I will call, the first period of the Anarchist movement. After more than twenty years of propaganda and struggle, after so much devotion and so many martyrs, we are to-day nearly strangers to the great popular commotions which agitate Europe and America, and we find ourselves in a situation which permits the governments to foster, without plainly appearing absurd, hopes to suppress us by some police measures.

Let us reconsider our position.

To-day, that which always ought to have been our duty, which was the logical outcome of our ideas, the condition which our conception of the revolution and reorganization of society imposes on us, namely, to live among the people and to win them over to our ideas by actively taking part in their struggles and sufferings, to-day this has become an absolute necessity imposed upon us by the situation which we have to live under. Our ordinary means of propaganda—the press, meetings, groups of more or less convinced adherents of our ideas—at any rate for a certain time, will become more and more difficult to be used. It is only in working-men's associations, strikes, collective revolt where we can find a waste field for exercising our influence and propagating our ideas. But if we want to succeed, let us remember that people do not become Anarchists in a single day, by hearing some violent speeches, and let us above all avoid falling into the error common to many comrades, who refuse to associate with working men who are not already perfect Anarchists, whilst it is absolutely necessary to associate with them in order to make them become Anarchists.

20. THE GENERAL STRIKE AND THE REVOLUTION[1]

The tremendous commotion which some of the strikes of the past few years have produced in the social organization proves they may be something far more important than a mere means of resisting the demands of the masters and of obtaining advantages more or less transitory and illusory. The strike can and will probably be the starting point of the Social Revolution at least in great industrial countries like England and the United States. Anyhow it would be the best of all the many possible starting points which Socialists and Anarchists could wish for the Revolution.

The question often poses itself of how the Revolution will come about. How shall we be able to destroy this powerful organization of military and police which protects the Bourgeoisie. Where shall we find the strength and unity of action necessary for victory?

A great spontaneous insurrection with the avowed object of overthrowing the government and expropriating the Bourgeoisie is a very difficult, perhaps an impossible event, both on account of the mental condition of the masses and the powerful means of prevention and repression at the disposal of the governing classes. Plots and conspiracies can only embrace a very limited number of individuals and are usually impotent to start a movement amongst the people of sufficient importance to give a chance of victory. Isolated movements, more or less spontaneous, are almost always stifled in blood before they have had time to acquire importance and become general.

---

1 *The Torch* (London) 1, new series, no. 3 (August 1894). This is another little-known but remarkable article, not only for its content, but also for its context. The same issue of the *Torch* contained also an article by Émile Pouget—soon to become a leading figure of French revolutionary syndicalism—about the futility of political change. As syndicalism was about to rise, it is a telling sign of Malatesta's foresight and influence that it was his article, not Pouget's, the one to advocate the general strike as a revolutionary weapon. What makes this even more remarkable is that the first part of Malatesta's article restates arguments that he had already made in the 1889 article "About a strike."

One opportunity which might be used as a starting point for the Social Revolution would be a war, anyhow in the conquered country, or some political agitation of a section of the Bourgeoisie.

But war develops patriotic hatreds and may result in the people, wounded in their national pride, irritated by the insolence of foreign soldiers, and obliged besides to resist invasion, making common cause with the Bourgeoisie and forgetting their own grievances. And a political agitation presents the great danger of turning aside the people from the social question and making it fraternize with the Revolutionary section of the Bourgeoisie which will not fail to make show of the best intentions towards the Proletariat.

Besides wars and political agitations become daily more improbable for the Bourgeoisie would derive no great advantage from them and a growing fear of the Social Revolution and also because our propaganda and that of Socialists in general helps to make them impossible.

Thus, whilst ready to avail ourselves of any opportunity which may offer, and to use all means compatible with our principles and our object, we must seek elsewhere the means of starting amongst the masses the great movement which will sweep away the Bourgeois world, and the means which the events of the day point to is—the general strike.

A strike more or less general throughout one of the great industries such as the mining or railway, with the stoppage it would cause in dependent industries would draw into the struggle enormous masses of people and could with comparative ease be converted into a Revolution.

The government would not be able, short of setting public opinion against it, to resort at once to an energetic military repression; the people would have time to get gradually drawn into the movement and understand the necessity for radical changes, and besides one of the chief advantages would be that the question would necessarily be in the realm of economics and its solution would affect the very basis of social organization.

But for a strike to have such results, the strikers must, as the result of previous propaganda and through the influence of a certain number of men amongst them, [be] conscious of the goal to be obtained, understand the full import of the movement and consider themselves as men struggling not for a small private interest but in the interest of the whole proletariat.

A great strike before it can be converted into a Revolution causes real suffering to the mass of the people who are unwilling to undergo it in the interests of the strikers unless it sees at the end of the struggle some advantage for all. Besides there are always so many men whom hunger drives to replace the strikers that this tends to create antagonism between the militant section of the proletariat and those who would be most immediately benefited by the Revolution, such as the unemployed. The strikers must understand this and conduct themselves so as to draw along with them the whole population including the blacklegs.

A few facts selected from those which characterise recent strikes in the United States and which we extract from Stead's book *Chicago Today* will throw light on the situation.[2]

In April 1894 a strike broke out in the bituminous coal trade which spread to sixteen states. The strikers blocked the rail lines and were so energetic that for some time they controlled the whole coal trade. The sympathy or hostility of the public depended on the use they made of this power: they only took into account the special interests of their trade:

> Permission was refused to the town of Demoines to obtain the coal necessary to keep the city waterworks going.
>
> The Illinois Lunatic Asylum at Kantakee in which were 1100 inmates ran short of coal. To save the miserable lunatics from perishing of cold the strikers at first permitted them to have some coal but, on second thoughts, strike policy triumphed over humane considerations and the permission given on the 21st was rescinded on the 29th. Per contra permission was given to McBride, the president of the strikers and also a brewer, to obtain coal for his breweries where he had 5000 dollars worth of beer which would have spoiled if no coal could have been procured.

In the recent strike and boycott of the Pullman cars the strikers, helped by many sympathisers, had quite paralysed the railway traffic, and had at their mercy for a whole week the provisioning of Chicago.

2 William Thomas Stead was an English newspaper editor and a pioneer of investigative journalism. In 1893 he went to Chicago and launched a journalistic investigation of the city's social issues. His 1894 books, *Chicago Today: The Labour War in America* and *If Christ Came to Chicago*, were based on his experiences in that city.

In consequence the fruits and vegetables were rotting in the cars, and it has been calculated that the farmers lost £6000 per day as long as the strike lasted. Meat and fish rotted and the loads of ice melted away.

And in Chicago they were short of meat, vegetables, and coal, ice rose from 12s. a ton to 40s., beer ran short, except for corn, of which, fortunately there were large reserves, Chicago passed through days of want as painful as those Paris suffered during the siege. They began to fear that they would run short of water for Chicago pumps up all its water and the fuel for working the pumps had run low.

> Trains full of women and children were sometimes blocked for days and in one case at least a whole hundred of suffering passengers were compelled to lie blistering in the midsummer sun with scanty food and no water. The strikers refused to allow their miserable hostages this necessary of life for thirty hours at a stretch.

Again the strikers used the worst violence against the blacklegs, who, after all, are but the slaves of misery. Here, for instance, is what a blackleg told a journalist:

> I have been a railroader eight years. When business got slack last winter I was knocked off, and I have not worked five weeks altogether since the first of the year. I have a wife and three children depending on me and for six months we have been living from hand to mouth. When the agent who hired me to come to Chicago asked me if I would go, I told him I would see my wife first. I went home and found her in tears at the dreary outlook. My children were actually in want of bread and it didn't take me long to make up my mind to come to Chicago. I am a Union man at heart, but when wife and children are in danger of starving I feel it my duty to work for them, even should I be killed in the endeavour. There are lots of men here who feel the same way.

Why are the strikers so pitiless towards their brothers in misfortune whom they might have converted into brothers in arms, when we hear of no acts of personal violence against the big pots of the Railway and of Pullman City?

Clearly it was impossible for the strike to succeed, much less to turn into a Revolution when conducted on such lines. Indeed the reaction started in Chicago and if the troops had been powerless to destroy the strikers they would have been crushed by the populace.

When one is master of a situation one must take on oneself the responsibilities of that situation, otherwise one cannot hope to succeed.

Since the provisioning of Chicago depended on the strikers they should have undertaken it. And the mere attempt to provision a town in the interests of the population instead of in that of the capitalists and tradesmen, even if unsuccessful would have been the greatest stride forward in the right direction yet made by the Social Revolution.

At the time of the London Dock Strike in 89 when all work was suspended a ship loaded with ice arrived. The rumour spread that this ice was for the hospitals and immediately a large number of strikers turned up to unload the ship without raising the question of wages. They said that the sick, especially the sick in the hospitals, ought not to suffer through the strike.

This is a small fact but it proves the existence of human solidarity which if developed would give the labor movement a truly socialistic and Revolutionary aspect.

The grandest role the Anarchist could have in the worker's unions and in strikes would be to direct them in these lines.

21.
ANARCHY AND VIOLENCE[1]

From their first manifestations Anarchists have [been] nearly unanimous as to the necessity of recourse to physical force in order to transform existing society; and while the other self-styled revolutionary parties have gone floundering into the parliamentary slough, the anarchist idea has in some sort identified itself with that of armed insurrection and violent revolution.

But, perhaps, there has been no sufficient explanation as to the kind and the degree of violence to be employed; and here as in many other questions very dissimilar ideas and sentiments lurk under our common name.

As a fact, the numerous outrages which have lately been perpetrated by Anarchists and in the name of Anarchy, have brought to the light of day profound differences which had formerly been ignored, or scarcely foreseen.

Some comrades, disgusted at the atrocity and uselessness of certain of these acts, have declared themselves opposed to all violence whatever, except in cases of personal defence against direct and immediate attack. Which, in my opinion, would mean the renunciation of all revolutionary initiative, and the reserving of our blows for the petty, and often involuntary agents of the government, while leaving in peace the organizers of, and those chiefly benefited by, government and capitalist exploitation.

Other comrades, on the contrary, carried away by the excitement of the struggle, embittered by the infamies of the ruling classes, and assuredly influenced by what has remained of the old Jacobin ideas permeating the political education of the present generation, have hastily accepted any and every kind of violence, provided only that it be committed in the name of Anarchy; and they have claimed hardly less than the right of life and death over those who are not Anarchists, or who are not Anarchists exactly according to their pattern.

And the mass of the public, ignoring these polemics, and deceived by the capitalist press, see in Anarchy nothing but bombs and

1 Parts 1 and 2, *Liberty* (London) 1, nos. 9 (September 1894) and 10 (October 1894).

daggers, and habitually regard Anarchists as wild beasts thirsting for blood and ruin.

It is therefore needful that we explain ourselves very clearly as regards this question of violence, and that each one of us should take a position accordingly: needful both in the interests of the relations of practical co-operation which may exist among all those who profess Anarchism, as well as in the interests of the general propaganda, and of our relations with the public.

In my opinion, there can be no doubt that the Anarchist Idea, denying government, is by its very nature opposed to violence, which is the essence of every authoritarian system—the mode of action of every government.

Anarchy is freedom in solidarity. It is only through the harmonizing of interests, through voluntary co-operation, through love, respect, and reciprocal tolerance, by persuasion, by example, and by the contagion of benevolence, that it can and ought to triumph.

We are Anarchists, because we believe that we can never achieve the combined well-being of all—which is the aim of all our efforts—except through a free understanding among men, and without forcibly imposing the will of any upon any others.

In other parties there are certainly men who are as sincere and as devoted to the interests of the people as the best of us may be. But that which characterizes us Anarchists and distinguishes us from all others is that we do not believe ourselves in possession of absolute truth; we do not believe ourselves either infallible, or omniscient,—which is the implicit pretension of all legislators and political candidates whatever; and consequently we do not believe ourselves called for the direction and tutelage of the people.

We are, *par excellence*, the party of freedom, the party of free development, the party of social experimentation.

But against this very freedom which we claim for all, against the possibility of this experimental search after better forms of society, there are erected barriers of iron. Legions of soldiers and police are ready to massacre and imprison anyone who will not meekly submit to the laws which a handful of privileged persons have made in their own interests. And even if soldiers and police did not exist, yet so long as the economic constitution of society remains what it is, freedom would still be impossible; because, since all the means of life are under the control of a minority, the great mass of mankind is obliged to labour for the others, and themselves wallow in poverty and degradation.

The first thing to do, therefore, is to get rid of the armed force which defends existing institutions, and by means of the expropriation of the present holders, to place the land and the other means of production at the disposal of everybody. And this cannot possibly be done—in our opinion—without the employment of physical force. Moreover, the natural development of economic antagonisms, the waking consciousness of an important fraction of the proletariat, the constantly increasing number of unemployed, the blind resistance of the ruling classes, in short contemporary evolution as a whole, is conducting us inevitably towards the outbreak of a great revolution, which will overthrow everything by its violence, and the fore-running signs of which are already visible. This revolution will happen, with us or without us; and the existence of a revolutionary party, conscious of the end to be attained, will serve to give a useful direction to the violence, and to moderate its excesses by the influence of a lofty ideal.

Thus it is that we are revolutionists. In this sense, and within these limits, violence is not in contradiction with Anarchist principles, since it is not the result of our free choice, but is imposed upon us by necessity in the defence of unrecognized human rights which are thwarted by brute force.

I repeat here: as Anarchists, we cannot and we do not desire to employ violence, except in the defence of ourselves and others against oppression. But we claim this right of defence—entire, real, and efficacious. That is, we wish to be able to go behind the material instrument which wounds us, and to attack the hand which wields the instrument, and the head which directs it. And we wish to choose our own hour and field of battle, so as to attack the enemy under conditions as favourable as possible: whether it be when he is actually provoking and attacking us, or at times when he slumbers, and relaxes his hand, counting on popular submission. For as a fact, the bourgeoisie is in a permanent state of war against the proletariat, since it never for one moment ceases to exploit the latter, and grind it down.

Unfortunately, among the acts which have been committed in the name of Anarchy, there have been some, which, though wholly lacking in Anarchist characteristics, have been wrongly confounded with other acts of obviously Anarchist inspiration.

For my part, I protest against this confusion between acts wholly different in moral value, as well as in practical effects.

Despite the excommunication and insults of certain people, I consider it an essential point to discriminate between the heroic act of a man who consciously sacrifices his life for that which he believes will do good, and the almost involuntary act of some unhappy man whom society has reduced to despair, or the savage act of a man who has been driven astray by suffering, and has caught the contagion of this civilised savagery which surrounds us all; between the intelligent act of the man who, before acting, weighs the probable good or evil that may result for his cause, and the thoughtless act of the man who strikes at random; between the generous act of one who exposes himself to danger in order to spare suffering to his fellows, and the bourgeois act of one who brings suffering upon others for his own advantage; between the anarchist act of one who desires to destroy the obstacles that stand in the way of the reconstitution of society on a basis of free agreement of all, and the authoritarian act of the man who intends to punish the crowd for its stupidity, to terrorise it (which makes it still more stupid) and to impose his own ideas upon it.

Most assuredly the *bourgeoisie* has no right to complain of the violence of its foes, since its whole history, as a class, is a history of bloodshed, and since the system of exploitation, which is the law of its life, daily produces hecatombs of innocents. Assuredly, too, it is not political parties who should complain of violence, for these are, one and all, red-handed with blood spilt unnecessarily, and wholly in their own interest; these, who have brought up the young, generation after generation, in the cult of force triumphant; these, who when they are not actual apologists of the Inquisition, are yet enthusiastic admirers of that Red Terror, which checked the splendid revolutionary impulse at the end of last century, and prepared the way for the Empire, for the Restoration, and the White Terror.

The fit of mildness which has come over certain of the bourgeois, now that their lives and their purses are menaced, is, in our opinion, extremely untrustworthy. But it is not for us to regulate our conduct by the amount of pleasure or vexation which it may occasion the bourgeois. We have to conduct ourselves according to our principles; and the interest of our cause, which in our view is the cause of all humanity.

Since historical antecedents have driven us to the necessity of violence, let us employ violence; but let us never forget that it is a case of hard necessity, and in its essence contrary to our aspirations. Let us not forget that all history witnesses to this distressing fact—whenever resistance to oppression has been victorious it has always engendered new oppression, and it warns us that it must ever be so until the bloody tradition of the past be for ever broken with, and violence be limited to the strictest necessity.

Violence begets violence; and authoritarianism begets oppression and slavery. The good intentions of individuals can in no way affect this sequence. The fanatic who tells himself that he will save people by force, and in his own manner, is always a sincere man, but a terrible agent of oppression and reaction. Robespierre, with horrible good faith and his conscience pure and cruel, was just as fatal for the Revolution as the personal ambition of Bonaparte. The ardent zeal of Torquemada for the salvation of souls did much more harm to freedom of thought and to the progress of the human mind than the scepticism and corruption of Leo X and his court.

Theories, declarations of principle, or magnanimous words can do nothing against the natural filiation of facts. Many martyrs have died for freedom, many battles have been fought and won in the name of the welfare of all mankind, and yet the freedom has turned out after all to mean nothing but the unlimited oppression and exploitation of the poor by the rich.

The Anarchist idea is no more secured from corruption than the Liberal idea has proved to be, yet the beginnings of corruption may be already observed if we note the contempt for the masses which is exhibited by certain Anarchists, their intolerance, and their desire to spread terror around them.

Anarchists! let us save Anarchy! Our doctrine is a doctrine of love. We cannot, and we ought not to be either avengers, nor dispensers of justice. Our task, our ambition, our ideal is to be deliverers.

22. DOING GOOD BY FORCE[1]

Dear comrades of *L'Idée,*

In publishing my piece "*Devoir d'aujourd'hui*" in your 15 September 1894 issue, you made, in addition to a few other changes upon which I shall not dwell since they are of no account, one to which I must take exception on the grounds that it completely distorts my thinking and, indeed, strikes me as a negation of the very idea of anarchism, as I understand it at any rate.[2]

Where I say that "our ideas oblige us to put all our hopes in the masses, because we do not believe in the possibility of imposing the good by force," you have added "for the time being at least." Meaning that, later, once we are the strongest, we shall impose *Good*… or whatever we take to be such, by force.

What, in that case, is the difference between us and the authoritarian parties?

We are anarchists because we hold that no one owns the absolute truth, nor is anyone blessed with infallibility; because we think that the sort of social arrangement that should best answer everyone's needs and sentiments, can only be the result—the always adjustable result—of the free play of all the interested parties; and because we believe that force renders brutish both the user and the target, whereas only through freedom and the responsibility that derives from it can men better themselves morally and intellectually to a point where they can no longer bear government.

Besides, if, as you seem to reckon, a day will come when we too could and would impose *our* ideas by force, what, precisely, are the ideas that are to be imposed? Mine, say, or the ideas of comrade A or comrade B!… For you will agree that there are no four anarchists who see completely eye to eye with one another; which is all very natural, by the way, and a sign of the party's vitality.

I thought the essential point upon which we were all agreed and

1 Originally published as "Le bien par la force," *L'Idée* (Saint-Josse-ten-Noode, Belgium), no. 7 (15 October 1894). The present translation is from the reprint in *Le Réveil Anarchiste* (Geneva) 27 [*recte* 37], no. 972 (1 May 1937).

2 The article in question was a French translation of "The Duties of the Present Hour," included in the present collection.

that made anarchists of us was this principle; *no imposition and no force other than force of argument and example.* If I am wrong here, I cannot see that there is very much else to anarchism.

Now, if—perhaps on account of some lack of clarity on my part—you thought that I was referring to force as the means necessary to fend off the force of government, place all the means of production currently hogged by a few at bayonet-point at the disposal of all and open the way to free social evolution with everyone's contribution, then again I take exception to the phrase "*for the time being at least,*" which you have ascribed to me. It was not my intention in my article to turn to the issue of a recourse to arms; and it might well be that I am of the opinion that, in certain countries and in certain circumstances, right now might be the right time to ward off violence with violence.

I am relying, dear comrades, upon your sense of fairness and your love of truth in the publication of this letter. Like me, you will think that the best way for us to get acquainted with one another and achieve the greatest possible measure of agreement between us, is to leave each person the freedom to articulate his thoughts such as they are, without any sort of censorship.

Best wishes to you and to the cause,

E. Malatesta

23. SHOULD ANARCHISTS BE ADMITTED TO THE COMING INTERNATIONAL CONGRESS?[1]

Why not? Perhaps because, as they have said, we are not Socialists. Well, if there are any persons who delight in calling themselves Anarchists, and who are not Socialists, certainly they have nothing to do with a Socialist Congress, and they ought to have no desire to take part in it. But we Anarchist-Communists or Collectivists desire the abolition of monopolies of all kinds; we demand the complete abolition of classes and all domination and exploitation of man by man; we wish that the land and all the instruments of production and distribution, as well as the wealth accumulated by the labour of past generations, should become by the expropriation of its present holders the common property of all mankind, so that all that work shall be able to enjoy the full produce of their work, either in full Communism or by each man receiving according to his efforts, according to the will and agreement of those interested. We wish to substitute for competition and war among men fraternity and solidarity in work for the good of all. And we have spread this ideal, and have struggled and suffered for its realisation for long years, and in some countries—Italy and Spain—long before the birth of parliamentary Socialism. What honest and well-informed man will affirm that we are not Socialists?

Perhaps we are not Socialists because we wish the workers should conquer their rights by their organised efforts, and not to trust to the hope which we think vain and chimerical—that they will obtain them by concessions from any Government? Or because we believe that Parliament is not only a useless weapon for the workers, but that even without the resistance of the middle classes it will never, by the law of its nature, represent the interests and the will of all, and will

1 *The Labour Leader* (London) 8, new series, no. 119 (11 July 1896). The article was written on the eve of the London International Socialist Workers and Trade Union Congress of 1896, where a front of anti-parliamentary forces unsuccessfully opposed the resolution to exclude anarchists from the congresses of the Second International. Malatesta was among the most active anarchists in this battle.

always remain the instrument of the domination of a class or party? Or because we believe that the new society ought to be organised by the direct agreement of all concerned, from the circumference to the centre, freely, spontaneously, under the inspiration of the sentiment of solidarity and under the pressure of natural and social necessities, and because that if this organisation was made by means of decrees from a central body, either elected or a directorship, it will begin by being an artificial organisation, forcing and dissatisfying everybody, and it would end in the creation of a new class of professional politicians, who would seize for themselves all sorts of privileges and monopolies? It might easily be maintained with more justice that we are, if not the only Socialists, certainly the most thorough and logical, because we claim for every man, not only his entire portion of social wealth, but also his part in social power—that is to say, the real faculty of making his influence felt equally with that of others in the management of public affairs.

If we are Socialists then it is clear that a congress from which we are excluded cannot honestly call itself "The Socialist Workers' Congress," and that it ought to take the particular title of the party or parties admitted to its deliberations. For example, none of us would think of mixing with a congress which would be called a "Social Democratic Congress" or a "Congress of Parliamentary Socialists."

But let us leave alone this question of nomenclature, and neglect also the discussion of the question, if the London Committee has properly interpreted the resolutions of Zurich.[2] Let us go to the root of the matter. It is to the interest of all the enemies of our capitalist society that the workmen should be united and solid in the struggle against capitalism, and that they should be conscious that this struggle is of necessity of an economic character. It is not because we ignore the importance of political questions. We believe not only that government—the state—is an evil in itself, but that it is the armed defence of capitalism, and that the people cannot take possession of their own property without passing over the bodies of its armed police—really or figuratively, according to circumstances. Thus we ought necessarily to occupy ourselves in the political struggle against government. But it may be owing to the difference of conditions and of temperaments of the peoples of various countries, or the fact that

2 The resolution against the anarchists had been taken at the Zurich congress of 1893, but had then been subjected to contrasting interpretations.

the relations between the political constitution and the conditions of the masses are very complicated, hard to adapt and less capable of being treated in a way that seems good to everybody, that politics are in effect a great source of division, and the fact is that the conscious workers in the different countries whom it would be easy to solidly unite in the economic struggle, are by politics broken up into many fractions. Consequently an understanding between all the workers who fight for their emancipation is not possible, save on economic ground—and it is this that is of most consequence, because political action of the proletariat, parliamentary or revolutionary, is equally futile so long as it does not form a conscious organised economic force. Every attempt to enforce a single political opinion upon the labour movement tends to its disintegration and stops the progress of its economic organisation.

The Social Democrats evidently desire to force upon the workers their special programme. It might almost be said that they want to prevent those who do not accept the decisions of their party from fighting for human emancipation! They have had in this direction more or less success—perhaps they will have more—but that can only take place at the expense of a general understanding among the workers, and certainly without desiring it, serving the interests of the middle classes. If Socialists would only remember the history of the old International, which certainly the old among them know better than it is generally related. There were plenty of insults between Marxists and Bakunists. The truth is that both sections wished to make its special programme triumphant in the International, and in the struggle between Centralism and Federalism, between Statism and Anarchism, we neglected the class struggle and economic solidarity, and the International perished through it. To-day the Anarchists, though we owe to them in many countries the first Socialist trade unions, by a series of circumstances and errors which there is no need at present to examine, have not much influence—save in Spain—in the Labour movement. But this will not last long, and the Social Democrats would do wrong to reckon upon it.

Certainly the Anarchists will soon be brought by the logic of their programme and by the necessities of the struggle to put their strength and their hope in the international organisation of the masses of the workers. Already eloquent signs of this can be seen. What will happen then? Will there be again *two* Internationals, wasting in internal quarrels the strength which ought to be employed against the capitalist middle classes, and will they again end in killing each other?

We have no intention of demanding—far from that—that the different parties and schools should renounce their programme and their tactics. We hold to our own ideas, and we understand that the others will do the same. We only ask that division shall not be carried where it ought not to be; we demand the right for every worker to fight against capitalism hand in hand with his brothers, without distinction of political ideas; we ask that all shall fight as they think best, with those that believe as they believe, but that all shall be united in the economic struggle.

Then, if the Social Democrats persist in their attempt at military despotism, and thus sow dissension among the workers, may the latter be able to understand and bring to a glorious triumph the noble words of Marx: "Workers of the world, unite!"

24. ERRORS AND REMEDIES[1]

There is such a variety of folk calling themselves anarchists these days and peddling such a variety of disparate and contradictory ideas as anarchy, that it really is small wonder that the public, being new to our ideas and unable to make out at a glance the big differences lurking under the blanket of a common name, remains deaf to our propaganda and regards us with suspicion.

Of course we cannot stop others from adopting whatever title they choose; nor would our jettisoning the title of anarchists achieve anything beyond adding to the confusion, since the public would reckon that we had merely switched flags.

All we can do, and what we should do, is to differentiate ourselves clearly from those whose notion of anarchy differs from our own, or who draw from the very same theoretical concept practical consequences opposite to the ones we draw. And such differentiation should come from a clear exposition of our ideas and from the relentless repetition, frankly and loudly, of our view of all things that fly in the face of our ideas and morality, without regard to personalities or party. Such a purported party fellowship between people who ultimately did not belong and could not have belonged to the same party, has actually been one of the chief causes of the confusion. And a pass has been reached where lots of people praise, coming from "comrades," the very same actions that they rail against in the bourgeois; and it looks as if their only yardstick in gauging good and bad may be this: whether the author of the deed under examination adopts the name anarchist, or not.

***

A multiplicity of errors has led some into utter contradiction of the principles that they, in theory, profess, and others to countenance that contradiction; just as there are many reasons for the attraction into our ranks of folk who mock socialism and anarchy and anything that looks beyond their own personal interests.

---

1 Translated from "Errori e rimedi," *L'Anarchia* (London), August 1896. This was a one-off publication "edited by a socialist-anarchist group," as the masthead read.

I cannot embark upon a systematic and comprehensive survey of such errors here. I shall merely allude to a few of them in the order that they come to mind.

First and foremost, let us talk of morality.

It is commonplace to find anarchists who "deny morality." Initially, this is merely a figure of speech, signifying that, in terms of theory, they accept no absolute, eternal, immutable morality, and that, in practice, they defy the bourgeois morality that countenances exploitation of the masses and condemns those acts that pose a danger and a threat to the privileged. But then, gradually, as is customarily the case with so many other things, the rhetorical flourish is mistaken for a precise encapsulation of the truth. They forget that under the current moral code, in addition to the rules inculcated by priests and bosses in the interests of their ascendancy, there exist, and these account for the main substance of it, other rules that are the outworking of and preconditions for all social co-existence; they forget that rebelling against any rule imposed by force does not actually mean a rejection of all moral restraint and any sense of obligation towards others; they forget that, in order to wage a reasonable fight against one moral code, one has to measure it in theory and in practice, against a higher code of morality; and, if only temperament and circumstances contribute a little, they wind up becoming immoral in the absolute sense of the word; which is to say, men with nothing to regulate their conduct, no criterion to guide them in what they do, and who surrender passively to the impulses of the moment. Today they take the crust of bread from their own mouths in order to help a comrade; tomorrow they will slay a man for visiting a brothel!

Morality is that line of conduct that each man regards as good. The morality that prevails at a given point in time, in a particular place, in a given society may be found wanting; and in fact we hold bourgeois morality to be dire; but a society without some form of morality is inconceivable, nor can any thoughtful person manage without some yardstick by which to gauge what is good and what is bad as far as he and others are concerned. In fighting established society, we counter the individualistic morality of the bourgeois, the morality of strife and competition, with a morality of love and solidarity, and strive to establish institutions that live up to how we think of relations between people. How else could we see evil in the bourgeois's exploitation of the people?

Another damaging claim, honestly made by many, but in others merely an excuse, is that the current social climate does not allow us to be moral; and that, as a result, it is pointless our making efforts that can never succeed, and the wisest course would be to glean as much as one can for one's own benefit from the current set-up with nary a care for anyone else, except changing one's ways, come the change in the arrangement of society. Certainly any anarchist, any socialist will understand the economic factors at work that force a man today to vie with his fellow men, and any good observer will see the powerlessness of individual rebellion against the overwhelming might of the social environment. But it is equally certain that without the rebellion of the individual who joins forces with other individual rebels to stand up to that environment and try to alter it, that environment would never change.

All of us, without exception, are obliged to live lives pretty much at loggerheads with our ideals; but we are socialists and anarchists because of and to the extent that we are irked by this contradiction, and strive to reduce it to a minimum. On the day we conform to our surroundings, we would of course be spared the determination to change them and turn into mere bourgeois; penniless bourgeois, maybe, but for all that, bourgeois in our deeds and in our intentions.

***

Another source of very grave errors and blame has been the construction placed by many upon the theory of violence.

Today's society is underpinned by force of arms. No oppressed class has ever managed to emancipate itself without recourse to violence; the privileged classes have never surrendered a part, the tiniest fraction, of their privileges, except because of force or fear of force. Established social institutions are such that changing them by means of phased, peaceful reforms appears to be impossible; and the necessity for a violent revolution that, by breaching and trampling all over the law, re-founds human society upon fresh foundations cannot be avoided. The obstinacy and brutality with which the bourgeoisie reacts to even the most anodyne demand from the proletariat are proof of the inevitability of violent revolution. It is therefore logical and essential that socialists, and especially anarchists, form a revolutionary party and look forward to and expedite the revolution.

Unfortunately, however, people have a tendency to mistake the means for the end; and violence, which we see as being—and so it must stay—a harsh necessity, has for many turned into virtually the sole purpose of the struggle. History is awash with examples of men who, having embarked upon struggle for a lofty purpose, have then, in the heat of battle, lost the run of themselves and lost sight of their purpose and turned into ferocious butchers. And, as recent events have shown, many an anarchist has not avoided this terrifying danger in violent struggle. Irked by persecution, driven mad by the instances of blind savagery emanating daily from the bourgeoisie, they have begun to ape the example set by the bourgeois; and a spirit of vengeance, a spirit of hatred has replaced the spirit of love. And, like the bourgeois, they have described such vengeance and hatred as justice. Then, in order to justify such acts, which might be explained away as the effects of the proletariat's dire predicament and taken as yet further reason to call for the destruction of a state of affairs that can generate such dismal outcomes, a few have started devising the weirdest, most fanatical, most authoritarian theories; and, heedless of self-contradiction, they have depicted these as the very latest advance in anarchist thinking. Simultaneously claiming to be determinists, and denying the very notion of responsibility, they have set about tracking down those responsible for the present state of affairs, and have identified them not only in the conscious bourgeois who knowingly do evil, not only in the mass of bourgeois who are bourgeois by birth and who have never questioned their status, but also in the mass of workers who are the main prop of oppression by enduring it without rebelling; and have settled upon the... death penalty for them all. And there has even been the odd one who, raving about some "latent responsibility," has concluded that pregnant women and children deserve butchering! Rightly querying the right of bourgeois judges to impose as much as one hour's imprisonment, they set themselves up as arbiters in the life and death of others and go so far as to say that *those who do not think as we do deserve killing!* Which defies belief and which many refuse to credit! Yet only a few weeks back, there, in one "anarchist" newspaper for all to read, were these words: "A bomb went off in Barcelona at a religious procession, leaving 40 dead and who knows how many injured upon the ground. The police have arrested upwards of 90 anarchists in the hope of apprehending the heroic author of the outrage." No rationale, no meaning, nothing;

there is heroism in the slaughter of defenseless women, children, and men—because they were Catholics. This is a step beyond vendetta: it is the morbid fervor of bloodthirsty mystics, a blood sacrifice upon the altar of a God... or of an idea, which amounts to the same thing. Oh Torquemada! Oh Robespierre!

I hasten to say that the vast majority of Spanish anarchists spoke out against the demented deed. But there are those who purport to be anarchists and who exult in the act; and that is sufficient for governments to pretend to lump us all together and for the public to genuinely mix us up.

Let us shout it loudly at all times; anarchists should not and cannot be avengers; they are liberators. We bear hatred towards none; we are not fighting to avenge ourselves or to avenge anyone else; we seek love towards all, liberty for all.

Since existing social inevitability and the stubborn resistance from the bourgeoisie oblige the oppressed to have recourse to the last resort of physical force, we do not shrink from the harsh necessity and ready ourselves to employ it successfully. But let us have no unnecessary victims, not even in the enemy camp. The very purpose on behalf of which we struggle requires us to be kind and humane even in the heat of battle; so I fail to understand how one can fight for a purpose like ours without our being kindly and humane. And let us not forget that a liberating revolution cannot be born of massacre and terror, these having been—and ever so it shall remain—the midwives to tyranny.

On the other hand, another mistake, the opposite of the one the terrorists make, poses a threat to the anarchist movement. Partly by way of a backlash against the way that violence has been misused in recent times, partly due to lingering Christian notions and above all due to the influence of the mystical preaching of Tolstoy, whose genius and moral qualities have made it fashionable and conferred a cachet upon it, the supporters of passive resistance are starting to acquire a measure of significance among anarchists, their principle being that we must endure oppression and degradation in our own cases and in those of others rather than do harm to the oppressor. This is what has been described as *passive anarchy*.

Since some, impressed by my aversion to needless, harmful violence, have tried to credit me—I am none too sure whether the intention is to praise me or blacken me—with leanings in the direction of Tolstoyism, let me use this opportunity to state that, in my view, that doctrine, no matter how sublimely altruistic it might seem, is in reality the very negation of instinct and social obligations. A man may, if he is very... Christian, patiently endure all manner of vexation without using every available means to defend himself and perhaps remain a moral person. But in practice and much against his will, would he not be simply terrifically selfish if he were to let others suffer oppression without trying to come to their defence? If, say, his preference were to see some class ground into misery, some people downtrodden by the invader, some man suffer trespass against his life and liberty, rather than that a hair on the head of the oppressor be harmed?

There may be instances in which passive resistance is an effective weapon, in which case it would certainly be the most commendable weapon, in that it would be the most sparing one in terms of human suffering. But in most instances, professing passive resistance amounts to the oppressors' being reassured against the fear of rebellion and thus a betrayal of the cause of the oppressed.

Odd to note how the *terrorists* and the *Tolstoyans*, precisely because they, one and all, are mystics, arrive at pretty much the same practical consequences. Those who would not hesitate to destroy half of humanity as long as the *idea* emerged triumphant; and those who would let the whole of humanity be ground down by the weight of the greatest suffering rather than trespass against a principle.

As for myself, I would breach every principle in the world in order to save someone; in which I would in fact be upholding a principle, for, as I see it, all social and sociological principles boil down, essentially, to one: the welfare of men, of all men.

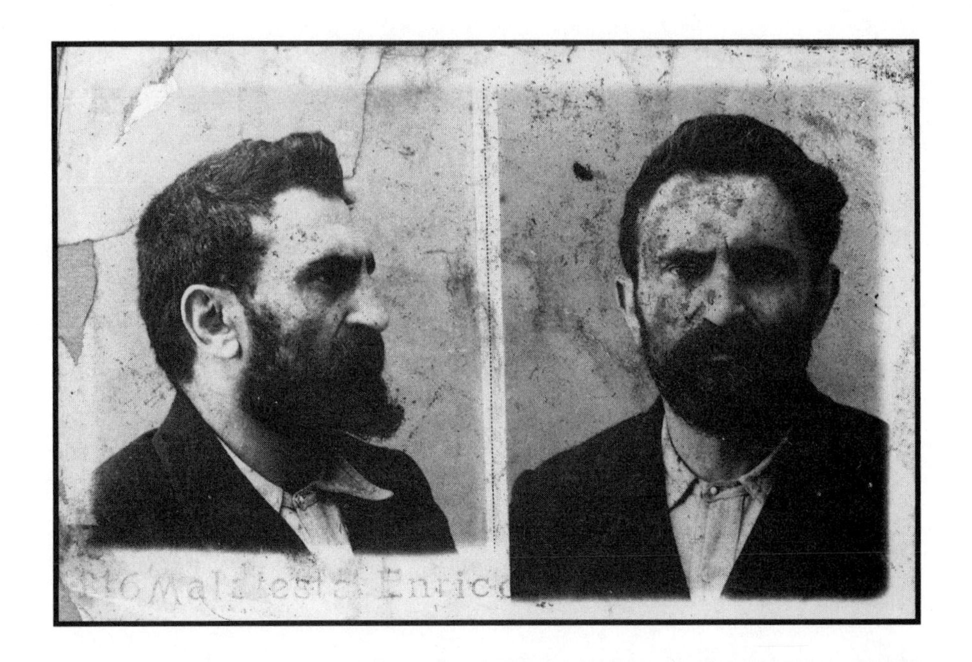

Malatesta's 1898 police photographs/ Source: Archivio Centrale dello Stato, Rome, Casellario Politico Centrale, box 2952

III.

"A Long and Patient Work...":
The anarchist socialism of *L'Agitazione*, 1897–98

In March 1897, Malatesta returned to Italy from his London exile to edit the weekly *L'Agitazione* in Ancona. In contrast with the insurrectionist wishful thinking and the isolation in which anarchists had increasingly fallen, and without repudiating revolution and anti-parliamentarianism, Malatesta began preaching novel tactics for Italy, advocating a "long and patient work of popular preparation and organization," by which anarchist socialism could grow in open daylight as an organized movement that drew its strength from the workers' movement. From the columns of *L'Agitazione* Malatesta emphasized the importance of labor unions; urged anarchists to be in the front line of workers' struggles; promoted the new tactics of workers' direct action that had already caught on in Britain and France; supported the legal struggle against *domicilio coatto* (forced residence); and claimed the anarchists' right of association. For Malatesta, society's direction was the composite resultant of multiple forces. Anarchists were to exert whatever influence their strength allowed them. Their action was simultaneously revolutionary and reforming: they aimed to build the workers' revolutionary strength, for emancipation could only come by revolution; at the same time they contributed to wrest from the bourgeoisie whatever concessions could be obtained in the present society.

25. THE SOCIALISTS AND THE ELECTIONS: A LETTER FROM E. MALATESTA[1]

London, 2 February 1897

Mr. Editor of the *Messaggero,*

I am informed that Italy's parliamentary socialists are putting it about that I, agreeing with Merlino, see some purpose in anarchist socialists taking part in election contests by voting for the most progressive candidate.

Since they honour me by even considering my opinion, I will not be thought presumptuous if I hasten to let them and the public know what I truly think on this issue.

I certainly do not query my friend Merlino's right to his own thoughts and to express them without holding back. It might have been better had he, prior to making a public announcement about a switch of tactics, which after all is worthless unless the comrades agree to it, discussed the matter at greater length with members of the party to which he has hitherto belonged and alongside which I hope he will be willing to carry on fighting. But the blame for that belongs, not so much to Merlino, as to the prolonged crisis by which our party has been beset and the, as yet, incipient stage of reorganization in which we find ourselves.

But it needs to be placed on record that what Merlino has said regarding parliamentarism and electoral tactics is merely a personal view, not binding upon whatever tactics are to be adopted by the anarchist socialist party.

For my own part, much though it may displease me to take issue on such an important matter with as worthy a fellow as Merlino, to

1 Translated from "I socialisti e le elezioni: Una lettera di E. Malatesta," *Il Messaggero* (Rome) 19, no. 38 (7 February 1897). This was a response to an open letter from Malatesta's comrade and friend Francesco Saverio Merlino, published in the same newspaper on January 29. In that letter Merlino proposed new tactics for the anarchists, which, in addition to direct action, were to include the ballot box.

whom I am bound by so many ties of affection, I feel it my duty to state that, as I see it, the tactics advocated by Merlino are damaging and would of necessity lead to the abandonment of the entire anarchist socialist programme. And I think I am speaking the thoughts of all, or nearly all, anarchists there.

The anarchists remain, as ever, resolutely opposed to parliamentarism and parliamentary tactics.

Opposed to parliamentarism because they believe that socialism should and can only be achieved through a free federation of producer and consumer associations, and that any government, parliamentary government included, is not merely powerless to resolve the social question and reconcile and satisfy everybody's interests, but of itself represents a privileged class, with ideas, passions, and interests contrary to those of the people, which it can oppress by means of the people's own strength. Opposed to the parliamentary tactics because they believe that, far from encouraging the development of popular consciousness, it has a tendency to disaccustom the people to the direct care of their own interests and schools the ones in slavishness and the others in intrigues and lies.

Far be it from us to ignore the importance of political freedoms. But freedoms are only secured once the people have shown themselves determined to have them; and, once obtained, they endure and have value only until such time as governments feel that the people would suffer their being abolished.

Accustoming the people to delegating to others the winning and defence of its rights is the surest means of giving a free hand to the whims of those who govern.

True, parliamentarism is better than despotism: but only if it represents a concession granted by the despot out of fear of worse.

Given a choice between a parliamentarism, embraced and boasted, and a despotism forcibly thrust upon minds that cry out for redemption, despotism is a thousand times better.

I am well aware that Merlino places small store by elections, and seeks, as we do, to ensure that the real battle is fought in the country and with the country. But, for all that, the two methods of struggle do not go together and whoever embraces them both inevitably winds up sacrificing any other consideration to the electoral prospect. Experience proves as much and the natural love of the quiet life explains it.

And Merlino demonstrates that he appreciates that danger when he says that the anarchist-socialists need not stand candidates of their own, since they do not aspire to power and have no notion what to do with it.

But is that a tenable position? If good can be done through Parliament, why others and not ourselves, when we reckon we know better than the others?

If we do not aspire to power, why would we help those who do? If we have no idea what to do with power, what would others do with it, other than wield it to the people's detriment?

Let Merlino be assured on this point: if we tell people today to go out and vote, tomorrow we will be telling them to vote for us. In which we would be logically consistent. Be that as it may, if it were up to me to give someone advice about voting, I would promptly advise them to vote for me, since I believe (and I am probably wrong here, but to err is human), since I believe that I am as good as anyone else and am perfectly certain as to my honesty and steadfastness.

To be sure, with the considerations above, I have not said everything that needed saying, but I would be loath to presume unduly upon your space. I shall explain myself more fully in a related article: and I hope, also, that some collective act will be forthcoming from the party to reaffirm the anarchist-socialists' anti-parliamentary principles and abstentionist tactics.

In the hope that you will find this letter useful in informing the public about the stance that will be adopted by the various parties in the coming elections and that you will therefore be willing to publish it, my thanks to you in anticipation.

Errico Malatesta
112, High Street, Islington N.
London

26. FROM A MATTER OF TACTICS TO A MATTER OF PRINCIPLE[1]

Merlino has some very fair things to say, things we ourselves would say; but by talking in generalities about the necessity of social living, he loses sight, or so it seems to us, of the dividing line between authoritarianism and anarchism and the rationale behind the difference. And so his entire argument could very well be used to argue the necessity of government and thus the impossibility of anarchy.

Let us straight away spell out the points of agreement between us, lest Merlino—or anyone else who might be inclined to engage us in argument—waste their time upbraiding us about ideas that are not ours and thereby finish up pushing at an open door.

We reckon that, in many cases, the minority, even though it might be sure that it is in the right, should defer to the majority, for otherwise life in society would be impossible—and any human life outside of society is impossible. And we know only too well that matters on which unanimity cannot be achieved and on which the minority needs to give way are not just matters of small consequence, but also, indeed especially, matters of vital importance to the collective economy.

We do not believe in the divine right of majorities, but neither do we hold that minorities always, as has been argued, stand for righteousness and progress. Galileo was right, despite all his contemporaries, but to this day there are some who maintain that the earth is flat and that the sun goes around it; but none will say that they are in the right merely because they have become the minority. Besides, whilst it is true that revolutionaries are always a minority, the exploiters and the goons are always minorities, too.

---

1 Translated from Malatesta's note to the article "Da una questione di tattica a una questione di principii," by Francesco Saverio Merlino, *L'Agitazione* (Ancona) 1, no. 3 (28 March 1897). Merlino's article and Malatesta's response are part of a long debate that started with the respective letters to the newspaper *Il Messaggero* and ended only with Malatesta's arrest in January 1898. The matter of principle mentioned in the title is whether the majority principle can be consistent with anarchism.

So, we agree with Merlino in accepting that there is no way that each man can do everything for himself, and that, even if it were possible, that would be extremely detrimental for everyone. Hence we agree to the division of labor, the delegation of roles and trusting others to represent our own views and interests.

And above all we reject as false and pernicious any notion of providentially or naturally ordained harmony within society, it being our belief that human society and the social individual himself are the products of a protracted and wearisome battle with nature, and that if man were to desist from exercizing his conscious will and surrender to nature, he would soon lapse back into animality and brutish strife.

But—and here is the reason why we are anarchists—we want minorities to defer voluntarily whenever necessity and the feeling of solidarity require it. We want the division of labour not to divide men into classes, turning some into directors and chiefs, exempt from any sort of off-putting work, and condemning others to serve as society's beasts of burden. We want men, when they delegate a role to others—which is to say, allocate a given task to others—not to be abdicating their own sovereignty and, wherever a representative may be called for, that he may serve as the spokesman for those from whom he receives his mandate or the executor of their wishes, rather than someone who makes laws and enforces acceptance of them. And we believe that any social arrangement that is not founded upon the free and considerate will of its members, leads to oppression and exploitation of the masses by a tiny minority.

Any authoritarian society survives through coercion. The anarchist society must be founded upon consent freely given. There, men must be acutely sensible and spontaneously accepting of the obligations of social living, and strive to orchestrate discordant interests and banish any source of internal strife; or at any rate, if conflicts do erupt, may they never be of such dimensions as to trigger the establishment of some moderating authority that would reduce everyone to the status of slave on the pretext of ensuring justice for all.

But what if the minority refuses to give way?, Merlino asks. What if the majority makes to abuse its strength?, we ask.

In both instances, plainly, anarchy is not a possibility.

For instance, we want no police. This naturally presupposes that our wives and children and we ourselves can proceed through the streets without being molested by anyone, or at any rate, that if anyone was to make to misuse his superior might against us we can look to our neighbors and passers-by for better protection than any hireling police force might offer. But on the other hand, what if gangs of blackguards roved the streets insulting and thrashing the weakest of them and what if the public were to gaze upon this spectacle with indifference? Then, naturally, the weak and those with a fondness for a quiet life would insist upon the establishment of a police force, and one would assuredly be raised. It might be argued that, in such circumstances, the police would be the lesser evil; but it certainly could not be argued that anarchy was achieved. The truth of the matter would be that with so many bullies on one side and so many cowards on the other, anarchy is not possible.

Therefore the anarchist has to have a lively sense of respect for the freedom and well-being of others, and ought to make such respect the over-arching purpose of his propaganda.

But, the objection will be raised, men these days are too selfish, too intolerant, too mischievous to respect other people's rights and defer voluntarily to the needs of society.

Actually, even in the most corrupt of men, we have always encountered something akin to a need to be held in good regard and to be loved and, in certain circumstances, such a capacity for sacrifice and such consideration for the needs of others as to give us hope that, once the on-going causes of the gravest antagonisms have been banished along with private ownership, it will not be hard to secure the freely given cooperation of each to the welfare of all.

Be that as it may, we anarchists are not the whole of mankind and we certainly cannot make the whole of human history on our own; but we can and should strive for the realization of our ideals by trying to banish strife and coercion from the life of society, insofar as this is feasible.

***

That said, Merlino is right to argue that parliamentarism cannot be banished entirely and that even in the society of our dreams there is going to be some trace of it left behind!

It is our belief that referring to the trading of services and distribution of social roles, without which there could be no society, as parliamentarism or a remnant of parliamentarism is an unreasonable tinkering with the accepted usage of the word and cannot help but cloud and confuse the issue.

Parliamentarism is a form of government; and government means legislative power, executive power, and judicial power; it means violence, coercion, forcible imposition of the will of the governors upon the governed.

An example will make our thinking plain.

The various states in Europe and around the world connect with one another, have their representatives to one another, organize international services, call congresses, explicitly or tacitly agree upon certain rights for the people, make peace or war without there being any world government, some legislative power making the laws for every state and an executive power imposing it upon them all.

These days, relations between the various states are still largely rooted in violence and in suspicion. Added to the lingering atavism of historic rivalries, racial and religious hatreds and the spirit of conquest, there is the economic rivalry generated by capitalism, so that the threat of war hangs over us every day and every day we watch as the bigger states do violence to the smaller.

But which of us would dare argue that, in order to rectify this state of affairs, every state would need to appoint representatives who, gathered together, would sort out between them and by majority vote the principles of international law and criminal sanctions to be used against transgressors, and little by little would lay down the law on every state-to-state issue; and be able to call upon a force to ensure that their decisions were abided by?

That would amount to parliamentarism applied to international relations; and, far from introducing harmony between the interests of the various states and banishing the causes of conflicts, the tendency would be for it to consolidate the ascendancy of the strongest and conjure up a new class of international exploiters and oppressors. Something of the sort already exists in germ in the "concert" of the great powers, and the freedom-murdering impact of that is there for us all to see.

***

And now, for a few more words about the issue of electoral abstentionism.

Merlino persists in talking about the propaganda activity that might be pursued by means of elections; but fails to consider what might happen if, repudiating electioneering, such activity was to be pursued in another theater more congruent with our principles and our purposes.

Merlino does not believe in capturing public office; but we cannot see any such capture being made, neither by ourselves nor by anyone else, not even if we were to believe it feasible. We are opposed to the principle of government and do not believe that anyone coming to government would then be in any hurry to surrender the power captured. The peoples who want freedom tear down the Bastilles; tyrants, on the other hand, wish to garrison and strengthen them, on the pretext of defending the people from its enemies. Hence it is not our wish that the people should get used to hoisting its friends, or alleged friends, into power and look to their rise to power for emancipation.

To us, abstentionism is a matter of tactics; but one of such importance that, when one forswears, it one finishes up foreswearing one's principles as well. Because of the natural connection between means and ends.

Merlino is sorry that he cannot see eye to eye completely, neither with us nor with the democratic socialists; but he says that he cannot renege upon what he has said.

We are certainly not asking him to renege upon it and go against his beliefs and his conscience. But permit us to make this observation to him.

No matter how good it may be, a tactic only has value to the extent that it is embraced by those tasked with implementing it. Now, rightly or wrongly, we and every other anarchist want no truck with the tactic being put forward by Merlino. Would he not be better sticking with us, with whom he shares his ideals and his chief methods of struggle, instead of squandering his efforts on a venture that we are sure will get nowhere, unless he turns his back on anarchy and looks to the ranks of his and our opponents for his supporters?

27. A FEW WORDS TO BRING THE CONTROVERSY TO AN END[1]

Merlino is developing an odd approach to debate. From what is said to him he picks out some phrase that he then wrenches out of its context, toying with it and twisting it and, because he then ignores the context, he manages to depict you as saying whatever suits him. Besides, he never answers questions put to him nor replies to rebuttals; but swoops on some incidental example or detail and addresses it, ignoring the essential point at issue; so that the subject of contention is never the same from one response to the next.

And actually, who could guess that we were in the throes of debating whether parliamentarism is or is not compatible with anarchy?

If things carry on like this, we can spend a good century arguing without ever discovering whether we agree or not.

Anyway, let us follow where Merlino leads.

Why is Merlino saying that "we are gradually becoming closer?"

Is it because we concede the need for cooperation and agreement between the component members of society and because we defer to conditions outside of which cooperation and agreement are not possible? But, sure, that is socialism and Merlino knows perfectly well that we have always been socialists and therefore always very "close."

The point, now, is whether socialism is to be anarchist or authoritarian, that is, whether agreement should be voluntary or imposed.

And what if people refuse to agree? Well, in that case, there will be tyranny or civil war, but not anarchy. Anarchy is not brought about by force; force can and should be used to sweep away the material stumbling blocks and allow the people a free choice as to how they wish to live; but, beyond that, it can achieve nothing.

So, if "a handful of good-for-nothings or hotheads, or even a single individual pig-headedly say no, is anarchy then to be ruled out?"

---

1 Translated from Malatesta's note to the article "Poche parole per chiudere la polemica," by Francesco Saverio Merlino, *L'Agitazione* (Ancona) 1, no. 6 (18 April 1897). This further exchange between Merlino and Malatesta follows directly the one of March 28, included here before the present one. In this further article, Merlino claims that the respective positions are "gradually becoming closer."

Damn it! Let's not bandy phoney arguments. Such individuals are free to say *no*, but they will not be able to stop others from pushing for *yes*—and so they will have to fit in as best they can. And if "good-for-nothings and hotheads" were sufficiently numerous as to be in a position to seriously thwart society and prevent it from blithely functioning, then ...sad to say, anarchy would still be a way off.

We do not depict anarchy as some idealized paradise indefinitely postponed precisely because it is too beautiful.

Men are too flawed, too used to competing with and hating one another, too brutalized by suffering, too corrupted by authority for a rearrangement of society to be likely to turn them all, overnight, into ideally good and intelligent beings. But no matter the measure of the impact we can expect that rearrangement to produce, the system needs changing and, in order to change it, we must bring about the essential preconditions that allow for such change.

Our reckoning is that anarchy is feasible in the near future, because we think that the requisite conditions for it to exist are already embedded in the social instincts of men today; so much so, that one way or another, they keep society afloat in spite of the disruptive, anti-social operations of government and property. And we reckon the remedy and bulwark against the noxious tendencies of some and against the dangers posed by the conflicts of interests and inclinations, is not government, whatever its hue, but freedom; being made up of men, any government cannot help but tilt the scales in favor of the interests and tastes of those who are in government. Freedom is the great reconciler of human interests, as long as it is rooted in equality of conditions.

Whilst we want to see anarchy made a reality, we are not waiting for crime or the possibility of crime to be banished from the face of society; but we want no police because we do not believe they have the ability to prevent crime or clear up after it, whereas the police themselves are the source of a thousand woes and a standing menace to freedom. Social defense must be taken care of by the whole society; if arms must be taken up in order to defend ourselves, we want to see everyone armed rather than a number of us constituted as some praetorian guard. We remember only too well the fable of the horse that submitted to the bridle and let itself be mounted by a man, the better to hunt the stag—and Merlino is well aware of how much of a lie there is in talk of "oversight by the citizenry," when those in need of such oversight are the very ones who command strength.

Nor is Merlino any more rigorous when he borrows our example of the "European Entente". We have never claimed that equality and justice were features of present day relations between states, any more than we have denied the need for a federative, libertarian orchestration of international interests. We merely said that the violence and injustice, which prevail in relations between states today, would not be remedied by some international government or Parliament. Greece today is under the yoke of the Great Powers and she resists it; if she was represented in some world Parliament and had agreed to abide by the determinations of the majority of that Parliament, she would be subject to an equal or greater violence, and would have no right to resist it.

Moreover, what is Merlino talking about when he says that we are mid-way between Individualism and Socialism?

Individualism is either a theory of struggle, "every man for himself and devil take the hindmost," or it is a teaching that everyone should think for himself and do as he pleases without a care for others, out of which universal harmony and happiness emerge, as if by some law of nature.

In either sense, we are the polar opposites of individualists, every bit as much as Merlino may be. The issue between him and us is an issue of freedom or authority and, to be quite frank, it strikes us that he has reached (or, rather, has strayed to) a position midway between authoritarianism and anarchism.

***

We come now to the matter of tactics.

Merlino is astounded that we should have rejoiced at the socialists' success.[2] We find his astonishment truly odd.

We rejoice when democratic socialists get one over on the bourgeois, just as we would celebrate if republicans got one over on the monarchists, or the liberal monarchists on the clericals.

We would be a lot happier still if we had managed to convert to anarchism those who cast their votes for the socialists, and had we managed to ensure that not a single vote was cast for the socialists. But in the present instance, had the hundred thousand-odd voters

2 The reference is to the socialists' success in the latest elections.

who did cast their votes for the socialists not done so, that would not have been because they were anarchists but because they would either have been various shades of conservatives, or folk who abstained out of sheer indifference, or who cast their votes indiscriminately for whoever was paying, promising, or threatening the most. And Merlino is astounded that we should rather know them to be socialists, or half-baked socialists?

Good and evil are quite relative; and a reactionary party may well represent a step forwards in comparison with an even more reactionary one.

We are always delighted to see a clerical turn into a liberal, a monarchist into a republican, a fence-sitter into something; but it does not follow from that that we—whose thinking is streets ahead of theirs—must become monarchists, liberals, or republicans.

Take an example: given the current status of the southern provinces, it would have been an excellent sign if the supporters of Cavallotti quite simply had met with success on a wide scale;[3] and we would have rejoiced at that, just as we reckon the democratic socialists would have as well. But that is not to say that the socialists and anarchists should have championed Cavallotti's supporters in southern Italy. Instead, the socialists stand their own candidates everywhere, even if that might lessen the chances of the less reactionary candidate—whereas we lobby everywhere for deliberate abstention, not bothered by whether or not it might favor this candidate or that. For us, it is not the candidate that counts, insofar as we do not see the point of having "good deputies"; what matters is some indication of people's frame of mind; and of the thousand and one bizarre frames of mind in which the voter may be found, the best is the one that opens his eyes to the pointlessness and dangers of returning someone to Parliament, and the one that impels him to work directly for what he wants through joining forces with all whose wishes are the same as his.

***

Finally, what possessed Merlino to finish his letter with innuendoes that are, to say the least, in poor taste, given the current status of his

3 Felice Cavallotti, leader of the radical Left, was a popular figure of Italian politics. He died in a duel in 1898.

relations with anarchists?[4] Merlino claims that he is still an anarchist and strives to get us to think of anarchy in his terms and to have us embrace his tactics; which he is entitled to do. But why adopt that tone, which may well be appropriate in dealings with an opponent that he does not care about wounding, but which is out of place towards comrades he is out to persuade and win over?

Some time ago, in responding in *Il Messaggero* to Malatesta[5] who had talked about the anarchist party's "incipient reorganization" Merlino was poking fun, while he *knew* that the anarchists actually were reorganizing and had already produced results, very modest results to be sure, but real for all that. And now here he is dredging up the history of self-styled abstentionist anarchists who vote; here he is, casting Azzaretti up to us, the very same Azzaretti we ourselves denounced in these columns.[6]

Well, if there abstentionists who vote - and we know that, actually, there are—that means that they are not fully aware of the views they profess; or else that they cannot find in the anarchist ranks the strength needed to stand up to outside influences; the cure lies, not in all of us abjuring our programme or adding to the causes of confusion and weakness, but in nurturing individuals' consciousness and bolstering the party's organization.

And if, after that, there are still knaves who sell out, it merely remains for them to be unmasked and driven out.

---

4 The closing paragraph of Merlino's article reads: "One last word. You claim that all anarchists are abstentionists. How wrong you are! The fiercest abstentionists vote for the republicans, for the socialists, for their personal friends, not to mention the Azzarettis, which are quite a few! What is gained by abstentionist tactics is to take part in elections not in the name of our own principles, but under a false name and to the advantage of other parties." Antonino Azzaretti was a Sicilian anarchist who had expressed public support for a certain right-wing candidate.

5 Malatesta is referring to himself in third person because his editorial note is unsigned.

6 Malatesta had harshly criticized Azzaretti three weeks before in an article titled "Cose sporche" (dirty stuff).

28. LET US BE OF GOOD CHEER![1]

Using as its pretext an outrage that we certainly could not have wanted since, as was foreseeable, we are the only ones to suffer any serious damage from it, further persecution is in the coming.[2]

Of the outrage itself we shall say nothing. We seek peace and love between men and because we genuinely crave peace and love, we strive, at constant cost to ourselves, to bring about a society where there will be no more grounds for hatred and every man will see every other as his brother.

At the feet of the champions of the most outrageous privileges, planters of the seeds of hate; those who expose the workers to the horrific temptations of hunger; those who plant disconsolation and despair in the hearts of the wretched; those who reply to any remonstrance, any civilized form of struggle for emancipation of the oppressed classes, with police thuggery, imprisonment, *domicilio coatto*, or jesuitical maneuvers that deny work and bread to the family of the man who has the misfortune to be in bad odor with the police, if not with shootings, the gallows and torture—on them we place the entire responsibility for the blood-letting that disfigures this supposedly civilized society.

And on we go, committed, come what may, to the striving after good.

We appeal with confidence to all comrades to stand up to the blows from our adversaries and to breathe fresh life into our party with renewed activity, renewed commitment and further sacrifices.

The tactics now foisted upon us by the circumstances are as follows: since we cannot secure a greater margin of freedom right now, let us at least use that which the law does afford us; but let us exploit it to the fullest extent. If, as they too often do, the defenders of the law breach it in our persons and in our acts, we shall cash in on the

---

1 Translated from "In alto i cuori," *Agitiamoci per il Socialismo Anarchico* (Ancona), 1 May 1897, a one-time publication in lieu of no. 8 of *L'Agitazione*.

2 On 22 April 1897, the anarchist Pietro Acciarito made an unsuccessful attempt on the life of the Italian king, Humbert I, in Rome. Many anarchists were arrested, including part of the *Agitazione*'s editorial staff. For this reason the periodical had to be replaced by a one-off publication for a few weeks.

anti-law propaganda that is spontaneously generated by every act of whimsy on the part of the powers-that-be.

So, they mean to strip us of our right to engage in propaganda? —Let us, always, proudly and openly and relentlessly proclaim our principles. They would haul us in front of the courts? —Let us ensure that the proceedings become an occasion for greater, more sensational propaganda.

They mean to strip us of our right of association? Treat us as criminal conspirators? Then let us associate even more, publicly and demonstrably; wherever we can, let us convene in public venues; let us publish the programme and the addresses of our groups, circles, and federations in the press. The public will eventually wonder who these strange new *malefactors* are who, rather than lurking in the shadows, insist upon the light of day and who gladly suffer on behalf of an openly avowed cause—and every man with a heart will feel, in his heart of hearts, that he is something of a *malefactor* himself.

They mean to deny us the right to speak in public? Let every one of us capable of saying a few words seize every opportunity to make our voice heard and, where the opportunity does not arise, strive to create one.

They mean to isolate us and deny us every means of prosecuting our activities? Let us live side by side with the toiling masses, let us join their associations, let us share in their struggles and grievances, let us dedicate ourselves wholly to their welfare, always leading the way when it comes to work, danger, and sacrifices.

They mean to dispatch many of us to *domicilio coatto*?[3] Seize the occasion of so many comrades' being together and in contact with those poor unwitting victims, the ordinary *coatti*, for them to come to some mutual agreement and ready themselves for even more fruitful efforts and, at the same time, spread the good news to those poor wretches who have thus far known nothing of society but its wretchedness and brutishness. Others will be driven out of the country? Wherever they may go, let them set up centers of propaganda and agitation and raise the means to sustain the movement in Italy. Others will be going to prison? Let them go in the knowledge that they have done all their duty, in the certainty that fresh militants will step into their shoes.

3 "Domicilio coatto" was the legal term for "forced residence" and "coatti" were the victims of this institution, who were usually sent to small islands in the Mediterranean Sea.

There are enough of us so that if everybody does his duty, persecution cannot halt our progress.

No matter how great the reactionary fury of our oppressors, they cannot imprison, deport or drive into exile more than a tiny fraction of us.

It falls to those left behind to convince the government that ideas cannot be refuted nor destroyed through the handiwork of butchers.

Onwards, ever onwards, for the sake of the blessed cause of human redemption!

29. THE DUTY OF RESISTANCE

Anarchists and the Law[1]

There are huge disparities in economic circumstances, political liberties and civic status between the proletariats of the various countries around the world. And *our* Italy occupies one of the lowest rungs. Few countries are as afflicted with poverty, few have a government so given to brazen prevarication or so ferociously thuggish—and none dispatches out into the world so many offspring who, being used, in their homeland, to a way of life that looks brutish to workers elsewhere, then compete with the native workforce, bringing hatred and contempt down on their own heads.

What did we do to earn such a dismal primacy?

Elsewhere, as in Italy, society is founded upon the individualistic principle of man versus man and class versus class, so there is a constant tendency in the direction of growing tyranny by the few and slavishness for the many. The institutions are essentially the same everywhere; private property and government are everywhere. So how come the consequences in Italy are even more disastrous than elsewhere?

Because in Italy people do not resist—and resistance from the people is the only boundary set upon the bullying of the bosses and rulers.

In Italy there is no resistance—and there is no resistance because the spirit of cooperation, of association is missing. The Italian reacts violently, overly so, to personal insults received from one of his peers; yet he supinely endures the boss's arbitrariness and the constable's bullying, because, left to his own personal devices, he feels powerless to resist the very person who can starve or imprison him and he winds up taking his punishment and becoming inured to mistreatment.

If current conditions are to be improved upon, if they are to be prevented from becoming even worse, if we are to pave the way to the future, then, first and foremost, every Italian must learn how to join forces and act collectively and look to mutual aid and solidarity

---

1 Translated from "Il dovere della resistenza: Gli anarchici e la legge," *L'Agitazione* (Ancona) 1, no, 12 (30 May 1897).

for the opportunity to resist effectively, and for an appreciation of that opportunity.

And if we anarchists want to live up to the mission imposed upon us by our program, and unless we mean to remain impotent dreamers day-dreaming about an ideal without a care for bringing about the conditions that make its implementation feasible, we must strive actively and methodically to prepare, organize and inspire popular resistance in every aspect of life in which the people suffer injustice or violence; economic resistance to the bosses' exploitation, political resistance to trespasses against liberty, moral resistance to anything that tends to ensure that the worker is looked upon and treated as some lesser breed.

That is our duty; that is our concern.

***

Led astray by a narrow, one-sided doctrinaire approach, anarchists have often lost interest in practical struggle and have thereby contributed to that moral collapse whereby the police today can thrash and murder citizens without provoking a backlash likely to stop them in their tracks.

Or else, they have reacted individually and paid back the boss and the constabulary in their own coin, the upshot being that, to their credit but to the detriment of the cause, they have been hauled off to prison and rendered hors de combat without having done a thing to encourage the people to resist and to fight.

Against the backdrop of a cowed people such as the people of Italy are today, any act of revolt in which the *law still has might on its side,* helps not so much to invite imitators, but rather to confirm the people's superstition that authority is invincible and to the upkeep of the vague terror that is authority's only strength.

Enough of rebellions *for art's sake*. Our thoughts today need to be of winning: we need to seek out means conducive to victory. True, we must come into conflict with the law some day; but let it be whenever the likelihood is that might is no longer on the side of the law or at least that it does not easily prevail and remain unscathed.

Meanwhile, let us do today whatever we usefully can do. And since we have not yet managed to amass the strength to resist the law, let us at least resist and let us urge the people to resist within the limits of the law. Even so we already have a fair way to go.

***

We are opposed to *legalism* which consists of seeking to resolve the social question and secure emancipation by means of law; but this is not to say that we refuse to avail of whatever means we feel useful when the law has not, perchance, outlawed them and only because it has not outlawed them.

We produce a newspaper, which is a perfectly lawful thing: we are in association with one another—that too is lawful; and we seek to hold popular rallies, speak in public, demonstrate, etc., etc., all of these being lawful activities, albeit that the police, cashing in on the people's docility and our weakness, now frequently dare to ban them.

Besides, it has never occurred to any revolutionary to stop breathing, eating or walking, etc., merely because the law was kind enough not to have banned them!

***

But we would do well to explain this point a little more.

The law is essentially the weapon of the privileged; it is made by them for the purpose of enshrining their power and the people need to dismantle it entirely if they means to be genuinely free.

But there are some laws that signal a people's victory in that they rescinded earlier and more oppressive laws or set a limit on the bosses' whims. When the people insist upon a right and do so vigorously, those in power, finding themselves with no option but to grant the people some relief, *pass a law*, which, whilst giving away as little as possible, and striving to make that concession as hollow as it can, is an attempt to ward off a greater danger and, unfortunately, is often successful in this.

It is a bad thing that the people should let themselves be taken in and demand a law and be appeased by that, instead of seizing for themselves the entirety of the right they demand. And it falls to us and to our party to demolish this cult of law, and encourage the people on to de facto gains that are absorbed into custom and practice and that are the only serious definitive gains. But it is even worse that the people, having extracted some concession from throwing a scare into its masters, should then blithely allow it to be snatched back, only for the same old struggles to begin all over again. And it falls to us also to see to it that the people, even as they fight on for greater gains, do not let gains already made be snatched away from them.

***

This is the point we are at in Italy today: all the political freedoms bought at the cost of so much bloodshed by our forefathers—freedom of the press, the right of association, the right of assembly, the inviolability of the home, the secrecy of the mail, freedom of the person—are done for, or are about to be done for, unless a strong resurgence of public opinion applies the brakes to the police's arrogance.

It is in our interest more than anyone else's that public opinion be roused and resistance organized, both because we are more under threat and targeted than others and chiefly because the loss of acquired freedoms would do very great damage by shifting the struggle back on to political terrain and overshadowing the economic issue that is the most important one.

30. ORGANIZATION[1]

I

For years now this has been a matter of great contention between anarchists. And, as is often the case when heat enters an argument and when insistence that one is in the right is injected into the search for the truth, or when arguments around theory are merely an attempt to vindicate practical behavior prompted by quite other motives, a great muddling of ideas and words is the result.

Incidentally, and just to get them out of the way, let us run through the straightforward semantic quibbles that have occasionally reached the utmost heights of absurdity, such as, say, "We are for harmonization, not organization"; "we are against association but are for agreement"; "we want no secretary and no treasurer, these being authoritarian features, but we put a comrade in charge of correspondence and another looks after our funds"—and let us get down to serious discussion.

Those who stake a claim to the title "anarchists," with or without a range of adjectives, fall into two camps: the advocates and the opponents of organization.

If we cannot see eye to eye, let us at least understand each other.

And for a start, since there are three parts to the question, let us make a distinction between organization in the general sense, as the principle and condition of social living, today and in the society of the future; the organization of the anarchist party; and organization of popular forces, especially that of the laboring masses with an eye to standing up to government and capitalism.

The need for organization in social life—even the synonymy between organization and society, I would be tempted to say—is so self-evident that it is mind-boggling that it could ever have been questioned.

In order to appreciate this, we need to remember what the specific, characteristic calling of the anarchist movement is, and how

---

1 Translated from "L'organizzazione," parts 1–3, *L'Agitazione* (Ancona) 1, nos. 13–15 (4, 11, and 18 June 1897).

men and parties are liable to become consumed by the issue that most directly affects them, forgetting all related issues, paying greater heed to form than to substance, and, finally, viewing matters from one angle only and thereby losing any proper grasp upon reality.

The anarchist movement began life as a backlash against the spirit of authority that prevails in civil society, as well as in all parties and workers' organizations and has been gradually swollen by all of the revolts promoted against authoritarian and centralizing trends.

It is therefore only natural that many anarchists were just about mesmerized by this fight against authority, and that believing, having had an authoritarian education, that authority is the soul of social organization, combated and repudiated the latter as a means of combating the former.

And, in truth, the mesmerism has gone so far that it has them supporting some things that truly defy belief.

Cooperation and agreement of any sort were rejected, the argument being that association was the very antithesis of anarchy. The case was made that in the absence of accords, of reciprocal obligations, everything would fall spontaneously into place if each person was to do whatever crossed his mind without troubling to find out what his neighbor was doing; that anarchy means every man should be sufficient unto himself and do for himself in everything without trade-off or pooled effort; that the railways could operate very well without organization, indeed, that this was already happening over yonder in England(!); that the postal service was not necessary and that anyone in Paris wanting to write a letter to Petersburg... could take it there himself(!!), and so on and so on.

But this is gibberish, you may say, and hardly deserving of mention.

Yes, but this sort of gibberish has been uttered, printed, and circulated; and accepted by much of the public as an authentic articulation of anarchist thinking; and still provides ammunition for our bourgeois and non-bourgeois adversaries in search of an easy victory over us. Then again, such *gibberish* is not without its value, insofar as it is the logical outworking of certain premises and may serve as the acid test of the truthfulness or otherwise of those premises.

A few individuals of limited intellect but endowed with mightily logical turns of mind, once they have embraced some premises, draw every last consequence that flows from them and, if logic so dictates, can blithely arrive at the greatest nonsense and negate the most self-evident facts without flinching. There are others as well, better educated and more open-minded, who can always come up with some way of arriving at pretty reasonable conclusions, even should they have to ride roughshod over logic; and in the case of the latter, theoretical errors have little or no influence upon their actual behavior. But, all in all, and until such time as certain fundamental errors are shunned, there is still the threat of the die-hard syllogizers and of our having to start all over again.

The fundamental error of the anarchists opposed to organization is to believe that organization is impossible without authority—and, once that hypothesis has been accepted, they would rather give up any organization than accept a modicum of authority.

Now, that organization, meaning association for a specific purpose and adopting the forms and means required in order to achieve that purpose, is a fundamental pre-requisite of living in society strikes us as self-evident. The isolated man cannot live even the life of a brute: other than in the tropics and when the population is exceedingly sparse, he cannot even feed himself; and remains, without exception, incapable of achieving a standard of living any better than the beasts'. Obliged, therefore, to combine forces with other people, and actually finding himself united with them as a result of the prior evolution of the species, he must either defer to the will of others (be a slave), or impose his own will on others (be an authority figure), or live in fraternal agreement with others for the sake of the greater good of all (be a partner). None can escape this need: and the most extravagant anti-organizers are not only subject to the overall organization of the society in which they live, but—even in purposeful acts in their own lives, and in their wrangles with organization—they come together and share the tasks and *organize* together with those of like mind and employ the means that society places at their disposal... provided, of course, that these are things genuinely wanted and enacted, rather than just vague, platonic aspirations and dreams dreamt.

Anarchy signifies *society organized without authority*, authority being understood as the ability to *impose* one's own wishes and not the inescapable and beneficial practice whereby the person who best understands and is most knowledgeable about the doing of something finds it easier to have his opinion heeded and, in that specific instance, serves as a guide for those less capable.

As we see it, authority is not only not a pre-requisite of social organization, but, far from fostering it, is a parasite upon it, hindering its evolution and siphoning off its advantages for the special benefit of one given class that exploits and oppresses the rest. As long as a harmony of interests exists within a community, as long as no one is inclined or equipped to exploit others, there is no trace of authority. Once internal strife comes along and the community is broken down into winners and losers, then authority arises, being naturally vested in the stronger, and helping to confirm, perpetuate, and magnify their victory.

That is what we believe and that is why we are anarchists; if, instead, we believed that organization without authority is unfeasible, we would rather be authoritarians, for we would prefer authority—which hobbles and stunts existence—to the disorganization that renders it impossible.

Besides, how things turn out for us is of little account. If it were true that the engineer and engine-driver and station-master simply had to be authorities, rather than partners performing certain tasks on everybody's behalf, the public would still rather defer to their authority than make the journey on foot. If there was no option but for the post-master to be an authority, anyone in his right mind would put up with the post-master's authority rather than deliver his own letters.

In which case... anarchy would be the stuff of some people's dreams, but could never become reality.

II

Accepting the possibility of there being a community organized in the absence of authority, that is, in the absence of coercion—and anarchists have to accept it, for anarchy would otherwise be meaningless—let us move on to deal with the anarchist party's own organization.

Here too organization strikes us as useful and necessary. If "party" means the ensemble of individuals who share a common purpose and strive to achieve that purpose, it is only natural that they should reach agreement, pool their resources, divide up the work, and adopt all measures that are thought likely to further that purpose and are the raison d'être of an organization. Staying isolated, with each individual acting or seeking to act on his own without entering into agreement with others, without making preparations, without marshalling the flabby strength of singletons into a mighty coalition, is tantamount to condemning oneself to impotence, to squandering one's own energies on trivial, ineffective acts and, very quickly, losing belief in one's purpose and lapsing into utter inaction.

But here again the thing strikes us as so self-evident that, rather than laboring direct proof, we shall try to answer the arguments of organization's adversaries.

Pride of place goes to the—so to speak—pre-emptive objection. "What is this talk of a party?" they say. "We're no party, we have no program." A paradox that is meant to indicate that ideas move on and are forever changing and that they refuse to accept any fixed program that might be fine for today but that will assuredly be obsolete tomorrow.

That would be perfectly fair if we were talking about academics questing after truth without a care for the practical applications. A mathematician, a chemist, a psychologist or a sociologist can claim not to have a program or to have none beyond the search for truth; they are out to discover, not to *do* something. But anarchy and socialism are not sciences; they are purposes, projects that anarchists and socialists mean to implement and that therefore have to be formulated as specific programs. The science and art of construction advance day by day; but an engineer wishing to build or indeed merely to demolish something, has to draw up his plans, assemble his equipment and operate as if science and art had ground to a halt at the point at which he found them when he embarked upon his task. It may very well be the case that he can find a use for new advances made in the course of the project without giving up on the core of his plan; and it may equally be that fresh discoveries made and new resources devised by the industry are such as to open his eyes to the need to drop everything and start all over again. But in starting over again, he will need to draw up a new plan based on what he knows and possesses at that point and he is not going to be able to devise and set about implementing some *amorphous* construction, with tools *not to hand,* just because, some time in the future, science might just come up with better forms and industry supply better tools!

By anarchist party we mean the ensemble of those who are out to help make anarchy a reality and who therefore need to set themselves a target to achieve and a path to follow; and we happily leave the lovers of absolute truth and unrelenting progress to their transcendental musings; never subjecting their notions to the test of action, they finish up doing nothing and discovering less.

The other objection is that organization creates leaders, authority figures. If that is true, if anarchists are incapable of coming together and reaching agreement with one another without deferring to some authority, that means that they are still far from being anarchists and that, before giving any thought to establishing anarchy in the world, they should spare a thought for equipping themselves to live anarchically. But the cure hardly lies in non-organization, but instead in expanding the consciousness of the individual members.

For sure, if an organization heaps all of the work and all of the responsibility upon a few shoulders, if it puts up with whatever those few do rather than put effort in and try to do better, those few will, albeit against their wishes, eventually substitute their own will for that of the community. If the members of an organization, all of them, do not make it their business to think, to try to understand, to seek explanations for that which they do not understand, and to always bring their critical faculties to bear on everything and everyone, and instead leave it up to the few to do the thinking for all, then those few are going to be the leaders, the directing intelligences.

But, let us say it again, the cure does not lie in non-organization. On the contrary: in small societies and in large, apart from brute force, which is out of the question in our case, the source and justification of authority lie in social disorganization. When a collective has needs and its members fail to organize themselves spontaneously, by themselves, in order to get by, someone, some authority figure pops up to cater for that need by deploying everyone's resources and directing them according to his whim. If the streets are not safe and the people cannot cope, a police force emerges that has itself maintained and paid for what few services it renders and it lords it and grows tyrannical; if there is a need for a product and the community fails to come to some arrangement with faraway producers to trade in return for local produce, up pops the merchant who cashes in on the need of some to sell and of others to buy, and charges producers and consumers whatever price he likes.

Look at what has happened in our own ranks: the less organized we have been, the more we have been at the mercy of a few individuals. And that was only natural.

We feel the need to be in contact with comrades elsewhere, to receive and send news, but we cannot, each of us individually, correspond with every other comrade. If we were organized we might charge some comrades with handling our correspondence for us, change them if they are not to our satisfaction and keep abreast of developments without depending on somebody's good grace for our news. If we are disorganized on the other hand, there will be someone with the means and willingness to correspond who will take all intercourse into his own hands, passing on or not passing on news depending on his choice of subject or person and, if he is active and clever enough, will be able, unbeknownst to us, to steer the movement in whatever direction he wants without our (the bulk of the party's) having any means of control and without anyone's having the right to complain, since that person is acting on his own, with mandate from none and with no obligation to give an account of his actions to anyone.

We feel the need to have a newspaper. If we are organized we can raise the funds for its launch and get it going, put a few comrades in charge of running it and monitor its direction. The paper's editors will assuredly, to a greater or lesser degree, discernibly stamp their personality upon it, but they will still be folk selected by us, and whom we can change if we are not happy with them. If, on the other hand, we are disorganized, someone with enough get-up-and-go will launch the paper on his own accord; he will find among us his correspondents, distributors, and subscribers and will bend us to his purposes, without our knowledge or consent; and, as has often been the case, we will accept and support that paper even if it is not to our liking, even if we find that it is damaging to the cause, because of our own inability to come up with one that offers a better representation of our thinking.

So, far from conjuring up authority, organization represents the only cure for it and the only means whereby each of us can get used to taking an active and thoughtful part in our collective endeavor and stop being passive tools in the hands of leaders.

If we do nothing at all and everybody remains perfectly idle then, to be sure, there will be no leaders and no flock, no order-givers and no order-followers, but that will be an end of propaganda, an end of the party and of arguments about organization as well... and that, let us hope, nobody will see as an ideal solution.

But an organization, they say, implies an obligation to coordinate one's own actions with those of others and thus infringes freedom and hobbles initiative. It seems to us that what actually snatches away freedom and renders enterprise impossible is the isolation that leaves one impotent. Freedom is not some abstract right, but the capability of doing something: this is as true in our own ranks as it is in society at large. It is in cooperation with his fellows that man finds the means of furthering his own activity and the power of his initiative.

To be sure, organization means coordinating resources for a common purpose and a duty upon the organized not to act contrary to that purpose. But where voluntary organizations are concerned, when those belonging to the same organization actually do share the same aim and are supportive of the same means, the mutual obligations upon them work to everybody's advantage. And if anyone sets aside any belief of his own for the sake of unity, it is because he finds it more beneficial to drop an idea that he could not in any case implement unaided, rather than deny himself the cooperation of others in matters he thinks are of more significance.

If, then, an individual finds that none of the existing organizations encapsulates the essence of his ideas and methods and that he cannot express himself as an individual according to his beliefs, then he would be well advised to stay out of those organization; but then, unless he wishes to remain idle and impotent, he must look around for others who think as he does and become the founder of some new organization.

Another objection, and the last one upon which we shall dwell, is that, being organized, we are more exposed to government persecution.

On the contrary, it seems to us that the more united we are, the more effectively we can defend ourselves. And actually every time we have been caught off guard by persecution while we were disorganized, it threw us into complete disarray and wiped out our preceding efforts; whereas when and where we were organized, it did us good rather than harm. And the same applies to the personal interests of individuals: the example of the recent persecutions that hit the isolated as much as they did the organized—and perhaps even worse—is enough. I am speaking, of course, of those, isolated and otherwise, who at least carry out individual propaganda. Those who do nothing and keep their beliefs well hidden are certainly in much less danger, but their usefulness to the cause is less as well.

In terms of persecution, the only thing to be achieved by being disorganized and preaching disorganization is to allow the government to deny us the right of association and pave the way for these monstrous criminal conspiracy trials that it would not dare mount against folk who loudly and openly assert their right to be and condition of being associated, or, if the government were to dare it, would backfire on it and benefit our propaganda.

Besides, it is only natural for organization to take whatever form circumstances commend and impose. The important point is not so much formal organization as the inclination to organize. There may be cases in which, due to the lingering reaction, it may be useful to suspend all correspondence and refrain from all gatherings; that will always be a set-back, but if the will to be organized survives, if the spirit of association endures, if the previous period of coordinated activities has widened one's personal circle, nurtured sound friendships and conjured up a genuine commonality of ideas and actions among comrades, then the efforts of individuals, even isolated individuals, will have a contribution to make to the common purpose, and a means will soon be found of getting together again and repairing the damage done.

We are like an army at war and, depending on the terrain and the measures adopted by the enemy, we can fight in massive or in scattered formations. The essential thing is that we still think of ourselves as belonging to the same army, that we abide by all of the same guidelines and hold ourselves ready to form up again into compact columns when necessary and feasible.

Everything that we have said is directed at those comrades who are authentically against the organization as a principle. To those who resist organization only because they are reluctant to join or have been refused entry into a given organization and because they are out of sympathy with the individuals belonging to that organization, we say: set up another organization of your own, along with those who see eye to eye with you. We should certainly love it if we could all see eye to eye and bring all of anarchism's forces together into one mighty phalanx; but we have no faith in the soundness of organizations built upon concessions and subterfuge and where there is no real agreement and sympathy between the members. Better dis-united than mis-united. But let us see to it that everyone bands together with his friends and that there are none who are isolated and no efforts going to waste.

III

We still have to talk about the organization of the laboring masses for the purposes of standing up to government and the bosses.

We have stated it before: in the absence of organization, be it free or imposed, there can be no society; in the absence of considered, deliberate organization, there can be neither freedom, nor guarantees that the interests of the component members of society will be respected. And anyone that fails to organize, fails to seek out the cooperation of others and volunteer his own cooperation on a reciprocal basis of fellowship, inescapably places himself in a condition of inferiority and plays the part of a thoughtless cog in the machinery of society that others operate according to their whims and to their own advantage.

The workers are exploited and oppressed because, being disorganized in everything having to do with safeguarding of their own interests, they are compelled by hunger or brute force to comply with the wishes of the rulers for whose benefit society is presently being run and must themselves supply the force (soldiers and capital) that helps hold them in subjection. Nor will they ever be able to emancipate themselves until such time as they look to unity for the moral, economic, and physical might needed to defeat the organized might of the oppressors.

There have been some anarchists—and a few of them are still around—who, while conceding the need for organization in the society of the future and the need to get organized today for propaganda and action purposes, are hostile to all organizations that do not have anarchy as their immediate objective and that do not espouse anarchist methods. And some of them have remained apart from all workers' organizations designed to stand up to and improve conditions in the current state of affairs, or have meddled in them with the express intention of disorganizing them, while others have conceded that membership of existing resistance societies may be legitimate, but have looked upon attempts to organize new ones as bordering upon defection.

To those comrades it looked as if all of the forces marshalled for a less than radically revolutionary purpose were forces siphoned away from the revolution. Our view, by contrast, is that their approach would doom the anarchist movement to perpetual sterility, and experience has already vindicated us only too well.

Before one can carry out propaganda, one has to be in people's midst, and it is in the workers' associations that the working man encounters his fellows and especially those most inclined to understand and embrace our ideas. But even if it were feasible to carry out as much propaganda as one might like outside of the associations, this would not have any discernible impact on the laboring masses. Aside from a tiny number of individuals who are better educated and better equipped for abstract thinking and theoretical fervor, the working man cannot arrive at anarchy in one fell swoop. For him to become a bona fide anarchist rather than an anarchist in name only, he needs to start to be sensible of the fellowship that binds him to his comrades, to learn to cooperate with others in the defence of shared interests and, battling the bosses and the boss-supporting government, to appreciate that bosses and governments are useless parasites and that the workers could run the apparatus of society on their own. And, having understood that, he is an anarchist even though he may not use the title.

Besides, the fostering of all manner of popular organizations is the logical consequence of our fundamental ideas and should therefore be part and parcel of our program.

An authoritarian party out to take power, so as to impose its own ideas has an interest in the people remaining a formless mass incapable of doing for itself and therefore easily dominated. And, therefore, logically, it should want organization only to the extent and of the sort that suits its coming to power—electoral organization, if it looks to get there by lawful means, or military organization if, instead, it relies upon violent action.

But we anarchists are not out to *emancipate* the people; we want to see the people *emancipate themselves*. We do not believe in blessings from on high, imposed by force. We want to see a new social order emerge from within the people, and we want it to match the degree of development reached by men and for it to be able progress as men themselves make progress. So what matters to us is that every interest and every opinion encounters, in conscious organization, some scope for asserting itself and bringing its influence to bear upon collective life, in keeping with its importance.

We have made it our task to combat the existing organization of society and clear away the obstacles hampering the advent of a new society wherein everyone is assured of freedom and well-being. To which end we have come together as a party and are out to become as many and as mighty as we possibly can. But if there was nothing organized other than our party, if the workers were to be left isolated like so many units, indifferent to one another and linked only by the common bonds; if, besides being organized as a party, we were not organized alongside the workers in our capacities as workers ourselves, we would not be in a position to bring anything off, or, at best, would only be able to impose ourselves... in which case we would not have the triumph of anarchy, but our triumph. We might then very well call ourselves anarchists, but in actual fact we would be mere governors and as incapable of doing good as any other governor is.

Revolution is often spoken of, the belief being that the word represents the ironing out of every difficulty. But what should this revolution that we long for be and what could it be?

Established authorities toppled and property rights pronounced dead. Fine. A party could do as much... though that party should still rely, in addition to its own strength, upon the sympathy of the masses and on sufficient preparation of public opinion.

Then what? The life of society accepts no interruptions. During the revolution—or insurrection, whatever we want to call it—and in its immediate aftermath, people have to eat and clothe themselves and travel around and publish and treat the sick, etc., and these things do not do themselves. At present the government and the capitalists have them done so as to extract profit from them; once we are rid of the government and the capitalists, the workers are going to have to do them all for everybody's benefit; otherwise, whether under those designations or something different, new governments and new capitalists will emerge.

And how could workers be expected to provide for pressing needs unless they were already used to coming together to deal jointly with their common interests and, to some extent, ready to embrace the legacy from the old society?

The day after the city's grain merchants and bakery bosses lose their property rights and thus have no further interest in catering for the market, there must be vital bread supplies available in the shops to feed the public. Who is going to see to that, if the bakery workers are not already associated and ready to manage without bosses, and if, pending the arrival of the revolution, it has not occurred to them to work out the city's needs and the means of meeting them?

We do not mean by that that we must wait until all workers are organized before the revolution can be made. That would be impossible, given the proletariat's circumstances; and, luckily, there is no need. But at the least there must be some nuclei around which the masses can rally once freed of the burden oppressing them. If it is utopian to want to make revolution once everybody is ready and once everybody sees eye to eye, it is even more utopian to seek to bring it about with nothing and no one. There is measure in all things. In the meantime, let us strive for the greatest possible expansion of the conscious and organized forces of the proletariat. The rest will follow of itself.

31. ANARCHISM'S EVOLUTION

(Apropos of an Interview)[1]

An interview I had with my friend Ciancabilla, which was published by him in *Avanti!*, has drawn some comment, which I was not expecting.[2]

Not having been able to get my hands on the edition of *Avanti!* in which the interview was published, since it has been impounded, how my words were reported I cannot tell; but the esteem in which I hold Ciancabilla gives me every confidence that he has not at all misrepresented my thinking.

How comes it that commentators have drawn inferences from it, which I, as the principal concerned, emphatically reject?

I am not talking about the correspondent from *Il Resto del Carlino* who finds that my thinking "comes very close to that of the legalitarian socialists." He is a bourgeois journalist and therefore cannot place much store by the distinctions between socialists, and may well have no grasp of them. We socialists of every persuasion all want to end the bourgeoisie's domination, and naturally we are all the same as far as the bourgeois are concerned. The same way as atheists, Protestants, Jews, and anybody else who contests the Pope's authority are all the same as far as Catholic priests are concerned.

I can only hope that the day is near when today's bourgeois, stripped of the privileges that mar their judgment today, will be able, in practical terms, to scrutinize and level-headedly gauge the differences between the various methods advocated for implementing socialism.

Given that it is socialist and an authoritative source for socialists, *Avanti!* deserves fuller consideration when it finds in what I told

1 Translated from "Evoluzione dell'anarchismo (A proposito di un'intervista)," *L'Agitazione* (Ancona) 1, no. 31 (14 October 1897).

2 The interview appeared in the *Avanti!* of 3 October 1897, under the title "L'evoluzione dell'anarchismo: Un'intervista con Errico Malatesta." The interviewer, Giuseppe Ciancabilla, was at the time a socialist, but shortly thereafter he went over to the anarchist camp, embracing anti-organizationist ideas. He later emigrated to the United States. When Malatesta, in 1899–1900, sojourned in that country, a drawn-out controversy arose between the two, which started on theoretical-tactical ground, but later became bitterly personal.

Ciancabilla an unmistakable indication of "anarchism's evolving in the direction of Marxist socialism."[3]

Claiming that we are moving in their direction is a long-established ploy of the democratic socialists (when they are trying to treat us with kid gloves rather than reiterating with Liebknecht that we are "the favorite sons of the bourgeoisie and governments of all countries"). For instance, I remember that a few years ago, the lawyer Balducci from Forlì—seizing on the occasion of the publication of a private letter of mine by a friend, in which I advocated organization of the toiling masses—wrote that I had "watered down my wine" and congratulated me on this, as if this was new ground for me, although, ever since 1871, I have not exactly been one of the lesser-known advocates of the International in Italy and was out of the country precisely on account of my having been convicted of membership in the International.

Let us be clear: in my estimation there is nothing that is anything but honourable about *evolving,* provided that that evolution is the fruit of genuine conviction.

The fact is that, on account of the corruption of politickers and the huge influence that self-seeking and class interests wield over politics, that which in a scientist would be deemed a sign of cretinous pig-headedness—never having shifted in one's opinions—is widely regarded as a point of honor.

But I have too much moral courage not to articulate my changes of mind, because of deference to some pointless, ridiculous reputation for immutability, even if these changes, as is alleged in this instance, set me at odds with my friends and with myself. And I have too much pride to be stopped for a single moment longer by the notion that others might think that I was motivated by cowardice or playing the odds.

The shift in opinion, however, has to have actually occurred and it needs to have been as claimed.

Now anarchists certainly have evolved, and I along with them, and the likelihood is that they will carry on evolving as long as they remain a living party capable of harnessing the lessons of science and experience, and adapting to the variables in life. But I utterly

3 This concept, already expressed in an introductory editorial note to the interview, and clearly reflected by the interview's title, was then restated in a further commentary in *Avanti!* the next day.

deny that we have evolved or are evolving in the direction of "Marxist socialism." And I believe, rather, that one of the most remarkable and most widespread features of our evolution is that we have rid ourselves of Marxist prejudices, which, at the beginning of our movement, we embraced too lightly and have been the source of our gravest mistakes.

Avanti! has probably succumbed to an illusion.

If it really believes what it has said time and time again about anarchism—that anarchism is the very opposite of socialism—and if it carries on sitting in judgment of us on the basis of the misrepresentations and calumnies with which the German marxists, aping the example set by Marx in his dealings with Bakunin, disgraced themselves, then the fact is that, every time it may deign to read something we have written or listen to one of our speeches, it will be pleasantly surprised to discover an "evolution" in anarchism pointing in the direction of socialism, which it seems is almost synonymous with Marxism as far as *Avanti!* is concerned.

But anyone with even a superficial grasp of our ideas and history knows that, since its inception, anarchism has been merely the outworking and integration of the socialist idea and thus could not and cannot evolve *towards* socialism, which is to say towards itself.

The very mistakes, hare-brained schemes, crimes ventilated and committed by anarchists are proof of anarchism's substantially socialist nature, just as an organism's pathology assists a better understanding of its physiological features and functions.

What was there in what I said to Ciancabilla that could justify *Avanti!*'s conclusion?

We certainly have many ideas that we hold in common with democratic socialists and, above all, we share a sentiment that prompts and incites us to fight for the advent of a society of free equals... albeit that we are of a mind that the logic of their preferred system leads to the negation of freedom and equality.

As the essential cornerstone of our program we have the abolition of private property and the organization of production for the benefit of all and achieved through the cooperation of all—which is, or ought to be, the cornerstone of any sort of socialism. And by our reckoning, given that the workers are the main casualties of the existing society and those with the most direct interest in its changing, and given that the matter is to establish a society in which all are workers, the new revolution simply has to be, chiefly, the handiwork of the organized working class, conscious of the irreconcilable antagonism between its interests and those of the bourgeois class –the formulation, propagation, and conversion of that notion into the driving force behind all modern socialism being Marx's greatest achievement.

But *Avanti!* would be hard pressed to talk about evolution in all of this since we are talking here about purposes and convictions that are part and parcel of anarchism and anarchists have always peddled them—and were doing so many years before there were ever Marxists in Italy.

So in order to find out if we actually have evolved in the direction of democratic socialism, which *Avanti!* very questionably terms *marxist socialism,* we would need to investigate the differences that divide, and have always divided us from the democratic socialists.

We need not enter into a discussion of Marx's economic and historical theories, which appear to me (albeit that I am scarcely qualified to say) partly wrong and partly to consist simply of the articulation in abstruse language of truths (made to ring strange and esoteric) that are clear, plain, and commonplace, if a more common parlance is used. The democratic socialists have long since stopped paying them any heed in their practical programme and, unless I am mistaken, are also about to drop them from their science too.

What matters to us, as party men, is what parties do and mean to do—rather than the theoretical notions by which they have been inspired or with which they seek, after the event, to explain away and justify their actions.

Right now, therefore, we are at odds with and in a fight with the democratic socialists because they are out to change the present society by means of laws and by carrying over into the future society the government, the State that they claim will become the organ of everybody's interests. Whereas we want society to be changed through the people's own efforts and we want the complete destruction of the machinery of State, which, we say, will always be an agency of oppression and exploitation and will tend, by its very nature, to establish a society founded on privilege and class warfare.

We may be right, we may be wrong, but where is the suggestion, seen by *Avanti!*, that we are flirting with its authoritarian conception of socialism?

Avanti!'s party being an authoritarian party, it logically has its sights set on "capturing public office."

Have we perhaps stopped directing our efforts into the purpose of rendering public office, which is to say, government, redundant and doing away with it? Or have we maybe begun putting our faith in this nonsense about *taking possession of the government, the better to dismantle it,* that a number of unduly naïve... or unduly crafty socialists prattle about?

Quite the opposite. No one delving deeply into a study of anarchism will have any difficulty understanding that in the movement's early days there was a strong residue of Jacobinism and authoritarianism within us, a residue that I will not make so bold as to say we have destroyed utterly, but which has definitely been and still is on the wane. Once upon a time, it was a commonly held view in our ranks that the revolution had to be authoritarian as a matter of necessity and there was more than one of us caught in the curious contradiction of wanting to see "Anarchy achieved by force." Whereas, these days, the general belief among anarchists is that anarchy cannot be delivered by authority, but must arise from on-going struggle against all and any imposition, whether in slowly evolving times or in tempestuously revolutionary periods and that our purpose should be to see to it that the revolution itself is, right from the very outset, the implementation of anarchist ideas and methods.

The *Avanti*'s party is a parliamentary party, both in terms of its aims for the future and its present tactics; whereas we are against parliamentarism both as a form of re-cast society and as a current method of struggle, so much so that we regard anarchist socialism and anti-parliamentary socialism as synonymous, or thereabouts.

Has *Avanti!* perhaps spotted some lessening of the aversion to parliamentarism that has always been a distinguishing feature of our party? Have we, perhaps, stopped committing a sizable part of our efforts to ridding workers' minds of the new-born belief in parliaments and parliamentary means that the democratic socialists are out to plant there? Has abstentionism maybe been dropped as the almost material badge by which we recognize our comrades?

Quite the opposite. When our movement started up, several of us still entertained the notion of participation in administrative elections and later from our ranks came the initiative of running Cipriani as a candidate, which we backed.[4] Today, we are all of one mind in regarding administrative elections every bit as pernicious as political ones and perhaps even more so, and we also repudiate protest candidacies, to avoid any misunderstanding.

So where is the evolution in the direction of Marxist socialism?

In keeping with my belief that a party of the future such as ours must bring an on-going and stringent critique to bear on itself and should not be afraid to confess its errors and sins in public, I told Ciancabilla about some of the factors that reduced the anarchist party to such a state of isolation and disintegration as to render it unable to offer any resistance to Crispi's reaction and to inspire any stirring of sympathy in the public.[5]

I told him how the youthful illusion (which we inherited from Mazzinianism) of imminent revolution achievable through the efforts of the few without due preparation in the masses had left us alienated from any long and patient work to prepare and organize the people.

I told him how, in the belief that no improvement could be extracted in the absence of prior radical transformation of the entire politico-social order, and imbued with that old prejudice that the revolution becomes easier the more wretched the people are—we gazed with indifference, if not hostility, upon strikes and kindred worker struggles, and looked to the organization of the working class almost exclusively for recruits for the armed insurrection:—which, on the one hand, left us open to unnecessary persecutions that were forever interrupting and unravelling our efforts, which thus never had long to mature and were always stalled in the launch stages, and, on the other, eventually alienated from us the most forward-looking workers who, having managed through digging in their heels to extract a few improvements from the bosses, looked upon the results they achieved as a refutation of what we went preaching.

---

4 Amilcare Cipriani was a popular Italian revolutionary. In 1882 he was convicted to twenty-five years in jail for an episode that occurred fifteen years before. A widespread campaign for his liberation arose. One of the initiatives was Cipriani's "protest candidacy," which aimed at getting him out of jail by electing him to Parliament. In 1884, Malatesta supported the initiative, linking it to his campaign against Andrea Costa's legalitarian turn. From the columns of his periodical, *La Questione Sociale,* he urged Costa to resign from Parliament to yield his seat to Cipriani.

5 Francesco Crispi was the prime minister who undertook the harsh repression that followed the Sicilian Fasci movement and the Carrara uprising in 1894. On these events, see the article "Let Us Go to the People."

And I told him how these days we look to the labour movement for the basis of our strength and an assurance that the coming revolution may well prove to be socialist and anarchist, and how we rejoice at any improvement the workers manage to win, in that it boosts the working class's consciousness of its strength, triggering further demands and fresh claims, and brings us closer to the crunch point where the bourgeois have nothing left to give unless they renounce their privileges and where violent conflict becomes inevitable.

All of this and much more that I could have told him certainly signals an evolution in our thinking and practice, but, far from representing some "evolution in the direction of marxism," it is the result of our jettisoning what little marxism we had embraced.

Indeed, was our old tactic not, perhaps, the logical outcome of the strict and unilateral interpretation of the *law of wages* devised by the marxist school of thought?[6] Was it not a mirror image of the influence of Marx's economic fatalism? And isn't the authoritarian spirit, which still lingered within us, the spirit by which Marxists are prompted and which lingers, unaltered, through all their own, not always forward-looking, evolutions?

No: allow me to dispel *Avanti!*'s illusions: we are not about to turn into marxists. Rather we look forward to marxists, refreshed through contact with the spirit of the people, going to turn, if not into anarchists, then at least into liberals, in the good sense of the term.

---

6 As Malatesta explains elsewhere, the conclusion that anarchists drew from the law of wages was that, "given private property, wages must be necessarily limited to the bare minimum needed by the worker to live and reproduce," and no workers' effort could increase the amount of goods allocated to the proletariat or decrease the amount of working hours at the capitalists' service. For Malatesta, this interpretation neglected the influence that workers' resistance could have and did have on the workings of that "law."

32. THE DECLINE OF THE REVOLUTIONARY SPIRIT AND THE NEED FOR RESISTANCE[1]

Dear Comrades

In reporting the talk against *domicilio coatto* that I delivered in Jesi, the correspondent for *L'Avanti!* newspaper, states: "... (the speaker) *added that a heavy blame* (for the supine docility with which the people have put up with vexations from the government and from the capitalists) *should be laid on the anarchist party and republican party*, which, having been preaching revolution so long, realized that making it was an impossibility since the people, lacking all consciousness, would not follow them."

This is what I actually did say: but the italics, of course, have been added by the correspondent himself, and what italics they are in a democratic socialist newspaper, helping to highlight (and with some bragging perhaps) that I, whilst critical of my own party and the republican party, omitted the democratic socialists from that criticism.

Which calls for something of an explanation.

In Jesi, I spoke of the disillusionments that followed upon the hopes raised by the Italian nationalist revolution, and I stated how, on the one hand, the proletariat's economic conditions were growing more and more dismal, and, on the other, how what morsel of freedom that revolution had won was being lost, to the extent of returning to a state the same as or worse than that in which we found ourselves under the toppled governments.

And I sought to explain this fact in the light of two rationales:

For a start, there is the tendency on the part of social institutions to evolve in a given direction and bring forth their natural consequences: the tendency of political authority always to widen its sphere of activity and grow ever more oppressive; and private ownership's tendency to capture all the means of production,

1 Translated from "La decadenza dello spirito rivoluzionario e la necessità della resistenza," *L'Agitazione* (Ancona) 1, no. 28 (23 September 1897). The article was signed under the pseudonym "Giuseppe Rinaldi" because at the time Malatesta was still in Italy clandestinely, though he occasionally managed to speak in public.

stepping up the exploitation of the workers more and more and turning all new advances in science and social progress to the detriment of the proletariat.

Secondly, there is the absence of popular resistance. And, looking past other more general factors that fell outside of the scope of that talk, I pinned the blame for that missing resistance on republicans and anarchists.

Both groups, cognisant of the fundamental unfairness of certain institutions and of the damaging consequences they inevitably entailed, had only troubled themselves with the utter and sudden destruction of those same institutions, sneering at anything that might soften those damaging consequences and yearning instead for them to arrive in their starkest possible form, in the hope that that might bring about and expedite the collapse of the institutions.

Republicans, naturally averse to the monarchy, traced all woes to the form of constitution and either did not think possible or, for tactical reasons, affected to sneer at any improvements or any reform that was not predicated upon the abolition of the monarchy.

For anything good, anarchists, being inimical to all governments and therefore to the monarchy, and being adversaries of private ownership, looked, on grounds similar to those of the republicans, to the radical overhaul of social organization, sneering at any improvements the current regime might be susceptible to and even looking forward to increased oppression and impoverishment in the hope of hastening conflict.

Thus the entire activity of both parties boiled down to preaching revolution. As to making it possible and laying preparations for it, the best they could come up with was recruiting their necessarily sparse supporters into their respective organizations and stockpiling weapons which, due to a lack of funds and the vigilance of the government, were always few in number and poor in quality, and generally they finished up being seized or rusting and becoming unusable. To which the Mazzinians first and the anarchists later added the distraction of the occasional more or less harmless bomb.

Meanwhile, as a result of waiting idly for the revolution to arrive, their affiliates ended up dropping off entirely to sleep; and the bulk of the people, or at any rate that portion of them with some glimmer of awareness and who could have done something, being told time and time again that there was nothing to be achieved without the revolution, let the government and the bosses blithely carry on oppressing and exploiting... and waited for the revolution to come. The revolutionary spirit aroused in Europe by the great French revolution and kept alive in Italy more than anywhere else throughout the first half of the century, gradually petered out since the revolution could no longer be made using the old methods due to changes in conditions and changes in goals, and in the end the government could do as it pleased without having to fret about any serious resistance. And it was very frequently the case that workers, once they had managed to organize themselves unaided and extract a few improvements, drifted further away than ever from the revolutionaries, whose forecasts and aims contradicted the progress achieved. And rather than these having, as they should have and could have, helped bring the utter emancipation of the people that much closer, they provided additional arguments for conservatism.

I countered these mistakes and the methodology of the classic revolutionaries to which we ourselves had long subscribed, with my own belief, which has come to be shared by almost all our comrades: that bourgeois institutions, cornered by resistance and popular menace, still have a lot of concessions to make before they reach the point where they must succumb to a more or less violent demise; that it is in the interests of revolutionaries to squeeze every possible concession out of the government and bosses, both in order to ease the current suffering of the people and to hasten the final showdown; and that the better the people's material and moral conditions are and the more it has become aware of its own strength and inured to and skilled in struggle, through resistance and relentless struggles for improved conditions, the better equipped the people is for revolution. I therefore closed by urging resistance to the law on *domicilio coatto*, which is to be the first, and we hope successful, sample of what the people can do, starting right now, even peacefully and within the law, to counter government bullies, if it will but show its determination.

In all of this, I made no allusion to the democratic socialist party, for the straightforward reason that it did not exist during the period of Italian history to which I was referring. It was spawned in Italy precisely as a result of the mistakes we made and the decline in the people's revolutionary spirit; and it will collapse or be reduced to a party of mere politicos the day that we, learning from the experience of our past failures, can spread our activities in the bosom of the masses and when the dormant revolutionary spirit within the Italian people springs back to life.

Besides, the democratic socialists would be wrong to try to make capital out of these "confessions of an anarchist", since our mistakes, shared by all the older schools of revolutionaries, are in large measure something we owe to marxist theory, of which all us anarchists were once upon a time more consistent or even more orthodox advocates than those who professed to be Marxists and, perhaps, than Marx himself, and we have been discarding those mistakes as we have been shrugging off marxism's mistakes.

But more of that some other time.

Your comrade
GIUSEPPE RINALDI

33.
ANARCHISM IN THE WORKERS' MOVEMENT[1]

We would draw our readers' attention to the Toulouse (France) workers' congress, which we report in this edition, and to the speech delivered to said congress by our comrade Delessalle, which we are reprinting under the heading "Workers' Resistance."[2]

The Toulouse congress was a significant victory for our persuasion and tactics—a victory that was predictable from the stance of the majority of the French delegation at the recent London International Congress and which was made that much easier for our friends in France by the authoritarian, intolerant behavior of the marxists.[3]

To be sure, the Toulouse congress was no anarchist congress—and it is a good thing that this was the case. Anarchist congresses should be held by anarchists, not by the workers at large... unless the latter have already become anarchists, in which case anarchy would have carried the day and no more congresses would be held for propaganda and struggle purposes, but only technical congresses to thrash out practicalities arising in the life of society.

It is not our intention to impose our program on the masses who have yet to be persuaded, much less are we out to put on a show of strength by using ambush and more or less *clever* intrigues to get workers to vote through statements of principles that workers have yet to embrace. We are not out to have our party take the place of the life of the people; but we strive to ensure that said life may be comprehensive,

---

1 Translated from "L'anarchismo nel movimento operajo," *L'Agitazione* (Ancona) 1, no. 30 (7 October 1897).

2 At the 3rd Congress of the *Confédération Générale du Travail* (General Confederation of Labor), held in Toulouse from 20 to 25 September 1897, the principle of the general strike was reaffirmed and the use of boycott and ca'canny (French *sabotage*) tactics, as illustrated in Paul Delesalle's report, was approved. Delesalle, a leading figure of the French syndicalist movement, for the next decade was to serve as joint secretary of both the CGT and the other major syndicalist organization, the *Fédération des Bourses du Travail* (Federation of Labor Exchanges).

3 At the London congress of the Second International, held from 27 July to 1 August 1896, the French delegation voted against the anarchists' exclusion from the congress. Malatesta was part of that delegation, representing the Amiens metalworkers.

thoughtful, and thriving and so our party can bring to bear upon it whatever influence may naturally derive from the activity and intelligence it can inject into its propaganda and its entire action as a party.

And one of the main reasons for our most recent fall-outs with the democratic socialists was their ambition to take over the workers' movement, in defiance of our demand for full freedom for all, to foist their democratic socialist creed upon it and harness it for their own electoral purposes—an ambition that has received a severe set-back in Toulouse, as far as France goes, and that will be utterly defeated, we believe, the world over at the great international congress in preparation for 1900.[4]

For us, it is enough if workers learn to do for themselves, acknowledge the conflict of interests between them and the bosses, and seek, through union and all manner of resistance, to shrug off the state of degradation and wretchedness in which they find themselves. Conscious, systematic socialism and anarchism will come little by little, as the conflict widens and deepens and as the need for radical organic remedies becomes apparent to all.

The Toulouse congress shows that the thoughtful part of the French proletariat, even though it may not understand or may not accept our general principles, can discern the path that must lead to the ending of human exploitation—and we are proud to record the important part that our comrades have played in this.

May their example spur us on.

***

The short-term practical means of struggle embraced by those attending the Toulouse congress—striking when possible and appropriate, *boycotting* traders and bosses as circumstances allow, and easing up on the quantity and quality of work, squandering raw materials and ruining machinery and tools until such time as the boss caves in to the demands put by the workers—may appear (especially those last two) ill-suited to the social conditions in Italy and to the state of public opinion.

This is because, up until a few years ago, workers not entirely brutalized by poverty and ignorance, fell in behind bourgeois parties

---

4 The organization of an international congress to be held in 1900 was one of the resolutions taken at the Toulouse congress. The congress, which was to be held in Paris, was eventually prohibited by the police.

and looked for improvement to the kindness of the bosses or to the arrival in power of one or the other faction of the bourgeoisie. There was no collective awareness of class antagonisms, and only now the first inklings of it are breaking through. At a personal level, every worker has always thought of the boss as his enemy, and has sought to give him as little work as possible and often to do him as much harm as he could; but, lacking the illumination of an ideal, lacking the purpose of the general good, such feelings were merely the instinctive and almost unthinking backlash against hurt. They were unable to generate any lasting, general impact and boiled down to personal hatreds and rivalries, which, for the most part, led to barbarism in practices, falling levels of sociability and a debasement of everybody's level of morality.

It is up to us, up to the socialists generally, to cultivate in the proletariat a consciousness of the class antagonism and the need for collective struggle, and a yearning to have an end of struggle and to resolve differences by establishing equality, justice, and freedom for everyone. And as that new consciousness and those new ideals spread, the tactics advocated in France and already being practiced in England will be feasible and useful even here in Italy, through adaptation to changing circumstances of time, place, or person.

The odd friend of ours may think this small potatoes: and there will be no shortage, either, of voices calling us "legalitarians."

This is mere rhetoric, the sort of thing we have not yet completely outgrown!

As individuals and as a party, we have grown up under the sway of admiration and craving for the classic, traditional forms of revolution: barricades, armed bands, gunfire, etc. And we are still of the view that those are superb forms… as long as they do not have the drawback of not being practicable and of remaining pious wishes.

We also say: such education and desire of ours will prove greatly useful to us come the day of final crisis, and it would be a mistake and a sin to let them fall into disrepute and oblivion.

But let us remember that neglecting small means when greater means cannot be deployed, and wallowing in inertia on the pretext of wanting to only engage in big things, eventually leads to our becoming impotent and incapable of doing a lot or a little.

This is how the legalitarians, the parliamentarists have managed to make headway. The revolution is a beautiful thing, they say;

but since you do not make it, allow us to do what we can: enter Parliament.

We, on the other hand, have to demonstrate that even while waiting for the revolution to arrive, we can fight, and fight to some effect, without dragging the masses down the unwinnable byways of parliamentarism. Once we pull that off, parliamentary socialism's days will be numbered.

Moreover let us not forget that, even when they are possible, barricades erected without a measure of awareness in the people lead only to the replacement of one government by another—and that such awareness can only develop gradually, through the day-to-day struggle, which cannot be barricade warfare.

So let us not scorn the "petty means." They will hoist us into a position where we can deploy major ones.

34. OUR TACTICS[1]

Rhetoric is an affliction hard to cure, and no mistake. And we are not talking about the sort of hypocritical rhetoric of the charlatans and bamboozlers, but the sort that honestly mirrors an exuberance of sentiment not tempered by a proper consideration of reality.

Some friends of ours, whom we hold in the highest esteem on account of their boundless devotion to the cause and the useful contribution they have made and are making to our common endeavors, are unhappy with us, on the grounds that... we are not revolutionary enough.

We readily admit as much. But is that stance on our part something we have freely chosen, or is it, rather, something forced upon us by circumstances? We are inclined to believe the latter, given that so many of the comrades who would have us do more and who are that much worthier than us, in practice do no more than we do.

You are out, they write us, to introduce *Anglicism* into Italy (we would not even dream of doing so and the reasons are set out below);[2] but, as a country, Italy is not cut out for legal resistance and slow-moving organizations. "Even if legal resistance could achieve anything of note, it would promptly *degenerate* into rebellions and upheavals, for the Italian people knows no middle way: it being the lamb or the tiger." What! A lamb if you must, but a tiger? We shall let it go, having no wish to offend tigers. For two or three dozen years we have been going around saying such things and each time we made to take to the streets or go out into the countryside, we were lucky if we could muster fifteen people!

Your paper-and-chatter agitation (they mean the one against *domicilio coatto*) is pointless; if the law does not get passed it will be because of backstairs parliamentary intrigues rather than because of any agenda of yours. "We cannot fathom how on earth the *domicilio coatto* issue could have become the stuff of backstairs parliamentary

---

1 Translated from "La nostra tattica," *L'Agitazione* (Ancona) 1, no. 35 (11 November 1897).

2 The charge refers to Malatesta's advocacy of direct action labor tactics, such as boycott and ca'canny, which had been used by the British labor movement for a long time and had been recently adopted by French syndicalists.

horse-trading, had the people not done a little protesting and some parliamentary parties not been made to realize that voting the law through might have been dangerous; it is certainly not out of any genuine love of liberty that the likes of Zanardelli and Rudinì would have found fault with this freedom-killing project![3] But we agree entirely that the present campaign is a paltry affair and paltrier still the part we play in it; but what are we to do if others refuse and we are not strong enough to do more?

The need would be for noisy, impressive, threatening public demonstrations; if, they write us, demonstrations like the one the shopkeepers organized in Rome were to be mounted simultaneously in twenty or thirty Italian cities, then something might be achieved.[4] Agreed, but one would need to be in a position to do that – or otherwise, have the patience to work away and wait until one can pull it off.

If only the peasants of Molinella had...whatever you like, but the peasants did not, and none of our critics (among whom there are some who did have the material means) stepped in to do it for them.[5] And this is not to put them down, for we are convinced that, had they stepped in, they would have succeeded only in having themselves arrested as *agents provocateurs*. In order to reach out to strikers and harness the strike for the advantage of our propaganda and steer it in a direction we think best serves the workers' cause, one would need to have had some involvement in the preparations for the strike or at least have previously mounted propaganda in the area and won the people's sympathy; rather than showing up at the eleventh hour, knowing no one and known to none.

In short, the counsel received from our friends is what all of us have been doing, or trying to do, for many a long year, without getting

---

3 Antonio di Rudinì was the Italian prime minister. Giuseppe Zanardelli was the president of the chamber of deputies and, as of December 1897, the minister of justice in Rudinì's new cabinet. *Domicilio coatto* (forced residence) had been in use for years in Italy. Its use was extended by exceptional laws, introduced by Prime Minister Francesco Crispi in 1894. In 1897, a new bill was proposed that meant to make *domicilio coatto* part of the permanent legislation, *de facto* introducing deportation for political reasons as an ordinary procedure.

4 On 11 October 1897, a demonstration against taxes promoted by the Roman shopkeepers turned into a street riot, during which a young worker was killed and many people wounded by the police.

5 Molinella, near Bologna, was a labor stronghold. Earlier that year, its paddy workers had won a labor dispute after a forty-day strike that had prompted the government to dispatch ten thousand soldiers to the area.

anywhere; and if our reputation is still good and we still have the potential to do better, this is simply because we have always paid the price. We do not intend to travel, over and over for all eternity, roads that might be summed up like this: six months of quiet activity, followed by a few microscopic uprisings—or, more often, mere threats of uprisings—then arrests, flights abroad, interruption of propaganda, disintegration of the organization... Just to start the whole thing all over again two or three years further down the line.

We are now convinced (and it took some time!) that before one can do, one must have the strength to do; and if it takes time to build up that strength, we will have the patience to wait as long as it takes.

Got that?

Do not call upon us to employ violent language in the newspaper. We would then be systematically confiscated: our readers would receive the paper with entire columns blanked out, which would constitute the least violent and least persuasive of all languages, and then... Well, you yourselves would be the first to write us off as fools for not knowing how to avoid being impounded.

Do not bemoan the fact that nothing is being done and no one is being urged to do anything: instead, let us all work in unison to get ourselves to a position where we can achieve something of note.

And don't talk to us of *Anglicism*. If the word means anything, it means economic resistance as an end in itself, as practiced by the "old" trade unions, which, though out to improve the workers' conditions, embraced and respected the capitalist system and all bourgeois institutions.

We, on the other hand, believe (and even the English are beginning to catch on to this) that workers' organizations and economic resistance and the whole gamut of more or less law-abiding ways of resisting, are merely avenues leading to the utter transformation of society. In the absence of such a transformation, not only can emancipation not be achieved, but neither will be any overall, lasting, significant improvement. And we believe, as we have stated time and again, that that transformation is not going to be achieved peacefully.

Once again, got that?

Malatesta at the time of his 1899–1900 sojourn in the USA / Source: International Institute of Social History, Amsterdam, BG A8/785

IV.

“Toward Anarchy”:
Malatesta in America, 1899–1900

In April 1899, Malatesta escaped from forced residence in Lampedusa Island, where he had been relegated after the 1898 bread riots ended with the cannon shots of general Bava Beccaris in Milan. After a short stay in London, Malatesta undertook an eight-month sojourn in the United States, where he took on the editorship of *La Questione Sociale* of Paterson, New Jersey, one of the few surviving voices of Italian anarchism in the world. The anarchist-socialist project of operating and growing in broad daylight had been shattered by the Italian government’s brutality and willingness to crush with bloodshed even the demand for bread. The lesson of experience led Malatesta to take a radical tactical turn, beginning to advocate an alliance among the Italian revolutionary parties for an insurrection that toppled the Savoy monarchy, the “obstacle in the way of any progress and every improvement.” At the same time, he made it clear that “it is not a matter of achieving anarchy today, tomorrow, or within ten centuries, but that we walk toward anarchy today, tomorrow, and always.” Combining theoretical coherence and pragmatism, Malatesta thus laid the foundations of an original gradualist view of anarchism.

35. AGAINST THE MONARCHY[1]

(Appeal to all forward-looking men)

The House of Savoy has cast aside the last remaining shreds of the mask it used to pose as the representative of the people's interests and aspirations, and is brazenly, brutally riding roughshod over those vestiges of freedom for which our forebears paid such a high price in martyrs and blood-letting.

In addition to the ghastly poverty afflicting the masses of the laboring folk, the growing idleness of the middle classes, the swift decline with which a nonsensical tax policy was damning every national pursuit, now today we have the violent eradication of any murmur of civil society. The arbitrariness and persecution that have been a distinguishing feature throughout its reign have swollen into a system of consistent, permanent tyranny reminiscent of the darkest days of foreign overlordship.

What is the way out of this situation, which, if it were to last, would reduce Italy to such a condition of abjection as to leave her forever incapable of raising herself up by her own efforts to the dignity of civil life ever again?

Any illusions about peaceful progress have by now been dispelled.

Parliament, which, under the current constitution, is the lawful means by which that tiny fraction of the people with access to political life should be able to enact its wishes, has shown itself to be powerless to guarantee, not just the people's interests, but even those of the class it represents. And it is condemned to obey the king's wishes and those of the royal cabal, or be dismissed like some impudent slave.

The most tentative, the most anodyne reforms are looked upon as subversive and their champions treated like malefactors. The very laws underpinning the constitution, and that were in any event made

1 Translated from *Contro la Monarchia* ([London], 1899). This work was published as an anonymous pamphlet, presumably during Malatesta's short stay in London between his escape from Lampedusa Island at the end of April 1899 and his departure for America in early August. The pamphlet's cover bore the false title *Aritmetica Elementale*, clearly in order to ease its circulation by deflecting police attention.

in the sole interests of the ruling class, are breached at will by the government when they do not suit enough the wishes of the reaction. With freedom of the press, of assembly, of association and to strike done away with, every civil means of articulating one's own opinion and asserting one's rights has been abolished. And in the meantime, the country is bled dry by a tax burden out of all proportion to its resources; the people are starved so that police and soldiers can be maintained, in turn enriching a gang of latifundists and politickers and the very well springs of production are sucked dry by inanely stupid taxation arrangements.[2]

Is it not time that all of us who are not complicit in or beneficiaries of the tyranny and who refuse to resign ourselves to the current horrible state of affairs looked into what policy the circumstances commend and thought about acting upon it?

There is no need to drone on and on about the government arrangement that afflicts Italy and the circumstances to which she has been reduced.

Oppressive taxes, a customs arrangement designed to favor certain classes of privileged persons without a care for the damage caused to the mass of the citizenry and to the nation's output; pointless public works schemes carried out simply to line the pockets of contractors or favor the electoral interests of deputies in the pocket of the government, whilst, elsewhere, ventures of greater significance to public wealth and health are neglected; armaments on a colossal scale, pompous politics, alliances running counter to the nation's sympathies and interests but imposed by the interests of the dynasty... and all of it out of control, with no sense of proportion or thought for the future.

Outcome: record-breaking criminality and illiteracy; record-breaking emigration due to poverty; lower wages and higher prices for life's basic essentials than in any civilized country; rickety production and trade; land badly farmed or simply left fallow; three in every four towns without drinkable water, without sewerage, without schools; unemployment; hunger—hunger in a land where the soil is among the most fertile in the world and in a people renowned for their capacity to work and, alas, for the paucity of their needs!

---

2 In order to reach as wide an audience as possible, the argument is framed in terms of "national" interests rather than "class" interests.

And if Italy could be reduced to this when the people still had some measure of control left, what is to become of her now that the government acknowledges no restraints any more?

To be sure, the government's self-interest and that of the class that depends on the government ought to pause on a slippery slope at the foot of which universal ruination may wait. But it is a general feature of ruling classes that they stick to the wrong course all the more obstinately when threatened with ruination—and the Italian government is certainly showing no sign of wishing to be an exception to the rule. Besides, there is no denying that the Italian monarchy is by now so committed to the path of reaction that it could not turn back without hastening its own downfall; and it would not be reasonable to wait for it to be willing to commit deliberate suicide or perish before it has turned to extreme defensive measures.

Highs and lows in the reaction may well be still possible; maybe awareness of the danger and the House of Savoy's traditional wiliness will prompt it to try to throw dust in the people's eyes one more time; but the fact is that the monarchy now has only the sabre to rely upon and ultimately it will entrust its protection, and that of the class that has stood by it, to the sabre.

The thing is therefore to fight force with force; once again a popular insurrection looms as the means required to topple the tyranny.

But rising up is not enough; one must also win.

The kingdom's history is awash with popular revolts. Right from the start of the reign, from when the people, called upon to back the national movement in the name of freedom and the commonwealth, watched as the revolution was exploited by a pack of greedy speculators and as their conditions were made even worse than before, countless revolts have signalled their unhappiness and conviction that there was nothing to be hoped for, except from violence. But those revolts have been almost always small, sparked by poverty and the bullying of a local, government-backed *camorra,* and not out for radical, thoroughgoing changes. They have been easily crushed, with no discernible impact other than slaughter and ferocious persecution mounted by the authorities. And even when broader and more enlightened upheavals have shaken the country, the absence of preparations, agreement, and a specified target have ensured that the government has easily stemmed them and exploited them as the pretext for fiercer reaction.

So, if there is the will to win, rather than face periodical and pointless slaughter, we must lay preparations appropriate for the force we are going to have to confront.

***

In Italy, as everywhere else, there are several parties that, while all honestly desirous of the general good, differ radically from one another both about the chief causes of society's woes and about the remedies that might end them.

Some are believers in the inviolability of lawfully acquired private property, and in the intrinsic fairness of profit and interest and these contend that democratic institutions that afford everyone access to property by means of work and economies are possible and desirable; whereas others see private ownership of the land and the means of production as the primary cause of all injustice and wretchedness.

Some believe that, with the monarchy abolished, we should look for society to be changed by laws passed by the representatives of the people, elected by universal suffrage; whereas others hold that any government is of necessity an instrument of oppression in the hands of some privileged class, and these want to see the arrangement of society be the direct handiwork of the freely associated workers.

Some believe in a harmony of interests between property owners and proletarians, whereas others are convinced that there is an irreconcilable antagonism between the two classes and thus that the propertied class must, of necessity, disappear, as all of its members are absorbed into the class of useful workers. And so on.

We need not enter here into which of the various contenders may be right, nor side with any given view. What we do wish to establish here is that everybody suffers from lack of freedom, that they all have a common foe in the Monarchy, and that as none of the parties are strong enough to overthrow it by themselves, there is a shared interest in joining forces in order to rid ourselves of this obstacle in the way of any progress and every improvement.

Not that we mean to suggest that the various parties abjure their own ideas, their own hopes, their own autonomous organization and amalgamate into one; and if we were to suggest any such thing we should most certainly go unheeded since the differences that divide them, one from another, are too serious and too fundamental.

Those who believe in the legitimacy of private ownership, and contend that the establishment of a government is useful and necessary could certainly not countenance expropriation and anarchy. Conversely, the opponents of property and governmentalism would refuse to recognize the acquired rights of owners and defer of their own free will to some new government.

Let each of them therefore remain who they are and let them get on with propaganda on behalf of their own ideas and their own side. But, no matter how great they may be, the differences separating the various parties should not stop them from coming together for a specific purpose, whenever there really is some interest they all share in common.

And what more pressing interest could there be than winning the essential conditions of freedom without which the people slide into brutishness and become incapable of reacting and where the parties have no means of spreading their ideas?

In face of the brutality of certain situations, all discussion is of necessity cut short: what is needed is action.

When a man falls into the water and is drowning, one does not stand around debating why he fell in and what needs to be done to prevent him from falling in again; what matters is getting him out of the water and preventing his death.

When a country is invaded by some savage horde that mistreats, pillages, and massacres the inhabitants, the priority above all else is to drive the invader out of the country, no matter the scale of the grievance that one part of the population may have against the other part or how different the interests of the various classes and the aspirations of the various parties may be.

This is the sort of situation in which Italy finds herself today: that of a country under military occupation, where, save for the *camorra* surrounding the government and supporting it as the spring of its life, all of the inhabitants, no matter to which class they may belong, are threatened and aggrieved in their property and in their freedom and subject to the most unbearable soldierly arrogance.

What party, being in no position to slay the enemy on its own, would doom itself and the entire people to the indefinite continuation of its current slavishness, rather than join with the other parties opposed to the monarchy and seek, through union, the power to win?

Besides, even if, due to some inexcusable sectarianism that would ultimately show its lack of confidence in the validity and practicability of its own program, one of them was to opt instead to let the status quo continue, rather than act in concert with the other parties, necessity would anyway impose union on anyone not content to remain a passive onlooker, and thus effectively let down his own ideas and his own party.

Given the circumstances in Italy and of her government, the fact is that, sooner or later, a fresh eruption of the people's wrath is on its way and it will be drowned in blood if, yet again, it has nothing but stones with which to answer rifles and cannons. The subversive parties, if they have learned anything at all from past experience and have some sense of their duty and their own interest, will throw themselves into the fray and afford the people the aid of resources and plans readied in advance. So, if the various revolutionary parties participate in the struggle and there is no one able, even if he could, to prevent others from helping and thus deny them whatever morsel of influence over the future course of the revolution will accrue to them from the part they played in the victory, would it not be a very grave mistake for each of them to act on their own without any agreement, and run the risk of thwarting each other, with the advantage going to the common enemy? Instead, should they not try, through concerted action, to ensure the sort of material victory that is the essential precondition for any transformation of the established order?

Afterwards, if everybody respects freedom, as they say they do, and affords anyone else the right and the means to spread and try out their own ideas, freedom will bring forth that which it can, and those methods and institutions that best cater for the material and moral conditions of the moment will carry the day. Otherwise, the downfall of the monarchy will still mean that the worst of our enemies has been dealt with—and the fighting will start all over, but in more humane and more civilised circumstances.

***

We are dealing here with a material issue that will prevail with all brute force over the economic and moral problems by which the country is exercised.

The government has its soldiers, cannons, rapid means of communication, and transport; it has a whole mighty organization ready for the task of repression; and it has demonstrated the extent to which it is ready and willing to deploy it.

The government has not hesitated to massacre citizens by the hundreds just to snuff out some agitation that came down to harmless demonstrations and minor disturbances easily assuaged by abolition of some levy or some other anodyne concessions.[3] What might the uniformed beasts in the king's service not be capable of, if they were threatened by some grave danger?

A city that rises up, in the hope that others might respond to its example, would probably be reduced to rubble before the news could reach the outside world. A populace out to make a vigorous display of its own unhappiness, but lacking appropriate weaponry, would be drowned in blood before its rebellion could get off the ground.

We must therefore strike with consensus, with force and with determination. Before the authorities can recover from their surprise, the people, or—to be more accurate—groups previously organized for action, will need to have seized as many army and government leaders as possible. Each rebel group, each unruly mob needs to have a sense that it is not on its own, so that, encouraged by the hope for victory, it sticks with the struggle and pursues it to the bitter end. Soldiers need to realize that they are confronted by a genuine revolution and to feel the temptation to desert and fraternise with the people, before the intoxication of bloodletting turns them into savages. Useful intelligence needs to be spread at speed and troop movements obstructed by every possible means. The troops must be attracted away from the places targeted for action by means of diversionary maneuvers, and rapid-fire rifles and cannons must be answered with bombs, mines, and arson. In short, there must be an appropriate response to the enemy's weapons of war, to a determined crackdown that will stop at nothing. A response must be made in the shape of action even more determined. This is war and so everything commended by the science of warfare but applied to the conditions of a risen people that has to face regulars equipped with the most up to date weaponry must be pressed into service.

But none of this can be improvised at a moment's notice: experience should have proved that to everybody. At the moment of truth, arms are in short supply unless they have been prepared in advance and unless the means of seizing them by force and by surprise have

3 The reference is to the bread riots of 1898.

been looked into. Agreement on the allocation of roles in the erection of barricades, the bringing of fire-power to bear wherever required, and implementation of some battle-plan—these cannot be done at the drop of a hat, once the fighting is already under way. Synchronisation of insurrections in various places or at least such a swift spread of the conflagration as to prevent the government from marshalling its troops and snuffing out the various insurgent centers one at a time—this is not achievable unless the action groups have agreed beforehand to liaise with one another.

We invite all the enemies of the monarchy who are seriously determined to end it to engage with this work of practical preparation.

Let men of good will seek one another out and liaise in the preparation of the insurrection. Their several initiatives will meet and federate with one another, thereby accumulating the strength required to steer the next popular uprising to victory.

The not so distant future will tell if we were mistaken in counting upon the Italian people's revolutionary energies.

August 1899

36.
SIGNOR MALATESTA EXPLAINS[1]

Signor E. Malatesta wishes to amend certain views, not reflective of his thinking, carried in the report sent to us by third parties on the talk he gave on the evening of the 16th inst., in Paterson, NJ.

To which end he has sent us this letter in which he asks that we accommodate him, which we are happy to do as follows.

750 Clay St., Paterson, 20.08.99
Dear Editor-in-chief,

I read in your edition of today's date that I am supposed to have stated in Paterson that "henceforth it is no longer a matter of class struggle against the bourgeoisie as the older socialist schools wished us to believe."

Since this does not accurately reflect my thinking, allow me to reiterate for your readers what I actually did say.

As I see it, it is not the case that the bourgeoisie forms a single body in the struggle against the proletariat and that government, army, bench, church, etc. have no reason to exist other than the protection of bourgeois interests, just as the various schools of socialism believed once upon a time.

The current position in Europe is there as evidence, even for the most pig-headed, that the bourgeoisie is split into a number of factions competing among themselves, and that the various political, court, military, religious institutions, etc., not only champion the bourgeoisie against the proletariat, but indeed have interests of their own, which they protect even at the expense of placing bourgeois interests in jeopardy.

This situation represents a benefit and a danger as far as the laboring population is concerned; a benefit insofar as the enemy is

---

1 Translated from "Il signor Malatesta si spiega," *Il Progresso Italo-Americano* (New York) 20, n. 200 (23 August 1899). Malatesta had arrived in America on 12 August and held his first conference in Paterson, New Jersey, on 16 August. The *Progresso Italo-Americano,* one of New York's Italian newspapers, had published a report of Malatesta's speech in its 20 August issue. The address provided by Malatesta is that of Pedro Esteve and his wife Maria Roda, with whom he was staying. Esteve was the Spanish anarchist with whom Malatesta had toured Spain in 1891. Esteve had since emigrated to America.

divided; a danger in that it might lead the workers to forget that "all" bourgeois are its enemies.

So we anarchist socialists should cash in on the divisions within the enemy camp; and, if it can be done to some purpose, ally ourselves with this or that bourgeois faction in order to rid ourselves of the most immediate obstacles such as, in Italy, the monarchy; but we must always remain what we are, namely, implacable enemies of capitalism and authoritarianism, and, insofar as we have it in us so to do, prevent the workers from being used yet again as footstool for new rulers and new exploiters.

The point is not to give up on the class struggle but rather to prevent the workers from straying from the Polar Star of class struggle in the complex struggles at the present hour and in the near future.

The debate centers on a de facto matter, to wit, the influence, exclusive or otherwise, of the class struggle in a wide variety of historical events. But all socialists, of no matter what school of thought, are—or ought to be—in agreement on the necessity of the proletariat's always being guided by the interests of the working class; given that, as far socialists are concerned, there is no equitable solution to the social question other than the destruction of all parasitical classes through the eradication of private ownership and the conversion of all able-bodied men into useful workers.

In the hope that you will be willing to publish these few lines for the sake of the truth, thanking you in anticipation.

Yours
ENRICO MALATESTA

37. AN ANARCHIST PROGRAMME[1]

We have nothing new to say.

Propaganda is not, and cannot be, but the incessant, tireless repetition of those principles that must guide our conduct in the diverse circumstances of life.

Hence we will restate, with more or less different words but along the same lines, our old revolutionary-anarchist-socialist program.

We believe that most of the ills that afflict mankind stem from a bad social organisation; and that Man could destroy them if he wished and knew how.

Present society is the result of age-long struggles of man against man. Not understanding the advantages that could accrue for all by cooperation and solidarity; seeing in every other man (with the possible exception of those closest to them by blood ties) a competitor and an enemy, each one of them sought to secure for himself, the greatest number of advantages possible without giving a thought to the interests of others.

In such a struggle, obviously the strongest or more fortunate were bound to win, and in one way or another subject and oppress the losers.

So long as Man was unable to produce more than was strictly needed to keep alive, the conquerors could do no more than put to flight or massacre their victims, and seize the food they had gathered.

Then when with the discovery of grazing and agriculture a man could produce more than what he needed to live, the conquerors found it more profitable to reduce the conquered to a state of slavery, and put them to work for their advantage.

---

1 In *Errico Malatesta: His Life and Ideas,* compiled and edited by Vernon Richards (London: Freedom Press, 1965; reprinted in 1993), p. 182–198. Originally published as "Il nostro programma," parts 1–4, *La Questione Sociale* (Paterson, NJ) 5, new series, nos. 1–4 (9, 16, 23, and 30 September 1899) and reissued, with modifications, as *Programma Anarchico, accettato dall'"Unione Anarchica Italiana" nel Congresso di Bologna del 1–4 Luglio 1920* (Bologna: Commissione di Corrispondenza dell'U.A.I., 1920). Richards's translation, which we have preferred to earlier ones as more faithful, is from the 1920 edition. Where the two Italian editions differ, we have modified Richards's text so as to reflect the original 1899 edition.

Later, the conquerors realised that it was more convenient, more profitable and certain to exploit the labour of others by other means: to retain for themselves the exclusive right to the land and working implements, and set free the disinherited who, finding themselves without the means of life, were obliged to have recourse to the landowners and work for them, on their terms.

Thus, step by step through a most complicated series of struggles of every description, of invasions, wars, rebellions, repressions, concessions won by struggle, associations of the oppressed united for defence, and of the conquerors for attack, we have arrived at the present state of society, in which some have inherited the land and all social wealth, while the mass of the people, disinherited in all respects, is exploited and oppressed by a small possessing class.

From all this stems the misery in which most workers live today, and which in turn creates the evils such as ignorance, crime, prostitution, diseases due to malnutrition, mental depression and premature death. From all this arises a special class (government) which, provided with the necessary means of repression, exists to legalise and protect the owning class from the demands of the workers; and then it uses the powers at its disposal to create privileges for itself and to subject, if it can, the owning class itself as well. From this the creation of another privileged class (the clergy), which by a series of fables about the will of God, and about an after-life etc., seeks to persuade the oppressed to accept oppression meekly, and (just as the government does), as well as serving the interest of the owning class, serves its own. From this the creation of an official science which, in all those matters serving the interests of the ruling class, is the negation of true science. From this the patriotic spirit, race hatred, wars and armed peace, sometimes more disastrous than wars themselves. From this the transformation of love into torment or sordid commerce. From this hatred, more or less disguised, rivalry, suspicion among all men, insecurity and universal fear.

We want to change radically such a state of affairs. And since all these ills have their origin in the struggle between men, in the seeking after well-being through one's own efforts and for oneself and against everybody, we want to make amends, replacing hatred by love, competition by solidarity, the individual search for personal well-being by the fraternal cooperation for the well-being of all, oppression and imposition by liberty, the religious and pseudo-scientific lie by truth.

Therefore:

1. Abolition of private property in land, in raw materials and the instruments of labour, so that no one shall have the means of living by the exploitation of the labour of others, and that everybody, being assured of the means to produce and to live, shall be truly independent and in a position to unite freely among themselves for a common objective and according to their personal sympathies.

2. Abolition of government and of every power which makes the law and imposes it on others: therefore abolition of monarchies, republics, parliaments, armies, police forces, magistratures and any institution whatsoever endowed with coercive powers.

3. Organisation of social life by means of free association and federations of producers and consumers, created and modified according to the wishes of their members, guided by science and experience, and free from any kind of imposition which does not spring from natural needs, to which everyone, convinced by a feeling of overriding necessity, voluntarily submits.

4. The means of life, for development and well-being, will be guaranteed to children and all who are prevented from providing for themselves.

5. War on religions and all lies, even if they shelter under the cloak of science. Scientific instruction for all to advanced level.

6. War on patriotism. Abolition of frontiers; brotherhood among all peoples.

7. Reconstruction of the family, as will emerge from the practice of love, freed from every legal tie, from every economic and physical oppression, from every religious prejudice.

This is our ideal.

Ways and Means

We have outlined under a number of headings our objectives and the ideal for which we struggle.

But it is not enough to desire something; if one really wants it adequate means must be used to secure it. And these means are not arbitrary, but instead cannot but be conditioned by the ends we aspire to and by the circumstances in which the struggle takes place, for if we ignore the choice of means we would achieve other ends, possibly diametrically opposed to those we aspire to, and this would be the obvious and inevitable consequence of our choice of means.

Whoever sets out on the highroad and takes a wrong turning does not go where he intends to go but where the road leads him.

It is therefore necessary to state what are the means which in our opinion lead to our desired ends, and which we propose to adopt.

Our ideal is not one which depends for its success on the individual considered in isolation. The question is of changing the way of life of society as a whole; of establishing among men relationships based on love and solidarity; of achieving the full material, moral and intellectual development not for isolated individuals, or members of one class or of a particular political party, but for all mankind—and this is not something that can be imposed by force, but must emerge through the enlightened consciences of each one of us and be achieved with the free consent of all.

Our first task therefore must be to persuade people.

We must make people aware of the misfortunes they suffer and of their chances to destroy them. We must awaken sympathy in everybody for the misfortunes of others and a warm desire for the good of all people.

To those who are cold and hungry we will demonstrate how possible and easy it could be to assure to everybody their material needs. To those who are oppressed and despised we shall show how it is possible to live happily in a world of people who are free and equal; to those who are tormented by hatred and bitterness we will point to the road that leads to peace and human warmth that comes through learning to love one's fellow beings.

And when we will have succeeded in arousing the sentiment of rebellion in the minds of men against the avoidable and unjust evils from which we suffer in society today, and in getting them to understand how they are caused and how it depends on human will to rid ourselves of them; and when we will have created a lively and strong desire in men to transform society for the good of all, then those who are convinced, will by their own efforts as well as by the example of those already convinced, unite and want to as well as be able to act for their common ideals.

As we have already pointed out, it would be ridiculous and contrary to our objectives to seek to impose freedom, love among men and the radical development of human faculties, by means of force. One must therefore rely on the free will of others, and all we can do is to provoke the development and the expression of the will of the people.

But it would be equally absurd and contrary to our aims to admit that those who do not share our views should prevent us from expressing our will, so long as it does not deny them the same freedom.

Freedom for all, therefore, to propagate and to experiment with their ideas, with no other limitation than that which arises naturally from the equal liberty of everybody.

* * *

But to this are opposed—and with brute force—those who benefit from existing privileges and who today dominate and control all social life.

In their hands they have all the means of production; and thus they suppress not only the possibility of free experimentation in new ways of communal living, and the right of workers to live freely by the product of their own efforts, but also the right to life itself; and they oblige whoever is not a boss to have to allow himself to be exploited and oppressed if he does not wish to die of hunger.

They have police forces, a judiciary, and armies created for the express purpose of defending their privileges; and they persecute, imprison and massacre those who would want to abolish those privileges and who claim the means of life and liberty for everyone.

Jealous of their present and immediate interests, corrupted by the spirit of domination, fearful of the future, they, the privileged class, are, generally speaking incapable of a generous gesture; are equally incapable of a wider concept of their interests. And it would be foolish to hope that they should freely give up property and power and adapt themselves to living as equals and with those who today they keep in subjection.

Leaving aside the lessons of history (which demonstrates that never has a privileged class divested itself of all or some of its privileges, and never has a government abandoned its power unless obliged to do so by force or the fear of force), there is enough contemporary evidence to convince anyone that the bourgeoisie and governments intend to use armed force to defend themselves, not only against complete expropriation, but equally against the smallest popular demands, and are always ready to engage in the most atrocious persecutions and the bloodiest massacres.

For those people who want to emancipate themselves, only one course is open: that of opposing force with force.

* * *

It follows from what we have said that we have to work to awaken in the oppressed the conscious desire for a radical social transformation, and to persuade them that by uniting they have the strength to win; we must propagate our ideal and prepare the required material and moral forces to overcome those of the enemy, and to organise the new society. And when we will have the strength needed we must, by taking advantage of favourable circumstances as they arise, or which we can ourselves create, make the social revolution, by using force to destroy the government and to expropriate the owners of wealth, and by putting in common the means of life and production, and by preventing the setting up of new governments which would impose their will and hamper the reorganisation of society by the people themselves.

* * *

All this is however less simple than it might appear at first sight. We have to deal with people as they are in society today, in the most miserable moral and material condition; and we would be deluding ourselves in thinking that propaganda is enough to raise them to that level of intellectual development which is needed to put our ideas into effect.

Between man and his social environment there is a reciprocal action. Men make society what it is and society makes men what they are, and the result is therefore a kind of vicious circle. To transform society men must be changed, and to transform men, society must be changed.

Poverty brutalises man, and to abolish poverty men must have a social conscience and determination. Slavery teaches men to be slaves, and to free oneself from slavery there is a need for men who aspire to liberty. Ignorance has the effect of making men unaware of the causes of their misfortunes as well as the means of overcoming them, and to do away with ignorance people must have the time and the means to educate themselves.

Governments accustom people to submit to the Law and to believe that Law is essential to society; and to abolish government men must be convinced of the uselessness and the harmfulness of government.

How does one escape from this vicious circle?

Fortunately existing society has not been created by the inspired will of a dominating class, which has succeeded in reducing all its subjects to passive and unconscious instruments of its interests. It is the result of a thousand internecine struggles, of a thousand human and natural factors acting indifferently, without directive criteria; and thus there are no clear-cut divisions either between individuals or between classes.

Innumerable are the variations in material conditions; innumerable are the degrees of moral and intellectual development; and not always—we would almost say very rarely—does the place of any individual in society correspond with his abilities and his aspirations. Very often individuals accustomed to conditions of comfort fall on hard times and others, through exceptionally favourable circumstances succeed in raising themselves above the conditions into which they were born. A large proportion of the working class has already succeeded either in emerging from a state of abject poverty, or was never in such a situation; no worker to speak of, finds himself in a state of complete social unawareness, of complete acquiescence to the conditions imposed on him by the bosses. And the same institutions, such as have been produced by history, contain organic contradictions and are like the germs of death, which as they develop result in the dissolution of institutions and the need for transformation.

From this the possibility of progress—but not the possibility of bringing all men to the necessary level to want, and to achieve, anarchy, by means of propaganda, without a previous gradual transformation of the environment.

Progress must advance contemporaneously and along parallel lines between men and their environment. We must take advantage of all the means, all the possibilities and the opportunities that the present environment allows us to act on our fellow men and to develop their consciences and their demands; we must use all advance in human consciences to induce them to claim and to impose those major social transformations which are possible and which effectively serve to open the way to further advances later.

We must not wait to achieve anarchy, in the meantime limiting ourselves to simple propaganda. Were we to do so we would soon exhaust our field of action; that is, we would have converted all those who in the existing environment are susceptible to understand and accept our ideas, and our subsequent propaganda would fall on sterile ground; or if environmental transformations brought out new popular groupings capable of receiving new ideas, this would happen without our participation, and thus would prejudice our ideas.

We must seek to get all the people, or different sections of the people, to make demands, and impose itself and take for itself all the improvements and freedoms that it desires as and when it reaches the state of wanting them, and the power to demand them; and in always propagating all aspects of our programme, and always struggling for its complete realisation, we must push the people to want always more and to increase its pressures, until it has achieved complete emancipation.

The Economic Struggle

The oppression which impinges most directly on the workers and which is the main cause of the moral and material frustrations under which they labour, is economic oppression, that is the exploitation to which bosses and business men subject them, thanks to their monopoly of all the most important means of production and distribution.

To destroy radically this oppression without any danger of it re-emerging, all people must be convinced of their right to the means of production, and be prepared to exercise this basic right by expropriating the land owners, the industrialists and financiers, and putting all social wealth at the disposal of the people.

But can this expropriation be put into effect today? Can we today pass directly, without intermediate steps, from the hell in which the workers now find themselves to the paradise of common property?

The proof that the people is not capable of expropriating the owners, yet, is that it does not expropriate them.

What must be done until the day of expropriation comes?

Our task is the moral and material preparation of the people for this essential expropriation; and to attempt it again and again, every time a revolutionary upheaval offers us the chance to, until the final triumph. But in what way can we prepare the people? In what way must one prepare the conditions which make possible not only the material fact of expropriation, but the utilisation to everybody's advantage of the common wealth?

We have already said that spoken and written propaganda alone cannot win over to our ideas the mass of the people. A practical education is needed, which must be alternately cause and effect in a gradual transformation of the environment. Parallel with the workers developing a sense of rebellion against the injustices and useless sufferings of which they are the victims, and the desire to better their conditions, they must be united and mutually dependent in the struggle to achieve their demands. And we as anarchists and workers, must incite and encourage them to struggle, and join them in their struggle.

But are these improvements possible in a capitalist regime? Are they useful from the point of view of a future complete emancipation of the workers?

Whatever may be the practical results of the struggle for immediate gains, the greatest value lies in the struggle itself. For thereby workers learn that the bosses interests are opposed to theirs and that they cannot improve their conditions, and much less emancipate themselves, except by uniting and becoming stronger than the bosses. If they succeed in getting what they demand, they will be better off: they will earn more, work fewer hours and will have more time and energy to reflect on the things that matter to them, and will immediately make greater demands and have greater needs. If they do not succeed they will be led to study the causes of their failure and recognise the need for closer unity and greater activity and they will in the end understand that to make their victory secure and definitive, it is necessary to destroy capitalism. The revolutionary cause, the cause of the moral elevation and emancipation of the workers must benefit by the fact that workers unite and struggle for their interests.

But, once again, can the workers succeed in really improving their conditions in the present state of society?

This depends on the confluence of a great number of circumstances.

In spite of what some say, there exists no natural law (law of wages) which determines what part of a worker's labour should go to him; or if one wants to formulate a law, it could not be but that: wages cannot normally be less than what is needed to maintain life, nor can they normally rise such that no profit margin is left to the boss.

It is clear that in the first case workers would die, and therefore would stop drawing any wages, and in the second the bosses would stop employing labour and so would pay no more wages. But between these two impossible extremes there is an infinite scale of degrees ranging from the nearly bestial conditions of most land workers to the almost respectable conditions of skilled workers in the large cities.

Wages, hours and other conditions of employment are the result of the struggle between bosses and workers. The former try to give the workers as little as possible and get them to work themselves to the bone; the latter try, or should try to work as little, and earn as much, as possible. Where workers accept any conditions, or even being discontented, do not know how to put up effective resistance to the bosses demands, they are soon reduced to bestial conditions of life. Where, instead, they have ideas as to how human beings should live and know how to join forces, and through refusal to work or the latent and open threat of rebellion, to win the bosses respect, in such cases, they are treated in a relatively decent way. One can therefore say that within certain limits, the wages he gets are what the worker (not as an individual. of course. but as a class) demands.

Through struggle, by resistance against the bosses, therefore, workers can up to a certain point, prevent a worsening of their conditions as well as obtaining real improvement. And the history of the workers' movement has already demonstrated this truth.

One must not however exaggerate the importance of this struggle between workers and bosses conducted exclusively in the economic field. Bosses can give in, and often they do in face of forcefully expressed demands so long as the demands are not too great; but if workers were to make demands (and it is imperative that they should) which would absorb all the bosses' profits and be in effect an indirect form of expropriation, it is certain that the bosses would appeal to the government and would seek to use force to oblige the workers to remain in their state of wage slavery.

And even before, long before workers can expect to receive the full product of their labour, the economic struggle becomes impotent as a means of producing the improvements in living standards.

Workers produce everything and without them life would be impossible; therefore it would seem that by refusing to work they could demand whatever they wanted. But the union of all workers, even in one particular trade, and in one country is difficult to achieve, and opposing the union of workers are the bosses' organisations. Workers live from day to day, and if they do not work they soon find themselves without food; whereas the bosses, because they have money, have access to all the goods in stock and can therefore sit back and wait until hunger reduces their employees to a more amenable frame of mind. The invention or the introduction of new machinery makes workers redundant and adds to the large army of unemployed, who are driven by hunger to sell their labour at any price. Immigration immediately creates problems in the countries where better working conditions exist, for the hordes of hungry workers, willy nilly, offer the bosses an opportunity to depress wages all round. And all these facts, which necessarily derive from the capitalist system, conspire in counteracting and often destroying advances made in working class consciousness and solidarity.[2]

Soon then, those workers who want to free themselves, or even only to effectively improve their conditions, will be faced with the need to defend themselves from the government, with the need to attack the government, which by legalising the right to property and protecting it with brute force, constitutes a barrier to human progress, which must be beaten down with force if one does not wish to remain indefinitely under present conditions or even worse.

From the economic struggle one must pass to the political struggle, that is to the struggle against government; and instead of opposing the capitalist millions with the workers' few pennies scraped together with difficulty, one must oppose the rifles and guns which defend property with the more effective means that the people will be able to find to defeat force by force.

Political Struggle—Revolutionary Action

By the political struggle we mean the struggle against government. Government is the *ensemble* of all those individuals who hold the reins of power, however acquired, to make the law and to impose it on the governed, that is the public.

Government is the consequence of the spirit of domination and violence with which some men have imposed themselves on other, and is at the same time the creature as well as the creator of privilege and its natural defender.

---

2 In the 1920 edition, this paragraph continues as follows: "And in every case the overriding fact remains that production under capitalism is organised by each capitalist for his personal profit and not, as would be natural, to satisfy the needs of the workers in the best possible way. Hence the chaos, the waste of human effort, the organised scarcity of goods, useless and harmful occupations, unemployment, abandoned land, under-use of plant and so on, all evils which cannot be avoided except by depriving the capitalists of the means of production and, it follows, the organisation of production."

It is wrongly said that today government performs the function of defender of capitalism but that once capitalism is abolished it would become the representative and administrator of the general interest. In the first place capitalism will not be destroyed until the workers, having rid themselves of government, take possession of all social wealth and themselves organise production and consumption in the interests of everybody without waiting for the initiative to come from government which, however willing to comply, would be incapable of doing so.

But there is a further question: if capitalism were to be destroyed and a government were to be left in office, the government, through the concession of all kinds of privileges, would create capitalism anew for, being unable to please everybody it would need an economically powerful class to support it in return for the legal and material protection it would receive.

Consequently privilege cannot be abolished and freedom and equality established firmly and definitely without abolishing government—not this or that government but the very institution of government.

As in all questions of general interest, and especially this one, the consent of the people as a whole is needed, and therefore we must strain every nerve to persuade the people that government is useless as well as harmful, and that we can live better lives without government.

But, as we have repeated more than once, propaganda alone is impotent to convince everybody—and if we were to want to limit ourselves to preaching against government, and in the meantime waiting supinely for the day when the public will be convinced of the possibility and value of radically destroying every kind of government, then that day would never come.

While preaching against every kind of government, and demanding complete freedom, we must support all struggles for partial freedom, because we are convinced that one learns through struggle, and that once one begins to enjoy a little freedom one ends by wanting it all. We must always be with the people, and when we do not succeed in getting them to demand a lot we must still seek to get them to want something; and we must make every effort to get them to understand that however much or little they may demand should be obtained by their own efforts and that they should despise and detest whoever is part of, or aspires to, government.

Since government today has the power, through the legal system, to regulate daily life and to broaden or restrict the liberty of the citizen, and because we are still unable to tear this power from its grasp, we must seek to reduce its power and oblige governments to use it in the least harmful ways possible. But this we must do always remaining outside, and against, government, putting pressure on it through agitation in the streets, by threatening to take by force what we demand. Never must we accept any kind of legislative position, be it national or local, for in so doing we will neutralise the effectiveness of our activity as well as betraying the future of our cause.

* * *

The struggle against government in the last analysis, is physical, material.

Governments make the law. They must therefore dispose of the material forces (police and army) to impose the law, for otherwise only those who wanted to would obey it, and it would no longer be the law, but a simple series of suggestions which all would be free to accept or reject. Governments have this power, however, and use it through the law, to strengthen their power, as well as to serve the interests of the ruling classes, by oppressing and exploiting the workers.

The only limit to the oppression of government is the power with which the people show themselves capable of opposing it. Conflict may be open or latent; but it always exists since the government does not pay attention to discontent and popular resistance except when it is faced with the danger of insurrection.

When the people meekly submit to the law, or their protests are feeble and confined to words, the government studies its own interests and ignores the needs of the people; when the protests are lively, insistent, threatening, the government, depending on whether it is more or less understanding, gives way or resorts to repression. But one always comes back to insurrection, for if the government does not give way, the people will end by rebelling; and if the government does give way, then the people gain confidence in themselves and make ever increasing demands, until such time as the incompatibility between freedom and authority becomes clear and the violent struggle is engaged.

It is therefore necessary to be prepared, morally and materially, so that when this does happen the people will emerge victorious.

* * *

A successful insurrection is the most potent factor in the emancipation of the people, for once the yoke has been shaken off, the people are free to provide themselves with those institutions which they think best, and the time lag between passing the law and the degree of civilisation which the mass of the population has attained, is breached in one leap. The insurrection determines the revolution, that is, the speedy emergence of the latent forces built up during the "evolutionary" period.

Everything depends on what the people are capable of wanting.

In past insurrections unaware of the real reasons for their misfortunes, they have always wanted very little, and have obtained very little.

What will they want in the next insurrection?

The answer, in part, depends on our propaganda and what efforts we put into it.

We shall have to push the people to expropriate the bosses and put all goods in common and organise their daily lives themselves, through freely constituted associations, without waiting for orders from outside and refusing to nominate or recognise any government, any body that claims the right to lay down the law and impose its will on others.

And if the mass of the population will not respond to our appeal we must—in the name of the right we have to be free even if others wish to remain slaves and because of the force of example—put into effect as many of our ideas as we can, refuse to recognise the new government and keep alive resistance and seek that those communes where our ideas are received with sympathy reject all governmental interference and insist on wanting to live their own lives.

We shall have to, above all, oppose with every means the re-establishment of the police and the armed forces, and use any opportunity to incite workers to a general strike that lays the most far reaching demands we can induce them to make.

And however things may go, to continue the struggle against the possessing class and the rulers without respite, having always in mind the complete economic, political and moral emancipation of all mankind.

Recapitulation

What we want, therefore, is the complete destruction of the domination and exploitation of man by man; we want men united as brothers by a conscious and desired solidarity, all cooperating voluntarily for the well-being of all: we want society to be constituted for the purpose of supplying everybody with the means for achieving the maximum well-being, the maximum possible moral and spiritual development; we want bread, freedom, love, and science for everybody.

And in order to achieve these all-important ends, it is necessary in our opinion that the means of production should be at the disposal of everybody and that no man, or group of men, should be in a position to oblige others to submit to their will or to exercise their influence other than through the power of reason and by example.

Therefore: expropriation of landowners and capitalists for the benefit of all; and abolition of government.

And while waiting for the day when this can be achieved: the propagation of our ideas; unceasing struggle, violent or non-violent depending on the circumstances, against government and against the boss class to conquer as much freedom and well-being as we can for the benefit of everybody.

38. THE ANARCHISTS' TASK[1]

What should we do?

That is the question facing us, as indeed it does all who have ideas to put into effect and interests to defend, in every moment of our party life.

We want to do away with private ownership and authority, which is to say we are out to expropriate those who cling to the land and capital, and to overthrow government, and place society's wealth at the disposal of everyone so that everyone may live as he pleases with no other restriction than those imposed by natural and social necessity, *freely* and *voluntarily* recognized and accepted. In short, we are out to implement the anarchist-socialist program. And we are convinced (and day to day experience confirms us in this belief) that the propertied and governments use physical force to protect their ascendancy, so, in order to defeat them, we must of necessity resort to physical force, to violent revolution.

As a result, we are the foes of all privileged classes and all governments, and inimical to all who, albeit with the best of intentions, tend, by their endeavors, to sap the people's revolutionary energy and substitute one government for another.

But what should we do to ensure that we are up to making our revolution, a revolution against all privilege and every authority and that we win?

The best tactic would be for us to spread our ideas always and everywhere; to use all possible means to nurture in proletarians the spirit of combination and resistance and to egg them on to ever greater demands; to be unrelenting in our opposition to every bourgeois party and every authoritarian party and remain unmoved by their complaints; to organize among those who have been won over and are being won over to our ideas and to provide ourselves with the material means needed for struggle; and, once we have built up enough strength to win, to rise up alone, on our own exclusive behalf, to implement our program in its entirety, or, to be more exact, to

1 Translated from "Il compito degli anarchici," *La Questione Sociale* (Paterson, NJ) 5, new series, no. 18 (2 December 1899).

secure for every single person unrestricted freedom to experiment, practice and progressively amend that form of social living that he may feel is best.

But, unfortunately, this tactic cannot always be strictly adhered to and there is no way that it can achieve our purpose. The effectiveness of propaganda is, to say the least, limited, and when, in any given context, all individuals likely, by virtue of their moral and material conditions, to understand and embrace a given set of ideas have been brought on board, there is little more to be achieved by means of the spoken and written word until such time as an alteration in the context elevates a fresh stratum of the population to a position where it can value those ideas. Likewise, the effectiveness of labor organization is limited by the very same factors as inhibit the indefinite spread of propaganda; as well as by broad economic and moral factors that weaken or entirely neutralize the impact of resistance by conscious workers. Our having a strong, vast organization of our own for the purposes of propaganda and struggle runs into a thousand hurdles in ourselves, our lack of resources, and, above all, government repression. And even if it were possible, over time, to arrive by means of propaganda and organization at sufficient strength for us to make the revolution, striking out directly in the direction of anarchist socialism, every passing day, well ahead of our reaching that point of strength, throws up political situations in which we are obliged to take a hand lest we not only lose the benefits to be reaped from them, but indeed lose all sway over the people, thwart part of the work done thus far, and render future work the more daunting.

The problem therefore is to come up with some means whereby, insofar as we can, we bring about those changes in the social environment that are needed if our propaganda is to make headway, and to profit from the conflicts between the various political parties and from every opportunity that presents itself, without surrendering any part of our program, and doing this in such a way as to render victory easier and more imminent.

In Italy, for instance, the situation is such that there is the possibility, the probability sooner or later of an insurrection against the Monarchy. But it is equally certain that the outcome of the next insurrection is not going to be anarchist socialism.

Should we take part in laying the groundwork for, or in mounting, this insurrection? And how?

There are some comrades who reckon that it is not in our interest to engage with a rising that will leave the institution of private property untouched and will simply replace one government with another, that is to say, establish a republic, that would be every bit as bourgeois and oppressive as the monarchy. They say: let us leave the bourgeois and would-be governors to lock horns with one another, while we carry on down our own path, by keeping up our anti-property and anti-authoritarian propaganda.

Now, the upshot of any such abstention on our part would be, first, that in the absence of our contribution, the uprising's chances of success would be lessened and that therefore it might be because of us if the monarchy wins—this monarchy that, particularly at the present moment, when it is fighting for its survival and rendered fierce by fear, bars the way to propaganda and to all progress. What is more, if the rising went ahead without our contribution, we would have no influence over subsequent developments, we would not be able to extract any advantages from the opportunities that always crop up during the period of transition from one regime to the next, we would be discredited as a party of action, and it would take us many a long year before we could accomplish anything of note.

It is not a case of leaving the bourgeois to fight it out among themselves, because in any insurrection the source of strength, material strength at any rate, is always the people and if we are not in on the rising, sharing in the dangers and successes and striving to turn a political upheaval into a social revolution, the people will be merely a tool in the hands of ambitious types eager to lord it over them.

Whereas, by taking part in the insurrection (an insurrection we would never be strong enough to mount on our own), and playing as large a part as we can, we would earn the sympathy of the risen people and would be in a position to push things as far as possible.

We know only too well and never weary of saying so and proving it, that republic and monarchy are equally bad and that all governments have the same tendency to expand their powers and to oppress their subjects more and more. We also know, however, that the weaker a government is, the stronger the resistance to it from among the people, and the wider the freedom available and the chances of progress are. By making an effective contribution to the overthrow of the monarchy, we would be in a position to oppose more or less effectively the establishment or consolidation of a republic, we could remain armed and refuse to obey the new government, and we would be able, here and there, to carry out attempts at expropriation and organization of society along anarchist and communist lines. We could prevent the revolution from being halted at step one, and the people's energies, roused by the insurrection, from being lulled back to sleep. All of these things we would not be able to do, for obvious reasons of popular psychology, by stepping in afterwards, once the insurrection against the monarchy had been mounted and succeeded in our absence.

On the back of these arguments, other comrades would have us set aside our anarchist propaganda for the moment in order to concentrate solely on the fight against the monarchy, and then resume our specifically anarchist endeavours once the insurrection has succeeded. It does not occur to them that if we were to mingle today with the republicans, we would be working for the sake of the coming republic, throw our own ranks into disarray, send the minds of our supporters spinning, and when we wanted to would then not be strong enough to stop the republic from being established and from embedding itself.

Between these two opposite errors, the course to be followed seems quite clear to us.

We must cooperate with the republicans, the democratic socialists, and any other anti-monarchy party to bring down the monarchy; but we must do so as anarchists, in the interests of anarchy, without disbanding our forces or mixing them in with others' forces, and without making any commitment beyond cooperation on military action.

Only thus, as we see it, can we, in the coming events, reap all the benefits of an alliance with the other anti-monarchy parties without surrendering any part of our own program.

39.
TOWARD ANARCHY[1]

It is a general opinion that we, because we call ourselves revolutionists, expect Anarchy to come with one stroke—as the immediate result of an insurrection which violently attacks all that which exists and which replaces it with institutions that are really new. And to say the truth this idea is not lacking among some comrades who also conceive the revolution in such a manner.

This prejudice explains why so many honest opponents believe Anarchy a thing impossible; and it also explains why some comrades, disgusted with the present moral condition of the people and seeing that Anarchy cannot come about soon, waver between an extreme dogmatism which blinds them to the realities of life and an opportunism which practically makes them forget that they are Anarchists and that for Anarchy they should struggle.

Of course the triumph of Anarchy cannot be the consequence of a miracle; it cannot come about in contradiction to the laws of development (an axiom of evolution that nothing occurs without sufficient cause), and nothing can be accomplished without the adequate means.

If we should want to substitute one government for another, that is impose our desires upon others, it would only be necessary to combine the material forces needed to resist the actual oppressors and put ourselves in their place.

But we do not want this; we want Anarchy which is a society based on free and voluntary accord—a society in which no one can force his wishes on another and in which everyone can do as he pleases and together all will voluntarily contribute to the well-being of the community. But because of this Anarchy will not have definitively

---

1 *Man!* (San Francisco) 1, no. 1 (April 1933). Originally published as "Verso l'anarchia," *La Questione Sociale* (Paterson, NJ) 5, new series, no. 14 (9 December 1899). The actual title of *Man!*'s edition and all successive reprints is "Toward anarchism." We have replaced "anarchism" with "anarchy" in the title and throughout the text to rectify a gross mistranslation. The whole article is based on the distinction between "anarchy," the ultimate ideal, and the incessant effort to approach that ideal, which is what "anarchism" is about. Thus translating "anarchia" as "anarchism" completely obfuscates the article's main thrust. We have also made changes in a few places where the translation was unclear or incorrect.

and universally triumphed until all men will not only not want to be commanded but will not want to command; nor will Anarchy have succeeded unless they will have understood the advantages of solidarity and know how to organise a plan of social life wherein there will no longer be traces of violence and imposition.

And as the conscience, determination, and capacity of men continuously develop and find means of expression in the gradual modification of the new environment and in the realization of the desires in proportion to their being formed and becoming imperious, so it is with Anarchy; Anarchy cannot come but little by little—slowly, but surely, growing in intensity and extension.

Therefore, the subject is not whether we accomplish Anarchy today, tomorrow or within ten centuries, but that we walk toward Anarchy today, tomorrow and always.

Anarchy is the abolition of exploitation and oppression of man by man, that is the abolition of private property and government; Anarchy is the destruction of misery, of superstitions, of hatred. Therefore, every blow given to the institutions of private property and to the government, every exaltation of the conscience of man, every disruption of the present conditions, every lie unmasked, every part of human activity taken away from the control of the authority, every augmentation of the spirit of solidarity and initiative, is a step towards Anarchy.

The problem lies in knowing how to choose the road that really approaches the realization of the ideal and in not confusing the real progress with hypocritical reforms. For with the pretext of obtaining immediate ameliorations these false reforms tend to distract the masses from the struggle against authority and capitalism; they serve to paralyze their actions and make them hope that something can be attained through the kindness of the exploiters and governments. The problem lies in knowing how to use the little power we have—that we go on achieving, in the most economical way, more prestige for our goal.

There is in every country a government which, with brutal force, imposes its laws on all; it compels all to be subjected to exploitation and to maintain, whether they like it or not, the existing institutions. It forbids the minority groups to actuate their ideas, and prevents the social organizations in general from modifying themselves according to, and with, the modifications of public opinion. The normal peaceful course of evolution is arrested by violence, and thus with violence it is necessary to reopen that course. It is for this reason that we want a violent revolution today; and we shall want it always—so long as man is subject to the imposition of things contrary to his natural desires. Take away the governmental violence, ours would have no reason to exist.

We cannot as yet overthrow the prevailing government; perhaps tomorrow from the ruins of the present government we cannot prevent the arising of another similar one. But this does not hinder us, nor will it tomorrow, from resisting whatever form of authority—refusing always to submit to its laws whenever possible, and constantly using force to oppose force.

Every weakening of whatever kind of authority, each accession of liberty will be a progress toward Anarchy; always it should be conquered—never asked for; always it should serve to give us greater strength in the struggle; always it should make us consider the state as an enemy with whom we should never make peace; always it should make us remember well that the decrease of the ills produced by the government consists in the decrease of its attributions and powers, not in increasing the number of rulers or in having them chosen by the ruled. By government we mean any person or group of persons in the state, country, community, or association who has the right to make laws and inflict them upon those who do not want them.

We cannot as yet abolish private property; we cannot regulate the means of production which is necessary to work freely; perhaps we shall not be able to do so in the next insurrectional movement. But this does not prevent us now, or will it in the future, from continually opposing capitalism. And each victory, however small, gained by the workers against their exploiters, each decrease of profit, every bit of wealth taken from the individual owners and put to the disposal of all, shall be a progress—a forward step toward Anarchy. Always it should serve to enlarge the claims of the workers and to intensify the struggle; always it should be accepted as a victory over an enemy and not as a concession for which we should be thankful; always we should remain firm in our resolution to take with force, as soon as it will be possible, those means which the private owners, protected by the government, have stolen from the workers.

The right of force having disappeared, the means of production being placed under the management of whomever wants to produce, the rest must be the fruit of a peaceful evolution.

It would not be Anarchy, yet, or it would be only for those few who want it, and only in those things they can accomplish without the cooperation of the non-anarchists. This does not necessarily mean that the ideal of Anarchy will make little or no progress, for little by little its ideas will extend to more men and more things until it will have embraced all mankind and all life's manifestations.

Having overthrown the government and all the existing dangerous institutions which with force it defends, having conquered complete freedom for all and with it the right to the means of production, without which liberty would be a lie, and while we are struggling to arrive to this point, we do not intend to destroy those things which we little by little will reconstruct.

For example, there functions in the present society the service of supplying food. This is being done badly, chaotically, with great waste of energy and material and in view of capitalist interests; but after all, one way or another we must eat. It would be absurd to want to disorganize the system of producing and distributing food unless we could substitute it with something better and more just.

There exists a postal service. We have thousands of criticisms to make, but in the meantime we use it to send our letters, and shall continue to use it, suffering all its faults, until we shall be able to correct or replace it.

There are schools, but how badly they function. But because of this we do not allow our children to remain in ignorance—refusing their learning to read and write. Meanwhile we wait and struggle for a time when we shall be able to organise a system of model schools to accomodate all.

From this we can see that, to arrive at Anarchy, material force is not the only thing to make a revolution; it is essential that the workers, grouped according to the various branches of production, place themselves in a position that will insure the proper functioning of their social life—without the aid or need of capitalists or governments.

And we see also that the Anarchist ideals are far from being in contradiction, as the "scientific socialists" claim, to the laws of evolution as proved by science; they are a conception which fits these laws perfectly; they are the experimental system brought from the field of research to that of social realization.

London, May 1912. Malatesta awaiting trial at the Central Criminal Court

V.

"The Armed Strike": The Long London Exile of 1900–13

The twentieth century, which opened with Gaetano Bresci's killing of king Humbert I, also marked the beginning of Malatesta's longest exile in London. During these years Malatesta coherently reasserted the two pillars of his tactics: the reliance on the workers' movement and the anarchists' necessity to be at its forefront; and the inescapability of insurrection as a step toward emancipation, and therefore the necessity to prepare for it. The target of Malatesta's argument had changed, though. Whereas, in the previous decade, it was the former point he had to argue for, the rising of syndicalism—with its theory of the self-sufficiency of the workers' movement—had now made it necessary to emphasize the latter point. Therefore Malatesta countered the syndicalist idea of the general strike as the decisive revolutionary weapon with the advocacy of the "armed strike." In re-asserting his distinction between inclusive workers' unions, open to workers of all political colors, and organizations with a clear anarchist orientation, Malatesta showed that he had learned from the mistakes of the First International, at the same time that he had remained true to its spirit.

40. THE MONZA TRAGEDY[1]

Another act of bloodshed has come along to cast a pall over sensitive souls... and to remind the mighty that placing oneself above the people and riding roughshod over the great precept of equality and human solidarity is not without its risks.

Gaetano Bresci, worker and anarchist, has killed Humbert the king. Two men: one prematurely dead, the other condemned to a life of torments a thousand times worse than death! Two families plunged into grief!

Where does the blame lie?

Whenever we criticize established institutions and point out the unspeakable pain and countless deaths they cause, we never fail to caution that such institutions are harmful, not just to the broad proletarian masses thrust into poverty, ignorance, and all the other woes that spring from poverty and ignorance because of them, but also to the very privileged minority that suffers, physically and morally, from the tainted environment that it conjures up and that lives in constant fear of the people's wrath making it pay a high price for its privileges.

Whenever we look forward to redemptive revolution, we are always talking about the benefits for all men without distinction; and we mean that, regardless of the competing interests and party loyalties by which they are divided today, they should all set aside hatred and resentments and join as brothers in shared striving for the well-being of all.

And every time that capitalists and governments perpetrate some extraordinarily criminal act, every time that innocents are tortured, every time the savagery of the powerful erupts into bloodshed, we deplore that fact, not merely because of the pain it directly generates

1 Translated from "La tragedia di Monza," *Cause ed Effetti, 1898–1900* (London), September 1900. This was a one-off publication that meant to provide an anarchist perspective on the killing of King Humbert I by the anarchist Gaetano Bresci, which occurred in Monza on 29 July 1900. The title translates as "causes and effects," and the date range that follows provides the key to the title: 1898 was the year of the bread riots that tragically ended in May with the cannon shots by which the troops of general Bava Beccaris killed hundreds of workers in Milan. A few weeks later, King Humbert conferred a decoration to the general for his services rendered "to the institutions and to civilization." That was the cause. Bresci's bullets, by which he avowedly intended to avenge the Milan bloodshed, were the effect.

and for the trespass against our sense of fairness and mercy, but also on account of the legacy of hatred it leaves in its wake and the seed of vengeance it plants in the minds of the oppressed.

But our warnings go unheeded; on the contrary, they are used as a pretext for persecution.

And then, when the pent-up anger of protracted tortures bursts into a storm, when a man driven to despair or a generous soul moved by the suffering of his brethren and impatient for sluggish justice to arrive, raises an avenging arm and strikes at what he reckons is the cause of the woe, then the guilty parties, the ones responsible... are us.

It is always the lamb that gets the blame!

Nonsensical conspiracies are concocted, we are fingered as a threat to society; they pretend to believe—and maybe some actually do believe—that we are bloodthirsty criminals whose only choice should be between the penitentiary and the criminal asylum...

Besides, it is only natural that things should be so. In a land where the likes of Crispi, Rudinì, Pelloux, and all those who have slaughtered and starved the people can live free, are powerful and are feted, there can be no place for the likes of us who protest and rebel against massacre and famishment!

But let us leave the incorrigible police personnel to one side; let us leave to one side the interested parties who lie in the full knowledge that they are lying; let us leave aside the cowards who turn on us in order to ward off any blows that might land also upon them—and let us reason for a moment with people of good faith and common sense.

***

For a start, let us bring things back into proportion.

A king has been killed; and since a king is, for all that, still a man, that fact is to be deplored. A queen has been made a widow; and since a queen is, for all that, still a woman, she has our sympathy in her loss.

But why all the brouhaha over the death of one man and over the tears of one woman when the fact that so many men are being killed on a daily basis and so many women left to weep because of wars, accidents at work, revolts crushed by gunshots, and thousands of crimes spawned by poverty, spirit of vengefulness, fanaticism, and alcoholism is accepted as natural?

Why such an outpouring of sentimentality over one particular misfortune when thousands and millions of human beings are perishing of starvation and malaria, to the indifference of those who might have the wherewithal to stop this?

Perhaps it is because, this time, the victims are not vulgar workers, not some nondescript man and woman, but a king and a queen? ... Actually, we take a greater interest in the case and our grief is more poignant, livelier, more authentic, when we are dealing with a miner crushed by a landslide while working and a widow left behind to perish of hunger with her little children!

Nevertheless, the sufferings of royals are human suffering too and are to be deplored. But lamentations are pointless if one does not look into the root causes and try to eliminate them.

***

Who is it that provokes the violence? Who is it that makes it necessary and inescapable?

The entire established social order is founded upon brute force harnessed for the purposes of a tiny minority that exploits and oppresses the vast majority; all of the education delivered to children boils down to an unrelenting paean to brute force; the whole atmosphere in which we live is an unbroken parade of violence, a continual incitement to violence.

The soldier, which is to say the murderer-by-profession, is revered. And most revered of all is the king, whose most distinguishing feature, historically, has been that he commands soldiers.

By brute force, the laborer is obliged to suffer the theft of the product of his labors; by brute force, weaker nations are robbed of their independence.

The kaiser of Germany urges his troops to give the Chinese no quarter; the British government treats Boers who refuse to bow to the foreign bully as rebels and puts their farms to the torch, hunts down housewives and even pursues non-combatants and re-enacts Spain's ghastly feats in Cuba; the Sultan has the Armenians slaughtered by the hundreds of thousands; and the American government massacres the Filipinos, having first cravenly betrayed them.

Capitalists send workers to their deaths in the mines, on the railways, in the paddy fields by refusing to make the necessary expenditure on safety at work. They summon in soldiers to intimidate and, if need be, gun down workers calling for better conditions.

Again we ask: from whom, therefore, comes the incitement, the provocation to violence? Who is it that makes violence look like the only way out of the existing state of affairs, the only means whereby one may not be eternally subjected to the violence of others?

And in Italy, things are worse than elsewhere. The people are perennially hungry; our lordlings are more cavalier than during the Middle Ages; the government competes with the property owners, bleeding the people in order to line the pockets of its favorites and squandering the rest on dynastic ventures; the police have the power of yea or nay over citizens' freedom, and every cry of protest, every stifled lament is strangled by gaolers and smothered in blood by soldiers.

The list of massacres here is a lengthy one: ranging from Pietrarsa to Conselice, Caltabiano, Sicily, etc.

The king's troops massacred the defenseless people just about two years ago; just days ago the king's troops afforded the landowners of Molinella the support of their bayonets and their conscript labor against famished, desperate workers.

Who is to blame for the rebellion, who is to blame for the revenge that erupts from time to time: the provocateur, the offender, or the man who denounces the offence and seeks to banish its cause?

But the king is not responsible, they say!

We certainly do not take the farce of constitutional shadow play seriously. The "liberal" newspapers, which now contend that the king is not accountable, were well aware, when it came to themselves, that above parliament and ministers there was a powerful influence, a "higher echelon," that the king's prosecutors would not countenance to be alluded to too bluntly. And the conservatives currently looking forward to a vigorous "new age" from the new king, indicate that they know that—in Italy at any rate—when it comes to identifying responsibility, the king is not the puppet they would have us believe. And besides, even if he does not do the harm directly, any man who fails to prevent it, though is able to do so, is still answerable for it—and the soldier-commanding king can always, at the least, stop his soldiers from opening fire on the defenseless populace. And is still responsible if, unable to prevent evil's being done, he allows it to be done in his name rather than abjure the benefits of his office.

True, if factors such as heredity, education, ethos are taken into account, the personal responsibility of the mighty is greatly attenuated and may well evaporate altogether. But then, if the king is not answerable for his actions and his omissions—for the people's being massacred in his name—and allegedly had to remain in the highest office in the land, why on earth should Bresci be held to account? Why on earth must Bresci pay with a lifetime of unspeakable suffering for one deed that, no matter how wrong-headed one might like to think it, no one can deny was prompted by altruistic intentions?

But this business of tracing responsibility is of mediocre interest to us.

We are not believers in the right to punish, we repudiate revenge as a barbaric notion; we do not mean to be either executioners or avengers. The calling of liberators and peacemakers strikes us as a holier, nobler, more productive calling.

We would gladly reach out our hand to kings, oppressors, and exploiters just as soon as they made up their minds to be again men like any others, equals surrounded by equals. But for as long as they persist in revelling in the existing order of things and defending it by the use of force, thereby leading to torment, brutalization, and death from exhaustion for millions of human creatures, we need and are obliged to meet force with force.

***

Meet force with force!

Does that mean that we revel in melodramatic conspiracies and are always in the throes of or bent on stabbing some oppressor?

Nothing like that. As a matter of sentiment and principle, we abhor violence and always do whatever we can to avoid it; only the necessity of resisting evil through suitably effective means could induce us to have recourse to violence.

We know that such singular acts of violence, in the absence of sufficient preparation by the people, remain futile and indeed, by triggering backlashes against which one cannot stand, they generate incalculable injury to the very cause they were intended to serve.

We know that the essential, incontrovertibly purposeful act lies not in the physical killing of a king but in killing all kings—from courts, parliaments and factories—in the hearts and minds of people; meaning the eradication of belief in the authority principle worshipped by so many of the people.

We know that the less ripe revolution is, the bloodier and more uncertain it proves to be.

We know that, violence being the font of authority—indeed, at its core, one and the same as the authority principle—the more violent the revolution turns out to be, the greater the risk that it may spawn fresh forms of authority.

And so, before deploying the ultimate arguments of the oppressed, we strive to acquire that moral and material strength that is needed to minimize the violence needed to bring down the system of violence to which humanity is presently subjected.

Will we be left in peace to get on with our propaganda work and our organizing and preparations for revolution?

In Italy, they prevent us from speaking, writing, and associating. They ban workers from joining together to struggle peaceably, not just for emancipation but also for the slightest improvement in their uncivilized and inhumane living conditions. Prisons, *domicilio coatto*, and bloody repressions are the means deployed not just against us anarchists, but against anyone who dares to contemplate a more civilized state of affairs.

Is it any wonder if, having lost all hope of fighting successfully in their own cause, ardent spirits let themselves be swept up into acts of vengeful justice?

***

The police measures that always victimize the least dangerous; the zealous search for non-existing instigators, which looks grotesque to anyone with the slightest grasp of the spirit that prevails among anarchists; and the thousands of farcical extermination schemes advanced by dabblers in police work, all of these serve only to highlight the savagery lurking inside the heads of the ruling classes.

If a bloody revolt by the victims is to be utterly ruled out, there is no course of action except the abolition of oppression by means of social justice.

If eruptions are to be reduced and disarmed, there is no recourse other than to allow everybody freedom to propagandize and organize; for the disinherited, the oppressed, and the discontented to be left the option of civilized campaigning; for them to be afforded the hope that, albeit piecemeal, they might secure their own emancipation by bloodless methods.

The government of Italy will have none of this; it will carry on with its repression... and it will carry on reaping what it sows.

While we deplore the short-sightedness of rulers who make the contest unnecessarily harsh, we shall carry on fighting for a society without violence, in which all will have bread, freedom, and science, and where love is the supreme law of existence.

41.
THE ARMED STRIKE[1]

We are promised the likely appearance of a new Spanish-language anarchist newspaper, entitled *The Armed Strike.*

Its title defines its program.

Whether the planned publication comes off or not, we hope that the title will be taken up and become the motto of a brand new approach to revolutionary tactics. Words and slogans are of great importance in popular movements; and the expression "armed strike" may prove very useful, in that it is the happiest encapsulation of a pressing need at the present time. And it is good that it has come from Spain where there is already a mass of organized and conscious workers who have already shown what they are worth and who are better placed than anyone else to demonstrate the new tactics by practical example.

The propaganda for the general strike has done and is still doing an immense amount of good.

By pointing out to workers an effective means with which they can emancipate themselves, it demolishes blind and harmful belief in parliamentary and legislative methods; it banishes from the workers' movement the ambitious types on the look-out for a springboard to power; it provides revolutionaries with the means of involving the great toiling masses in the struggle and poses that struggle in such terms that a radical transformation of social relations must naturally and well-nigh automatically ensue.

But the big benefits of this propaganda and the success it has had, have given rise to a grave danger that threatens the very cause it promotes.

The illusion has been forming that the revolution can be made almost peaceably, by folding one's arms and reducing the bosses to discretion by simply refusing to work for them. And by dint of repetition of the great importance of the economic struggle, it has been all but overlooked that, beside and defending the boss who keeps us hungry, there is the government that famishes and kills.

---

1 Translated from "Lo sciopero armato," *Lo Sciopero Generale* (London) 1, no. 3 (2 June 1902).

In Barcelona, in Trieste, in Belgium, the price of this illusion has already been paid in the blood of the people.[2] The strike has almost entirely been mounted without arms and without any definite intention of deploying what very few there were—and with a few volleys the governments have restored order.

When thought of as merely a law-abiding, peaceful strike, the general strike is a nonsensical idea.

To begin with, given the proletariat's circumstances and the specific nature of farm production, it can be *general* only in a manner of speaking; in actuality, it will merely be the handiwork of a more forward-looking minority—a forceful minority capable of deploying its moral and material energies on the steering of events—but it will always be a numerically tiny minority that could only have a brief impact on the scales of production and consumption. But even if we supposed the strike to be authentically general, that would makes things even more nonsensical—provided, we say again, that it be thought of in terms of a lawful, peaceable movement.

What would there be to eat? What would be used to purchase life's necessities?

The workers will have starved to death well before the bourgeois are forced to give up any morsel of their surplus.

So, if one wants to mount a general strike, one has to be ready to seize possession of the means of existence, despite any of the alleged rights of private ownership. But then along come the troops and one must flee or fight.

So, if we know that the strike will necessarily lead to a clash with armed force and turn into a revolution, why not say so and make our preparations?

Must this inept farce of periodical clashes, in which proletarian deaths are numbered in the hundreds with scarcely a soldier or policeman struck by a stone, carry on for all eternity?

Let us go on strike, but let us do so in circumstances in which

---

2 In February 1902, a strike of the Barcelona metal workers developed into a city-wide general strike, during which about thirty workers were killed in street fighting. In Trieste, it was a strike of the stokers at Lloyd Austriaco's shipping company that gave rise to a general strike in the city. A great demonstration took place on 15 February 1902, at the end of which fourteen workers were left dead. In Belgium, a general strike against the plural vote system was called on 13 April 1902. On the night of 18 April, the civil guard fired into a crowd of protestors, injuring fourteen and killing six.

we can defend ourselves. Since the police and the troops show up wherever a clash between bosses and workers occurs, let us ensure that we are in a position to command their respect.

Revolutionaries should arm themselves so that they are ready to make the revolution whenever the opportunity arises. Non-revolutionary workers should arm themselves as well, if only to avoid being beaten like so many sheep.

Even with their savings, proletarians will never be in a position to amass the capital needed to fight the bosses' capital; but with a modicum of good will they may well get their hands on a revolver. And a mob of strikers armed with revolvers or any other weapons commands a lot more respect than one blessed with a strike fund, no matter how swollen.

Long live the general strike, but let it be an ARMED STRIKE.

42. IN RELATION TO STRIKES[1]

The United States, France, and Spain are the scene of important and more or less violent strikes. Because of a strike, in the past fortnight Geneva has seen civic life brought to a standstill, republican troops combing the street sabring the population, and the government arresting, expelling, and harassing.

The intervals between editions of our newspaper and distance from the places for which it is bound preclude us from chronicling the events that the comrades should be monitoring attentively through the daily newspapers. All we can do is draw attention to the lessons deriving from them.

The ever-growing frequency of strikes and the scale that these are achieving, now deeply disrupting the life of society and rattling the very foundations of the State, clearly show that simultaneous suspension of work as determined and implemented by the workers for whatever reason has now become a great training ground, and will very likely be the occasion from which will spring the final insurrection that will end Society's current, nonsensical and murderous make up.

Hence, it is of the utmost importance for us anarchists, who want to spark that insurrection, to place ourselves in a position where we can exercise a decisive influence upon the course of these strikes and on the organization of labor from which the strikes derive. So the greatest and most pressing issue claiming our attention and requiring our consideration at the present moment is none other than the purpose by which we should be guided and the tactics that are to be espoused in our engagement with the workers' organization and strikes.

Of the workers' organization, more on another occasion: today we shall have something to say about strikes.

***

If economic forces were all that was involved in disputes between capitalists and proletarians, the strike would be doomed to inevitable

1 Translated from "A proposito di scioperi," *La Rivoluzione Sociale* (London), no. 2 (18 October 1902).

defeat. In the battle between millions and pennies, between the propertied gambling with a part of their wealth and the workers who have no bread for tomorrow and are racked by the screams of their famished offspring, the latter are usually routed by the former. And even when due to some exceptionally favorable circumstance, a strike proves successful, its outcome, in terms of the wages that the worker gets and the purchasing power of those wages, proves to be an illusion. Having been, for a pretty long time without a wage and having braved often harrowing suffering, the successful striker sees his meagre earning boosted by a few pennies... but then realizes that the bosses recoup these from consumers, that the cost of things rises as wages rise and that, ultimately, even with more money, he cannot afford any more than he used to buy and is, consequently, as badly off as ever.

But there are moral and political forces at work that change the terms of the problem and lead, or may lead, to different outcomes.

Besides being an economic dispute, a strike is a moral revolt. The worker who goes on strike and risks famishment for himself and his loved ones in order to win some improvement in his conditions is no longer the docile and compliant slave who endures oppression without a murmur as if it were some inescapable inevitability. He asserts his rights, or at any rate some of his rights, and demonstrates that he has realized that for the acknowledgment of those rights he should await neither the grace of God nor the beneficence of the mighty, but must look to his own strength in association with the strength of those in his same position. And this means that he gets better treatment, because, when all is said and done, collectively speaking, the bosses can only treat folk as badly as folk will allow. And meanwhile, the worker comes to desire a better standard of living and acquires a clear appreciation of the antagonism there is between his interests and the bosses' interests and of the need to do away with the master class so that labor can be emancipated.

That, in essence, is the only good that can come of strikes and so anarchists should take an interest in them from the point of view of the economics and try to steer them to victory, not through passive resistance sustained over as long a time as possible thanks to strike funds and subscriptions, but by espousing an aggressive attitude and having recourse to all possible means in order to show that the workers are serious about wanting what they want and will not allow it to be withheld with impunity.

***

Two phenomena, not new to be sure, but which are becoming increasingly serious and widespread, can be discerned in the current strikes.

One is the meddling of the State, in the form of gendarmes and soldiers, in clashes between capital and labor. Whether we are talking about feudal, monarchist Spain, or about France, Switzerland, or America—republican, democratic countries—always and everywhere the government massacres strikers.

Must we give up on every demand and submit unconditionally to the whims of the capitalists, or allow ourselves to be slaughtered eternally?

Let us leave the preaching of patience and calm to those who view the slaughter of the people as an opportunity for them to go fishing for a parliamentary seat... and issue an interpellation to the minister. We, who know the worth of deputies and their interpellations and who seek ultimately to revolutionize the world by means of agitation and revolts, should be pointing out to the workers how, these days, every strike is wide open to military repression and coax them to prepare themselves just as they would for an insurrection.

These days, strike funds are not the issue any more. With the mass strikes being mounted these days and the coalitions the bosses have learned to form, it would be extremely laughable of the workers to try to compete in monetary terms. The workers are starting to realize this and are showing a tendency to turn to different means. Governments are fully aware of the dangers of this trend and are placing their rifles and artillery at the bosses' disposal. The point is to counter those rifles and artillery with suitable weaponry: that is all.

The other phenomenon is that the *scabs* or "*yellows,*" as they are called in France these days, are beginning to stand up brazenly to the organized workers and even to pit organization against organization. This is a very serious development because it triggers strife between one worker and another, which is wholly to the benefit of the bosses and generates hostility, begrudgery, and hatred that may yet prove a tremendous obstacle to the success of the proletarian revolution.

"Scabbing"—to wit, the existence of workers who feel and practise no solidarity with their fellow workers and who are on the bosses' side and work for cut-price wages and take the strikers' jobs—is a sadly necessary feature of a society that cannot provide work for all its members and reduces so many men to the condition of starving livestock who care nothing and can care nothing except for the pursuit of a crust of bread. At the same time, it is largely the fault of the organized workers themselves, who purport to be conscious of their class interests. Eager to take the capitalists on within the confines of the law, they have sought to restrict the availability of jobs as much as possible, and so, whilst on the one hand they insist that the bosses should not hire non-union labor, on the other, as soon as their unions have felt strong enough, they have placed obstacles in the path of new members' joining their number, reduced the numbers of apprentices and gone to war on foreign labor... and have thereby been a mighty help to the growth of scabbery. Heedless of the needs of the jobless and unskilled, have they any real right to whine if the latter do not feel bound to them by bonds of solidarity and steal their jobs out from under them when the opportunity presents itself?

In the ranks of the enemy, there are certainly some of a slavish turn of mind; they are poor unfortunates who might attain human consciousness and dignity only by means of material comfort and fraternal treatment. But there are those, too, who feel repugnance at what they are doing and do it only out of harsh necessity. We can still remember what one American scab told a reporter a few years back: "That mine is a thuggish and odious part, I know," he said, "but there you have it! I haven't been able to find regular employment for years. I can't get into the factories because I am not a member of the union and they won't have me in the union because I am out of work and can't pay the entrance fee. The strike has opened up my chances of working. I know that once the strike is over there will be no more job for me, but then I knew it would not have been there even had I stood four-square by the strikers. My kids were starving to death and I had to send them out and go myself to pick through the garbage cans for leftovers; and my wife held me to blame for our wretchedness. A chance to eat came along and I grabbed it. Did I do wrong? I don't know; in the meantime I eat and I can see smiles on the faces of my kids who knew only how to cry! Now the strikers are threatening me and might attack me at any moment. I go armed and may well kill somebody. It's ghastly! ... but I cannot let myself be killed without fighting back. Like it or not, my sense of duty towards my kids stops me from doing so."

Who would dare to condemn that man in the name of labor

solidarity, of which he has borne all the brunt without ever having tasted any of the benefits?

Yet it is only natural and human for strikers to feel angry with those who turn up to take their jobs, but we who are guided by loftier principles must temper that anger with a dose of logic and justice. Why attack scabs, who are our brothers, albeit a little more ignorant and a lot more unfortunate than us, rather than the bosses who are the source of both of our misfortunes? In any event, no matter which comes under attack, the police step in and we have to toe the line or fight back. Better to attack the real enemy, therefore.

***

If the current trend towards big and fairly general strikes is to deliver the beneficial revolutionary effects with which it is laden, rather than petering out gradually due to weariness and loss of heart, giving way to long years of monotonous calm, the workers have to get it into their heads that the strike should not be an end in itself but rather a tool for transforming society. And the task of getting this across to them falls to the anarchists.

Let us take the example of the coalminers' strike in America.

This tragicomedy has been going on for years now. The workers ask for improvements, and the bosses, who have large stocks of coal to fall back on, refuse them. The workers go on strike and suffer and leave the public—the poorer, coal-less part of the public—to suffer. Meanwhile the bosses sell off their stocks at higher prices. Once those stocks are approaching the point of exhaustion, negotiations and compromises set in and the workers are granted some of what they were asking for. Then, gradually, as the stocks are rebuilt, the bosses snatch back the concessions they made until the workers put new demands ... and it starts all over again.

Likewise, this time around. By the time of writing, the dispute will probably have been settled. The miners' long months of suffering, of wretchedness and distress and the countless deaths caused among the poorer classes of Americans by lack of coal will have served only as yet another act in the usual farce.

But what great consequences might ensue from the situation if only the strikers' mentality and that of their leaders were different!

The miners' strike can get nowhere unless the railwaymen simultaneously refuse to carry the coal that the bosses are holding in reserve. In America, the railwaymen are organized just as the miners are and are federated with them; and if there was no rail strike, this was because the leaders could not be sure where going down that road might lead them and were afraid of seeing their economic and political standing compromised.

The impoverished population of the big American cities, to whom coal shortage matters as much as bread shortage does to us, were irritated and full of menace. If the miners and railwaymen had by common consent set about working the mines and shipping the coal themselves on the people's behalf, organizing distribution free of charge along the route and receiving whatever folk might have been willing to give them in return, the populace would have vigorously backed the strikers' bold initiative.

The government would assuredly have stepped in … come of that what might. But the world's great revolutions were made with more paltry causes and means and much more modest principles!

***

The objection will be made that this is all more easily said than done and we readily agree with that. We will be told that the people are not ready, not ripe for such things, and we agree. Had the people been ready, had the people been ripe, they would have done so without waiting for advice from us.

But everything has to start somewhere. Today, and right from the outset, the American labor movement seems to have been made more for the benefit of its leaders than for the workers. Starting with the president who enjoys a ministerial salary and wields considerable political influence, and right down to the merest branch secretary, there is a whole hierarchy of employees who live off the movement and, having lost the habit of working and developed a taste for being regarded as important personages, fear nothing so much as they fear having to return to the mines and toil like common working men. This is the main reason why the entire movement boils down to a monotonous round inside a vicious circle. They deal with the government and threaten and make concessions and enter into compromises … but ultimately they take care that everything is done according to the law, quietly, and ending in blessed peace. That way they can hang on to the friendship or at any rate tolerance of the government and the bosses, their sway over the workers and their salaries.

If the workers could be persuaded to break free of all these parasites and look after their own affairs themselves, strikes would soon take on a different character. And with relentless active propaganda, propaganda by spoken word and example, what may look today like a utopia might soon become a fact.

The road may be long or may be short, depending on circumstances—what counts above all else is the direction in which one moves.

43. THE WORKERS' NEW INTERNATIONAL[1]

The grandiose workers' movement that is emerging across the whole of the civilized world and the ever-more apparent need for solidarity between workers in every land so that they may stand up to the progressive internationalization of capitalism inevitably had to plant and have planted in the heads of many the idea of establishing a new International Working Men's Association. And the international Federations established between the workers from certain trades, such as the fossil coal miners and transport workers are themselves a step in the direction of a general union of all workers conscious of their class interests.

It might not be without its uses at this point to remind ourselves of the lessons of past experience, scrutinizing what the mission of the old International was and the reasons that led to its demise.

The life of the renowned International Working Men's Association was brief but glorious. Born into a time similar to the present, a time of labor awakening, it died quickly and genuinely succeeded in shaking the world. It weaned the workers away from following bourgeois parties and endowed them with a class consciousness, a program of their own and a policy of their own; it broached and debated all the most essential social issues and devised the whole of modern socialism, which some writers then claimed was the product of their own heads; it set the mighty quaking, roused the ardent hopes of the oppressed, inspired sacrifices and heroism... and just as it most looked fated to lay capitalist society to rest, it disintegrated and perished.

How come?

The break-up of the International is conventionally ascribed either to persecution or to the personal frictions that emerged within its ranks, or to the manner of its organization, or to all of the above.

I am of a different mind.

---

1 Translated from "La nuova Internazionale dei Lavoratori," *La Rivoluzione Sociale* (London), no. 4 (5 November 1902).

Persecution would have been powerless to break up the Association and often fostered its popularity and growth.

The personal frictions were actually only a secondary concern and, as long as the movement was vibrant, were inclined rather to spur the various factions and most prominent personalities into action.

The manner of its organization, having grown centralistic and authoritarian thanks to the handiwork of the General Council in London and especially of Karl Marx who was the driving force behind it, actually resulted in the International's splitting into two branches: but the federalist, anarchist branch that included the federations from Spain, Italy, francophone Switzerland, Belgium, southern France, and individual sections from other countries did not long outlive the authoritarian branch. It will be argued that even within the anarchist branch the authoritarian blight endured and that, there too, a few individuals were able to do and undo in the name of the masses who passively followed them. And that is the truth. But it is worth noting that in this instance, the authoritarianism was unintended and did not derive from the organizational format nor from the principles informing it, but was the natural and logical consequence of the phenomenon to which I chiefly ascribe the break-up of the Association and which I am about to spell out.

Within the International, founded as a federation of resistance societies in order to provide a broader base for the economic struggle against capitalism, two schools of thought very quickly surfaced, one authoritarian and the other libertarian; these split the Internationalists into two hostile factions, which, at least in their extreme wings, were associated with the names of Marx and Bakunin.

One group was out to turn the Association into a disciplined body under the command of a Central Committee, whereas the others wanted a free federation of autonomous groups; one group was out to bring the masses in line in order to do it good by force, according to the hoary authoritarian superstition, whereas the others were out to raise them up and get them to set themselves free. But the inspirations behind both factions had one distinguishing feature in common, and that is that each side passed on their thoughts to the body of the membership, reckoning that they had converted them when they had actually only secured their pretty much unthinking support.

Thus we saw the International quickly turning mutualist, collectivist, communist, revolutionary, and anarchist at a rate of development documented in the proceedings of its congresses and in the periodical press, but which simply could not have been reflective of any actual and simultaneous evolution in the vast majority of members.

Since there were no separate agencies for the economic struggle and the political and ideological struggle, and every Internationalist did all his thinking and fighting activity within the International, the inevitable outcome was either that the most advanced individuals would have had to stoop to and stay at the level of the slow-moving, backward mass or, as happened, stride ahead and proceed on their way with the illusion that the masses understood and was following them.

These more advanced elements pondered, debated, discovered the needs of the people; they framed the vague intuitions of the masses into concrete programs; they affirmed socialism; they affirmed anarchy; they divined and prepared for the future—but they killed the Association: the sword had worn out the sheath.

Not that I am saying that this was a bad thing. Had the International remained a straightforward federation for resistance and not been buffeted by the storm of ideas and partisan passions, it might have survived as the English Trade Unions have, as things useless and perhaps even harmful to the cause of human emancipation. It was better that it should have perished and tossed its fertile seeds to the winds.

But I hold that today the old-school International cannot and should not be remade. Today there are thriving socialist and anarchist movements; the illusion and error that sustained the old International are no longer possible today.

The factors that ultimately killed off the old International—namely, the frictions between authoritarians and libertarians on the one hand and the gulf between the thinkers and the semi-conscious masses driven only by interests, on the other—are likely today to thwart the birth and growth of a new International, should it be, as the first one was, simultaneously a society for economic resistance, a workshop of ideas, and a revolutionary association.

The new International can only serve as an association designed to marshal all workers (which is to say, as many as it can), without regard to social, political, or religious outlook, in the fight against capitalism. Thus it should be neither individualist, nor collectivist, nor communist; it must be neither monarchist nor republican, nor anarchist; and should be neither religious nor anti-religious. It should have a single shared thought upon which entry into it is conditional: a willingness to fight the bosses.

Hatred of the bosses is the beginning of salvation.

If later on, enlightened by propaganda, educated by the struggle in tracing the causes of woes and searching for radical remedies, and encouraged by the example of the revolutionary parties, the bulk of the membership were to burst into socialist, anarchist, and anti-religious assertions so much the better; since the progress would then be real rather than illusory.

Of course, it is not that I would not like to see the new International Working Men's Association be socialist and anarchist; I would just like it to be genuinely so.

And for that to be a possibility, it needs to happen freely and gradually, as consciences expand and understanding spreads.

AN OLD INTERNATIONALIST

44. BOURGEOIS SEEPAGE INTO SOCIALIST DOCTRINE[1]

For some time now, in order to justify the path of surrender upon which they have embarked, the reformist socialists have begun tinkering, not merely with socialism's tactics but also with its theories. And so, little by little, a number of essentially bourgeois ideas and even moral, political, and economic prejudices have been seeping into socialist doctrine.

Just how serious this situation is can readily be understood if we think that this is nowadays evident, not just among the more moderate factions of the democratic socialist party, but other factions, which brag of being more revolutionary and uncompromising, are also being blighted.

For instance, even Arturo Labriola, the celebrated Italian socialist intransigent, a while ago—so the newspapers reported—argued in a talk he gave that "the issue requiring urgent resolution is not the issue of wealth distribution, but that of the rational organisation of production."

This is so wrong, that we would do well to dwell upon it, because it compromises the very foundations of the socialist doctrine, and conclusions that can logically be deduced from it are anything but socialist.

***

Ever since Malthus, conservatives of every hue have argued that poverty derives, not from the unfair distribution of wealth, but from limited productivity or inadequate human industry.

In terms of its historical origins and very essence, socialism is a rebuttal of this contention; it amounts to an emphatic assertion that the social question is primarily an issue of social justice, a distribution issue. But ever since socialists began negotiating with power and with the propertied classes—that is, ever since they stopped being socialists—they have, albeit in a slightly more modern form, begun to embrace the conservative argument.

---

1 Translated from "Infiltrazioni borghesi nella dottrina socialista," *Il Pensiero* (Rome) 3, no. 10 (16 May 1905).

If the thesis backed by Labriola were true, it would then be untrue that the antagonism between bosses and workers is irreconcilable, since the solution to it would be the shared interest that bosses and wage earners have in boosting the quantum of goods; that is, socialism would be wrong, at least as a means of solving the social question. And actually, we have already heard Turati argue that during strikes the workers must take care not to ruin the boss and his industry; and, before Turati, Ferri held that socialists should help the bourgeois enrich themselves; and the whole spectrum of Italian democratic socialism's most distinguished representatives thunder in our ears about Italian proletarians' supposed interest in being ruled by a wealthy, civilized, "modern" bourgeoisie.

This new message from the socialists, which tends to induce the conscious proletariat to turn away from the straight and narrow of class struggle and herd it down the blind alleys of bourgeois reformism, is especially dangerous in that it takes as its premise a genuine fact, that current production is not equal to meeting everyone's needs, even to a limited extent, and, having stunned the public with a demonstration of this fact, it takes just a slight sophist stratagem to turn effect into cause and, without seeming to, to draw the mistaken conclusions that served their purposes.

We need to lift the veil off the system.

It is a fact that production as a whole, especially production of basic necessities, is meager and inadequate and almost laughably small compared with what it should and could be.

The starveling passing stores bulging with grocery supplies, the destitute watching the lengths to which shopkeepers go to sell off goods surplus to public demand may well believe that there is a universal abundance of supply, and that all that is missing is the wherewithal to buy them. Some anarchists, bedazzled by the more or less mystifying statistics and perhaps also at having a stunning argument in their propaganda arsenal—one readily understood by the ignorant masses—have been able to contend that actual output is far in excess of all reasonable need and that the people have merely to assume possession of it all, and we can all live in the land of plenty. And the recurrent crises of so-called over-production (meaning that work is in short supply because the bosses cannot find a market for the goods they have stockpiled) help embed such superficial impressions in the public mind.

But a little more cool-headed analysis soon makes it clear that any such alleged sea of wealth simply has to be a delusion.

The goods that most of the population consumes are not enough to satisfy their basic needs; the vast majority of people are little and poorly fed, poorly clothed, poorly housed, poorly off in everything; indeed lots of them perish of hunger and cold. If enough is really being churned out to meet everyone's needs, and since the majority under-consumes, where on earth would the yearly surplus production be stockpiled? And by what unimaginable aberration would capitalists who produce for the market and for profit persist in producing that which they cannot sell?

Because of inter-capitalist competition and the mutual ignorance of the quantity of goods the others might be able to put on the market at any given point, because of the speculator mind-set, the greed for gain and mistakes in forward planning, it can be and very often is the case that, especially in the manufacturing industries where output potential is more elastic, production exceeds demand at a certain point; but then along comes the crisis and work is suspended for a time in order for balance to be restored—and usually, in the long run, production does not outstrip demand. It is demand that dictates output and not the other way around.

Besides, in regard to foodstuffs, these being the most vital necessities, one has only to look at the ghastly consequences visited upon a farming region by a failed harvest, and one will see that, even eating as poorly as is normally the case, barely enough is being produced to survive from one year to the next.

If the sum of the wealth produced annually, over half of which goes to a tiny number of capitalists, were to be equally shared between all, it would bring little improvement in the conditions of the working man; indeed, his share would be increased, not in terms of necessities but rather of thousands of virtually useless, if not positively harmful gewgaws. As to bread, meat, housing, clothing and other basic necessities, the fraction over-consumed or squandered by the rich would, if shared out around the countless masses, make no discernible difference.

Therefore production is falling short and needs boosting: on that we agree.

But how come more is not being produced right now? Why is so much land left untilled or poorly worked? How come so many machines are inoperative? Why are so many workers out of jobs? How come homes are not being built for everybody, clothes not being made for everybody, etc. when there is plenty of materials for doing so, plus men able and eager to put those materials to use?

The reason is obvious and should not come as a surprise to any self-styled socialist. It is because the means of production—the soil, raw materials, instruments of labor—are not in the hands of those who need what they can produce, but are privately owned by a small number of people who use them to put other folk to work for them, and then only as much and in the manner that suits their own interests.

Today, man has no entitlement to any share in production on the basis of his manhood alone; he eats and he lives only because the capitalist, the owner of the means of production, has an interest in putting him to work in order to exploit him.

Now, the capitalist has no interest in production being increased beyond a certain point; indeed his interest lies in preserving a relative shortage. To put that another way, he is all for production as long as the product can be sold for more than its cost to him and he steps up production as long as the increase in his profits can keep pace. But once he sees that in order to sell his goods he might have to cut his prices too much, and that a glut would lead to an overall decrease in profits, he stops production and often—and there are thousands examples of this—destroys some of the stock of products available in order to force up the value of the rest.

So, if we want to see production grow to the extent that it can fully meet everyone's needs, it needs to be tailored to the needs that require satisfying, rather than the private profits of the few. Everybody must have an entitlement to enjoy products; everybody needs to have an entitlement to use the means of production.

If somebody suffering from hunger had the right to bread, we would need to see to it that there is bread enough to fill us all; and the land would be put to work, and outmoded methods replaced by more productive farming methods. On the other hand, if, as is the case at present, existing assets in the form of means of the production and stockpiled goods belong to a special class of people, and that class, being blessed with everything, can have the hungry, who are too noisy, arrested at gunpoint, production will keep stopping at the line set by capitalist interests.

In conclusion, the reason for meager output today is limited distribution; and if we would destroy the effect, we need to remove the cause.

In order to produce enough for everyone, it is necessary for everyone to have a right to consume enough.

Thereby proving the socialist thesis that the poverty question is primarily a distribution problem.

45. ANARCHISM AND SYNDICALISM[1]

The question of the position to be taken in relation to the Labour movement is certainly one of the greatest importance to Anarchists.

In spite of lengthy discussions and of varied experiences, a complete accord has not yet been reached—perhaps because the question does not admit of a complete and permanent solution, owing to the different conditions and changing circumstances in which we carry on the struggle.

I believe, however, that our aim may suggest to us a criterion of conduct applicable to the different contingencies.

We desire the moral and material elevation of all men; we wish to achieve a revolution which will give to all liberty and well-being, and we are convinced that this cannot be done from above by force of law and decrees, but must be done by the conscious will and the direct action of those who desire it.

We need, then, more than any the conscious and voluntary co-operation of those who, suffering the most by the present social organisation, have the greatest interest in the Revolution.

It does not suffice for us—though it is certainly useful and necessary—to elaborate an ideal as perfect as possible, and to form groups for propaganda and for revolutionary action. We must convert as far as possible the mass of the workers, because without them we can neither overthrow the existing society nor reconstitute a new one. And since to rise from the submissive state in which the great majority of the proletarians now vegetate, to a conception of Anarchism and a desire for its realisation, is required an evolution which generally is not passed through under the sole influence of the propaganda; since the lessons derived from the facts of daily life are more efficacious than all doctrinaire preaching, it is for us to take an active part in the life of the masses, and to use all the means which circumstances permit to gradually awaken the spirit of revolt, and to show by these facts the path which leads to emancipation.

---

1 *Freedom* (London) 21, no. 223 (November 1907). The article was published shortly after the International Anarchist Congress of Amsterdam, where the center stage was taken by the debate between Pierre Monatte and Malatesta on syndicalism and the general strike.

Amongst these means the Labour movement stands first, and we should be wrong to neglect it. In this movement we find numbers of workers who struggle for the amelioration of their conditions. They may be mistaken as to the aim they have in view and as to the means of attaining it, and in our view they generally are. But at least they no longer resign themselves to oppression nor regard it as just—they hope and they struggle. We can more easily arouse in them that feeling of solidarity towards their exploited fellow-workers and of hatred against exploitation which must lead to a definitive struggle for the abolition of all domination of man over man. We can induce them to claim more and more, and by means more and more energetic; and so we can train ourselves and others to the struggle, profiting by victories in order to exalt the power of union and of direct action, and bring forward greater claims, and profiting also by reverses in order to learn the necessity for more powerful means and for more radical solutions.

Again—and this is not its least advantage—the Labour movement can prepare those groups of technical workers who in the revolution will take upon themselves the organisation of production and exchange for the advantage of all, beyond and against all governmental power.

But with all these advantages the Labour movement has its drawbacks and its dangers, of which we ought to take account when it is a question of the position that we as Anarchists should take in it.

***

Constant experience in all countries shows that Labour movements, which always commence as movements of protest and revolt, and are animated at the beginning by a broad spirit of progress and human fraternity, tend very soon to degenerate; and in proportion as they acquire strength, they become egoistic, conservative, occupied exclusively with interests immediate and restricted, and develop within themselves a bureaucracy which, as in all such cases, has no other object than to strengthen and aggrandise itself.

It is this condition of things that has induced many comrades to withdraw from the Trade Union movement, and even to combat it as something reactionary and injurious. But the result has been that our influence diminished accordingly, and the field was left free to those who wished to exploit the movement for personal or party interests that had nothing in common with the cause of the workers' emancipation. Very soon there were only organisations with a narrow spirit and fundamentally conservative, of which the English Trade Unions are a type; or else Syndicates which, under the influence of politicians, most often "Socialist," were only electoral machines for the elevation into power of particular individuals.

Happily, other comrades thought that the Labour movement always held in itself a sound principle, and that rather than abandon it to the politicians, it would be well to undertake the task of bringing them once more to the work of achieving their original aims, and of gaining from them all the advantages they offer to the Anarchist cause. And they have succeeded in creating, chiefly in France, a new movement which, under the name of "Revolutionary Syndicalism," seeks to organise the workers, independently of all bourgeois and political influence, to win their emancipation by the direct action of the wage-slaves against the masters.

That is a great step in advance; but we must not exaggerate its reach and imagine, as some comrades seem to do, that we shall realise Anarchism, as a matter of course, by the progressive development of Syndicalism.

Every institution has a tendency to extend its functions, to perpetuate itself, and to become an end in itself. It is not surprising then, if those who have initiated the movement, and take the most prominent part therein, fall into the habit of regarding Syndicalism as the equivalent of Anarchism, or at least as the supreme means, that in itself replaces all other means, for its realisation. But that makes it the more necessary to avoid the danger and to define well our position.

Syndicalism, in spite of all the declarations of its most ardent supporters, contains in itself, by the very nature of its function, all the elements of degeneration which have corrupted Labour movements in the past. In effect, being a movement which proposes to defend the present interests of the workers, it must necessarily adapt itself to existing conditions, and take into consideration interests which come to the fore in society as it exists to-day.

Now, in so far as the interests of a section of the workers coincide with the interests of the whole class, Syndicalism is in itself a good school of solidarity; in so far as the interests of the workers of one country are the same as those of the workers in other countries, Syndicalism is a good means of furthering international brotherhood; in so far as the interests of the moment are not in contradiction with the interests of the future, Syndicalism is in itself a good preparation for the Revolution. But unfortunately this is not always so.

Harmony of interests, solidarity amongst all men, is the ideal to which we aspire, is the aim for which we struggle; but that is not the actual condition, no more between men of the same class than between those of different classes. The role to-day is the antagonism and the interdependence of interests at the same time: the struggle of each against all and of all against each. And there can be no other condition in a society where, in consequence of the capitalist system of production—that is to say, production founded on monopoly of the means of production and organised internationally for the profit of individual employers—there are, as a rule, more hands than work to be done, and more mouths than bread to fill them.

It is impossible to isolate oneself, whether as an individual, as a class, or as a nation, since the condition of each one depends more or less directly on the general conditions of the whole of humanity; and it is impossible to live in a true state of peace, because it is necessary to defend oneself, often even to attack, or perish.

The interest of each one is to secure employment, and as a consequence one finds himself in antagonism—i.e., in competition—with the unemployed of one's country and the immigrants from other countries. Each one desires to keep or to secure the best place against workers in the same trade; it is the interest of each one to sell dear and buy cheap, and consequently as a producer he finds himself in conflict with all consumers, and again as consumer finds himself in conflict with all producers.

Union, agreement, the solidary struggle against the exploiters,—these things can only obtain to-day in so far as the workers, animated by the conception of a superior ideal, learn to sacrifice exclusive and personal interests to the common interest of all, the interests of the moment to the interests of the future; and this ideal of a society of solidarity, of justice, of brotherhood, can only be realised by the destruction, done in defiance of all legality, of existing institutions.

To offer to the workers this ideal; to put the broader interests of the future before those narrower and immediate; to render the adaptation to present conditions impossible; to work always for the propaganda and for action that will lead to and will accomplish the Revolution—these are the objects we as Anarchists should strive for both in and out of the Unions.

Trade Unionism cannot do this, or can do but little of it; it has to reckon with present interests, and these interests are not always, alas! those of the Revolution. It must not too far exceed legal bounds, and it must at given moments treat with the masters and the authorities. It must concern itself with the interests of sections of the workers rather than the interests of the public, the interests of the Unions rather than the interests of the mass of the workers and the unemployed. If it does not do this, it has no specific reason for existence; it would then only include the Anarchists, or at most the Socialists, and would so lose its principal utility, which is to educate and habituate to the struggle the masses that lag behind.

Besides, since the Unions must remain open to all those who desire to win from the masters better conditions of life, whatever their opinions may be on the general constitution of society, they are naturally led to moderate their aspirations, first so that they should not frighten away those they wish to have with them, and next because, in proportion as numbers increase, those with ideas who have initiated the movement remain buried in a majority that is only occupied with the petty interests of the moment.

Thus one can see developing in all Unions, that have reached a certain position of influence, a tendency to assure, in accord with rather than against the masters, a privileged situation for themselves, and so create difficulties of entrance for new members, and for the admission of apprentices in the factories; a tendency to amass large funds that afterwards they are afraid of compromising; to seek the favour of public powers; to be absorbed, above all, in co-operation and mutual benefit schemes; and to become at last conservative elements in society.

After having stated this, it seems clear to me that the Syndicalist movement cannot replace the Anarchist movement, and that it can serve as a means of education and of revolutionary preparation only if it is acted on by the Anarchistic impulse, action, and criticism.

Anarchists, then, ought to abstain from identifying themselves with the Syndicalist movement, and to consider as an aim that which is but one of the means of propaganda and of action that they can utilise. They should remain in the Syndicates as elements giving an onward impulse, and strive to make of them as much as possible instruments of combat in view of the Social Revolution. They should work to develop in the Syndicates all that which can augment its educative influence and its combativeness,—the propaganda of ideas, the forcible strike, the spirit of proselytism, the distrust and hatred of the authorities and of the politicians, the practice of solidarity towards individuals and groups in conflict with the masters. They should combat all that which tends to render them egoistic, pacific, conservative,— professional pride and the narrow spirit of the corporate body, heavy contributions and the accumulation of invested capital, the service of benefits and of assurance, confidence in the good offices of the State, good relationships with masters, the appointment of bureaucratic officials, paid and permanent.

On these conditions the participation of Anarchists in the Labour movement will have good results, but only on these conditions.

These tactics will sometimes appear to be, and even may really be, hurtful to the immediate interests of some groups; but that does not matter when it is a question of the Anarchist cause,—that is to say, of the general and permanent interests of humanity. We certainly wish, while waiting for the Revolution, to wrest from Governments and from employers as much liberty and wellbeing as possible; but we would not compromise the future for some momentary advantages, which besides are often illusory or gained at the expense of other workers.

Let us beware of ourselves. The error of having abandoned the Labour movement has done an immense injury to Anarchism, but at least it leaves unaltered the distinctive character.

The error of confounding the Anarchist movement with Trade Unionism would be still more grave. That will happen to us which happened to the Social Democrats as soon as they went into the Parliamentary struggle. They gained in numerical force, but by becoming each day less Socialistic. We also would become more numerous, but we should cease to be Anarchist.

46. ANARCHISTS AND THE SITUATION[1]

The First of May having become a sort of annual review of the Labor forces, it is well on such an occasion for Anarchists to ask themselves what their action should be in view of the constantly changing position of the movement.

This year also the First of May has passed very quietly, without anything exciting (in a revolutionary sense) happening. And yet never before has the situation been so full of promise and encouragement as in this year.

It is especially France which, retaining the vantage conquered during the revolutions of the past century, gives a revolutionary character to the situation.

The workers show clearly that they have at length lost all confidence in Governmental parties, even when these call themselves Socialist. They begin to understand that for emancipation they can count only on themselves, on direct action against Capitalism and against the State. Labour resistance becomes daily more intense, solidarity develops, strikes follow each other with increasing energy and combativeness. Already for the politicians—so-called Labour or Socialist, who go forth to preach peace and arbitration, to promise beneficent laws, profiting by the occasion to climb into some place as Deputy or Municipal Councillor—already for such there is no longer room on the field of strikes. Now, if "Socialists" wish to be elected, they must seek the support of some section of the bourgeoisie.

Conscious workers act—and already we begin to see blazing factories and fleeing masters. These are the first scenes of the great Revolution which will put towns and countryside in flames and produce a radical transformation in every social relation.

The peasants also emerge from their passivity and begin to throw off that prejudice against town-workers which has for so long been a power for reaction.

Again, the State employees who until recently boasted of their position as public functionaries, and held themselves aloof from the industrial proletariat—these commence to understand their true

1 *Freedom* (London) 23, no. 242 (June 1909).

interests and to test their capacity for paralysing the State by disorganising its services. The postmen's strike and the meeting in the Paris Hippodrome, where thousands of State employees fraternised with workmen in private industries in the name of the Social Revolution to be accomplished, marked a decisive step forward along the road to emancipation. And whatever may be the immediate result (still uncertain at the moment I am writing) of the second postmen's strike, it is indisputable henceforth that the revolt has penetrated amongst the employees of the State, and is bound to grow.

On the other hand, the patriotic prejudice has been breached with success, and antimilitarism filtering through the ranks of the Army saps at the base a society which only maintains itself by the brutal strength of soldiers and police.

As in France, so more or less everywhere the spirit of revolt grows; direct action takes the place of a blind confidence in the elected and the protection of the law.

The Revolution is advancing.

Such are the Anarchistic ideas which force themselves even upon those who resist them. Anarchists, by their position as vanguard and their high ideals, have ever been unable to be more than a numerically small minority; they have been decried, calumniated, and persecuted in every way—and yet the new outlook of the whole contemporaneous social movement is due to the infiltration of their ideas.

Revolutionary Trade Unionism (Syndicalism), which sums up the new tendencies, is certainly not Anarchism; but the spirit that animates it is Anarchist, and all that it has of good is Anarchist.

But this is matter of history. What is important at present is to see what should now be our actual conduct when rendering to the revolutionary cause the services we are prepared to render.

***

It is evident that the dominant class will not permit the revolutionary tide to submerge them without making every possible effort to arrest it.

The methods which the Governments and the bourgeoisie can employ in order to check the revolutionary movement may be summed up under four heads—(1) persecutions, to smother the movement in the germ; (2) war, to evade the storm by provoking an outbreak of the atavistic savageness which still manifests itself in race and national hatreds; (3) corruption, in order to turn the movement aside from its emancipatory aims; (4) ferocious repression, the bloodshed which drains the best forces of a people and postpones the struggle for another fifty years.

The ordinary persecutions of police and magistracy have failed; and although Governments, owing to the anti-freedom instinct which forms the basis of their nature, do not renounce these, it is evident that they now only serve to render the conflict more bitter and violent.

War has become a little too dangerous, and could well precipitate rather than prevent the Revolution. War will not take place. In any case, we should simply have to intensify our antipatriotic and antimilitarist propaganda to render war less probable and ever more dangerous to the Government which had recourse to it.

There remain, therefore, two principal dangers for us to guard against—corruption and repression.

Corruption has already completely succeeded with the Parliamentarian Socialists, in such wise that in every country where Socialism was somewhat of a real menace to the existing system there has arisen an aristocracy formed of Socialist Deputies or would-be Deputies, which has become one of the best forces at the disposition of the bourgeoisie to divert or strangle the popular movement.

The same course will be tried with Revolutionary Trade Unionism.

Revolutionary Trade Unionism is not safe from corruption and degeneration. Apart from the question of individuals, who are always subject to mistakes and weaknesses, Trade Unionism by its very nature is a movement which cannot remain stationary. It must advance, develop; and its development either will approach more and more to Anarchism and make the Revolution, or modify itself, assume a bureaucratic character, adapt itself to the claims of capitalism, and become a factor in social conservation. To endeavour to lead Trade Unionism in the latter direction is at present the effort of every intelligent Conservative.

Old-age pensions, arbitration, the official recognition of Trade Union delegates, collective contracts, profit-sharing, co-operative societies, the recognised right of Trade Unions to hold property and to appear in a law court, are some of the methods employed by the bourgeoisie to arrest revolutionary impulse, and to stifle the growing desire for full emancipation and liberty by the ephemeral and illusory concession of some immediate ameliorations, and especially by the formation of a self-satisfied bureaucracy which will absorb the most intelligent and active elements among the proletariat.

It is, in the first place, against this danger that we must direct our forces. We must take a more and more active part in the Trade Union movement, strenuously oppose the formation in its midst of a bureaucracy of paid and permanent officials, propagate our tactics, fight against every idea of conciliation and compromise with the enemy, as well as against every tendency towards the pride and selfishness of individual Trade Unions. We must especially prevent the "workers secretaries" taking the place of Members of Parliament, and see that Direct Action does not in its turn become a lie like the so-called sovereignty of the people.

In this way we can enable Syndicalism to retain its revolutionary character and become an increasingly powerful instrument of emancipation.

But then we will be faced with a final crisis. Of itself, and driven by the alarmed bourgeoisie, the Government will wish to put an end to the movement. Repression will commence seriously, and the Army, not as yet sufficiently permeated with the antimilitarist propaganda to be inoffensive, will be called upon to play its murderous rôle.

Will the revolutionists be in a position to successfully face military repression? This is the question upon which all depends: according to which way it is answered, it will be triumphant revolution and the inauguration of a new civilisation or rampant reaction for twenty years and more.

We must, then, prepare ourselves for a struggle in arms.

How is it to be done?

It cannot be done in Trade Unions, nor in public groups open more or less to everybody. Neither can it be discussed in the newspapers. And yet it must be done.

Let Anarchists, and all who foresee the coming Revolution and would have it triumphant, ponder over the matter.

***

The above, having been written for Englishmen, may strike some as fantastic. England has not reached this point yet; but she will reach it, and sooner than is expected.

To-day, even if it would, a civilised country cannot remain separated from other civilised countries; and the French and Continental movement will not be without influence on the proletariat of this side of the Channel.

Besides, English workers have the solid qualities of perseverance, the spirit of organisation, and personal independence, which will soon enable them to regain the time lost, once they escape from the noxious influence of politicians.

47. CAPITALISTS AND THIEVES

Regarding the Tragedies in Houndsditch and Sidney Street[1]

In a backstreet in the City, there is an attempted robbery at a jewellers shop and the thieves, startled by the police, shoot their way out using their revolvers. Later, two of the robbers, tracked down to a house in the East End, use their guns again to defend themselves and perish in the exchange.[2]

At bottom, nothing particularly out of the ordinary in today's society, except for the exceptional vigour of the fight the robbers put up.

But these thieves were Russians, perhaps Russian refugees, and maybe they also went to an Anarchist club on days of public meetings, when they were open to everybody. And naturally the capitalist press avails itself to declare war upon the Anarchists. If one were to believe the bourgeois papers one would think that anarchy, that dream of love and justice among men, is nothing but theft and assassination; and with these lies and calumnies they certainly succeed in turning away from us many people who would be with us if they only knew what we want.

Thus it will not be useless to state once more the position of Anarchists respecting the theory and practice of theft.

---

1 "Capitalists and Thieves," *The Syndicalist* (London) 1, no. 5 (June 1912). Originally published as "Capitalistes et voleurs: A propos des tragédies de Houndsditch et Sidney Street," *Les Temps Nouveaux* (Paris) 6, no. 23 (18 February 1911). The English version is abridged. We have integrated it with an original translation of the missing parts. According to Rudolf Rocker, the first version to appear was actually the Yiddish one published in London by *Der Arbeter Fraint* on 27 January 1911. Though we have not been able to track down this version, there is no doubt that it must have been itself a translation from a Malatesta manuscript, which, in all likelihood, was in French.

2 The Houndsditch robbery occurred on 16 December 1910, and the so-called "siege of Sidney Street" on 4 January 1911. The double outrage caused enormous stir in Great Britain. Malatesta got marginally involved, as the investigations revealed that an oxygen cylinder that had been used in the robbery came from his workshop. However, he was able to prove that he had no knowledge of the use the cylinder would be put to.

One of the fundamental points of Anarchism is the abolition of the monopoly of the land, raw material, and the instruments of production, and thereby the abolition of the exploitation of other people's labour by those who hold the means of production. Any appropriation of other people's labour, everything that serves to enable a man to live without giving to society his quota of production is, from the Anarchist and Socialist point of view, a theft.

The landlords, the capitalists have stolen from the people, by violence or by fraud, the land and all the means of production, and in consequence of this initial theft they are enabled, day by day, to take away from the workers the products of labour. But they were happy thieves, for they became strong: they made laws in order that they might justify their situation, and they have organised a whole system of repression to defend themselves against the claims of the workers as well as against those who would like to replace them by doing as they did themselves. And to-day their theft is called property, commerce, industry, etc., the name of "thief" being reserved, in common language, for those who would like to follow the example of the capitalists, but, because they arrived too late and in adverse circumstances, cannot do it without putting themselves in conflict with the law.

However, the difference of names currently used does not suffice to hide the moral and social character of the two situations. The capitalist is a thief who has succeeded either by his merits or by those of his ancestors; the thief is an aspiring capitalist who is but waiting to succeed to become a capitalist, in fact, and live without working on the product of his theft, that is to say, on other people's labour.

As enemies of the capitalists, we cannot sympathise for the thief who aspires at becoming a capitalist. And being in favour of their expropriation by the people for the profit of all, we cannot, as Anarchists, have anything in common with an operation whose object is to get some wealth to pass from the hands of one owner into those of another.

I am speaking, of course, about the professional thief, the one who rejects work and casts around for ways of leading a parasitical existence on the back of other people's labours. A man denied the opportunity to work by society and who steals rather than starve to death and watch his children perish of starvation is something different. In his case, thievery (if such it can be called) is a rebellion against social injustice and may well become the most sacred of rights and the most imperious of duties. But the capitalist press avoids mentioning such cases, because if it did, it might have to indict the social order whose mission it is to champion.

To be sure, the professional thief is also in large part a victim of the social order. The example set by the higher-ups, the education bestowed, the repulsive conditions in which one is often obliged to work, readily explain why some men, who are morally no better than their contemporaries, when faced with a choice between being exploited or being exploiters, opt for exploiter and strive by any means open to them to become just that. But such extenuating circumstances might as readily apply to the capitalists: the essential sameness of the two callings could scarcely be better demonstrated.

Thus anarchist ideas cannot drive people to become thieves any more than to become capitalists. On the contrary, by giving to the discontented an ideal of superior life, and a hope of collective emancipation, they turn away, as far as possible in the present midst, from all these legal or illegal doings which are but an adaptation to the capitalist system and tend towards perpetuating it.

Notwithstanding all this, the social midst being so strong and personal temperaments so different, there might possibly be amongst the Anarchists a few who go in for thieving as there are some who go in for commerce or industry; but in that case both are acting, not because of their Anarchist ideas, but in spite of these.

48. THE WAR AND THE ANARCHISTS[1]

There is no nefarious deed, no criminal passion that interested parties do not try to excuse, justify, and even glorify by means of noble reasons. This is, in essence, a source of comfort, for it shows that certain loftier ideals devised by humanity over the course of its evolution have by now seeped into the universal consciousness and linger and prevail even in times of the greatest aberration. But this does not make it any less necessary that the deception be exposed, and the sordid interests and atavistic brutality lurking under the cloak of noble sentiments be denounced.

Thus, lying assurances that the undertaking would be simple, and about the great benefits the Italian proletariat would reap from it were not enough to justify and persuade the people to embrace the loot-and-pillage war that the Italian government meant to wage on the people of Libya. It would be really too outrageous if a man, other than a complete brute, were to be incited to carry out a murder on the assurance that the intended victim is defenseless and has lots of money and that there is no risk of being discovered and punished. So other, loftier motives had to be marshalled, and the naïve persuaded that this was a rare opportunity when one might become rich while performing a selfless act of magnanimity. And they came up with the need to exercise "the nation's energies" and show the world what "our folk" are worth, their right and duty to spread civilization and, first and foremost, love of country and the glory of Italy.

We shall not bother here with the supposed material benefits, first of all because, in our view, these could never justify aggression, and then because these days few people have any belief left in such benefits, unless we are talking about the profiteering by a tiny band of monopolists and military suppliers. But it is worth our while to take a closer look at the moral arguments that have been deployed to justify the war.

---

1 Translated from "La guerra e gli anarchici," *La Guerra Tripolina* (London), April 1912. This was a one-off publication edited by Malatesta's group against the Italo-Turkish war, which was declared the year before by the Italian government against the Ottoman empire to gain colonies in North Africa by conquering the provinces of Tripolitania and Cyrenaica, corresponding to today's Libya.

***

Italy, they say, is not given her due place in this world. Italians are oblivious of their latent energies; they need to be shaken out of their lethargy. Life is energy, strength and action and struggle, and we want to live.

All well and good. But since we are men and not brute beasts and since the life we are out to live is a human life, there are going to have to be certain qualifications about the energy that is to be expended. Is it, perhaps, the vigor of the predatory beast to which we aspire? Or that of the blackguard, the brigand, the goon, the executioner? Or—and this may well be the example that best fits in this instance—that of the cowardly thug who, having got a sound thrashing in town, heads for home and demonstrates his courage … by beating his wife?

The vigor of civilized people, the force that genuinely brings an intensity to life is not the sort expended on inter-human strife, bullying the weak or oppressing the defeated. But it is the sort deployed in the contest against the adverse powers of nature, in the performance of useful toil, in the demanding researches of science, in helping to spur forward those who have been left behind, in lending a helping hand to those who stumble, in securing ever greater powers and well-being for every human being.

Yes, it is true, Italians are lacking in vigor. Mean and lazy, our bourgeoisie do not even have it in them to exploit the available workforce and forces it to move away to be exploited abroad; and our workers let themselves be driven from their homeland in search of a crust of bread and now they are being dispatched to Libya to be slaughtered for the profits of a few grasping speculators, to win fresh territory for those who stop them enjoying the land of Italy. But war is not the source of their vigor and determination to improve, any more than turning to a life of thievery and prostitution invigorates those who cannot and will not work.

Work and enjoyment of the entire fruits of their labour—that is what the Italians need, like every other people.

***

The warmongers say: we are bringing civilisation to the barbarians.

Let us take a little look at that.

Civilization means wealth, science, freedom, brotherhood, and justice; it means material, moral, and intellectual advancement; it means the abandonment and condemnation of brutish strife and the advancement of solidarity and conscious, willing cooperation.

Above all, civilising involves inspiring the sentiments of freedom and human dignity, raising the value of life, encouraging activity and enterprise, respecting individuals and whatever natural or voluntary associations into which men may enter.

Is that what the soldiers of Italy, in the hire of the Bank of Rome, are off to Africa to do?

In spite of Verbicaro[2] and the Camorra, in spite of illiteracy, in spite of lands left untilled and malaria-infested and the thousands of waterless, streetless, sewerless townships, Italy is still more civilized than Libya. She has strong, skilled workers; she has her doctors, engineers, agronomists, and artists; she has great traditions and a clever and gentle people that have always proved themselves capable of the most exacting, noblest tasks, when not oppressed by poverty and tyranny. She could climb quickly to the highest rungs of human civilisation and become a mighty factor for progress and fairness in the world.

Instead, deceived and intoxicated by those who oppress and exploit her and prevent her from developing her finer qualities and her wealth, she ships soldiers and priests to Africa, bringing carnage and looting, and in the vile endeavour to reduce a foreign population to slavery, she makes a brute and a slave of herself.

Let the time for reformation be fast approaching!

***

We come now to the ultimate argument: patriotism.

The patriotic sentiment undoubtedly holds great sway in every country and serves the people's exploiters wonderfully well by blinding its eyes to class frictions and, in the name of an idealized solidarity based on stock and nation, draws the oppressed into reluctant service of the interests of their oppressors. And this is all

2 When the Calabrian town of Verbicaro was hit by an epidemic of cholera in 1911, a violent revolt exploded against the local authorities, who were considered responsible for the epidemic. The episode made sensation and tended to be seen as a manifestation of barbaric primitivism. Giovanni Giolitti's government addressed the revolt more as an issue of law and order than of public health. An intense repressive action ensued, and the town was militarily occupied by the army for the next three years.

the more successful in a country like Italy which was for so long oppressed by the foreigner and was released from that only yesterday after cruel, glorious struggle.

But what, precisely, does patriotism consist of?

Love of birthplace, or rather, greater love for wherever we were reared, wherever we received our mothers' caresses, where we as children played with other children, and as striplings won our first kiss from a beloved girlfriend, a preference for the language we understand best and, therefore, our most intimate dealings with those who speak it: these are natural phenomena and blessings. Blessings because, while they quicken the beating heart and create firmer ties of solidarity within a range of human groups and nurture the originality of a range of types, they do no harm to anyone and are a help rather than a hindrance to progress over all. And as long as those preferences do not blind us to the merits of others and to our own shortcomings, as long as they do not make us contemptuous of a broader culture and wider relations, as long as they do not lead to a laughable vanity and conceitedness that makes us believe that we are better than the next fellow just because we were born in the shadow of a certain bell-tower or within certain borders, then they can turn out to be an essential element in the future development of mankind. Since, once distances have been nearly abolished by advances in machinery, political obstacles cleared away by freedom, and economic obstacles banished by general comfort, those preferences remain as the best guarantee against the rapid influx of huge masses of immigrants into those areas best favored by nature or best prepared by the labours of bygone generations; something that would pose grave threat to the peaceful progress of civilisation.

But these are not the only feelings upon which so-called patriotism feeds.

In antiquity, man's oppression of his fellow man was effected chiefly by means of warfare and conquest. It was the victorious outsider who seized the land, forcing the natives to work it on his behalf, and he was, if not the only master, then certainly the harshest and most despised. And whereas that state of affairs has all but disappeared from the nations of Europe, where the master is now, in most cases, a fellow countryman of his victims, it still remains the chief characteristic of Europeans' dealings with peoples of different areas. Consequently the fight against the oppressor has had, and retains, the character of a fight against the outsider.

Unfortunately, but understandably, hatred of the outsider as the oppressor turned into hatred of the outsider as outsider, and turned gentle love of homeland into that feeling of antipathy and rivalry, vis à vis other peoples, which usually goes by the name of patriotism, and which the native-born oppressors in various countries exploit to their own advantage. Civilisation's mission is to scatter this poisonous error and bring every people together as brothers in the fight for the common good.

We are internationalists, meaning that, just as the tiny homeland that revolved around a tent or a bell-tower and was at war with neighboring tribes or towns has been superseded by the larger region- and nation-sized homeland, so we extend our homeland to the whole world, feel ourselves to be brothers of every other human being, and seek well-being, freedom, and autonomy for every individual and group. Just as, back in the days when Christianity was believed and heartfelt, Christians regarded the whole Christendom as their homeland and the outsider that needed converting or destroying was the pagan, so we regard all of the oppressed and all who struggle for human emancipation as our brothers. And all oppressors, all whose own prosperity is built upon the woes of others, as our enemies—no matter where they were born nor the language they speak.

We abhor war, which is always fratricidal and damaging, and we want a liberating social revolution; we deplore strife between peoples and champion the fight against the ruling classes. But if, by some misfortune, a clash were to erupt between one people and another, we stand with the people that are defending their independence.

When Austrian soldiery were trawling the plains of Lombardy and Franz Josef's gallows were going up in the town squares of Italy, the Italians' revolt against the Austrian tyrant was noble and holy. Now that today's Italy invades another country and Victor Emmanuel's infamous gallows are being erected and put to work in the marketplace in Tripoli, it is the Arabs' revolt against the Italian tyrant that is noble and holy.

For the sake of Italy's honor, we hope that the Italian people, having come to its senses, will force a withdrawal from Africa upon its government: if not, we hope that the Arabs may succeed in driving it out.

With such thoughts, it is we, the "anti-patriots," who will have salvaged whatever part of Italy's honor can be salvaged in the face of history, in the face of humanity. We shall be the ones to show that there is still a gleam of the sentiments that moved Mazzini and Garibaldi and that whole glorious crew of Italians, whose bones are strewn across every battlefield in Europe and the Americas where a holy battle was fought, and who endeared the name of Italy to all men, everywhere, whose hearts thrilled to the cause of freedom, independence, and justice.

Malatesta around 1913.

"Is Revolution Possible?": *Volontà*, the Red Week, and the War, 1913–18

In 1913, Malatesta returned to Ancona after fifteen years. In his new weekly, by the telling title of *Volontà,* he started giving full expression to themes that had long underpinned his thinking, such as voluntarism and the separation between science and human values. The periodical was also meant to support work of a more practical nature. At a time when the insurrectionary prospect seemed to have lost purchase, Malatesta provocatively asked "Is revolution possible?" and reiterated that nobody knew when the times were ripe for revolution. Indeed, few weeks later, in June 1914, the insurrectionary Red Week broke out in Ancona and elsewhere. Though the uprising was not pre-arranged, the alliance of revolutionary forces that backed it was reminiscent of the scenario that Malatesta had urged since his 1899 pamphlet against the monarchy. Back to London for another long exile in that city, Malatesta had the opportunity to confirm the firmness of his ideas in the storm of the Great War, when he reasserted anarchist anti-militarism in the clearest terms, in the face of the confusion that had not spared the anarchist camp.

49. LIBERTY AND FATALISM, DETERMINISM AND WILL[1]

We say that a revolution is necessary, that we want one, and that we are devoting our energies to awakening and uniting the wills intent upon this end.

But a fundamental objection is opposed to us. "Revolution," we are told, "is not made by the caprice of man; it comes (if it does come) only when the time is ripe for it. History does not move by chance but develops in accordance with natural laws which are immutable, irresistible, and against which the will of man can do nothing."

In practice, at least in the majority of cases, this objection involves nothing but a polemic, or a political expedient. Just because a thing is not desired it is affirmed that it is impossible; the power of will is denied when one is called upon to make an effort in a direction which is not convenient; and, (since now nearly all who know the alphabet set themselves up as scientists and philosophers) desire itself is rationalized and science and philosophy are called upon to act as go-betweens for the little schemes of individuals and parties. On the other hand when a thing is interesting and pleasing, all theories are forgotten, one makes the necessary effort and, if concurrence of others is needed, one appeals to their willingness and exalts the power of will instead of denying it.

In spite of this, however, it is certain that every man who thinks, feels the need to put his conduct into harmony with his intellectual convictions, and, when he acts, he likes to take account of the efficacy and the quality of his actions. Every man who thinks and observes and who is learning the innumerable facts of nature and of history, feels the need of organizing his acquired impressions into a system, and of finding some general principle which will unify and explain them.

From this need of comprehension and of mental adjustment, have originated both the theological and the naturalistic systems of

1 *Man!* (San Francisco) 3, no. 2 (February 1935), translated by Eli J. Boche. Originally published as "Libertà e fatalità: Determinismo e volontà," *Volontà* (Ancona) 1, no. 24 (22 November 1913).

philosophy. From this need are born the inquiries and the discussions concerning the problem of Will, that is, of the power of man (or of any conscious being) to sway the course of events. This is the fundamental problem of any philosophy—it has fatigued, and continues to fatigue, the thinkers of all schools.

This fact would not have been otherwise than advantageous to the intellectual development of man and for the better utilization of human forces, had it not been that, very often, by a common mental illusion, that which is a simple product of the imagination was mistaken for the real objective and more or less comfortable hypotheses were mistaken for certified facts with which it was attempted to unify and explain known facts. Worse still, when simple words without any precise and definite significance were taken for real things.

Thus were invented God and the Immortal Soul; thus were invented Matter, Force, Energy (all with capital letters) and all the other mental concepts designed to explain by words, the universe which is not understood.

But above all these entities, which it is well to treat with prudent and smiling skepticism, there is a superior principle which seems truly unassailable—or at least such that the human mind cannot conceive its negation; thus is the principle of Causality which, all by itself constitutes the philosophy called Determinism. Nothing creates itself and nothing destroys itself; no effect without sufficient cause; no cause without its proportionate effect.

Very well. If, to the human mind, this seems to be a necessary and absolute truth then logical reasoning is also a necessity of the mind, and it is also true that every premise leads to its obvious conclusion. Now the logical conclusion of the principle of causality, understood as the universal and unavoidable principle, is that, starting out of eternity, everything is a necessary concatenation of events which could not be other than as determined, and that therefore, man is nothing but a conscious automaton, will is an illusion, and liberty is non-existent and impossible.

It is a fact that, reasoning in the abstract, many willingly arrive as far as the ultimate consequences and they say, with Laplace, that, if a man could know all the existing forces in the universe at a given moment, with all their points of application, their intensities and directions, he could calculate all that has happened, and everything that will happen, at any moment whatever in eternity and at any point whatever in infinite space—everything from a star in its orbit to the verse of a poet, from an earthquake shock to a newspaper article.

This is, in its most consequent expression, the philosophical system which is commonly called Determinism, and which, starting from the concepts of Nature and Necessity, and following rational and scientific method, arrives at the same conclusions as those reached by the ancients with their Fate and the theologians with their Predestination.

There are also some who seek to restrict and attenuate the meaning of the system and to elude its consequences, trying to conciliate the idea of necessity with that of liberty. But these are, as we see it, vain and illogical attempts for, a "necessity" which is not always necessary, which admits restrictions and exceptions, can no longer be called by that name.

Determinism responds admirably to certain needs of the intellect and it is a sure guide in the study of the physico-chemical world. But it indubitably paralyzes and denies the will and makes useless and laughable any effort directed toward any end.

Nevertheless, while every man more or less thinks and acts by deterministic logic, there aren't any who actually translate their philosophy into life—at any rate, we do not know of any. This is not strange because, if there were any such they must find it useless to make known and to propagate their ideas, convinced, as they must be, that that which must occur (even the cerebral antics of each one) will occur fatalistically at the determined time, and that nothing can possibly prevent it, nor retard it, nor hasten it.

Obviously the determinists—who are, in general, studious, active and desirous of progress, and who have become determinists not only thru reasoning but also thru reaction against the prejudices, the impositions, and the obscurantism of religions—are floundering about in a continuous contradiction. They deny free will and, therefore, responsibility, and then they become indignant against the judge who punishes the irresponsible. As if the judge were not himself determined and therefore also irresponsible! They say that all things that take place (natural phenomena, human history, actions, passions, and individual thoughts) do so in an uninterrupted and necessary sequence of cause and effect, reducible to physico-chemical facts which are subject to mechanical laws. Then they assign great importance to education and to propaganda! They are the apostles of charity, tolerance, and liberty. As if evil, intolerance, and tyranny were not, since they exist, necessary things which the laws of mechanics should explain! Often they are revolutionists, struggling and sacrificing themselves for something which, according to their system, will happen and must necessarily happen of its own accord, when the time comes.

It is true that it could be answered that the determinist who thus contradicts himself is also determined and cannot help contradicting himself, just as we cannot do otherwise than point out the contradiction.—But, then, one may as well say that doing is equal to not doing and that all this reasoning and striving is but a comic opera, tiresome or diverting, but—also necessary. How are we to escape from these difficulties?

***

The absolute Free Will of the spiritualists is contradicted by facts and is repugnant to the intellect. The negation of Will and Liberty by the mechanists is repugnant to our feelings. Intellect and sentiment are constituent parts of our egos and we know not how to subjugate one to the other.

We may not know how to deny the principle of causality but neither can we look upon ourselves as automata. Nor if we seek and desire the explanation of all things, do we deny their existence simply because we do not succeed in explaining them. For there are many more things in the universe than in all the systems of philosophy! Science and philosophy are but attempts, still infinitely imperfect, to explain the universe. And while science searches and philosophy syllogizes, we ought to live—to live like men who will obtain from life the maximum possible satisfaction.

What is Will in its essence? We do not know. But do we know what, in their essence, are Matter and Energy? Efficacious will must be the power to introduce into the chain of events, new factors which are not necessary and not pre-existent—it must be, in fact, the power to produce and effect without a cause. This immediately repels the intellect educated to the scientific method. But isn't it true that upon retracing the path of the chain of events and regardless of the philosophical system one takes as a guide, one always arrives at an unknown and perhaps inconceivable First Cause—that is to say, at an effect without a cause? "We do not know." To us, this seems to be the last word that can be said, at least for the present, by wise philosophy.

But we want to live a conscious and creative life, and such a life demands, in the absence of positive concepts, certain necessary presuppositions which may be unconscious but which are always nevertheless, in the soul of everyone. The most important of these presuppositions is the efficacy of the will. All that can usefully be sought are the conditions which limit or augment the power of the will.

50. SCIENCE AND SOCIAL REFORM[1]

The great scientific discoveries of the nineteenth century and the victorious criticism which science made against the lies and the errors of religions, had the effect upon progressive spirits, of making them enthusiastic admirers if not intelligent and patient cultivators, of science. These progressives exaggerated the importance of science by attributing to it the power to solve and understand everything; they made of science a new religion.

Social reformers of every kind that is, of every kind which, by whatever means and ends, wished to modify the existing social order believed themselves obliged to found their aspirations upon Science. Similarly, the conservatives also, when they saw that religious faith was vacillating and that it was no longer sufficient to keep the people in subjection, sought to justify the existing regime by means of science. It was verily a state of intellectual intoxication (not yet vanished) which caused the loss of a clear concept of nature and of the methods and scope of science, and it was to the utter detriment of scientific truth and social action.

Hardly anyone was saved; and if we anarchists were saved from the ridiculousness of calling ourselves scientific anarchists, it was perhaps only because the adjective "scientific" had already been taken and rendered antipathetic by Marxian socialism. In fact, many of our Comrades (and among them some of the most deserving and illustrious) actually maintained that Anarchism is a deduction consolidated with scientific truths, and, furthermore, that it is nothing but the application of the mechanical conception of the universe to human interests.[2]

Meanwhile, the fact that they remain anarchists even while science progresses and changes, demonstrates the fallacy of their scientific-ism and demonstrates likewise, that their anarchism is derived from their sentiments and not from their scientific convictions. But, in spite of their professed objectivism, in practice they will not admit

---

1 *Man!* (San Francisco) 3, no. 2 [*recte* 3] (March 1935), translated by Eli J. Boche. Originally published as "Scienza e riforma sociale," *Volontà* (Ancona) 1, no. 29 (27 December 1913).

2 The implicit but obvious reference is to the theories of Peter Kropotkin.

facts or accept theories which seem to contradict their anarchical aspirations. And, if they had not had the opportunity to pursue scientific studies, or science did not exist and human knowledge had remained in the state in which it was centuries ago,[3] they would probably be anarchists just the same because, being good and sensible men, they would suffer because of human sorrows and would want to find a remedy and because, being proud and just men, they would rebel against oppression and would want complete liberty for themselves and for all. In addition they recognize the quality of conscious anarchism in that immense majority of Comrades who do not know science, and, when they do propaganda work, they do just as we do, that is, they seek to awaken in men the sentiments of personal dignity and love of others; they strive to excite the passion for liberty and justice; they speak of general well-being and of human brotherhood; they bring to light the social ills and they arouse the desire to destroy them; and they do not wait until the people have studied mathematics, astronomy, and chemistry.

The study of the sciences is an excellent thing and we will speak later of those things which they serve. But to pretend that anarchism (and the same holds true for socialism or any other human aspiration) is a scientific deduction and especially, therefore, a consequence of one of those vast cosmogonical hypotheses in which philosophy takes such great delight, is a thing which is false per se and is pernicious because of the consequent effect it can have upon the intellectual development of individuals and upon their capacity as combatants.

The idea of a personal god, creator of all things, which is the oldest, the most ingenuous, and the most grossly absurd of these hypotheses, has done immense harm because it has accustomed people to believing without understanding and, by suffocating the spirit of examination, it has made intellectual slaves, well prepared to support political and economic slavery.

But do not scientific hypotheses do the same when they are presented as firm facts and as motives for actions, to those who know little or nothing of science and who are therefore in no position to judge? Some vague notions of scientific facts, more or less true, and the knowledge of a few strange words, are not enough to make of a

3 The words from "science did" to "knowledge had" were missing from the English version. They have been added on the basis of the Italian original.

man a scientist or even one who knows what he is talking about or who can choose from among the things that he is told.

For the public in general Moses and Haeckel are equally mythical figures and the belief in the monism of the one rather than in the genesis of the other just because it happens to be in style in the present environment, does not make one any the less ignorant, any the less superstitious, or any the less religious.[4] And to speak to the unbelievers of atoms, ions, and electrons (which are only hypotheses for explaining and binding certain categories of fact—convenient hypotheses useful to the ends of scientific research, but, nevertheless, only hypotheses, simple mental concepts, and not at all positive discoveries, pace friend Cassisa)[5]—to speak, I say, without adequate preparation, of mysterious and incomprehensible things to one who does not understand, is the same as to speak of god and of angels. It means the teaching of words as things and the accustoming of the mind to contenting itself with affirmations which it can neither understand, nor prove, nor define.

This would be only a change in religion because it would still be a religion in the sense of blind submission to a revealed truth, which can be neither controlled nor comprehended. If it were true that anarchy is a scientific truth, then there would be no real anarchists except the very few scientists who would call themselves such; all we others would constitute a non-conscious herd which would blindly follow a few holy men who had been initiated into the reasons for faith!

Nor is there any difference in the moral deductions or in the social applications which can be obtained out of the various cosmogonical theories. The priests had God say the things which were convenient to them and they used him as a medium for justifying and strengthening the dominion of the victors.

However, in the course of history there was no lack of rebels who, in the name of God, preached justice and equality. It is said that everything occurs by the will of God and that, therefore, we must accept with resignation our own position. But it can also be said that

4 Ernst Haeckel (1834–1919) was a German scientist who promoted and popularized Darwin's theories. His philosophical monism proposed the unity of organic and physical nature, including social phenomena and mental processes.

5 In the article "L'Anarchia è atea" (Anarchy is atheistic), which appeared in the previous issue of *Volontà*, the anarchist Gian Salvatore Cassisa had taken issue with Malatesta on religion and science. Taking a strongly positivistic stance, he had maintained that Anarchy was the synthesis of a new "scientific civilization."

rebellion is holy since it does occur and hence must be willed by God. It can also be said that, if God is the common father, we are all brothers and ought, therefore, to be equal. In sum, this idea may be turned in any manner, to suit any taste—for example, we know that Mazzini invented God of goodness, of love, and of progress, who was entirely different from the ferocious God of Pius IX.

Bakunin used to say that, if God exists, men can have neither liberty nor dignity. Another might say—and many, in fact, have said it—that if all is matter, if everything is subject to natural laws, the will is an illusion, liberty a chimera and man nothing but an automaton.

So it is that, if the convictions and the moral aspirations are based upon the mobile foundations of philosophic hypotheses, they are always uncertain and mutable. Like the catholic who, basing his conduct upon belief in God, is left without any moral criterion as soon as his faith is shaken, so the anarchist, if he were really an anarchist because of scientific convictions, would have to continually consult the latest bulletins of the Academy of Science in order to determine whether he can continue to be an anarchist.

Cassisa furnishes an example of how, by means of philosophy, the simplest and most evident things can be confounded. According to him, "the principle of property is based upon the false belief in creation from nothing." I, truly, do not understand what he wants to say: but it seems to me that if, before having a revolution and expropriating the holders of social wealth, we must first attend to nothing but the question of the origin of the world, then the capitalists may sleep in tranquility! Oh, isn't it much more simple, much more comprehensible, to say that, however the world may have been formed, it is here and ought to serve the needs of all, and to incite the workers to take it and to work it on their own account, and to no longer permit themselves to be despoiled by those who, by violence or fraud, have made themselves the owners?

***

If then, from the clouds of philosophy, we descend to the more solid domain of the positive sciences and of the so-called social sciences, we find here, too, that they can serve to defend the most diverse political regimes, the most contradictory social aspirations. From the immense heap of more of less established facts, each one chooses those which support his own position, and each one formulates theories which in reality, become programs, desires, and objectives which he proposes and which he, deluding himself as well as others, calls scientific truths. In the interpretation of the facts of natural history, in anthropology, in the philosophy of history, in political economy, and in every phase of sociology, at every turning of a page we come upon dubious affirmations which say "it is" when they should say "it ought to be" or, better, "I wish it were." The result is that scientific, objective, and impartial investigation suffers; the social struggle passes from the ardent field of passion and interest which are its very own, to degenerate itself in the chattering of the academicians and the pedants.

Science gathers facts, classifies them, and, when it finds that these facts are necessary and that they necessarily reproduce themselves every time the same conditions are set up, formulates natural laws. The latter are, for this reason, nothing but affirmations that under given conditions certain definite phenomena occur. But this does not tell man what to desire, whether he should love or hate, be good or bad, just or unjust. Goodness, justice, and right are concepts which science ignores completely.

Science tends to delimit the field between fatalism and free will. The more science advances the more powerful does man become because he learns what are the the necessary conditions which he must fulfill in order to be able to execute his will. But this will, executed or not, remains an extra scientific force with its own origins and its own tendencies.

Toxology teaches us the physiology of poisons, but it does not tell us whether we should use the acquired knowledge to poison or to cure people. Mechanics discovers the laws of equilibrium and of the resistance of materials, it teaches us to build bridges, steamships, and aeroplanes, but it does not tell us whether it is better to build the bridge where it may serve the greed of a proprietor, or where it may serve the interests of all; it does not tell us whether ships and planes should be used to carry soldiers and to hurl bombs upon the people or to spread throughout the world, civility, well-being, and brotherhood. Science is a weapon that can serve for good or for evil; but it ignores completely the idea of good or evil.

So then, we are not anarchists, because sciences tell us to be: we are, instead, anarchists because, among other reasons, we want everyone to be able to enjoy the advantages and the joys that science can procure for us.

51. IS REVOLUTION POSSIBLE?[1]

Needless to say, we cannot know what may happen in the near future.

But whatever the future may bring, should it be the government caving in to the railway workers' demands, coming to the rescue of the monarchist order and the masters' interests yet again, or tackling the strike with all its uncertainties, the fact is that the crisis by which Italy is at present beset represents a great lesson that is not going to go to waste.[2]

For many years now, the "hard-headed" types out to resolve the heavyweight of making an omelette without breaking eggs have been going around preaching that revolution is no longer an option. Breach-loading rifles; machine-guns; rapid communications; the old cities being cleared of narrow, twisting streets spelled certain defeat for any attempt at popular insurrection.

We were the "1848 fossils," the "romantics," the "classic revolutionaries" overtaken by the onward march of time.

We stood condemned by science—that dutiful maid of all work—"Science."

By then, in order to save the world and transform society, what was needed was lots of fear... and the election of deputies to the parliament.

Now, lo and behold, at one fell swoop and because of a minor pay issue—because of the simple fact that one category of workers has caught on that when one works, one has, at the very least, a right to eat and to rest, and is vigorously calling for some improvements—the whole of "science" can be ignored and the laws of "evolution" forgotten: and we seem to hark back to the days of barbarism when revolutionaries were less well versed in science but also had less fear.

---

1 Translated from "È possibile la rivoluzione?" *Volontà* (Ancona) 2, no. 16 (18 April 1914).

2 A great agitation of the railway workers had taken place between the fall 1913 and the spring 1914, contributing to the resignation of Prime Minister Giovanni Giolitti in March 1913. The labour dispute continued under the new ministry of Antonio Salandra and was still open at the time of the present article, with the railway workers threatening to go on strike.

There is indeed a strike-back atmosphere. One can sense fresh hopes stirring in the popular classes, and the ruling, which is to say, oppressor classes, are entirely overrun by ill-concealed worry.

People wonder—if the railwaymen were really to refuse to work, if ill-intentioned people were to sabotage the rolling stock and railway tracks making even a skeleton service impossible, if the most wide awake segment of the proletariat was to support the action by means of general strikes—what would the government do with its soldiers, even if the latter were to forget that they are proletarians who were forcibly conscripted and have parents, brothers, and chums in the strikers' ranks? And how could the established order carry on then?

Revolution would become a necessity: only it could ensure that the life of society carried on.

Maybe this is not going to happen today. But why would it not, tomorrow?

Nobody can tell in advance when the time will be ripe, and the fatal hour could arrive at any moment.

Let everybody hold themselves in readiness for tomorrow… or today.

52. THE GENERAL STRIKE AND THE INSURRECTION IN ITALY[1]

The events which have taken place recently in Italy are of the greatest importance, not so much in themselves, but as an indication of the disposition of the Italian people and of what we can anticipate in the near future.

The immediate cause of the outbreak was a massacre of unarmed demonstrators by the gendarmes of the town of Ancona.

For over a year the revolutionary and Labour organisations of all political shades had been carrying on an agitation in favour of several victims of military despotism and for the abolition of *disciplinary battalions*, to which are sent all young soldiers known to hold anti-monarchical and anti-bourgeois opinions. The treatment is barbarous, and the unhappy young men are submitted to all kinds of moral and physical tortures.

As the meetings and demonstrations were held all over Italy, but on different dates, they seemed to make but little impression on the Government; and the Trades Council of Ancona proposed, therefore, to organise manifestations in the whole country on the same day, that day to be the date of the official celebration of the establishment of Italian unity and the Monarchy. As on these occasions great military reviews are always held, the comrades thought that the Government would be obliged to postpone the review in order to hold the troops ready to preserve "order," and the attention of the whole public would be drawn to the object of the demonstration.

The idea put forward by the Ancona comrades was everywhere received with enthusiasm by all the opposition parties. The Minister ordered the police to prevent any public demonstrations. Of course, that did not deter us. In fact, we had counted on the police prohibition to give more publicity to the demonstration and to instigate the masses to resistance.

To stop the people who were leaving a meeting-hall from going to the central square to demonstrate, the gendarmes fired on the unarmed

---

1 *Freedom* (London) 28, no. 303 (July 1914). In the article, written shortly after his escape from Italy and return to London, Malatesta provides an account of the Red Week, which broke out on 7 June 1914 in Ancona, where Malatesta lived.

crowd, killing three workers, and wounding twenty more. After this massacre, the gendarmes, frightened, rushed to the barracks for shelter, and the people were left masters of the town. Without anybody even mentioning the word, a general strike was soon complete, and the workers collected at the Trades Council to hold a meeting.

The Government tried to prevent the events of Ancona from being telegraphed to other parts of the country; but nevertheless by-and-by the news became known, and strikes broke out in all the towns of Italy. The two Federal Labour organisations of Italy, the General Confederation of Labour, which is reformist, and the Labour Union,[2] with revolutionary tendencies, proclaimed a general strike, and the same was done by the Railwaymen's Union.

These strikes and demonstrations in several towns provoked new conflicts with the police, and new massacres. At once, without any common understanding, one place ignorant of what the other was doing, as communications were broken off, the movement assumed everywhere an insurrectional character, and in many places the Republic, which meant for the people the autonomous Commune, was proclaimed.

All was going splendidly; the movement was developing, and the railway strike, spreading on all lines, paralysed the Government; the workers were beginning to take measures of practical Communism in view of reorganising social life on a new basis; when suddenly the Confederation of Labour, by an act which has been qualified as treachery, ordered the strike off, thereby throwing the workers into confusion and discouraging them.

The Government was not slow to profit by this condition, and began to restore "order."

If it had not been for the betrayal of the Confederation, though we could not yet have made the revolution for lack of necessary preparation and understanding, the movement would certainly have assumed larger proportions and a much greater importance.

In every way these events have proved that the mass of the people hate the present order; that the workers are disposed to make use of all opportunities to overthrow the Government; and that when the fight is directed against the common enemy—that is to say, the Government and the bourgeoisie—all are brothers, though the names of Socialist, Anarchist, Syndicalist, or Republican may seem to divide them.

Now it is up to revolutionaries to profit by these good dispositions.

---

2 In Italian: *Unione Sindacale Italiana* (USI).

53. ANARCHISTS HAVE FORGOTTEN THEIR PRINCIPLES[1]

At the risk of passing as a simpleton, I confess that I would never have believed it possible that Socialists—even Social Democrats—would applaud and voluntarily take part, either on the side of the Germans or on that of the Allies, in a war like the one that is at present devastating Europe. But what is there to say when the same is done by Anarchists—not numerous, it is true, but having amongst them comrades whom we love and respect most?

It is said that the present situation shows the bankruptcy of "our formulas"—i.e., of our principles—and that it will be necessary to revise them.

Generally speaking, every formula must be revised whenever it shows itself insufficient when coming into contact with facts; but it is not the case to-day, when the bankruptcy is not derived from the shortcomings of our formulas, but from the fact that these have been forgotten and betrayed.

Let us return to our principles.

I am not a "pacifist." I fight, as we all do, for the triumph of peace and of fraternity amongst all human beings; but I know that a desire not to fight can only be fulfilled when neither side wants to, and that so long as men will be found who want to violate the liberties of others, it is incumbent on these others to defend themselves if they do not wish to be eternally beaten; and I also know that to attack is often the best, or the only, effective means of defending oneself. Besides, I think that the oppressed are always in a state of legitimate self-defence, and have always the right to attack the oppressors. I admit, therefore, that there are wars that are necessary, holy wars: and these are wars of liberation, such as are generally "civil wars"—i.e., revolutions.

---

1 *Freedom* (London) 28, no. 307 (November 1914). The article was part of a "Symposium on the War," a few months after German troops had invaded neutral Belgium. The other three articles in the symposium, by the French Jean Grave, the Russian Warlaam Tcherkessoff, and the Belgian Frans Verbelen, were all in favor of intervention.

But what has the present war in common with human emancipation, which is our cause?

To-day we hear Socialists speak, just like any bourgeois, of "France," of "Germany," and of other political and national agglomerations—results of historical struggles—as of homogenous ethnographic units, each having its proper interests, aspirations, and mission, in opposition to the interests, aspirations, and mission of rival units. This may be true relatively, so long as the oppressed, and chiefly the workers, have no self-consciousness, fail to recognise the injustice of their inferior position, and make themselves the docile tools of the oppressors. There is, then, the dominating class only that counts; and this class, owing to its desire to conserve and to enlarge its power, even its prejudices and its own ideals, may find it convenient to excite racial ambitions and hatred, and send its nation, its flock, against "foreign" countries, with a view to releasing them from their present oppressors, and submitting them to its own political and economical domination.

But the mission of those who, like us, wish the end of all oppression and of all exploitation of man by man, is to awaken a consciousness of the antagonism of interests between dominators and dominated, between exploiters and workers, and to develop the class struggle inside each country, and the solidarity among all workers across the frontiers, as against any prejudice and any passion of either race or nationality.

And this we have always done. We have always preached that the workers of all countries are brothers, and that the enemy—the "foreigner"—is the exploiter, whether born near us or in a far-off country, whether speaking the same language or any other. We have always chosen our friends, our companions-in-arms, as well as our enemies, because of the ideas they profess and of the position they occupy in the social struggle, and never for reasons of race or nationality. We have always fought against patriotism, which is a survival of the past, and serves well the interests of the oppressors; and we were proud of being internationalists, not only in words, but by the deep feelings of our souls.

And now that the most atrocious consequences of capitalist and State domination should indicate, even to the blind, that we were in the right, most of the Socialists and many Anarchists in the belligerent countries associate themselves with the Governments and the bourgeoisie of the respective countries, forgetting Socialism, the class struggle, international fraternity, and the rest.

What a downfall!

It is possible that present events may have shown that national feelings are more alive, while feelings of international brotherhood are less rooted, than we thought; but this should be one more reason for intensifying, not abandoning, our antipatriotic propaganda. These events also show that in France, for example, the religious sentiment is stronger, and the priests have a greater influence than we imagined. Is this a reason for our conversion to Roman Catholicism?

I understand that circumstances may arise owing to which the help of all is necessary for the general well-being: such as an epidemic, an earthquake, an invasion of barbarians, who kill and destroy all that comes under their hands. In such a case the class struggle, the differences of social standing must be forgotten, and common cause must be made against the common danger; but on the condition that these differences are forgotten on both sides. If any one is in prison during an earthquake, and there is a danger of his being crushed to death, it is our duty to save everybody, even the gaolers—on condition that the gaolers begin by opening the prison doors. But if the gaolers take all precautions for the safe custody of the prisoners during and after the catastrophe, it is then the duty of the prisoners towards themselves as well as towards their comrades in captivity to leave the gaolers to their troubles, and profit by the occasion to save themselves.

If, when foreign soldiers invade the *sacred soil of the Fatherland,* the privileged class were to renounce their privileges, and would act so that the "Fatherland" really became the common property of all the inhabitants, it would then be right that all should fight against the invaders. But if kings wish to remain kings, and the landlords wish to take care of *their* lands and of *their* houses, and the merchants wish to take care of *their* goods, and even sell them at a higher price, then the workers, the Socialists and Anarchists, should leave them to their own devices, while being themselves on the look-out for an opportunity to get rid of the oppressors inside the country, as well as of those coming from outside.

In all circumstances, it is the duty of the Socialists, and especially of the Anarchists, to do everything that can weaken the State and the capitalist class, and to take as the only guide to their conduct the interests of Socialism; or, if they are materially powerless to act efficaciously for their own cause, at least to refuse any voluntary help to the cause of the enemy, and stand aside to save at least their principles—which means to save the future.

***

All I have just said is theory, and perhaps it is accepted, in theory, by most of those who, in practice, do just the reverse. How, then, could it be applied to the present situation? What should we do, what should we wish, in the interests of our cause?

It is said, on this side of the Rhine, that the victory of the Allies would be the end of militarism, the triumph of civilisation, international justice, etc. The same is said on the other side of the frontier about a German victory.

Personally, judging at their true value the "mad dog" of Berlin and the "old hangman" of Vienna, I have no greater confidence in the bloody Tsar, nor in the English diplomatists who oppress India, who betrayed Persia, who crushed the Boer Republics; nor in the French bourgeoisie, who massacred the natives of Morocco; nor in those of Belgium, who have allowed the Congo atrocities and have largely profited by them—and I only recall some of their misdeeds, taken at random, not to mention what all Governments and all capitalist classes do against the workers and the rebels in their own countries.

In my opinion, the victory of Germany would certainly mean the triumph of militarism and of reaction; but the triumph of the Allies would mean a Russo-English (i.e., a knouto-capitalist) domination in Europe and in Asia, conscription and the development of the militarist spirit in England, and a Clerical and perhaps Monarchist reaction in France.

Besides, in my opinion, it is most probable that there will be no definite victory on either side. After a long war, an enormous loss of life and wealth, both sides being exhausted, some kind of peace will be patched up, leaving all questions open, thus preparing for a new war more murderous than the present.

The only hope is revolution; and as I think that it is from vanquished Germany that in all probability, owing to the present state of things, the revolution would break out, it is for this reason—and for this reason only—that I wish the defeat of Germany.

I may, of course, be mistaken in appreciating the true position. But what seems to me elementary and fundamental for all Socialists

(Anarchists, or others) is that it is necessary to keep outside every kind of compromise with the Governments and the governing classes, so as to be able to profit by any opportunity that may present itself, and, in any case, to be able to restart and continue our revolutionary preparations and propaganda.

54.
PRO-GOVERNMENT ANARCHISTS[1]

A manifesto has just appeared, signed by Kropotkin, Grave, Malato, and a dozen other old comrades, in which, echoing the supporters of the Entente Governments who are demanding a fight to a finish and the crushing of Germany, they take their stand against any idea of "premature peace."

The capitalist Press publishes, with natural satisfaction, extracts from the manifesto, and announces it as the work of "leaders of the International Anarchist Movement."

Anarchists, almost all of whom have remained faithful to their convictions, owe it to themselves to protest against this attempt to implicate Anarchism in the continuance of a ferocious slaughter that has never held promise of any benefit to the cause of Justice and Liberty, and which now shows itself to be absolutely barren and resultless even from the standpoint of the rulers on either side.

The good faith and good intentions of those who have signed the manifesto are beyond all question. But, however painful it may be to disagree with old friends who have rendered so many services to that which in the past was our common cause, one cannot—having regard to sincerity, and in the interest of our movement for emancipation—fail to dissociate oneself from comrades who consider themselves able to reconcile Anarchist ideas and co-operation with the Governments and capitalist classes of certain countries in their strife against the capitalists and Governments of certain other countries.

During the present war we have seen Republicans placing themselves at the service of kings, Socialists making common cause with the ruling class, Labourists serving the interests of capitalists; but in reality all these people are, in varying degrees, Conservatives—believers in the mission of the State, and their hesitation can be understood when the only remedy lay in the destruction of every Governmental chain and the unloosing of the Social Revolution. But such hesitation is incomprehensible in the case of Anarchists.

We hold that the State is incapable of good. In the field of international as well as of individual relations it can only combat aggression

1 *Freedom* (London) 30, no. 324 (April 1916).

by making itself the aggressor; it can only hinder crime by organizing and committing still greater crime.

Even on the supposition—which is far from being the truth—that Germany alone was responsible for the present war, it is proved that, as long as governmental methods are adhered to, Germany can only be resisted by suppressing all liberty and reviving the power of all the forces of reaction. Except the popular Revolution, there is no other way of resisting the menace of a disciplined Army but to try and have a stronger and more disciplined Army; so that the sternest anti-militarists, if they are not Anarchists, and if they are afraid of the destruction of the State, are inevitably led to become ardent militarists.

In fact, in the problematical hope of crushing Prussian Militarism, they have renounced all the spirit and all the traditions of Liberty; they have Prussianised England and France; they have submitted themselves to Tsarism; they have restored the prestige of the tottering throne of Italy.

Can Anarchists accept this state of things for a single moment without renouncing all right to call themselves Anarchists? To me, even foreign domination suffered by force and leading to revolt, is preferable to domestic oppression meekly, almost gratefully, accepted, in the belief that by this means we are preserved from a greater evil.

It is useless to say that this is a question of an exceptional time, and that after having contributed to the victory of the Entente in "this war," we shall return, each into his own camp, to the struggle for his own ideal.

If it is necessary to-day to work in harmony with the Government and the capitalist to defend ourselves against "the German menace," it will be necessary afterwards, as well as during the war.

However great may be the defeat of the German Army—if it is true that it will be defeated—it will never be possible to prevent the German patriots thinking of, and preparing for, revenge; and the patriots of the other countries, very reasonably from their own point of view, will want to hold themselves in readiness so that they may not again be taken unawares. This means that Prussian Militarism will become a permanent and regular institution in all countries.

What will then be said by the self-styled Anarchists who to-day desire the victory of one of the warring alliances? Will they go on calling themselves anti-militarists and preaching disarmament, refusal to do military service, and sabotage against National Defence, only to become, at the first threat of war, recruiting sergeants for the Governments that they have attempted to disarm and paralyse?

It will be said that these things will come to an end when the German people have rid themselves of their tyrants and ceased to be a menace to Europe by destroying militarism in their own country. But, if that is the case, the Germans who think, and rightly so, that English and French domination (to say nothing of Tsarist Russia) would be no more delightful to the Germans than German domination to the French and English, will desire first to wait for the Russians and the others to destroy their own militarism, and will meanwhile continue to increase their own country's Army.

And then, how long will the Revolution be delayed? How long Anarchy? Must we always wait for the others to begin?

The line of conduct for Anarchists is clearly marked out by the very logic of their aspirations.

The war ought to have been prevented by bringing about the Revolution, or at least by making the Governments afraid of the Revolution. Either the strength or the skill necessary for this has been lacking.

Peace ought to be imposed by bringing about the Revolution, or at least by threatening to do so. To the present time, the strength or the skill is wanting.

Well! there is only one remedy: to do better in future. More than ever we must avoid compromise; deepen the chasm between capitalists and wage-slaves, between rulers and ruled; preach expropriation of private property and the destruction of States as the only means of guaranteeing fraternity between the people and Justice and Liberty for all; and we must prepare to accomplish these things.

Meanwhile it seems to me that it is criminal to do anything that tends to prolong the war, that slaughters men, destroys wealth, and hinders all resumption of the struggle for emancipation. It appears to me that preaching "war to the end" is really playing the game of the German rulers, who are deceiving their subjects and inflaming their ardour for fighting by persuading them that their opponents desire to crush and enslave the German people.

To-day, as ever, let this be our slogan: Down with Capitalists and Governments, all Capitalists and all Governments!

Long live the peoples, all the peoples!

A portrait of Malatesta around 1920

"United Proletarian Front": The Red Biennium, *Umanità Nova* and Fascism, 1919–23

When Malatesta returned to Italy, on 24 December 1919, the effects of the war and the galvanizing example of Russia had created a situation that gave ground for strong revolutionary hopes. Malatesta was received with enthusiasm and even hailed as the "Lenin of Italy." As he warned against such excesses, he set to work as editor of the anarchist daily *Umanità Nova,* which began publication in February 1920. First in the heat of the factory occupation, then after the revolutionary hopes had faded, and finally after the rise of fascism, Malatesta further elaborated his view, idealist and pragmatist at the same time, of the revolutionary process: he advocated a united front of all revolutionary forces, none of which was strong enough to win alone; he insisted on the practical measures and constructive work required in times of revolution, when no interruption in the provision of collective goods could be afforded; and he illustrated the humanist side of his anarchism, arguing that material interests were insufficient to bring about a revolution if they were not backed by an ideal, and re-asserting love as the fundamental spring of anarchism.

55. THE DICTATORSHIP OF THE PROLETARIAT AND ANARCHY[1]

Dearest Fabbri:

Upon the question that so occupies your mind, that of the dictatorship of the proletariat, it seems to me that we are fundamentally in accord.

Upon this question it seems to me that there can be no doubt among anarchists, and in fact there was none prior to the Bolshevist revolution. Anarchy signifies non-government, and therefore for a greater reason non-dictatorship, which is an absolute government without control and without constitutional limitations.

But when the Bolshevist revolution broke several of our friends confused that which was the revolution against the pre-existent government and that which was the new government that came to superimpose itself upon the revolution so as to split it and direct it to the particular ends of a party... and they came themselves very close to claiming to be bolshevists.

Now, the bolshevists are simply marxists, who have honestly and coherently remained marxist, unlike their masters and models—the Guesdes, the Plekanoffs, the Hyndmans, the Scheidemanns, the Noskes, who finished as you know. We respect their sincerity, we admire their energy, but as we have not been in accord with them on the ground of theory, we cannot affiliate with them when from theory they pass to action.

But perhaps the truth is simply this, that our Bolshevized friends intend with the expression "dictatorship of the proletariat" merely the revolutionary act of the workers in taking possession of the land and of the instruments of labor and trying to constitute a society for

1 *The Liberator* (New York) 4, no. 9 (September 1921). The letter was published in the body of the article "The Anarchists of Italy," by Norman Matson. Originally published as "La dittatura del proletariato e l'anarchia," *Volontà* (Ancona) 1, new series, no. 11 (16 August 1919), and reprinted as a preface to the book *Dittatura e Rivoluzione*, by Luigi Fabbri (Ancona: Bitelli, 1921). The original letter, of which only the part concerning Russia was published, was dated London, 30 July 1919. We have occasionally amended the translation where it was incorrect or incomplete.

organizing a mode of life in which there would be no place for a class that exploited and oppressed the producers.

Understood so the dictatorship of the proletariat would be the effective power of all the workers intent on breaking down capitalist society, and it would become anarchy immediately upon the cessation of reactionary resistance, and no one would attempt by force to make the masses obey him and work for him.

And then our dissent would have to do only with words. Dictatorship of the proletariat should signify dictatorship of all which certainly does not mean dictatorship, as a government of all is no longer a government, in the authoritarian, historic, practical sense of the word.

But the true partisans of the dictatorship of the proletariat do not understand the words so, as they have clearly shown in Russia. Obviously, the proletariat comes into it as the people comes into democratic regimes, that is to say, simply for the purpose of concealing the true essence of things. In reality one sees a dictatorship of a party, or rather of the heads of a party; and it is a true dictatorship, with its decrees, its penal laws, its executive agents and above all with its armed force that serves today also to defend the revolution for its external enemies, but that will serve tomorrow to impose upon the workers the will of the dictators, to arrest the revolution, consolidate the new interests and finally defend a new privileged class against the masses.

Bonaparte also served to defend the French revolution against the European reaction, but in defending it he killed it. Lenin, Trotsky and their companions are certainly sincere revolutionaries—as they understand the revolution, and the will not betray it; but they prepare the governmental cadres that will serve those that will come, who will profit from the revolution and kill it. They will be the first victims of their method, and with them, I fear, will fall the revolution. And history will repeat itself; mutatis mutandis, it was the dictatorship of Robespierre that brought Robespierre to the guillotine and prepared the way for Napoleon.

These are my general ideas upon things in Russia. Inasmuch as the news we get from Russia is too contradictory to base upon it a judgement, it is possible that many things that seem bad are the fruit of the situation, and that in the peculiar circumstances in Russia it was impossible to do otherwise than was done. It is better to wait, much more so in that whatever we might say would have no influence upon the developments in Russia, and might be ill interpreted in Italy and seem to echo the interested calumnies of the reaction.

The important thing is what we must do. But there we go again, I am far away, and it is impossible for me to do my part…

56. THANK YOU, BUT ENOUGH ALREADY[1]

I am back in Italy thanks to the efforts of comrades and friends and I thank them for having afforded me the means to make my contribution to our common cause. It grieves me that my modest faculties do not allow me to do as much as I should like or as, perhaps, is expected of me; be that as it may, I shall strive with all my belief and all the enthusiasm that burns within my heart.

Permit me now to make one observation critical of comrades' actions towards me.

During the agitation that took place for my return, and during these first days since my return to Italy, things have been done and said which offend my modesty and sense of proportion.

The comrades should remember that the hyperbole is a rhetorical figure of speech which should not be abused. They should above all remember that the exhaltation of man is politically a dangerous thing and morally unhealthy as much for him who is exhalted as for those who do the exhalting.

And then I am so made that I find handclapping and cheering unpleasant, tending to paralyze me rather than encourage me to work.

I want to be a comrade among comrades, and if I have the misfortune of being older than others it cannot please me to be continually reminded of this by the deference and attentions which the comrades inflict on me.

Do we understand one another?

---

1 Translated from "Grazie, ma basta," *Il Libertario* (La Spezia) 18, no. 747 (8 January 1920). An abridged English version of the article was included in Malatesta's pamphlet *Anarchy* (Buffalo: Friends of Malatesta, [1971]). We have used this version and integrated it with an original translation of the missing parts. The article was written a fortnight after Malatesta's return to Italy.

57. UNITED PROLETARIAN FRONT[1]

Sad to say that even today, on the eve of battle, with the old world already wobbly and when it will require just a determined push to topple it once and for all, there are still some workers fighting and nearly hating other workers merely because these belong to different, rival organizations and parties.

Today the bourgeoisie's and government's only hope of salvation is such division in the workers' ranks, and so whoever, for whatever reason, fans the fires of discord rather than striving to bring all the forces of revolution together under a single umbrella is a traitor to the cause of human emancipation.

We are anarchists and we fight solely for the success of our ideal. But the first step along the way that is to lead us towards our radiant ideal is the overthrow of established institutions, and so all who fight those institutions are our comrades-in-arms.

Whereas others, driven by a spirit of rivalry and a lust for hegemony, may try to portray us as sectarians, we still reach out a hand to all men of sincerity and combat only those methods that seem to us to run counter to the revolution, and such men whenever they turn up, are plainly betraying the cause they purport to serve.

In Italy there are two major proletarian organizations that ostensibly have their sights set on destruction of the capitalist system: the *Confederazione Generale del Lavoro* and the *Unione Sindacale Italiana.*[2]

Most of our sympathies certainly lie with the *Unione Sindacale,* since there are lots of our comrades among its leaders and its direct-action methods suit our tactic best.

That said, there are many comrades of ours in the *Confederazione del Lavoro* and the masses affiliated to the *Confederazione* are—and this is what matters most—genuine workers actually prompted by the very same spirit as the mass membership of the *Unione Sindacale.*

1 Translated from "Fronte unico proletario," *Umanità Nova* (Milan) 1, no. 35 (8 April 1920).

2 The membership and leadership of the older and larger *Confederazione Generale del Lavoro* significantly overlapped with those of the socialist party, while the *Unione Sindacale Italiana,* founded in 1912, had a revolutionary syndicalist orientation.

Above all else, the masses from both organizations must fraternize with one another and fight as one.

If the *Confederazione*'s regulations are such as to thwart the honest expression of the wishes of the membership, those regulations need to be fought against and an effort made to change them; if many of the *Confederazione*'s leaders are, as they appear to us to be, collaborationists busily snuffing out any suggestion of revolt, smothering any movement, then those leaders have to be fought against and steps taken to ensure that the masses do not let themselves be led like sheep by bad shepherds.

But the masses need to be united and it would be a lethal error to try to dissolve one organisation in order to bolster the other. All organisations need to be pushed forward by our entering them and bringing our spirit to them.

Let the workers bear this in mind:

When the bosses exploit them, they pay no heed to party distinctions and starve them all the same; when the *carabinieri* pepper their chests with the king's lead, they do not bother to ask first what sort of membership card they carry in their pockets.

Let that at least be a lesson.

58. THIS IS YOUR STUFF![1]

From a few places around Italy, where rebel hearts beat harder, we hear rumors of a madcap notion.

Of the destruction of the crops.

Only recently in the Novara area the peasants maimed oxen just to spite their bosses; and we were reminded of the husband who maimed himself in the nether regions just to punish his wife.

Such acts would be understandable at a time when workers had no hope of imminent liberation, when the slave, having no way of freeing himself, looked for a moment of bittersweet delight by taking his master with him when he died.

But these days, such acts would look more like a suicidal mania.

Today the workers stand on the brink of becoming the masters of all they have produced; today the revolution is hammering at the gates and we should be sparing with all products, especially foodstuffs, so that we may assured of survival and success.

Or is there anyone out there who thinks that, come the revolution, the need to eat will be no more?

The destruction of goods would be tantamount to making it impossible for us to pull off a revolution that brings benefits; and, at the time, since the goods of only a few bosses would be destroyed, that would be playing into the hands of other bosses who would profit by the growing shortfall and would sell off their products at higher prices.

Rather than thinking about destroying stuff, the workers must get used to the idea that everything that there is, everything that is produced, is theirs, in the hands of thieves today, but to be wrested back tomorrow.

It never occurs to any robbery victim to destroy his possessions just to spite the thief, when he knows that he will shortly be getting his stuff back.

Rather than toying with the idea of destroying things, the workers should keep an eye out that the bosses do not waste it; they should prevent the bosses and the government from letting products go to

1 Translated from "È roba vostra!" *Umanità Nova* (Milan) 1, no. 88 (10 June 1920).

ruin through speculation or neglect, from leaving the land untilled and the workers jobless, or engaged in the churning out of useless or harmful goods.

Starting right now, the workers should think of themselves as the owners, and start acting like owners.

The destruction of stuff is the act of a slave—a rebellious slave, but a slave nonetheless.

The workers today do not want and do not have to be slaves any longer.

59. THE TWO ROUTES: REFORM OR REVOLUTION? FREEDOM OR DICTATORSHIP?[1]

I

The conditions within society at present cannot last forever—and we may state today that they cannot last much longer.

Everybody is agreed on that—those who give it any thought, at any rate.

There are no more conservatives in the proper sense of the term.

Instead, there are folk who aim to profit from the present moment and enjoy their privileges for as long as they may without worrying if, after them, the deluge will come. There are also rabid reactionaries who would like to turn back the clock, drown any attempt at liberation in blood, and subject the masses to the rule of the sword. All to no avail. The reaction may manage to dye the rising dawn a brighter blood red; but it will never succeed in preventing the coming catastrophe.

The masses refuse to be cowed any longer.

As long as the belief was that suffering was a punishment or some test set by God and that all of the evils borne down here would be repaid one-hundred fold in the next world, a system of iniquity could be installed and endure, a system whereby a handful of men impose their will on others, exploiting and oppressing them according to their whim.

But such belief has never been all that effective because it has never stopped folk from looking out for their own interests on this earth, which is why religion has not managed to snuff out progress entirely. And such belief has dwindled considerably: it is in the throes of disappearing. Even the clergy are obliged, in order to rescue

1 "The Two Roads," *Freedom* (London) 35, no. 386 (August 1921). Originally published as "Le due vie: Riforme o rivoluzione? Libertà o dittatura?" parts 1–3, *Umanità Nova* (Milan) 1, nos. 136, 142, and 145 (5, 12, and 15 August 1920). The English version is an abridgment of the article's second section. We have integrated it with an original translation of the missing parts.

religion and at the same time to be saved, to adopt the air of wanting to resolve the social question and ease the workers' afflictions.

From the moment that the workers' eyes are opened to the place that they occupy in society, it is impossible for them to carry on toiling and suffering forever, producing their whole lives long on behalf of their masters and with no prospect before them save the heartbreak of an old age when they will not have even the guarantee of shelter and bread. Since they are the producers of all wealth and know that they can produce in order to more than meet the needs of all, it is impossible for them to want to resign themselves forever to a wretched existence with the constant threat of unemployment and hunger. Being better educated, refined through contact with civilization, even it be for the benefit of others, and having tasted the strength that they can derive from unity and courage, it is impossible for them to make do with remaining a scorned lower class and for them not to stake their claim to a great share in life's joys.

Today the proletarian knows that, as a rule, he is doomed to remaining a proletarian for life, unless there is some widespread alteration to the social order. He knows that that alteration cannot come about without the aid of other proletarians, and this is why he looks to union for the strength needed to impose it.

The bourgeois and the governments that represent and defend them know this as well, and in order to avoid their being swept away in some awful social cataclysm, they appreciate the need to take some sort of steps; especially since there is no dearth of intelligent bourgeois who appreciate that society, as it stands at present, is a nonsense and, deep down, damaging even to those who are its beneficiaries.

So, sooner or later, by fits and starts or gradually, change must come.

But what will be the substance of that change and how far will it go?

Today's society is split into the propertied and the proletarian. It can change by doing away with the status of proletarian and by making each and every one co-owner of society's wealth; or it can change whilst retaining the distinction that underpins it but guaranteeing the proletarians better treatment.

In the first case, men would become free and socially equal; they would then organize society according to the wishes of each and every person, and the full potential of human nature could develop in its infinite variations. In the second case, the proletarians as useful and well-fed cattle, would resign themselves to their slavish condition and be happy with their kindly masters.

Freedom or slavery. Anarchy or slavishness.

Those two potential solutions lie at the root of two divergent trends represented in their most logical and coherent manifestations, by the anarchists on one hand and by the so-called reformist socialists on the other. With this difference: the anarchists know and state what they want, which is the destruction of the State, and society freely organized on a footing of economic equality; whereas the socialists are at odds with themselves; they purport to be socialists when their activity has a tendency to husband and perpetuate the capitalist system by rendering it more humane; and they thereby renege upon their socialism, the primary meaning of which is abolition of the division of people into the propertied and the proletarian.

The task of anarchists—and, let me say, or all real socialists—is to oppose this trend towards slavishness, towards a state of attenuated slavery that would strip humanity of its finest qualities, deny the operation of society of its finest potential—and, in the meantime, helps sustain the impoverishment and degradation into which the masses are thrust, by persuading them to be patient and to trust in the providence of the State and in the kindness and understanding of their masters.

All allegedly social legislation, all state measures designed to "protect" labour and guarantee workers a modicum of well-being and security, as well as all measures employed by astute capitalists to chain the worker to the factory by means of bonuses, pensions, and other benefits, unless they are lies or snares, are indeed a step in the direction of that state of enslavement, which poses a threat to the emancipation of the workers and the progress of humankind.

A legally prescribed minimum wage; legal limits placed upon the working day; mandatory arbitration; legally enforceable collective bargaining; legal status for workers' associations; government-prescribed hygiene measures in factories; state insurance against sickness, unemployment, accidents at work; old-age pensions; profit-sharing schemes, etc., etc.—these are all measures designed to ensure that the proletarians stay proletarians forever and the propertied propertied forever; all measures that afford the workers slightly more comfort and security (if that), but that rob them of what little freedom they have and that have a tendency to perpetuate the division of mankind into masters and slaves.

To be sure, until such time as the revolution gets here, it is a good thing—which brings revolution closer—for workers to try to earn more and work fewer hours and in improved conditions. It is a good thing for the jobless not to starve to death, for the sick and the elderly not to be abandoned. But these and other things can and should be won by the workers themselves, through direct struggle with their masters, through their own organizations; by means of individual and collective action and by nurturing every person's sense of personal dignity and awareness of his rights.

Gifts from the State and *gifts* from the bosses are poisoned fruit that carry within them the seeds of slavery. And should be refused.

II

If awarded and accepted as advantageous concessions granted by the State and the bosses, all reforms that leave the division of people into the propertied and the proletarian—and, therefore, some people's right to live off other people's toil—unaltered, cannot help but dampen the rebelliousness of the masses against their oppressors and lead to the introduction of a state of slavishness whereby humanity would be irreversibly split into ruling classes and slave classes. Once this is acknowledged, there is no other option but revolution: a radical revolution that demolishes the entire machinery of the State, expropriates those who cling to society's wealth, and places everybody on an equal footing, economically and politically.

That revolution will, of necessity, be violent, although violence per se is obnoxious. It has to be violent because it would be a nonsense to expect the privileged to wake up to the woes and injustice that sprout from their privileges and to make up their minds to forego them of their own volition. It has to be violent because transitory revolutionary violence is the only way of ending the greater and enduring violence that holds the vast majority of people in slavery.

We welcome reforms, if they are possible. They have a fleeting contribution to make and can rouse the masses to more ambitions and demands, provided that proletarians keep it well in mind that bosses and governments are their enemies and that whatever they grant is wrested from them by force or fear of force and would quickly be snatched back, should that fear be lifted. If, instead, reforms are secured by means of agreement and collaboration between the ruled and the rulers, they cannot help but strengthen the chains binding the workers to the chariot of the parasites.

Besides, these days, the danger of reforms lulling the masses to sleep and successfully consolidating and perpetuating the bourgeois order seems to have passed. Only deliberate treachery by those who have managed to win the workers' trust through their socialist propaganda could attach value to them.

The blindness of the ruling class and the natural evolution of the capitalist system, accelerated by the war, led to this, that any reform whatever which would be acceptable to the owners of property is powerless to solve the crisis under which the country labours.

Hence the revolution is imposing itself, the revolution is coming.

But how must this revolution be effected, and what development must it take?

It is, of course, necessary to begin by that insurrectional action which will sweep away the material obstacle, the armed forces of the government, which opposes every social change. For this insurrection, since here we live in a monarchy, the union of all the anti-monarchist forces is desirable, and possibly essential. It is necessary to be prepared, morally and materially, in the best possible way, and it is before all necessary to profit by all spontaneous movements and to endeavour to make them general and to transform them into decisive movements, in order that, whilst the parties are preparing themselves, the popular forces shall not be exhausted by isolated outbreaks.

But after the victory of the insurrection, after the fall of the government, what must be done then?

We, the anarchists, wish that in each locality the workers, or, more properly, that part of the workers which has the clearest insight of their position and the readiest spirit of initiative, should take possession of all the instruments of labour, all wealth, land, raw materials, houses, machinery, foodstuffs, etc., and should sketch out as far as possible the new form of social life. We wish that the agricultural labourers who now toil for their masters should no longer recognise the rights of any landlords, and should continue and intensify their work on their own account, entering into direct relations with the industrial and transport workers for the exchange of products; that the industrial workers, leading engineers and the technical staff included, should take possession of the factories, and should continue and intensify their work on their own account and that of the community, transforming rapidly all those factories which produce useless or harmful things into establishments for the production of articles which the people most urgently need; that the railway workers should continue to run the railways, but for the use of the community; that community or voluntary workers, locally elected, should, under the direct control of the masses, take possession of all available habitations, to shelter as best the hour will permit all the most indigent; that other committees, always under the direct control of the masses, should provide for the food supply and the distribution of articles of daily use; that all real bourgeois be placed under the necessity of merging with the mass of the former proletarians and of working like them in order to enjoy the same benefit as they. And all this must be effected quickly, on the same day as the victorious insurrection or the day after, without waiting for orders from central committees or any other authority whatever.

This is what the anarchists want and this also would naturally happen if the revolution is really to be a social revolution and not limited to a simple political change which, after some convulsions, would lead everything back to the starting-point.

For either the bourgeois class is rapidly stripped of its economic power or it will soon take back also the political power of which the insurrection deprived it. And to strip the bourgeois class of its economic power it is necessary to organise immediately a new economic order founded upon justice and equality. The economic services, at least the most important ones, admit of no interruption and must be satisfied quickly. "Central committees" either do nothing or begin to act when their work is no longer needed.

In opposition to anarchists, many revolutionists have no confidence in the constructive power of the masses; they believe themselves to be in possession of infallible recipes for universal happiness; they fear a possible reaction; they fear perhaps more the competition of other parties and other schools of social reformers, and they want, therefore, to possess themselves of all power and to replace the "democratic" government of to-day by a dictatorial government.

Dictatorship they mean; but who would be the dictators? Of course, so they think, the chiefs of their party. They still use the words *dictatorship of the proletariat,* either from habit or from a conscious desire to evade plain explanations; but this is to-day an exploded farce.

Here is the explanation from Lenin, or whoever wrote on his behalf (see *Avanti* of 20 July).[2]

*"Dictatorship means a toppling of the bourgeoisie by means of a revolutionary vanguard (*which is revolution rather than dictatorship*), in contrast to the notion that one must first secure a majority by means of elections. By means of the dictatorship the majority is obtained, not the dictatorship by means of the majority."* (Fine. But if we have a minority that has to win over the majority after it has seized power, all talk of a dictatorship of the proletariat is a lie. The proletariat is obviously the majority.)

"Dictatorship means the use of violence and terror." (By whom and against whom? Since the supposition is that the majority is hostile and, according to the dictatorship rationale, it cannot be a matter of an unrestrained mob that lays hands on public assets, the *violence and terror* must be those deployed against all those who do not bend to the whims of the dictators, by goons in the service of those dictators).

"Freedom of the press and of association would be tantamount to authorizing the bourgeoisie to poison public opinion." (So, after the installation of a dictatorship of the "proletariat," which is supposedly made up of the totality of workers, there is still going to be a bourgeoisie that, instead of working, will have the means to poison "public opinion," and a pubic opinion open to being poisoned, and separate from the proletarians who would be setting up the dictatorship? There will be all-powerful censors who will determine what can be published or not published, and prefects to whom one will have to apply for permission to hold a meeting. There is no need to talk about the freedom that would be afforded those who might not be loyal subjects of the rulers of the day.)

"Only after the propertied have been expropriated, only in the wake of victory will the proletariat win over the masses of the population, which hitherto followed the bourgeoisie." (Yet again we have to ask: what is this proletariat when it is not the mass of those who work? Does proletariat therefore mean those with a certain outlook and who belong to a certain party, rather than those who have no property?)

---

2 The article in question was a correspondence from Berlin signed "Geselle" and titled "Come Lenin rinunzia alla Dittatura del Proletariato" (How Lenin gives up the dictatorship of the proletariat). In response to "a legend borne out in social democratic circles," according to which "Lenin and the Russian would be softening their theories" to broaden the Third International's base, the article listed ten statements about the dictatorship of the proletariat, whose acceptance was a pre-condition for admission to the Third International.

So we will leave this wrong term of proletarian dictatorship, which leads to so many misunderstandings, and speak of dictatorship as it really is—that is, of the absolute domination of one or several individuals who, by the support of a party or of an army, become the masters of the social body and impose their will "with violence and with terror."

What their will may be depends upon the quality of those who in any particular case get hold of the power. In our case it is supposed to be the will of the communists, hence a will inspired with the desire of the common good.

This is rather doubtful already, because as a rule those who are best qualified to seize the reins of power are not the most sincere and the most devoted friends of the public cause, and when submission to a new government is preached to the masses, this means but paving the way for intriguers and ambitious persons.

But let us suppose that the new rulers, the dictators who will put into practice the aims of the revolution, are true communists, full of zeal, convinced that upon their work and their energy the happiness of mankind depends. They may be men of the Torquemada and Robespierre type, who, for a good purpose, in the name of private or public salvation, would strangle every discordant voice, destroy every breath of free and spontaneous life – and yet, powerless to solve the practical problems which they withdraw from competent handling by the interested parties themselves, they must willingly or unwillingly give way to those who will restore the past.

The principal justifications of dictatorship are the alleged incapacity of the masses and the necessity of defending the revolution against reactionary attempts.

If the masses were really a dumb flock unable to live without the staff of the shepherd, if a sufficiently numerous and conscious minority able to carry away the masses by persuasion and example did not already exist, then we would be able to understand the standpoint of the reformists who are afraid of a popular upheaval and fancy that they can, bit by bit, by small reforms, small improvements, undermine the bourgeois State and prepare the road to socialism; we would be able to understand the *educationists* who, underrating the influence of surroundings, hope to change society by previously changing all individuals; but we really cannot understand the partisans of dictatorship who want to educate and raise the masses "by violence and terror," and so must use gendarmes and censors as prime factors of education.

In reality, nobody could be in the position to establish a revolutionary dictatorship if the people had not previously made the revolution, thus showing effectively that it is able to make it; and in this case dictatorship would only step on the neck of the revolution, divert, strangle, and kill it.

In a political revolution proposing only to overthrow the government and leaving intact the existing social organisation, a dictatorship may seize power, place its men in the posts of the deposed functionaries, and organise a new régime from above.

But in a social revolution where all the foundations of social life are overthrown, where production must be quickly re-established for the benefit of those who work, where distribution must be immediately regulated according to justice, a dictatorship could do nothing. Either the people will provide for themselves in the various communities and industries or the revolution will be a failure.

Perhaps, at bottom (and some of them are now saying it openly) the supporters of dictatorship want to see nothing more than a political revolution in the short term; in other words, they would like to take power, and that's that, and then progressively change society by means of laws and decrees. In which case, they would probably be surprised to see others ensconcing themselves in power rather than themselves and, in any event, they would, above all, have to give some thought to raising an armed force (police), required if they are to enforce respect for their own laws. In the interim, the bourgeoisie would still hold the wealth, in essence, and once the critical point of popular anger has passed, it would prepare its backlash, pack the police with agents of its own, exploit the unease and disillusionment of those who had been expecting to see the earthly paradise achieved straight away... and would seize back power by winning over the dictators or replacing them with men of its own.

That fear of reaction, used to justify the dictatorial system, springs from the fact that it pretends to make the revolution whilst a privileged class, able to take hold again of power, is still permitted to exist.

If, on the contrary, the beginning is made by complete expropriation, then a bourgeois class will no longer exist, and all the living forces of the proletariat, all existing capacities, will be employed on social reconstruction.

After all, in a country like Italy (to apply these remarks to the country in which we work), where the masses are penetrated by libertarian and rebel instincts, where anarchists represent a considerable force by the influence which they can exercise quite apart from their organisations, an attempt at dictatorship could not be made without provoking civil war between workers and workers, and could not succeed unless it were by means of the most ferocious tyranny.

In that case, good-bye to communism!

There is only one possible way of salvation: LIBERTY.

60.
THE REVOLUTIONARY "HASTE"[1]

Let us deal again with G. Valenti's article republished by the Reggio Emilia newspaper *Giustizia*.[2]

Valenti dwells on enumerating all the masses that are indifferent or hostile to subversive propaganda. Writing about the United States, he claims that there are sixty (?) million Catholics organized in religious associations who go to church and pray to God, and he invites the anarchists to go and make propaganda among those sixty million, if they want to speed up the revolution. He claims that only four and a half million producers out of forty million are organized in groups, the majority of which, as a matter of fact, are still opposed to socialism. He also invites trade unionists to start working at organizing workers in unions, if they really want to speed up the revolution. He claims that only one million voters out of twenty-five million voted for Debs in the last polls; he recalls that in the South socialist speakers get beaten and driven out of towns by mobs intoxicated with patriotism; finally, he invites communists to go and propagandize their 21 points in the South, instead of "bugging socialists into accepting them."

This is all too true and right, if it means that we have to make propaganda and do our best to win over as many individuals, as many masses as possible to the ideas of emancipation.

On the other hand, the argument is completely wrong if it means that the demolition of capitalism has to wait until those 60 million Catholics become free thinkers, until all workers (or their majority) are organized for class struggle, and Debs gets out of prison thanks to the majority of voters.

Let us not misunderstand. It is an axiomatic, self-evident truth that a revolution can only be made when there is enough strength

1 Translated from "La 'fretta' rivoluzionaria," *Umanità Nova* (Rome) 2, no. 125 (6 September 1921).

2 *La Giustizia* was a socialist newspaper. Malatesta had already commented upon the article in question three days before, thus summarizing its content: "*La Giustizia* of Reggio Emilia, which should know better, reprints from the *Avanti* of Chicago an article by G. Valenti in which the successive splits between socialists and anarchists, socialists and syndicalists, socialists and communists, are explained as one and the same dissension."

to make it. However, it is a historical truth that the forces determining evolution and social revolutions cannot be reckoned with census papers.

Catholics in the United States and elsewhere will remain as numerous as they are, or even grow in numbers, as long as there is a class holding the power of wealth and science, and interested in keeping the masses in their intellectual slavery, in order to dominate them more easily. Workers will never be fully organized, and their organizations will always be subject to breaking down or degenerating, as long as poverty, unemployment, fear of losing one's job, and desire to improve one's conditions feed the antagonism among workers, giving the masters the opportunity to profit from any circumstances and any crises to make the workers compete against each other. And voters will always be sheep by definition, even if sometimes they happen to kick back.

Given certain economic conditions and a certain social environment, it is proven that the intellectual and moral conditions of the masses stay basically the same. Until an external, ideally or materially violent event comes and changes that environment, propaganda, education, and instruction remain helpless; they only act upon those individuals who can overcome the environment in which they are forced to live, by virtue of natural or social privileges. However, that small number, that self-conscious and rebellious minority, born by every social order, in consequence of those injustices to which the masses are subject, acts like a historical ferment, which suffices, as it always did, to make the world progress.

Every new idea and institution, all progress and every revolution have always been the work of minorities. It is our aspiration and our aim that everyone should become socially conscious and effective, but to achieve this end, it is necessary to provide all with the means of life and for development. It is therefore necessary to destroy with violence—since one cannot do otherwise—the violence that denies these means to the workers.

Naturally, the "small numbers," the minority, must be sufficient, and those who imagine that we want to have an insurrection every day without taking into account the forces opposing us, or whether circumstances are in our favor or against us, misjudge us. In the now-remote past, we were able, and did, carry out a number of minute insurrectionary acts that had no probability of success. But in those days we were indeed only a handful, and wanted the public to talk about us, and our attempts were simply means of propaganda.

Now it is no longer a question of uprising to make propaganda; now we can win, and so we want to win, and only take such action when we think we can win. Of course we can be mistaken, and on the grounds of temperament may be led into believing that the fruit is ripe when it is still green; but we must confess our preference for those who err on the side of haste as opposed to those who always play a waiting game and let the best opportunities slip through their fingers for they, through fear of picking a green fruit, then let the whole crop go rotten!

In conclusion, we completely agree with *La Giustizia* when it emphasizes the necessity of making a lot of propaganda and of developing proletarian struggle organizations as much as possible; but we definitely depart from it when it maintains that we should not take action until we have drawn the majority of that inert mass, which will only be converted by the events and will only accept the revolution after the revolution has begun.

61. CLASS STRUGGLE OR CLASS HATRED?: "PEOPLE" AND "PROLETARIAT"[1]

I expressed to the jury in Milan some ideas about class struggle and proletariat that raised criticism and amazement. I better come back to those ideas.

I protested indignantly against the accusation of inciting to hatred; I explained that in my propaganda I had always sought to demonstrate that the social wrongs do not depend on the wickedness of one master or the other, one governer or the other, but rather on masters and governments as institutions; therefore, the remedy does not lie in changing the individual rulers, instead it is necessary to demolish the principle itself by which men dominate over men; I also explained that I had always stressed that proletarians are not individually better than bourgeois, as shown by the fact that a worker behaves like an ordinary bourgeois, and even worse, when he gets by some accident to a position of wealth and command.

Such statements were distorted, counterfeited, put in a bad light by the bourgeois press, and the reason is clear. The duty of the press, paid to defend the interests of police and sharks, is to hide the real nature of anarchism from the public, and seek to accredit the tale about anarchists being full of hatred and destroyers; the press does that by duty, but we have to acknowledge that they often do it in good faith, out of pure and simple ignorance. Since journalism, which was once a calling, decayed into mere job and business, journalists have lost not only their ethical sense, but also the intellectual honesty of refraining from talking about what they do not know.

Let us forget about hack writers, then, and let us talk about those who differ from us in their ideas, and often only in their way of

1 Translated from "Lotta di classe o odio tra le classi?: 'Popolo' e 'proletariato,'" *Umanità Nova* (Rome) 2, n. 137 (20 September 1921). This was the fourth and last of a series of articles published under the common title "Intorno al mio processo" (About My Trial). Malatesta, who was the chief editor of the daily *Umanità Nova,* had been arrested in October 1920, together with other anarchists. They stood trial at the end of July 1921, after more than nine months of detention, and were all acquitted.

expressing ideas, but still remain our friends, because they sincerely aim at the same goal we aim at.

Amazement is completely unmotivated in these people, so much so that I would tend to think it is affected. They cannot ignore that I have been saying and writing those things for fifty years, and that the same things have been said by hundreds and thousands of anarchists, at my same time and before me.

Let us rather talk about the dissent.

There are the "worker-minded" people, who consider having callous hands as being divinely imbued with all merits and all virtues; they protest if you dare talking about people and mankind, failing to swear on the sacred name of proletariat.

Now, it is a truth that history has made the proletariat the main instrument of the next social change, and that those fighting for the establishment of a society where *all* human beings are free and endowed with all the means to exercise their freedom, must rely mainly on the proletariat.

As today the hoarding of natural resources and capital created by the work of past and present generations is the main cause of the subjection of the masses and of all social wrongs, it is natural for those who have nothing, and who are therefore more directly and clearly interested in sharing the means of production, to be the main agents of the necessary expropriation. This is why we address our propaganda more particularly to the proletarians, whose conditions of life, on the other hand, make it often impossible for them to rise and conceive a superior ideal. However, this is no reason for turning the poor man into a fetish just because he is poor; neither it is a reason for encouraging him to believe that he is intrinsically superior, and that a condition surely not coming from his merit or his will gives him the right to do wrong to the others as the others did wrong to him. The tyranny of callous hands (which in practice is still the tyranny of few who no longer have callous hands, even if they had once), would not be less tough and wicked, and would not bear less lasting evils than the tyranny of gloved hands. Perhaps it would be less enlightened and more brutal: that is all.

Poverty would not be the horrible thing it is, if it did not, when prolonged from generation to generation, produce moral brutishness as well as material harm and physical degradation. The poor have different faults than those produced in the privileged classes by wealth and power, but not better ones.

If the bourgeoisie produces the likes of Giolitti and Graziani and all the long succession of mankind's torturers, from the great conquerors to the avid and bloodsucking petty bosses, it also produces the likes of Cafiero, Reclus, and Kropotkin, and the many people that in any epoch sacrificed their class privileges to an ideal. If the proletariat gave and gives so many heroes and martyrs of the cause of human redemption, it also gives off the white guards, the slaughterers, the traitors of their own brothers, without which the bourgeois tyranny could not last a single day.

How can hatred be raised to a principle of justice, to an enlightened spirit of demand, when it is clear that evil is everywhere, and it depends upon causes that go beyond individual will and responsibility?

Let there be as much class struggle as one wishes, if by class struggle one means the struggle of the exploited against the exploiters for the abolition of exploitation. That struggle is a way of moral and material elevation, and it is the main revolutionary force that can be relied on.

Let there be no hatred, though, because love and justice cannot arise from hatred. Hatred brings about revenge, desire to be over the enemy, need to consolidate one's superiority. Hatred can only be the foundation of new governments, if one wins, but it cannot be the foundation of anarchy.

Unfortunately, it is easy to understand the hatred of so many wretches whose bodies and sentiments are tormented and harrowed by society: however, as soon as the hell in which they live is lit up by an ideal, hatred disappears and a burning desire of fighting for the good of all takes over.

For this reason, true haters cannot be found among our comrades, although there are many rhetoricians of hatred. They are like the poet, who is a good and peaceful father, but he sings of hatred, because this gives him the opportunity of composing good verses... or perhaps bad ones. They talk about hatred, but their hatred is made of love.

For this reason, I love them, even if they call me names.

62. REVOLUTION IN PRACTICE[1]

At the meeting held in Bienne (Switzerland) on the fiftieth anniversary of the Saint Imier Congress, comrade Bertoni and I expressed some ideas that comrade Colomer did not like. So much so, that he wrote in Paris's *Libertaire* that he is sure those ideas contrast the most lively tendencies of the contemporary anarchist movement. Had the comrades of Germany, Spain, Russia, America, etc. been present at that meeting, he writes, they would have got moved and nearly indignant ("*émus et presque indigné*"), as he himself did.

In my opinion, comrade Colomer slightly overstates his knowledge of the real tendencies of anarchism. In any case, it is an improper use of language, at the least, to talk about "indignation" when the matter is a discussion where everyone honestly tries to contribute to the clarification of ideas in the best interest of the common goal. Anyway, it is better to keep discussing in a friendly manner, as we did in Bienne.

Bertoni will certainly defend his ideas on the *Réveil;* I will do the same on *Umanità Nova,* as will Colomer on the *Libertaire.* Other comrades, I hope, will join in the discussion; and it will be to the benefit of all, if everyone takes care not to alter the contradictor's thought in the translations imposed by the diversity of languages. And it does not hurt to hope that nobody will get indignant if he hears something that he had never thought of.

Two topics were discussed in Bienne: "Relationships between syndicalism and anarchism", and "Anarchist action at the outbreak of an insurrection." I will come back to the former topic some other time and unhurriedly, as the readers of *Umanità Nova* must already know what I think about the issue. I will presently explain what I said on the latter topic.

***

We want to make the revolution as soon as possible, taking advantage of all the opportunities that may arise.

---

1 Translated from "La rivoluzione in pratica," *Umanità Nova* (Rome) 3, no. 191 (7 October 1922).

With the exception of a small number of "educationists," who believe in the possibility of raising the masses to the anarchist ideals before the material and moral conditions in which they live have changed, thus deferring the revolution to the time when all will be able to live anarchically, all anarchists agree on this desire of overthrowing the current regimes as soon as possible: as a matter of fact, they are often the only ones who show a real wish to do so.

However, revolutions did, do, and will happen independently from the anarchists' wish and action; and since anarchists are just a small minority of the population and anarchy cannot be made by force and violent imposition by few, it is clear that past and future revolutions were not and will not possibly be anarchist revolutions.

In Italy two years ago the revolution was about to break out and we did all we could to make that happen. We treated like traitors the socialists and the unionists, who stopped the impetus of the masses and saved the shaky monarchical regime on the occasion of the riots against the high cost of living, the strikes in Piedmont, the Ancona uprising, the factory occupations.

What would we have done if the revolution had broken out for good?

What will we do in the revolution that will break out tomorrow?

What did our comrades do, what could and should they have done in the recent revolutions that occurred in Russia, Bavaria, Hungary, and elsewhere?

We cannot make anarchy, at least not an anarchy extended to all the population and all the social relations, because no population is anarchist yet, and we cannot either accept another regime without giving up our aspirations and losing any reason for existence, as anarchists. So, what can and must we do?

This was the problem being discussed in Bienne, and this is the problem of greatest interest in the present time, so full of opportunities, when we could suddenly face situations that require for us to either act immediately and unhesitatingly, or disappear from the battleground after making the victory of others easier.

It was not a matter of depicting a revolution as we would like it, a truly anarchist revolution as would be possible if all, or at least the vast majority of the people living in a given territory were anarchist. It was a matter of seeking the best that could be done in favor of the anarchist cause in a social upheaval as can happen in the present situation.

The authoritarian parties have a specific program and want to impose it by force; therefore they aspire to seizing the power, regardless of whether legally or illegally, and transforming society their way, through a new legislation. This explains why they are revolutionary in words and often also in intentions, but they hesitate to make a revolution when the opportunities arise; they are not sure of the acquiescence, even passive, of the majority, they do not have sufficient military force to have their orders carried out over the whole territory, they lack devoted people with skills in all the countless branches of social activity... therefore they are always forced to postpone action, until they are almost reluctantly pushed to the government by the popular uprising. However, once in power, they would like to stay there indefinitely, therefore they try to slow down, divert, stop the revolution that raised them.

On the contrary, we have indeed an ideal we fight for and would like to see realized, but we do not believe that an ideal of freedom, of justice, of love can be realized through the government violence.

We do not want to get in power, neither we want anyone else to do so. If we cannot prevent governments from existing and being established, due to our lack of strength, we strive, and always will, to keep or make such governments as weak as possible. Therefore we are always ready to take action when it comes to overthrowing or weakening a government, without worrying too much (I say "too much," not "at all") about what will happen thereafter.

For us violence is only of use and can only be of use in driving back violence. Otherwise, when it is used to accomplish positive goals, either it fails completely, or it succeeds in establishing the oppression and the exploitation of the ones over the others.

The establishment and the progressive improvement of a society of free men can only be the result of a free evolution; our task as anarchists is precisely to defend and secure the evolution's freedom.

Here is our mission: demolishing, or contributing to demolish any political power whatsoever, with all the series of repressive forces that support it; preventing, or trying to prevent new governments and new repressive forces from arising; in any case, refraining from ever acknowledging any government, keeping always fighting against it, claiming and requiring, even by force if possible, the right to organize and live as we like, and experiment with the forms of society that seem best to us, as long as they do not prejudice the others' equal freedom, of course.

Beyond this struggle against the government imposition that bears the capitalistic exploitation and makes it possible, once we had encouraged and helped the masses to seize the existing wealth and particularly the means of production, once the situation is reached whereby no one could impose his wishes on others by force, nor take away from any man the product of his labour—only then could we act through propaganda and by example.

Destroy the institution and the machinery of existing social organizations? Yes, certainly, if it is a question of repressive institutions; but these are, after all, only a small part of the complex of social life. The police, the army, the prisons, and the judiciary, which exercise a parasitic function, are potent institutions for evil. Other institutions and organizations manage, for better or for worse, to guarantee life to mankind; and these institutions cannot be usefully destroyed without replacing them by something better.

The exchange of raw material and goods, the distribution of foodstuffs, the railways, postal services and all public services administered by the State or by private companies have been organized to serve monopolistic and capitalist interests, but they also serve real needs of the population. We cannot disrupt them (and in any case the people would not in their own interests allow us to) without reorganizing them in a better way. And this cannot be achieved in a day; nor as things stand, have we the necessary abilities to do so. We are delighted therefore if, in the meantime, others act, even with different criteria from our own.

Social life does not admit of interruptions, and the people want to live on the day of the revolution, on the morrow, and always.

Woe betide us and the future of our ideas if we shouldered the responsibility of a senseless destruction that compromised the continuity of life!

***

During the discussion of such topics, the issue of money, which is of the greatest importance, was raised in Bienne.

It is customary in our circles to offer a simplistic solution to the problem, by saying that money must be abolished. And this would be the solution if it were a question of an anarchist society, or of a hypothetical revolution to take place in the next hundred years, always assuming that the masses could become anarchist and communist before the conditions under which we live had been radically changed by a revolution.

But today the problem is complicated in quite a different way.

Money is a powerful means of exploitation and oppression; but it is also the only means (apart from the most tyrannical dictatorship or the most idyllic accord) so far devised by human intelligence to regulate production and distribution automatically.

For the moment, rather than concerning oneself with the abolition of money, perhaps one should seek a way to ensure that money truly represents the useful work performed by its possessors.

Anyway, let us come to the immediate practice, which is the issue that was actually discussed in Bienne.

Let us assume that a successful insurrection takes place tomorrow. Anarchy or no anarchy, the people must go on eating and providing for all their basic needs. The large cities must be supplied with necessities more or less as usual.

If the peasants and carriers, etc., refuse to supply goods and services for nothing, and demand payment in money, which they are accustomed to considering as real wealth, what does one do? Oblige them by force? In which case we might as well wave goodbye to anarchism and to any possible change for the better. Let the Russian experience serve as a lesson.

And so?

The comrades generally reply: But the peasants will understand the advantages of communism or at least of the direct exchange of goods for goods.

This is all very well; but certainly not in a day, and the people cannot stay without eating for even a day.

I did not mean to propose solutions.

What I do want to do is to draw the comrades' attention to the most important questions that we shall be faced with in the reality of a revolutionary morrow.

Let the comrades contribute their clarifications on the issue; and do not let friend and comrade Colomer be outraged or indignant.

If these issues are novel for him, getting so much scared by novelties is not like an anarchist.

63. FURTHER THOUGHTS ON REVOLUTION IN PRACTICE[1]

My latest article on this topic drew the attention of many comrades and procured me numerous questions and remarks.

Perhaps I was not clear enough; perhaps I also disturbed the mental habits of some, who love to rest on traditional formulas more than tormenting their brain, and are bothered by anything that forces them to think.

In any case I will try to make myself clearer, and I will be happy if those who consider what I say quite heretical will enter the discussion and contribute to define a practical program of action, which can be used as a guide in the next social upheavals.

So far our propagandists have been mainly concerned with criticizing the present society and demonstrating the desirability and possibility of a new social order based on free agreement, in which everyone could find the conditions for the greatest material, spiritual, and intellectual development, in brotherhood and solidarity and with the fullest freedom.

They strove, above all, to inflame with the idea of a condition of individual and social perfection, called "utopia" by some and "ideal" by us; they did good and necessary work, because they set the goal to which our efforts must aim, but they (we) were insufficient and almost indifferent with respect to the search of ways and means that can lead us to that goal. We were very much concerned with the necessity of radically destroying the bad social institutions, but we did not pay enough attention to the positive actions that we needed to take, or let others take, on the day and the morrow of the destruction, in order for individual and social life to be able to continue in the best possible way. We thought, or we acted as we thought, that things would fix themselves, by natural law, without any will consciously intervening to direct the efforts towards the goal previously set. This is probably the reason for the relative lack of success of our work.

---

1 Translated from "Ancora sulla rivoluzione in pratica," *Umanità Nova* (Rome) 3, n. 192 (14 October 1922).

It is about time to look upon the problem of social transformation in all its broad complexity, and try to examine more closely the practical side of the issue. The revolution could happen tomorrow, and we must enable ourselves to act within it in the most effective possible way.

Since at this transitory time the triumphant reaction prevents us from doing much to broaden our propaganda among the masses, let us use our time to examine more closely and clarify our ideas about what is to be done, while we try, by wishes and deeds, to hasten the time of acting and accomplishing.

***

I based my remarks upon two principles:

First: Anarchy cannot be made by force. Anarchist communism, applied in its full breadth and with all its beneficial effects, is only possible when it is understood and wanted by large popular masses that embrace all the elements necessary to creating a society superior to the present one. One can conceive selected groups, whose members live in relationships of voluntary and free association among them and with similar groups, and it will be good that such groups exist, and it will be our task to create them as experiments and examples; however, such groups will not constitute the anarchist-communist society, yet, rather they will be cases of devotion and sacrifice for the cause, until they succeed in involving all or a large part of the population. Therefore, on the morrow of the violent revolution, if it has to come to a violent revolution, it will not be a matter of accomplishing anarchist communism, but one of setting off towards anarchist communism.

Second: the conversion of the masses to anarchy and communism—and even to the mildest form of socialism—is not possible as long as the present social and economic conditions last. Since such conditions, which keep workers slave for the benefit of those privileged, are preserved and perpetuated by brutal force, it is necessary to change them violently through the revolutionary action of conscious minorities. Hence, if the principle is granted that anarchy cannot be made by force, without the conscious will of the masses, the revolution cannot be made to accomplish anarchy directly and immediately, but rather to create the conditions that make a rapid evolution towards anarchy possible.

The following sentence is often repeated: "The revolution will be anarchist or will not be at all." This claim may look very "revolutionary," very "anarchist"; however, it is actually nonsense, when it is not a means, worse than reformism itself, to paralyze good will and induce people to keep quiet, to peacefully put up with the present, waiting for the forthcoming heaven.

Evidently, either "the anarchist revolution" will be anarchist or it will not be at all. However, did not revolutions happen in the world, when the possibility of an anarchist society was yet to be conceived? Won't any revolution ever happen again until the masses are converted to anarchism? As we fail to convert to anarchism the masses brutalized by their life conditions, should we give up any revolution and submit to living in a monarchical and bourgeois regime?

The truth is that the revolution will be what it may be, and our task is to speed it up as much as possible and strive to make it as radical as possible.

***

However, let us be quite clear.

The revolution will not be anarchist if the masses are not anarchist, as unfortunately it is presently the case. However, we are anarchists, we must remain anarchists and act like anarchists before, during and after the revolution.

Without the anarchists, without the anarchists' activity, if the anarchists accepted any kind of government whatsoever and any so called transition constitution, the next revolution would bear new forms of oppression and exploitation even worse than the present, instead of marking a progress of freedom and justice and the start of a complete liberation of mankind. At best, it would only bring about a shallow improvement, largely delusive and by no means adequate to the effort, the sacrifices, the pain of a revolution, such as expected in a more or less near future.

After contributing to overthrow the present regime, our task is to prevent, or try to prevent a new government form arising; failing to do that, at least we must struggle to prevent the new government from being exclusive and concentrating all social power in its hands; it must remain weak and unsteady, it must not be able to have enough military and financial strength, and it must be acknowledged and obeyed as little as possible. In any case, we anarchists should never take part in it, never acknowledge it, and always fight against it as we fight against the present government.

We must stay with the masses, encourage them to act directly, to take possession of the production means and organize the work and the product distribution; to occupy housing; to perform public services without waiting for resolutions or commands from higher-ranking authorities. We must contribute to such work with all our forces, and to that end we must immediately start to engage in acquiring as many skills as possible.

However, as we must uncompromisingly oppose all restraining and repressing bodies and everything that tends to forcibly hinder the will of the people and the freedom of minorities, so we must take care not to destroy those things and disorganize those useful services that we cannot replace in a better way.

We must remember that violence, unfortunately necessary to resist violence, is no use to build anything good: it is the natural enemy of freedom, the procreator of tyranny, therefore it must be kept within the limits of strict necessity.

Revolution is useful, necessary to tear down the violence of governments and privileged people; however, the establishment of a society of free people can only result from a free evolution.

It is the task of the anarchists to watch over the freedom of evolution, which is always at risk as long as men are thirsty for domination and privileges.

***

A question of great, vital importance, nay, the question that must stand out on the revolutionaries' minds, is food.

There was a time when the prejudice spread out that industrial and farm products were so abundant that it would be possible to live on stockpiles for long, postponing the organization of production to a later time, after the accomplishment of the social transformation. It made an inviting propaganda item to be able to say: "People are out of everything, while everything abounds and the warehouses overflow with every good; people die of starvation and wheat rots in the granaries." Things were made so much simpler. An expropriation was enough to secure the well-being of everyone: there would be plenty of time to deal with all the rest.

Unfortunately, quite the opposite is true.

Everything is running out, and a bad harvest, or some major disaster, is enough to cause a complete shortage and the impossibility to provide for everyone's needs, even within the limits imposed by capitalism to the popular masses.

It is true that the production capacity has become almost unlimited, thanks to the means nowadays provided by mechanics, chemistry, scientific work organization, etc.

However, it's one thing to be able to produce and another to have produced. Owners and capitalists do not sufficiently exploit the means of production they own, and prevent others from exploiting them, partly for incompetence and indifference, and largely because of a system that often makes profits decrease with abundance and increase with shortage.

Because of the disorder inherent in the individualistic economy, there are unbalances between one place and the other, overproduction crises, etc., but all in all the general production is always on the verge of famine.

As a consequence, we must bear in mind that on the morrow of the revolution we shall be faced with the danger of hunger. This is not a reason for delaying the revolution, because the state of production will, with minor variations, remain the same, so long as the capitalist system lasts.

But it is a reason for us to pay attention to the problem, and of how, in a revolutionary situation, to avoid all waste, to preach the need for reducing consumption to a minimum, and to take immediate steps to increase production, especially of food.

This is a topic about which some essays already exist, but that needs to be investigated more thoroughly, mainly focusing on the technical means to bring the quantity of food to the level of needs.

64. INTERESTS AND IDEALS[1]

In a recent article of mine and apropos of the impossibility, under capitalist rule, of reconciliation between the actual interests of individuals and the ideals of fairness for all, I closed by saying: "All things considered interest is always conservative; and only the ideal is revolutionary. And it is men who prize ideal over interest who can determine the success of the revolution."[2]

And I received, for saying that, some compliments, which I had not been expecting.

Few days ago, in a chance encounter, I bumped into a gentleman with whom I had previously been rather superficially acquainted. The moment he spotted me he reached out his hand with a grin and told me what a great pleasure it was for him to see me in good health.

I noticed that he was wearing a fascist badge and I was at something of a loss,[3] but he immediately relieved me of my embarrassment and started to say:

"Look, I'm a fascist but I love and respect you and I would be a revolutionary too, if only all revolutionaries were like you."

And whilst I stared at him in wonder, none too sure of what to say, he went on briskly:

"Yes, yes, I read your piece on the economic struggle and I applaud your conclusions. Beyond the Ideal, there is nothing. Those socialist swine, who have taught workers to think only of their bellies, have been the ruination of Italy. They have derided and discredited all idealism, and now, for a little more money in the pay-packet, workers would condemn the country to ruination. Yes, you are right; there has to be a fight-back against this creeping materialism." And who

1 Translated from "Interesse ed ideale," *Umanità Nova* (Rome) 3, no. 196 (2 December 1922).

2 The article in question, "La lotta economica in regime capitalistico" (The economic struggle under capitalist rule), had appeared in *Umanità Nova* of 21 October.

3 By the time this article was published, fascists had been in power for little over than a month. In fact, this was the last issue of *Umanità Nova*. Its columns reported that the newspaper's offices had been occupied by fascist squads.

knows how much longer he might have continued in the same vein, had I not timidly slipped in a naïve question: "Using the cudgel?"

The fellow stopped for a moment, thrown, and I used the opportunity to say to him:

"Kindly let me know, what is your position in society?"

"I'm an industrialist," he replied, "I have a large factory and employ about a thousand workers. Oh, if only you knew what sort of folk they are! They are never content, never displaying any enthusiasm, any love in their work..."

"Whereas you," I interrupted him, "make sacrifices for them; and, since they are Italians like you are, you decline any possible profits for the sake of your workers and the collective generally, thinking that the best way of making Italy great is to make Italians morally and materially better off. Ah, if only Italy had lots of capitalists like you!"

The fellow picked up on the irony and made to disagree: but I shrugged him off, saying:

"Listen, number me among the materialists as well and among the swine, but know that my idealism has nothing in common with your own."

***

There was nothing to be gained by laboring the point. The idealism of which I speak is certainly not the false and lying "idealism" of the bourgeois who would love the workers to show contempt for their "bellies" so that they, the bourgeois, might comfortably grow fat; just like the interest that I describe as conservative is not the loftier interest of humanity, which is indistinguishable from the ideal.

Let me say it again: interest is conservative, and ideal, revolutionary. But that does not mean that interest, even though it be short term or petty or personal, is worthless, and that the revolutionary can and should live by ideals alone.

In order to be able and willing to improve, one must exist; in order to progress, one needs to conserve and consolidate the progress already achieved.

And since things are such that very often there is contradiction and incompatibility between short term, personal, material interests and the future, broader, moral interest that go to make up what we refer to as the ideal, the "revolutionary," the man who is out to combat society's woes, is always faced by the issue of how to reconcile today's needs with the ambitions for the future and how and to what extent needs can be met in such a way as to help, or at any rate not hinder, the greatest and swiftest possible achievement of the ideal to which one aspires.

And a solution to this grave problem generally implies a fairly substantial sacrifice of one's own well-being and one's own peace of mind, so that it could be argued that, the greater the capacity for sacrifice, the better the "revolutionary," the greater the intelligence with which his sacrifice is made, the more effective the revolutionary.

At the level of the individual, the sacrifice may extend to total renunciation, including even the loss of one's own liberty and life; then we have martyrs who are like shining beacons lighting humanity's path.

But when it comes to the collective, once a certain point has been reached, sacrifice is no longer feasible, nor would it be useful, nor desirable.

For the masses, sacrificing that minimum measure of wellbeing that has been achieved, unresisting, willing renunciation of meager gains made at the cost of past personal or collective sacrifices, would be tantamount to a lurch backwards, a lapse back into brutishness, running counter to the ideal of human uplifting. Whereas the fight to protect, the fight to secure every improvement feasible at the time, helps to preserve or conjure up conditions favoring further progress, the emergence of further desires and fresh claims and to lay the groundwork for the great uprising in pursuit of comprehensive emancipation once and for all.

Which is why revolutionaries, especially anarchists, whom we see as the only really thoroughgoing revolutionaries, must take an active hand in the workers' movement, be the first to take up battle stations and occupy the places of danger even when it comes to minor battles and minor dangers relating to minor matters. They must inspire the workers to ever more ambitious demands and avoid that contemplative, ecstatic, and absolutist state of mind that ultimately leads to inertia and passive waiting for some future paradise that will never be reached other than by a path strewn with tribulations and ambushes. But, in grappling with the battles of today, the anarchists should never lose sight of the higher interests of the future; they must fight the tendency towards accommodation, which is typical of the masses, and those methods of struggle that signify acceptance of the status quo.

In conclusion: inside the unions, certainly, and in the forefront of them; but let it always be on behalf of the revolution and anarchy.

65.
ANARCHISTS' LINE WITHIN THE TRADE UNION MOVEMENT[1]

(Report to the International anarchist Congress in Paris in 1923)

Charged with reporting on the trade union question at a time of crisis, when the old tactics need re-examining in the light of recent experiences so that they can be adapted to fresh circumstances, and when the arrest, exile, and harassment of so many of the active members of the *Unione* makes it hard to communicate with comrades and get an exact feel for their current thoughts and dispositions, I can only speak for myself here and on my own account—though I am convinced, on the basis of what I know of the movement, that what I am about to say will articulate the thoughts of the vast majority, and possibly the totality, of the anarchists that are members of the *Unione Anarchica Italiana*.[2]

We have always recognized the great significance of the workers' movement and the need for anarchists to be an active driving force within it. And it has frequently been at the instigation of our comrades that the liveliest and most pugnacious labor groupings have been established.

We have always been of the opinion that trade unionism is, today, a means whereby the workers begin to understand their slave status and to crave emancipation and get used to solidarity with all the oppressed in the fight against the oppressors—and that it will, tomorrow, serve as the essential core vital to continuity in the life of society and to the reorganizing of production without bosses or parasites.

---

1 Translated from "La condotta degli anarchici nel movimento sindacale," *Fede!* (Roma) 1, no. 3 (30 September 1923).

2 The *Unione Anarchica Italiana* was the main Italian anarchist organization. It was founded at the Bologna congress of 1920, replacing the *Unione Comunista Anarchica Italiana* that had been founded the year before. The Paris congress, where Malatesta's report was meant to be presented, did not take place. The difficulties to which Malatesta refers are those determined by the rise to power of fascism, which occurred less than a year before.

But we have always argued and often disagreed over the manner in which anarchist activity was to be pursued in dealings with the workers' organization.

Were we to enter the unions or else stay outside, albeit taking part in all of the agitations with an eye to making these as radical as possible and to taking the lead when there were things that needed doing and dangers to be braved?

And above all, once inside the unions, were we or were we not to take up leadership posts and thereby be part of the horse-trading, compromises, accommodations, dealing with the authorities and the bosses to which unions had to submit, according to the workers' own wishes on behalf of their short-term interests in day-to-day struggles, when revolution was not on the agenda but the securing of improvements or defence of gains already won were?

In the two years following the peace, and up until the eve of the reaction's triumph thanks to fascism, we found ourselves in a peculiar situation.

Revolution looked imminent, and actually all the material and spiritual conditions were in place to make it feasible and necessary.

But we anarchists fell well short of having the sort of strength needed to make the revolution using only our own methods and men; we needed the masses and, though they were ready for action, they were not anarchist. Moreover, even had one been possible, a revolution made without the participation of the masses could only have led to a brand new overlordship, which, even should it be wielded by anarchists, would always have been a negation of anarchism, would have corrupted the new overlords, and would have ended in restoration of the statist and capitalist order.

To have pulled out of the struggle and abstained on the basis that we were unable to do exactly what we might have wished, would have been tantamount to giving up on any present or future opportunity, any hope of steering the movement in the direction of our preference—and abandoning it not only this time but for good, since the masses would never be anarchist prior to a political and economic overhaul of society, and the same situation would be replicated every time that circumstances made an attempt at revolution feasible.

We therefore had to win the trust of the masses at any cost, equip ourselves to be able to push them on to the streets and, to that end, there seemed to be a purpose to our capturing positions of leadership within the workers' organizations. All the dangers of domestication and corruption were pushed into the background and, besides, the assumption was that they would not have time to come to pass.

The conclusion was therefore reached that everyone should be left free to sort himself out depending on his circumstances and however he saw fit, provided that he never forget that he was an anarchist and that he was guided at all times by the overriding interests of the anarchist cause.

But now, in the wake of recent experiences, and in view of the current situation, which allows for no temporary alliances but calls for a strict return to principles so that we may be that much better prepared and more deeply convinced in forthcoming developments, it strikes me that the right thing to do is to revisit this matter and see whether there is a case to be made for amending our tactics on this very highly important aspect of our activities.

I hope that Congress will scrutinize the issue with the attention that it deserves.

In my view, we need to get into the unions, because, from the outside, we look hostile to them; our criticisms are looked at askance and come the time to agitate we would be looked upon as trespassers and our assistance would be unwelcome.—I am talking, plainly, of real trade unions made up of workers freely associated for the purpose of defending their interests against the bosses and the government; and not about the fascist syndicates, which are often recruited at the point of the cudgel and the threat of starvation; they are an arm of government and an attempt to make the workers more deferential towards the demands of the bosses. We need to get into the unions and start driving them forwards so as to endow them with an ever more libertarian character and monitor, criticizes, and combat any possible weaknesses or disloyalties on the part of the leadership.

And as for our pursuit or acceptance of leadership positions, I reckon that generally speaking in times of calm, these would be better avoided. I think, however, that the harm and the danger resides not so much in the holding of a position of leadership—something that might even prove useful, indeed, vital, in certain circumstances—as in clinging to such posts. As I see it, the leadership line-up should be refreshed as often as possible, both in order to train the greatest possible number of workers into administrative duties, and to prevent the task of organizer from turning into a trade and prompting those who ply it to carry their preoccupation with not losing their jobs over into the workers' struggles.

All of this not just for the current interests of the struggle and of educating the workers, but also and chiefly with an eye to the rolling out of the revolution once it has started.

Anarchists are rightly opposed to authoritarian communism, which implies a government that, aiming to direct the whole life of the society and place the organization of production and the distribution of wealth under the control of its officials, cannot help but produce the most outrageous tyranny and leave all of society's live forces paralyzed.

The syndicalists, seemingly in agreement with the anarchists in their aversion to statist centralization, want to dispense with government by replacing it with syndicates; and they say that it is the latter that should assume ownership of wealth, requisitioning foodstuffs, distributing them, organizing production and exchange. And I would see no problems there, as long as the syndicates throw their doors wide open to the entire population and leave dissenters a free hand and let them claim their portion.

But such expropriation and such distribution cannot, in practice, be carried out by fits and starts, even by unionised masses, without there being a resultant squandering of resources and the sacrificing of the weak to those stronger and more brutal; much less could the relations between different areas be handled en masse or trade between the various producer bodies. So provision would have to be made through decisions made at popular assemblies and left to spontaneously volunteering or properly delegated groups and individuals to implement.

Now, if there is a select number of persons regarded as a result of their seniority as union leaders, if there are permanent secretaries and official organizers, then as a matter of course, they are the ones that will be put in charge of organizing the revolution and they will have a tendency to see trespassers and mavericks in those who might be inclined to take initiatives independently of them and will be out to impose their own will—albeit with the best of intentions—maybe by force.

Whereupon *syndicalist rule* would promptly turn into the same lie and the same tyranny into which the so-called *dictatorship of the proletariat* has turned.

The remedy against this danger, and the means by which the revolution can be made truly liberating, reside in the nurturing of a large number of persons capable of showing initiative and practical accomplishments, in getting the masses used to not surrendering the cause of all into the hands of the few, and, where delegation may be necessary, keeping delegation tied to specific tasks and then for a limited time only. And the union, if organized and run along genuinely libertarian lines, is a highly effective means of generating such a situation and ethos.

***

Allow me to add to everything that I have said on the subject of worker organization a few words on the subject of organizing anarchists, as the *Unione Anarchica Italiana* sees it.

The *Unione Anarchica Italiana* is a federation of autonomous groups united by mutual assistance in propaganda and in the implementation of a freely accepted programme. From time to time it holds congresses and between one congress and the next is represented by a *Corresponding Commission* appointed by the congress; its personnel and location change every time. The deliberations of its congresses are binding only upon those groups that agree with them after learning about them; for which reason, the form of representation, whatever it may be, is of no importance in that it cannot give rise to unfairness and bullying. Each group or individual federation of groups sends whatever delegates it can, no matter what the size of its membership and there is no problem with this, because the congress does not make laws binding on everyone but serves as an indicator of varying opinions; the prevailing opinion is articulated in resolutions that are then put to the groups and which carry no more weight than advice or suggestions.

The Corresponding Commission helps facilitate relations between groups, to raise support from others for the initiatives of each and to make agreed action easier. But it wields no authority and is not equipped to impose its own wishes.

Each group and each individual can correspond, as they see fit, directly with the rest without going through the channels of the Corresponding Commission; each of them is at liberty to publish whatever they please, to launch whatever initiatives they can, in short, to do whatever they please on behalf of the common cause. The only bond being the general program, acceptance of which is an essential pre-requisite for entry into the *Unione*.

These principles are accepted by all members of the *Unione*, in that they make up the compact by which they are united. And any who, out of ignorance or for ulterior motives, tries to suggest that the *Unione Anarchica Italiana* is an authoritarian organization, is at odds with the truth.

The *Unione* seeks no monopoly in the field of anarchist organizing. Each anarchist is free to remain isolated or join other organizations.

The *Unione* is happy with any anarchist activity pursued within or without its own ranks and is prepared to give aid to all and receive aid from all, provided this is in relation to matters that are not inconsistent with its programme.

On behalf of the Unione Anarchica Italiana
ERRICO MALATESTA

Malatesta in his seventies

ACHIEVABLE AND ACHIEVING ANARCHISM:
Pensiero e Volontà and Last Writings, 1924–32

In 1924, at seventy years of age and living in fascist Italy, Malatesta managed to put out in Rome a new anarchist journal, *Pensiero e Volontà*. Prevented from practical action, Malatesta was finally in a position to delve into some of the theoretical themes that had been at the heart of his anarchism for over half a century. In 1925, he wrote to his friend Luigi Fabbri: "You expect from me the achievable and achieving anarchism that takes a step forward from Bakunin and Kropotkin. As a matter of fact, I have not given up hope to fulfill your expectation." Indeed, from 1924 on Malatesta brought forth some of the most enlightening articles of the anarchist literature of all times. In his discussions of gradualism and the post-revolutionary economy, as well as in his scrutiny of various forms of anarchist revisionism, Malatesta's ability to reconcile coherence with principles and realism shines through. The revolution, he writes in the closing article of this collection, "must do immediately whatever it can, but no more than that … nothing should be destroyed unless there is something better to be put in its place."

66. "IDEALISM" AND "MATERIALISM"[1]

It has been noted thousands of times that men, before arriving at the truth, or at least as much relative truth as is attainable at various junctures in their intellectual and social development, are wont to fall into the most widely varying errors in looking at things, now from one side and now from the other, thereby lurching from one exaggeration to its opposite.

I wish to examine here a phenomenon of this sort, which is of great interest to the whole of contemporary social life.

A few years ago everybody was a "materialist." Invoking a "science" that was the harnessing of the general principles derived from a positive knowledge that was all too incomplete, it was expected to explain the whole of human psychology and the entire eventful history of humanity in terms of basic material needs alone. The "economic factor" explained all: past, present, and future. Every manifestation of thought and sentiment, every vagary in life, love as well as hate, passions good and bad, the condition of women, ambition, jealousy, racial pride, any sort of relations between individuals and peoples, war and peace, mass submissiveness or rebelliousness, sundry forms of family and society, political regimes, religion, morality, literature, art, science... all of these were merely the outworkings of the prevalent mode of production and distribution of wealth and of the instruments of labor in each epoch. And those with a broader, less simplistic notion of human nature and history were looked upon within the conservative and subversive ranks alike as throwbacks bereft of "science."

Naturally, this outlook influenced the practical behavior of parties and tended to lead to the sacrificing of every nobler ideal to material interests, economic issues, no matter how petty and insignificant these latter might be.

Today, the fashion has changed. These days everybody is an "idealist": everybody affects to sneer at the "belly," and treats man as if he were pure spirit, eating, dressing, and meeting physiological needs

1 Translated from "'Idealismo' e 'materialismo,'" *Pensiero e Volontà* (Rome) 1, no. 2 (15 January 1924).

being matters of no significance to him, matters not to be heeded, lest a moral decline set in.

I have no intention of concerning myself here with the sinister quirks that turn "idealism" into sheer hypocrisy and a weapon of deception; the capitalist who commends a sense of duty and spirit of sacrifice to his workers so that he may blithely slash their wages and boost his own profits; the "patriot" who, enthused by love of country and the national spirit, devours his own homeland and, given the chance, the homelands of others; or the soldier who, for the greater glory and honor of the flag, exploits the vanquished and oppresses them and rides roughshod over them.

I talk about honest folk: especially those of our comrades who, having seen that the fight for economic betterment ended up consuming the entire energy of the workers' organizations until all revolutionary potential there was spent, and now witnessing so much of the proletariat allowing itself to be stripped of any vestige of freedom and, albeit reluctantly, kissing the rod that smites them in the vain hope that they might be guaranteed employment and decent pay, are showing a tendency to jettison in disgust all economic concerns and struggles and to confine, or, if your prefer, raise our entire activity to the realms of education and revolutionary struggle proper.

The main problem, the basic need is the need for freedom, they argue; and freedom can only be won and retained through wearisome struggles and cruel sacrifices. It therefore falls to revolutionaries to pay no mind to petty matters relating to economic improvements, to oppose the selfishness that prevails among the masses, to spread the spirit of sacrifice and, instead of promising pie-in-the-sky, to imbue the crowd with a sacred pride in suffering on behalf of a noble cause.

Entirely agree—but let us not get carried away.

Freedom, full and complete freedom, is certainly the essential prize, because it represents the enshrinement of human dignity and is the only means whereby social problems can and ought to be resolved to the benefit of all. But freedom is a hollow word unless it is wedded to ability, which is to say, to the means whereby one can freely carry on his own activity.

The maxim "whoever is poor is a slave" is still true, though equally true is that other maxim that "whoever is a slave is or is made poor, and thus loses all of the best characteristics of the human being."

Material needs, the satisfaction of physiological needs, are indeed lesser and even contemptible matters, but they are the basic pre-requisite for any higher moral and intellectual existence. Man is prompted by myriad factors of the most varied sorts and these shape the course of history, but... He has to eat. "First live, and then philosophize."

To our aesthetic sensibilities, a bit of canvas, some oil, and a little colored earth are mean things when set alongside a Raphael painting; but without those relatively worthless materials, Raphael would never have been able to set down his dream of beauty.

I suspect that the "idealists" are all folk who eat on a daily basis and who can still be reasonably sure of eating the following day; and this is only natural, because in order to be able to think, to be able to aspire to loftier matters, a basic minimum, no matter how low, of material comfort is required. There have been and are men equal to the greatest heights of sacrifice and suffering, men who can blithely look hunger and torture in the face and carry on fighting heroically for their cause amid the most horrific suffering; but these are men who have grown up in relatively favorable circumstances and who have managed to store up a quantum of latent energy, which then comes into play as the need arises. That is the general rule, at any rate.

For many a long year I have dallied with workers' organizations, revolutionary groups, and educational associations and I have always noticed that the greatest activists, the greatest enthusiasts were those who were in the least straitened circumstances and who were attracted, not so much by their own needs, but by a desire to contribute to the doing of good and to feel ennobled by an ideal. The true, the greatest wretches, the ones who might appear to have the most personal and immediate interest in a change in things were either absent or played a passive role. I remember how tough and fruitless our propaganda work turned out to be in certain locations around Italy thirty or forty years ago when the farm-workers and much of the urban worker population were living in genuinely brutish conditions, which I should like to think are now a thing of the past, albeit the fears of their making a come-back may not be without foundation. Just as I have seen hunger-inspired popular unrest stilled at a stroke by the opening a few "cookhouses" and the distribution of a little cash.

From all of which, my deduction is that pride of place goes to the idea, which must activate the will, but certain conditions are required for the idea to be able to emerge and make an impact.

Thus our old program, that announced that moral, political, and economic emancipation could not be disentangled one from another, and that the masses need to be placed in such material conditions as may allow for the outworking of ideal needs, stands confirmed.

Fight for wholesale emancipation and, while waiting and preparing for the day on which that will be feasible, wrest from government and capitalists all political and economic improvements that might improve the conditions of our struggle and boost the numbers of conscious fighters. So, wrest them by means that imply no acknowledgment of the existing arrangements and which pave the way to the future.

Spread the sense of duty and the spirit of sacrifice; but bear in mind that example is the best form of propaganda and that one can not ask of others that which we ourselves do not do.

67.
IDEAL AND REALITY[1]

Let's skip the "philosophical" definitions, that is, the demanding, confused and… inconclusive ones. The ideal means: that which is desired. The real means: that which exists.

Unhappiness with what is, and the constant craving for something better, the aspiration to greater freedom, to more power and more beauty is a peculiarly human characteristic. The man who finds everything fine, who reckons that everything there is, is as it ought to be, and should not and cannot change, and who blithely accommodates himself, without a murmur, without any objection, without a gesture of rebelliousness, to the position and circumstances thrust upon him, would be less than human. He would be... a vegetable, if such a thing could be said without offending vegetables.

But on the other hand, man cannot be and cannot do everything that he wants, because he is curtailed and obliged, not only by brute natural environment, but also by the actions of every other man, by social solidarity which, like it or not, ties him to the fate of the entire human race.

Therefore, one must strive for what he wants, doing what he can.

Anybody who can accommodate himself to everything would be a poor thing, comparable, as I was saying, to a vegetable. On the other hand, someone who reckons he can do anything he wants without taking into consideration the wishes of others, the means required to achieve a purpose, the circumstances in which he finds himself, would be nothing but a cloud-chaser cast forever in the role of victim, without advancing the cause he so cherishes by as much as a single step.

So the problem facing us anarchists—since the aim of this publication is to have whatever impact it can on the anarchist movement—the problem facing us anarchists, who regard anarchy not so much as a beautiful dream to be chased by the light of the moon, but as an individual and social way of life to be brought about for the greatest good for all… the problem, as we say, is to so conduct

---

1 Translated from "Ideale e realtà," *Pensiero e Volontà* (Rome) 1, no. 3 (1 February 1924).

our activities as to achieve the greatest useful effect in the various circumstances in which history places us.

One must not ignore reality; but if reality is noxious, one must fight it, resorting to every means made available to us by reality itself.

Come the outbreak of the world war, the harmful consequences of which are still evident, there was in certain quarters, which purported to be and may once upon a time had been subversive, much talk of "reality." All half-baked consciences, all of those who were casting around for some honorable pretext upon which to make amends for their youthful transgressions and secure themselves a livelihood, all the weary who lacked the honest courage to admit that that was what they were and then retreat from public life—and there were many such in the ranks of the socialists and several in the anarchist ranks—embraced and preached the war "because it was a fact," relying on backing from some selfless types who, in all good faith and misled by a wrong-headed view of history and a whole propaganda based on lies, believed that this really was a war of liberation and got involved in it and paid the price.

Today there is no shortage of those who back fascism "because it is a fact" and they cover up or think they can justify their defection and treachery by arguing of fascism, as they once did of the war, that its aims are revolutionary.

Yes, the world war and "the peace" that came out of it are facts, just like every previous war was a fact, and all the massacres and all the people-trading. The fascist cudgel is a fact, as was the German rod that "cannot tame Italy!"

Furthermore, all the oppression, all the poverty, all the hatreds and crimes that assail, divide and degrade men are facts too.

Are we therefore to accept everything, and defer to everything because this is the situation in which history has placed us?

The whole of human progress has been made up of battling against natural facts and social facts. And we who want to see maximum progress, the greatest possible happiness for every single human being, are besieged and buffeted on every side by hostile realities, and we have to combat these realities. But before we can combat them, we must know about them and take them into the reckoning.

If it is to emerge triumphant or merely to stride towards its triumph, anarchy has to be thought of, not merely as a luminous, attractive beacon of light, but also as something feasible, achievable not only with the passage of centuries but in relatively short space of time and with no need for miracles.

We anarchists have greatly minded the ideal; we have devised a critique of all the moral falsehoods and all the social institutions that corrupt and oppress humanity and we have outlined, with whatever poetry and eloquence each of us may have possessed, a yearned-for harmonious society rooted in kindness and love; but there is no denying that we have scarcely troubled ourselves about the ways and means of turning our ideals into reality.

Granted the need for a revolutionary—or, rather, insurrectionary—upheaval that should demolish any material obstacles, political authority or hogging of the means of production, things that counter the spread and trialling of our ideals, we believed—or behaved as if we did—that everything would just fall into place, without any pre-conceived planning, in a natural, spontaneous way, and our response to prospective difficulties was abstract formulae and an optimism that runs counter to present facts and foreseeable ones. In short, we resolved the whole thing by theorizing that the people will want what we want, and that matters will work out precisely as we would wish.

Are all governments noxious? Well, "we shall do away with them all and stop new ones from being formed." How, though? With what resources? "The people or the proletariat will see to that." But what if they do not?

"Each person will do as he pleases." But what if all these individuals, who together make up the masses, were to want the opposite of what we want, were to kneel before a tyrant, or let themselves be used as instruments deployed against us?

What if the peasants were to refuse to keep the towns provisioned? "The peasants are no fools and will hasten to ship foodstuffs to the towns in return for industrial goods… or for promises of goods yet to be manufactured."

And what if folk refuse to work? "Work is a pleasure and no one will want to deny themselves that pleasure."

And if there are criminals who trespass against the lives and liberty of others? "There will be no more criminals."

And so on and so on, answering every query with blithe assertions and denials, ruling out all the bad things, and taking for granted all the good things.

There have even been a few, fired up with enthusiasm and maybe looking ahead centuries to the hoped-for outcomes of education and eugenics (the science and art of selective procreation) who have divined that, on the morrow of a successful insurrection, humanity will be made up entirely of kindly, intelligent, healthy, strong, and handsome folk!

The truth is that we have always been trapped in a vicious circle. While, on the one hand, we have been arguing that the masses cannot attain moral emancipation as long as the current conditions of political and economic subjection apply, on the other we have assumed that events would turn out as if those masses were already made up entirely, or for the most part, of conscious, forward-looking individuals jealous of their own freedom and respectful of the freedom of others. Even as we have been arguing that anarchy, of which freedom is the stock-in-trade, cannot be forcibly imposed, "by contradiction absolute forbid," it never occurred to us that we should prepare against the eventuality of other people's over-ruling us.

In short, we have lacked a practical program capable of being enacted the day after the victorious insurrection, one which, whilst not trespassing against anybody's freedom, might enable us to enact, or start to enact, the implementation of our ideas, and draw the masses to our side through example and through the tried and tested superiority of our methods.

Thus, that fraction of the people that aspires to emancipation and will forge a new history has not understood us and has largely embraced either the authoritarian, oppressive communism or hybrid syndicalism.

And we have found ourselves powerless just when circumstances seemed most to favor us.

It is high time that we sort out these shortcomings of ours so that we can be ready for future opportunities, which are assuredly on their way.

And we urge all our friends to partake in this task of drawing up a practical program for immediate implementation.

68. ON "ANARCHIST REVISIONISM"[1]

A comrade writes: "*After your act of contrition in No. 3, it is your duty to tell us openly what the practical means are for carrying out the revolution. Only then can we discuss it.*"[2]

Another asks me to "unbutton"; many others await for as it were a magic formula to resolve all the difficulties.

Strange mentality for anarchists!

Let me begin by saying that I have made no "act of contrition." I could easily document that what I am saying now I have been saying for years; and if now I place more emphasis on it and others pay more attention to it than before, it is because the times are riper, in that experience has persuaded many, who formerly luxuriated in that blessed Kropotkinian optimism—which I used to call "atheist providentialism"—to descend from the clouds and look at things as they are—so different from how we would like them to be.

But let us leave these recollections of personal interest behind us and come to the general and contemporary problem.

We, of this review, like our comrades from other anarchist publications, make no claim to have prepared some pre-packaged, infallible and universal solution to all problems that come to mind. But, recognizing the need for a practical programme that can be adapted to the various circumstances that may arise as society develops prior to, during and after the revolution, we have invited all comrades with ideas to present and proposals to make to take part in the drawing up of such a programme. Those, therefore, who feel that everything has so far gone well and that we should continue as we have been doing, need only defend their point of view, while those who, like us, think we need to prepare intellectually and materially for the practical task which awaits the anarchists, rather than wait passively upon our words should try to make their own contribution to the discussion where it interests them.

---

1 In *The Anarchist Revolution: Polemical Articles 1924–1931*, edited and introduced by Vernon Richards (London: Freedom Press, 1995), p. 87–91. Originally published as "A proposito di 'revisionismo anarchico,'" *Pensiero e Volontà* (Rome) 1, no. 9 (1 May 1924).

2 The reference is to the previous article, "Ideal and Reality."

For my part, I believe there is no "single solution" to social problems, but a thousand different and varying ones, just as the life of a society, in time and space, is diverse and changeable.

Basically all institutions, all projects, all utopias, would be equally good for resolving the problem, if that problem is defined as satisfying a people who all have the same desires and opinions and are all living in the same conditions. But such unanimity of thought and identity of conditions are impossible and, to tell the truth, would not even be desirable. And therefore in our present behaviour and in our projects for the future we must bear in mind that we do not live, nor shall we live tomorrow in a world populated exclusively by anarchists. On the contrary, we are and shall be for a long time a relatively small minority. To isolate ourselves is not, on the whole, possible, and even if it were it would be detrimental to the mission we have set ourselves. We must therefore find a way of living among non-anarchists in the most anarchic fashion possible and to the best possible advantage for our propaganda and the realisation of our ideas.

***

We want to make the revolution because we believe in the need for radical change and this, owing to the resistance of the powers-that-be, cannot be brought about peacefully. We believe in a need for change in the prevailing political and social order because we want to create a new social environment which would enable that moral and material elevation of the people that propaganda and education are helpless to create under present circumstances. But we cannot make the revolution exclusively "ours" because we are a small minority, because we lack the consent of the mass of the people and because, even if we were able, we would not wish to contradict our own ends and impose our will by force.

To escape from the vicious circle we must therefore content ourselves with a revolution that is as much "ours" as possible, favouring and taking part, both morally and materially, in every movement directed towards justice and liberty and, when the insurrection has triumphed, ensure that the pace of the revolution is maintained, advancing towards ever greater freedom and justice. This does not mean "hanging on" to the other parties, but spurring them forward, so that the people are able to choose between a range of options. We could be abandoned and betrayed, as has happened on other occasions. But we have to run that risk if we do not want to remain ineffectual and renounce the opportunity for our ideas and actions to have an influence on the course of history.

***

Another observation. Many anarchists, including some among the best known, and I would add among the most eminent, who—whether because they really believe it or because they think it useful for propaganda—have spread about the idea that the quantity of goods produced and in the warehouses of the landowners and proprietors is so great that all that would be required would be to draw freely from those stocks. These would amply satisfy the needs and desires of all, and some time would pass before we were obliged to worry over problems of work and production. And naturally, they found people who were willing to accept the idea. Unfortunately, people tend to avoid exertion and danger. Like the democratic socialists who found widespread support by persuading people that all they needed to do to emancipate themselves was to slip a piece of paper in the ballot box and entrust their fate to others, so certain anarchists have won others over by telling them that one day of epic struggle—without effort, or with only the minimum of effort—will suffice to be able to enjoy a paradise of abundance and liberty.

Now precisely the opposite is true. The capitalists go into production to sell at a profit; they therefore cease production when they realise that they are getting diminishing or no returns. They generally find a greater advantage in keeping the market relatively short of goods, and this is proved by the fact that a bad harvest is enough for products to really run short or disappear altogether. So that it can be said that the worst harm done by the capitalist system is not so much the army of parasites it feeds as the obstacles it presents to the production of useful things. The ragged and the hungry are dazed when they pass stores crammed with goods of all kinds. But try to distribute those riches among the needy and see how little there actually is for each person!

Socialism, in the widest sense of the term, the aspiration to socialism, involves a problem of distribution, in that it is the spectacle of the misery of the workers when confronted with the affluence and luxury of the parasites and the moral revolt against patent social injustice that has driven the victims and all generous people to seek and imagine better means of living together in society. But the bringing about of socialism -whether anarchist or authoritarian, mutualist or individualist—is predominantly a problem of production. If there are no goods there is no point finding a better means of distributing them and if people are reduced to quarrel over a crust of bread, feelings of love and solidarity run the great danger of giving way to a brutal struggle for survival.

Today, fortunately, the means of production abound. Engineering, chemistry, agriculture, etc., have increased a hundredfold the productive power of human labour. But it is necessary to work and to work usefully it is necessary to know: know how the work must be done and how labour can be economically organised.

If the anarchists want to act effectively among the various parties they must deepen their understanding of the field or expertise to which they feel most suited, and make a study of all the theoretical and practical problems of useful activity.

***

Another point. We no longer live at a time or in a country when a family could be content with a piece of land, a spade, a handful of seeds, a cow and a few hens. Today our needs have multiplied and become enormously complex. The unequal natural distribution of raw materials forces any agglomeration of men and women to have international relations. The very density of the human population makes it not only a miserable thing but utterly impossible to live a hermit's life—supposing there are many so inclined.

We need to import from all over the world; we want schools, railways, postal and telegraph services, theatres, public sanitation, books, newspapers, etc.

All this, the achievement of civilisation, may work well or badly; it works mainly for the benefit of the privileged classes. But it works and its benefits can, relatively easily, be extended to all, once the monopoly of wealth and power were to be abolished.

Do we want to destroy it?

Or are we in a position to organise it from the outset in a better way?

Especially at an economic level, social life does not permit of interruption. We need to eat every day; every day we must feed the children, the sick, the helpless; and there are also those who, after having been hard at it all day, want to spend the evening at the cinema. To supply all these unpostponable needs—forget about the cinema—there is a whole commercial organisation which may work badly, but somehow fulfills its task. This must clearly be used, depriving it as far as possible of its exploitative and profiteering nature.

It is time to have done with that rhetoric—because that is all it is, rhetoric—which seeks to summarise the whole anarchist programme in one word: "Destroy!"

Yes, let us destroy, or seek to destroy every tyranny, every privilege. But let us remember that government and capitalism are merely the superstructures which tend to restrict the benefits of civilisation to a small number of individuals, and to abolish them there is no need to renounce any of the fruits of the human mind and of human labour. It is much more a question of what we need to keep than what we need to destroy.

As for ourselves, we must not destroy what we cannot replace with something better. And in the meantime we must work in all areas of life for the benefit of all, ourselves included—refusing, of course, to accept or perform any coercive function.

69.
INDIVIDUALISM AND ANARCHISM[1]

Adamas's reply to my article in no. 13 shows that I did not express my thoughts well, and induces me to add some clarifications.

I claimed, that "individualist anarchism and communist anarchism are the same, or nearly so, in terms of moral motivations and ultimate goals."

I know that one could counter my claim with hundreds of texts and plenty of deeds of self-proclaimed individualist anarchists, which would demonstrate that an individualist anarchist and communist anarchist are separated by something of a moral abyss.

However, I deny that that kind of individualists can be included among anarchists, despite their liking for calling themselves so.

If anarchy means non-government, non-domination, non-oppression by man over man, how can one call himself anarchist without lying to himself and the others, when he frankly claims that he would oppress the others for the satisfaction of his *Ego*, without any scruple or limit, other than that drawn by his own strength? He can be a rebel, because he is being oppressed and he fights to become an oppressor, as other nobler rebels fight to destroy any kind of oppression; but he sure cannot be anarchist. He is a would-be bourgeois, a would-be tyrant, who is unable to accomplish his dreams of dominion and wealth by his own strength and by legal means, and therefore he approaches anarchists to exploit their moral and material solidarity.

Therefore, I think the question is not about "communists" and "individualists", but rather about anarchists and non-anarchists. And we, or at least many of us, were quite wrong in discussing a certain kind of alleged "anarchist individualism" as if it really was one

1 Translated from a note to the article "Individualismo e anarchismo" by Adamas, *Pensiero e Volontà* (Rome) 1, no. 15 (1 August 1924). In the article, Luigi Fabbri, under the pseudonym of Adamas, responded to Malatesta's article "Individualismo e comunismo nell'anarchismo," which appeared in the July 1 issue of *Pensiero e Volontà*. Malatesta had argued, as Fabbri put it, that "the distinction between communists and individualists, *so long as they are anarchist*, is more formal than substantial, because both want to achieve the emancipation of all human beings from any form of exploitation and oppression." Fabbri countered that, in his opinion, anarchism and individualism were irreconcilable, especially on the ground of practical action.

of the various tendencies of anarchism, instead of fighting it as one of the many disguises of authoritarianism.

However, Adamas says, "if one strips individualist anarchism of all that is not anarchist, there is no individualist anarchism whatsoever left". We disagree about this.

Morally, anarchism is sufficient unto itself; but to be translated into facts it needs concrete forms of material life, and it is the preference for one or other form that differentiates the various anarchist schools of thought.

In the anarchist milieu, communism, individualism, collectivism, mutualism, and all the intermediate and eclectic programs are simply the ways considered best for achieving freedom and solidarity in economic life; the ways believed to correspond more closely with justice and freedom for the distribution of the means of production and the products of labor among men.

Bakunin was an anarchist, and he was a collectivist, an outspoken enemy of communism because he saw in it the negation of freedom and, therefore, of human dignity. And with Bakunin, and for a long time after him, almost all the Spanish anarchists were collectivists (*collective property of soil, raw materials and means of production, and assignment of the entire product of labor to the producer, after deducting the necessary contribution to social charges*), and yet they were among the most conscious and consistent anarchists.

Others, for the same reason of defense and guarantee of liberty, declare themselves to be individualists, and they want each person to have as individual property the part that is due to him of the means of production and therefore the free disposal of the products of his labor.

Others invent more or less complicated systems of mutuality. But in the long run it is always the searching for a more secure guarantee of freedom that is the common factor among anarchists, and that divides them into different schools.

We are communist, because we believe that a way of social life based on brotherhood, with no oppressed nor oppressors, can be better accomplished through a freely established solidarity and a free cooperation in the interest of all, aiming at the fullest possible satisfaction of everyone's needs rather than the *right* to a higher or lower recompense.

We believe that the distribution of the natural means of production and the determination of the exchange-value of things, both necessary in every system except communism, could hardly be accomplished without struggle and injustice, which might eventually end up in the establishment of new forms of authority and governments. On the other hand, we readily admit the danger involved in trying to apply communism before its desire and awareness be deep-rooted, and to a larger extent than allowed by the objective conditions of production and social relations: a parasitic bureaucracy could arise, which would centralize everything in its hands and become the worst of governments.

Therefore we remain communist in our sentiment and aspiration, but we want to leave freedom of action to the experimentation of all ways of life that can be imagined and desired.

For us, it is necessary and sufficient that everyone have complete freedom, and nobody can monopolize the means of production and live on someone else's work.

***

Adamas also talks about the necessity of "an organized, homogeneous, continuative anarchist movement, connected for a common action of struggle and demand." He also says that our propaganda in deeds must not consist of "postponing action, initiative, organization, etc. until all who call themselves anarchists agree about what is to be done. Rather, we ourselves, who already agree, must take immediate action according to our general and tactical programs, without refraining from it for a silly fear of hurting the feelings of the dissenters belonging to the various fractions and tendencies."

I perfectly agree with him; however, I believe he is wrong when he thinks the "individualists" are to blame if what he wishes has not been done so far, or it has been done insufficiently and badly.

In my opinion, the blame is on a state of mind of the anarchists, deriving from wrong ideas spread since the origins of our movement, which made them balk at any practical plan of action. Such errors depend on a kind of *natural providentialism,* which led to believe that human events happen automatically, *naturally,* without preparation, without organization, without preconceived plans. Just as many among us think the revolution will come by itself, when *the time is ripe,* by the spontaneous action of the masses, so they also think that after the revolution the *popular spontaneity* will suffice for everything and that there is no need to foresee and prepare anything. This is the reason of the wrongs pointed out by Adamas, not the "individualists," who have always been a very small minority among us, after all, generally without credit and without influence.

The maxim "anarchy is the natural order," which, in my opinion, is diametrically opposed to the truth, was not invented by the individualists!

Anyway, we can talk about this some other time.

70. SYNDICALISM AND ANARCHISM[1]

The question of the relation between the labor movement and the progressive parties is an old and everlasting one. This question still is, however, and will remain of interest as long as there exists, on the one hand, a large portion of the masses tormented by unsatisfied needs and incited by sometimes fiery, but always vague and indefinite, aspirations to a better life, and, on the other hand, men and political parties who, having a particular conception of a better form of society and of the best means of establishing same, endeavor to obtain the consent of the masses, whose support is necessary for the realization of their projects. This question is of still greater importance now that, after the catastrophes brought about by the war and its aftermath, everyone is preparing, even if only spiritually, for a revival of activity which is to follow the fall of the still pugnacious though already tottering tyrannies.[2]

This is why I shall endeavor to show clearly what, in my opinion, the attitude of the Anarchists should be towards the labor organizations.

I do not think that, today, there still exists among us any one who would deny the usefulness and necessity of the organization of labor as a means of material and moral betterment of the masses, as a fertile field for propaganda and as a force indispensable to the social transformation we are aiming for. No one any longer doubts the importance of the organization of labor, which matters more to us Anarchists than to anyone else, for we believe that the new social order must not and can not be forcibly imposed by a new government, but must of needs result of the free and concerted effort of all. Moreover, the labor movement is now a powerfully and universally established fact; fighting against it would be joining hands with the oppressors, ignoring it would be remaining outside of the people's life and forever being condemned to impotency.

---

1 *The Road to Freedom* (Stelton, NJ) 1, no. 12 (October 1925). Originally published as "Sindacalismo e anarchismo," *Pensiero e Volontà* (Rome) 2, no. 6 (16 April–16 May 1925).

2 The reader should remember that Malatesta is writing under the yoke of fascism. Several of the previous issues of his journal had been seized. Therefore he is forced to use a vague language and avoid any direct reference to fascism.

Still, although we all, or almost all, agree as to the usefulness and necessity of the Anarchists' taking an active part in the labor movement, acting as its initiators and its supporters, we, nevertheless, disagree as to the form, the conditions and the limits of such participation.

Many comrades aspire to fuse into one the Labor and Anarchist movements; and, wherever they are able to do so, as for instance in Spain and Argentina, and also to a certain extent in Italy, France, Germany, etc. they do their utmost to give the labor organizations a purely anarchistic program. These are the comrades who call themselves "Anarcho-Syndicalists," or those who, uniting with others who in reality are not Anarchists, take the name of "Revolutionary Syndicalists."

It is necessary clearly to explain what is meant by "Syndicalism."

If it is the "future society" we desire, i.e.: if by "syndicalism," we mean the form of social organization which is to take the place of the capitalist society and of the state, then, either "syndicalism" is the same as "Anarchy" and is nothing but a confusing word, or it is something different from "Anarchy" and, for this very reason, it cannot be accepted by Anarchists. As a matter of fact, among the various ideas and plans concerning the future society, as expounded by this or that syndicalist, some are genuine anarchistic ideas and plans, but others are only duplicating, under different names and with different modalities, the same authoritarian structure, which is, to-day, causing the evils we deplore; they have, consequently, nothing whatever in common with "Anarchy."

But I am not going to deal here with syndicalism as a social system, for, as such, it cannot be of any value in determining the present action of the Anarchists with regard to the labor movement.

What we are concerned with, here, is the labor movement under a state and capitalist regime; and, under the name of "Syndicalism," are included all labor organizations, all unions which were created in order to resist oppression by employers and to lessen or, if possible, bring to an end, the exploitation of human labor by those who have taken hold of the raw materials and the instruments of labor.

Now, my contention is that these organizations cannot be anarchistic and that it is not right to want them to be such, for if they were, they would not any longer fulfill their aim and could not be used for the ends Anarchists have in view when taking part in them.

Unions are created with a view to defend, today, the present interests of the toilers, and to better their condition as much as possible until they are in a position to make the social revolution, which will change the present wage slaves into free workers, freely associated for the benefit of all.

In order for the union to accomplish its aim and to be, at the same time, a means of education and a field for propaganda tending to cause a future and radical social transformation, it must include all the workers or, at least, all those who aspire to better their condition, and enable them to offer some kind of resistance to their exploiters. Are we to wait until all workers have become anarchists before we invite them to organize themselves, and before we accept them as members of organizations, thus inverting the natural course of propaganda and of the psychological development of the individuals---organizing the resistance when resistance is no longer needed, the masses already being able to accomplish the revolution? In this case a union would be the very same thing as an anarchist group and would remain unable either to obtain better conditions or to bring about the revolution. Or, do we want to have the Anarchist Program written on paper and be satisfied with a formal, unconscious recognition of its principles, and thus gather together a flock sheepishly following their organizers and ready to scatter or go to the enemy when the first opportunity arises to prove that they are anarchists in earnest?

Syndicalism (I mean "practical syndicalism," not "theoretical syndicalism," of which each one has a different conception) is reformist by its very nature. All that we can expect of it is that the reforms it aims at and obtains be such and be obtained in such a way as to help education and revolutionary preparation and leave the door open for always greater demands.

Each fusion or confusion between Anarchist and Revolutionary movement and that of Syndicalism results either in rendering the union powerless to attain its specific aim, or in attenuating, falsifying and extinguishing the spirit of Anarchism.

A union may be founded with a socialistic, revolutionary or anarchistic program and, in fact, the various labor organizations generally were born with such programs. But they remain true to their program only so long as they are weak and powerless, that is, so long as they still are groups of propaganda, initiated and animated by a few enthusiastic and convinced individuals rather than organisms capable of any efficient action. Then, as they succeed in attracting the masses into their midst and in acquiring sufficient strength to demand and command ameliorations, their original program becomes nothing but an empty formula to which nobody pays any more attention; the tactics adapt themselves to the necessities as they arise and the enthusiasts of the first hour must either adapt themselves or give up their place to "practical" men, who pay attention to the present only, without giving any thought to the future.

Certainly, there are comrades, who, though they stand at the very head of the syndicalist movement, remain sincere and enthusiastic Anarchists. Just so are there labor organizations inspired by Anarchist thoughts. But bringing forth the thousands of cases in which these men and these organizations act in contradiction to the Anarchist principles, in every day practice, would be too easy criticism. A pitiful necessity, we admit! One cannot act purely as an Anarchist when one is compelled to bargain with employers and the authorities; one cannot make the masses do things for themselves when the masses refuse to do them and request, nay, insist on having leaders. But why confuse Anarchism with what is not Anarchism; and why assume, as Anarchists, responsibility for compromises made necessary by the very fact that the mass is not anarchistic even if it has written an Anarchist program into the constitution of its organizations?

***

In my opinion, Anarchists should not want the unions to be anarchistic; they should only work in them for anarchistic purposes as individuals, as groups and as federations of groups. Just as there are, or there should be, groups for study and discussion, groups for written or spoken propaganda among the masses, co-operative groups, groups working in offices, in the fields, in the barracks, in the schools, etc., special groups should also be created in the various organizations interested in the class struggle.

Naturally, the ideal would be that every one be an Anarchist and that the organizations function in an anarchistic manner; but then it is obvious that if this would be the case it would no longer be necessary to organize for the struggle against the exploiters, as there would be no more exploiters. Present conditions being what they are, the development of the masses in which we are working being as it is, Anarchist groups should not demand of the organizations that they act as if they were anarchistic; they should only endeavor to make these organizations use tactics as near the Anarchist tactics as possible. If, for the sake of the organization's life and needs, they find it truly necessary to come to terms, give in and come in foul contact with the authorities and with the exploiters, so be it; but let the others and not the Anarchists do it, for their mission is to demonstrate the insufficiency and precarious character of all ameliorations that can be obtained under the capitalist regime, and to steer the struggle toward ever more radical solutions.

In the unions, Anarchists should fight so that these remain open for all the workers, whatever opinion they may hold and to whatever party they may belong, the only provision being that they agree to unite with the others in the struggle against exploitation. Anarchists should oppose the narrow trade-union spirit and all pretexts to monopolize the organizations and the work. They should prevent the members of the unions from becoming mere tools in the hands of politicians for electoral or otherwise authoritarian ends; they should preach and practice direct action, decentralization, autonomy, free initiative; they should endeavor to make the members of the unions directly take part in the life of the organizations without the need of leaders and permanent functionaries.

They should, in a word, remain Anarchists, always keep in contact with the Anarchists and remember that the labor organizations do not constitute the end but only one of the various means, no matter how important it may be, of preparing the advent of Anarchy.

71.
GRADUALISM[1]

In the course of those polemics which arise among anarchists as to the best tactics for achieving, or approaching the creation of an anarchist society—and they are useful, and indeed necessary arguments when they reflect mutual tolerance and trust and avoid personal recriminations—it often happens that some reproach others with being *gradualists*, and the latter reject the term as if it were an insult.

Yet the fact is that, in the real sense of the word and given the logic of our principles, we are all gradualists. And all of us, in whatever different ways, have to be.

It is true that certain words, especially in politics, are continually changing their meaning and often assume one that is quite contrary to the original, logical and natural sense of the term.

Thus the word *possibilist*. Is there anyone of sound mind who would seriously claim to want the impossible? Yet in France the term became the special label of a section of the Socialist Party who were followers of the former anarchist, Paul Brousse—and more willing than others to renouce socialism in pursuit of an impossible cooperation with bourgeois democracy.

Such too is the case with the word *opportunist*. Who actually wants to be an in-opportunist, and as such renounce what opportunities arise? Yet in France the term *opportunist* ended up by being applied specifically to followers of Gambetta[2] and is still used in the pejorative sense to mean a person or party without ideas or principles and guided by base and short-term interests.

The same is true of the word *transformist*. Who would deny that everything in the world and in life evolves and changes? Who today is not a "transformer?" Yet the word was used to describe the corrupt and short-term policies pioneered by the Italian Depretis.[3]

---

1 In *The Anarchist Revolution: Polemical Articles 1924–1931*, edited and introduced by Vernon Richards (London: Freedom Press, 1995), p. 82–87. Originally published as "Gradualismo," *Pensiero e Volontà* (Rome) 2, no. 12 (1 October 1925).

2 Léon Gambetta was a prominent republican politician of the French Third Republic, until his death in 1882.

3 Agostino Depretis was Italian prime minister nine times between 1876 and 1887. During his uninterrupted premiership from 1881 to 1887 he changed his cabinet

It would be a good thing to put a brake on the habit of attributing to words a meaning that is different from their original sense and which gives rise to such confusion and misunderstanding. But how to do it is another matter, particularly when the change in meaning is a deliberate tactic on the part of politicians to disguise their iniquitous purposes behind fine words.

Maybe it is true, therefore, that the word *gradualist*, as applied to anarchists, could end up in fact describing those who use the excuse of doing things gradually, as and when they become possible, and in the last analysis do nothing at all—either that or move, if they move at all, in a contrary direction to anarchy. If this is the case the term has to be rejected. Yet the real sense of gradualism remains the same: everything in nature and in life changes by degrees, and this is no less true of anarchy. It can only come about little by little.

***

As I was saying earlier, anarchism is of necessity gradualist.

Anarchy can be seen as absolute perfection, and it is right that this concept should remain in our minds, like a beacon to guide our steps. But quite obviously, such an ideal cannot be attained in one sudden leap from the hell of the present to the longed-for heaven of the future.

The authoritarian parties, by which I mean those who believe it is both moral and expedient to impose a given social order by force, may hope—vain hope!—that when they come to power they can, by using the laws, decrees... and *gendarmes* subject everybody indefinitely to their will.

But such hopes and wishes are inconceivable for the anarchists, since anarchists seek to impose nothing but respect for liberty and count on the force of persuasion and perceived advantages of free cooperation for the realisation of their ideals.

This does not mean I believe (as, by way of polemic, one unscrupulous and ill-informed reformist paper had me believe) that to achieve anarchy we must wait till *everyone* becomes an anarchist. On the contrary, I believe—and this is why I'm a revolutionary—that under present conditions only a small minority, favoured by special circumstances, can manage to conceive what anarchy is. It would be

five times, supported by majorities that shifted from the Left to the Right, based on short-term convenience rather than long-term programmes.

wishful thinking to hope for a general conversion before a change actually took place in the kind of environment in which authoritarianism and privilege now flourish. It is precisely for this reason that I believe in the need to organise for the bringing about of anarchy, or at any rate that degree of anarchy which could become gradually feasible, as soon as a sufficient amount of freedom has been won and a nucleus of anarchists somewhere exists that is both numerically strong enough and able to be self-sufficient and to spread its influence locally. I repeat, we need to organise ourselves to apply anarchy, or that degree of anarchy which becomes gradually possible.

Since we cannot convert everybody all at once and the necessities of life and the interests of propaganda do not allow us to remain in isolation from the rest of society, ways need to be found to put as much anarchy as possible into practice among people who are not anarchist or who are only sympathetic.

The problem, therefore, is not whether there is a need to proceed gradually but to seek the quickest and sincerest way that leads to the realisation of our ideals.

***

Throughout the world today the way is blocked by the privileges conquered, as a result of a long history of violence and mistakes, by certain classes which in addition to an intellectual and technical superiority which they enjoy as a result of these privileges, also dispose of armed forces recruited among the subject classes and use them when they think necessary without scruples or restraint.

That is why revolution is necessary. Revolution destroys the state of violence in which we live now, and creates the means for peaceful development towards ever greater freedom, greater justice and greater solidarity.

***

What should the anarchists' tactics be before, during and after the revolution?

No doubt censorship would forbid us to say what needs to be done before the revolution, in order to prepare for it and to carry it out. In any case, it is a subject badly handled in the presence of the enemy. It is, however, valid to point out that we need to remain true to ourselves, to spread the word and to educate as much as possible, and avoid all compromise with the enemy and to hold ourselves ready, at least in spirit, to seize all opportunities that might arise.

***

And during the revolution?

Let me begin by saying, we can't make the revolution on our own; nor would it be desirable to do so. Unless the whole of the country is behind it, together with all the interests, both actual and latent, of the people, the revolution will fail. And in the far from probable case that we achieved victory on our own, we should find ourselves in an absurdly untenable position: either because, by the very fact of imposing our will, commanding and constraining, we would cease to be anarchists and destroy the revolution by our authoritarianism; or because, on the contrary, we would retreat from the field, leaving others, with aims opposed to our own, to profit from our effort.

So we should act together with all progressive forces and vanguard parties to attract the mass of the people into the movement and arouse their interest, allowing the revolution—of which we would form a part, among others—to yield what it can.

This does not mean that we should renounce our specific aims. On the contrary, we would have to keep closely united and distinctly separate from the rest in fighting in favour of our programme: the abolition of political power and expropriation of the capitalists. And if, despite our efforts, new forms of power were to arise that seek to obstruct the people's initiative and impose their own will, we must have no part in them, never give them any recognition. We must endeavour to ensure that the people refuse them the means of governing—refuse them, that is, the soldiers and the revenue; see to it that those powers remain weak... until the day comes when we can crush them once and for all.

Anyway, we must lay claim to and demand, with force if needs be, our full autonomy, and the right and the means to organise ourselves as we see fit and to put our own methods into practice.

***

And after the revolution—that is after the fall of those in power and the final triumph of the forces of insurrection?

This is where gradualism becomes particularly relevant.

We must pay attention to the practical problems of life:

production, trade, communications, relations between anarchist groups and those who retain a belief in authority, between communist collectives and individualists, between the city and the countryside. We must make sure to use to our advantage the forces of nature and raw materials, and that we attend to industrial and agricultural distribution—according to the conditions prevailing at the time in the various different countries—public education, childcare and care for the handicapped, health and medical services, protection both against common criminals and those, more insidious, who continue to attempt to suppress the freedom of others in the interests of individuals and parties, etc. The solutions to each problem must not only be the most economically viable ones but must respond to the imperatives of justice and liberty and be those most likely to keep open the way to future improvements. If necessary, justice, liberty and solidarity must take priority over economic benefit.

There is no need to think in terms of destroying everything in the belief that things will look after themselves. Our present civilisation is the result of thousands of years of development and has found some means of solving the problem of how millions and millions of people co-habit, often crowded together in restricted areas, and how their ever-increasing and ever more complex needs can be satisfied. Such benefits are reduced—and for the great majority of people virtually denied—due to the fact that the development has been carried out by authoritarian means and in the interests of the ruling class. But, if the rules and privileges are removed, the real gains remain: the triumphs of humankind over the adverse forces of nature, the accumulated weight of experience of past generations, the sociable habits acquired throughout the long history of human cohabitation, the proven advantages of mutual aid. It would be foolish, and besides impossible, to give up all this.

In other words, we must fight authority and privilege, while taking advantage from the benefits that civilisation has conferred. We must not destroy anything that satisfies human need however badly—until we have something better to put in its place.

Intransigent as we remain to any form of capitalist imposition or exploitation, we must be tolerant of all those social concepts that prevail in the various human groupings, so long as they do not harm the freedom and equal rights of others. We should content ourselves with gradual progress while the moral level of the people grows, and with it, the material and intellectual means available to mankind; and while, clearly, doing all we can, through study, work and propaganda, to hasten development towards ever higher ideals.

***

I have here come up with more problems than solutions. But I believe I have succinctly presented the criteria which must guide us in the search and application of the solutions, which will certainly be many and vary according to the circumstances. But, so far as we are concerned, they must always be consistent with the fundamental principles of anarchism: no-one orders anyone else around, no-one exploits anyone else.

It is the task of all comrades to think, study and prepare—and to do so with all speed and thoroughly because the times are "dynamic" and we must be ready for what might happen.

72. LET'S DEMOLISH—AND THEN?[1]

In No. 9 of *Pensiero e Volontá* I wrote a review of Galleani's book, *La Fine dell'Anarchismo?*[2] Benigno Bianchi replies:

> I hope you will not mind if I write to bring to your attention a sentence that would give rise to regrettable misunderstandings. I refer to the second paragraph of Galleani's words quoted in your article.
>
> In the passage in question Galleani spoke of the need to clear the decks for posterity, of prejudices, privileges, churches, prisons, barracks, brothels, etc. It is therefore necessary to destroy, not to construct.
>
> You honestly reply that "it would be ridiculous, and fatal, to want to destroy all unhygienic ovens, all anti-economic mills, all backward cultures, leaving to posterity the task of seeking better means of growing wheat, grinding flour and baking bread."
>
> Oh, Errico, yes indeed, baking bread, in one form or another is indispensable, as is growing wheat and grinding it, and wanting to destroy the means of doing so, and of destroying other similar processes would be worse than ridiculous, it would be madness!
>
> These things will be renewed, reformed, perfected; but there is no way I would wish to renew and perfect prisons, churches, barracks and brothels, nor yet the monopolies and privileges of which Galleani spoke.
>
> It seems to me that the comparison does not hold and therefore that the whole thrust of the article is lost.
>
> Such polemical distortions ill befit the seriousness of the Review and the authority of your writing.

---

1 In *The Anarchist Revolution: Polemical Articles 1924–1931*, edited and introduced by Vernon Richards (London: Freedom Press, 1995), p. 65–69. Originally published as "Demoliamo. E poi?" *Pensiero e Volontà* (Rome) 3, no. 10 (16 June 1926).

2 Luigi Galleani's book, which has been translated into English as *The End of Anarchism?*, was the reprint of a series of articles written in 1907–8, in response to an interview in which Francesco Saverio Merlino had declared anarchism a spent force. Malatesta's review had appeared in *Pensiero e Volontà* of 1 June 1926.

***

Naturally I do not in the least mind comrade Bianchi's comments. On the contrary, I thank him for giving me the opportunity to return to a question which I consider of vital importance for the development and success of our movement.

Let us leave Galleani aside. If I have misinterpreted him, then he is the best person to tell me so and I am always ready to make amends. Let us, rather, discuss the argument in itself.

My reference to bread strikes Bianchi as a polemical distortion. To me, on the other hand, it is fitting. I am in the habit—I don't know if it's a virtue or a fault—of always looking for the simplest, most obvious examples, because these don't permit of rhetorical tricks and plainly reveal the kernel of the question.

It is essential, says Bianchi, to have the means of making bread; it would therefore be madness to think of destroying rather than perfecting those means. But bread is not the only indispensable item. Indeed, I believe it would be very difficult to find any present institution, including the worst of them—even prisons, brothels, barracks, privileges and monopolies—that does not respond, directly or indirectly, to a social need and that it would be possible to truly destroy and for ever unless it was replaced by something that better satisfies the need that generated it in the first place.

Do not ask, a comrade said, what we should substitute for cholera. It is an evil, and evil has to be eliminated, not replaced. This is true. But the trouble is that cholera persists and returns unless conditions of improved hygiene have replaced those that first allowed the disease to gain a foothold and spread.

Bread is a need, yes. But the question of bread is more complicated than those who live in a small farming centre and produce wheat for their own families might suppose. Providing bread for all is a problem that involves an entire social organisation: type of land ownership, method of working the land, means of exchange, transport systems, importation of grain, should the amount produced at home not be enough, means of distribution to the various centres of population, and thereafter to the individual consumers. In other words, it means that solutions must be found to the questions of ownership, value, currency, trade, etc.

Present day production and distribution of bread are exploitative and humiliating for the workers; the consumers are robbed and a whole army of parasites benefits at the expense of both producers and consumers. We, on the other hand, want bread to be produced and distributed for the greater benefit of all, without draining energy and materials, without oppression and parasitism and with fairness and efficiency. And we must seek the means of realising this goal, or as great an approximation to it as we can manage. Our descendants will certainly do better than us; but we must do as we know and can—and do it at once, the very same day as the crisis breaks, because if there were an interruption in rail services, or the milling and baking bosses began manoeuvring and concealing the bread, the urban centres would not receive it (nor would they receive other basic necessities); the revolution would be lost and the forces of reaction would triumph under the guise of restoration of the monarchy or under the form of dictatorship.

By all means let us destroy the monopolies. But when they are not to do with shirt buttons or lipstick for the ladies, the big monopolies (water, electricity, coal, road, rail and sea transport, etc.) they are the response to a necessary public service, and such monopolies cannot be destroyed without bringing about their swift return—unless, in the act of dismantling them the service itself is not continued, possibly with more efficiency than before.

By all means let us destroy the gaols—those dismal regions of suffering and corruption, where brutalised screws end up worse than those they guard. But in the case of, say, some *satyr* who rapes and tortures the little bodies of children, there has to be some means of preventing him from doing harm if he is not to make other victims before falling to lynch violence. Shall we leave such a problem to our descendants? Surely not. We must concern ourselves with it now, because these things are happening now. Let us hope that in the future the advances of science and the changed social scene will make such monsters impossible.

Let us destroy the brothels, those vile dens of human shame—shame more for those who live outside them than within. By all means. But the brothels will return, either publicly or in secret, so long as there are women who cannot find a decent job or gainful employment. Labour needs to be organised in such a way that there is a place for all; consumption must be organised in such a way that everyone can satisfy their own needs.

Of course, let us abolish the *gendarme*, that man who protects all privilege by force and is the living symbol of the State. But to be able to abolish him for good, and not see him reappear under another name and in a different guise, we have to know how to live without him—that is, without violence, without oppression, without injustice, without privilege.

Yes, let us abolish ignorance. But obviously we need first to teach and educate, and before even this, to create the social conditions that would permit everyone to avail themselves of education and training.

"To leave to posterity a land without privileges, without churches, without tribunals, without brothels, without barracks, without ignorance, without stupid fears." Yes, this is our dream, and we fight to bring it about. But this means bequeathing to future generations a new social organisation, new and better moral and material conditions. You cannot clear the decks and leave them bare if people are living on them. You cannot destroy evil without substituting good, or at least something that is less bad.

This does not mean imposing nothing on our descendants. It is to be hoped, I repeat, that they will do better than us. But we must do here and now what we know and can, for our own benefit and hand down to future generations something more than fine words and vague aspirations.

***

There is a state of mind which, despite much propaganda to the contrary, persists in a number of comrades and which, to my view, should be changed as a matter of urgency.

The conviction, which I share, that a revolution is needed to eliminate those material forces which defend privilege and obstruct any real social progress, has meant that many have dwelt exclusively on the act of insurrection, without considering what needs to be done to prevent an insurrection becoming a sterile act of violence to which a further act of revolutionary violence responds. For these comrades all practical questions—means or organisation, method of supplying our daily bread, are idle questions for now: matters, they say, that will resolve themselves or be resolved by future generations.

I remember an episode in 1920, when I was editor of *Umanità Nova*. It was the period when the socialists were trying to impede the revolution, and unfortunately they succeeded. They said that if an insurrection took place the lines of communication with abroad would be severed and we would have all died of starvation as a result of the grain shortage. There were even those who said there could be no revolution because Italy did not produce rubber! Concerned with the basic question of food and convinced that the grain shortage could be made good by using all the available arable land for cultivation of plants and fast-growing nutritional grains, I asked our comrade, Dr G. Rossi, an experienced agronomist, to write a series of articles on practical concepts of agriculture, directed precisely at the goal we had in mind. Rossi kindly did so. His articles were obviously very useful, but also practical, and did not therefore please everyone. One comrade, annoyed that I had rejected some poem or short story of his—I no longer recall exactly what—said brusquely: "Yes, you prefer *Umanità Nova* to be about ploughs, chick-peas, beans, cabbages and stupid things like that!"

And another comrade, who then had pretensions of being some sort of super-anarchist, unwittingly expressed the logical consequences of this kind of mentality. Finding himself with his back to the wall in just such a discussion as this, he said to me: "But these are matters that don't concern me. Providing bread and so on is the responsibility of the leaders."

The conclusion, indeed, is this: either we all apply our minds to thinking about social reorganisation, and right away, at the very same moment that the old structures are being swept away, and we shall have a more humane and more just society, open to future advances; or we shall leave such matters to the "leaders" and we shall have a new government; and this will do exactly what governments have always done—make the masses pay for the limited and bad services it provides, taking away their freedom while allowing the parasites and the privileged of all stripes the freedom to exploit them by every means.

73. A PROJECT OF ANARCHIST ORGANISATION[1]

I recently happened to come across a French pamphlet (in Italy today, as is known, the non-fascist press cannot freely circulate), with the title "Organisational Platform of the General Union of Anarchists (Project)".

This is a project for anarchist organisation published under the name of a "Group of Russian Anarchists Abroad" and it seems to be directed particularly at Russian comrades.[2] But it deals with questions of equal interest to all anarchists; and it is clear, including the language in which it is written, that it seeks the support of comrades worldwide.[3] In any case it is worth examining, for the Russians as for everyone, whether the proposal put forward is in keeping with anarchist principles and whether implementation would truly serve the cause of anarchism.

The intentions of the comrades are excellent. They rightly lament the fact that until now the anarchists have not had an influence on political and social events in proportion to the theoretical and practical value of their doctrines, nor to their numbers, courage and spirit of self-sacrifice—and believe that the main reason for this relative failure is the lack of a large, serious and active organisation.

And thus far I could more or less agree.

Organisation, which after all only means cooperation and solidarity in practice, is a natural condition, necessary to the running of society; and it is an unavoidable fact which involves everyone, whether in human society in general or in any grouping of people joined by a common aim.

As human beings cannot live in isolation, indeed could not really become human beings and satisfy their moral and material needs

1 In *The Anarchist Revolution: Polemical Articles 1924–1931*, edited and introduced by Vernon Richards (London: Freedom Press, 1995), p. 93–103. Originally published as "Un progetto di organizzazione anarchica," parts 1 and 2, *Il Risveglio Anarchico*, supplement of *Le Réveil Anarchiste* (Geneva) 26, nos. 728 and 729 (1 and 15 October 1927).

2 Among the group's members were Nestor Makhno and Peter Arshinov.

3 At the time French was the most used language for international communication.

unless they were part of society and cooperated with their fellows, it is inevitable that those who lack the means, or a sufficiently developed awareness, to organise freely with those with whom they share common interests and sentiments, must submit to the organisations set up by others, who generally form the ruling class or group and whose aim is to exploit the labour of others to their own advantage. And the age-long oppression of the masses by a small number of the privileged has always been the outcome of the inability of the greater number of individuals to agree and to organise with other workers on production and enjoyment of rights and benefits and for defence against those who seek to exploit and oppress them.

Anarchism emerged as a response to this state of affairs, its basic principle being free organisation, set up and run according to the free agreement of its members without any kind of authority; that is, without anyone having the right to impose their will on others. And it is therefore obvious that anarchists should seek to apply to their personal and political lives this same principle upon which, they believe, the whole of human society should be based.

Judging by certain polemics it would seem that there are anarchists who spurn any form of organisation; but in fact the many, too many, discussions on this subject, even when obscured by questions of language or poisoned by personal issues, are concerned with the means and not the actual principle of organisation. Thus it happens that when those comrades who sound the most hostile to organisation want to really do something they organise just like the rest of us and often more effectively. The problem, I repeat, is entirely one of means.

Therefore I can only view with sympathy the initiative that our Russian comrades have taken, convinced as I am that a more general, more *united*, more enduring organisation than any that have so far been set up by anarchists—even if it did not manage to do away with all the mistakes and weaknesses that are perhaps inevitable in a movement like ours, which struggles on in the midst of the incomprehension, indifference and even the hostility of the majority—would undoubtedly be an important element of strength and success, a powerful means of gaining support for our ideas.

I believe it is necessary above all and urgent for anarchists to come to terms with one another and organise as much and as well as possible in order to be able to influence the direction the mass of the people take in their struggle for change and emancipation.

Today the major force for social transformation is the labour movement (union movement) and on its direction will largely depend the course events take and the objectives of the next revolution. Through the organisations set up for the defence of their interests the workers develop an awareness of the oppression they suffer and the antagonism that divides them from the bosses and as a result begin to aspire to a better life, become accustomed to collective struggle and solidarity and win those improvements that are possible within the capitalist and state regime. Then, when the conflict goes beyond compromise, revolution or reaction follows. The anarchists must recognise the usefulness and importance of the union movement; they must support its development and make it one of the levers in their action, doing all they can to ensure that, by cooperating with other forces for progress, it will open the way to a social revolution that brings to an end the class system, and to complete freedom, equality, peace and solidarity for everybody.

But it would be a great and a fatal mistake to believe, as many do, that the labour movement can and should, of its own volition, and by its very nature, lead to such a revolution. On the contrary, all movements based on material and immediate interests (and a big labour movement can do nothing else) if they lack the stimulus, the drive, the concerted effort of people of ideas, tend inevitably to adapt to circumstances, they foster a spirit of conservatism and fear of change in those who manage to obtain better working conditions, and often end up creating new and privileged classes, and serving to uphold and consolidate the system we would seek to destroy.

Hence there is an impelling need for specifically anarchist organisations which, both from within and outside the unions, struggle for the achievement of anarchism and seek to sterilise all the germs of degeneration and reaction.

But it is obvious that in order to achieve their ends, anarchist organisations must, in their constitution and operation, remain in harmony with the principles of anarchism; that is, they must know how to blend the free action of individuals with the necessity and the joy of cooperation; they must serve to develop the awareness and initiative of their members; and they must be means of education for the environment in which they operate and of moral and material preparation for the future we desire.

Does the project under discussion satisfy these demands?

It seems to me that it does not. Instead of arousing in anarchists a greater desire for organisation, it seems deliberately designed to reinforce the prejudice of those comrades who believe that to organise means to submit to leaders and belong to an authoritarian, centralising body that suffocates any attempt at free initiative. And in fact it contains precisely those proposals that some, in the face of evident truths and despite our protests, insist on attributing to all anarchists who are described as organisers.

***

Let us examine the Project.

First of all, it seems to me a mistake—and in any case impossible to realise—to believe that all anarchists can be grouped together in one "General Union"—that is, in the words of the Project, in a *single,* active revolutionary body.

We anarchists can all say that we are of the same party, if by the word "party" we mean all who are *on the same side,* that is, who share the same general aspirations and who, in one way or another, struggle for the same ends against common adversaries and enemies. But this does not mean it is possible—or even desirable—for all of us to be gathered into one specific association. There are too many differences of environment and conditions of struggle; too many possible ways of action to choose among, and also too many differences of temperament and personal incompatibilities for a *General Union,* if taken seriously, not to become, instead of a means for coordinating and reviewing the efforts of all, an obstacle to individual activity and perhaps also a cause of more bitter internal strife.

As an example, how could one organise in the same way and with the same group a public association set up to make propaganda and agitation publicly and a secret society restricted by the political conditions of the country in which it operates to conceal from the enemy its plans, methods and members? How could the *educationalists,* who believe that propaganda and example suffice for the gradual transformation of individuals and thus of society, adopt the same tactics as the *revolutionaries,* who are convinced of the need to destroy by violence a status quo that is maintained by violence and to create, in the face of the violence of the oppressors, the necessary conditions for the free dissemination of propaganda and the practical application of the conquered ideals? And how to keep together some people who, for particular reasons, do not get on with and respect one another, but could nevertheless be equally good and useful militants for anarchism?

Besides, even the authors of the Project (*Plateforme*) declare as "inept" any idea of creating an organisation which gathers together the representatives of the different tendencies in anarchism. Such an organisation, they say, "incorporating heterogeneous elements, both on a theoretical and practical level, would be no more than a mechanical collection (*assemblage*) of individuals who conceive all questions concerning the anarchist movement from a different point of view and would inevitably break up as soon as they were put to the test of events and real life."

That's fine. But then, if they recognise the existence of different tendencies they will surely have to leave them the right to organise in their own fashion and work for anarchy in the way that seems best to them. Or will they claim the right to expel, to *excommunicate* from anarchism all those who do not accept their programme? Certainly they say they "want to assemble in a single organisation" all the *sound elements* of the libertarian movement; and naturally they will tend to judge as *sound* only those who think as they do. But what will they do with the elements that are *not sound*?

Of course, among those who describe themselves as anarchists there are, as in any human groupings, elements of varying worth; and what is worse, there are some who spread ideas in the name of anarchism which have very little to do with anarchism. But how to avoid the problem? *Anarchist truth* cannot and must not become the monopoly of one individual or committee; nor can it depend on the decisions of real or fictitious majorities. All that is necessary—and sufficient—is for everyone to have and to exercise the widest freedom of criticism and for each one of us to maintain their own ideas and choose for themselves their own comrades. In the last resort the facts will decide who was right.

***

Let us therefore put aside the idea of bringing together *all* anarchists into a single organisation and look at this *General Union* which the Russians propose to us for what it really is—namely the Union of a particular fraction of anarchists; and let us see whether the organisational method proposed conforms with anarchist methods and principles and if it could thereby help to bring about the triumph of anarchism.

Once again, it seems to me that it cannot.

I am not doubting the sincerity of the anarchist proposals of those Russian comrades. They want to bring about anarchist communism and are seeking the means of doing so as quickly as possible. But it is not enough to want something; one also has to adopt suitable means; to get to a certain place one must take the right path or end up somewhere else. Their organisation, being typically authoritarian, far from helping to bring about the victory of anarchist communism, to which they aspire, could only falsify the anarchist spirit and lead to consequences that go against their intentions.

In fact, their *General Union* appears to consist of so many partial organisations with *secretariats* which *ideologically* direct the political and technical work; and to coordinate the activities of all the member organisations there is a *Union Executive Committee* whose task is to carry out the decisions of the Union and to oversee the "ideological and organisational conduct of the organisations in conformity with the ideology and general strategy of the Union."

Is this anarchist? This, in my view, is a government and a church. True, there are no police or bayonets, no faithful flock to accept the dictated *ideology*; but this only means that their government would be an impotent and impossible government and their church a nursery for heresies and schisms. The spirit, the tendency remains authoritarian and the educational effect would remain anti-anarchist.

Listen if this is not true.

"The executive organ of the general libertarian movement—the anarchist Union—will introduce into its ranks the principle of collective responsibility; the whole Union will be responsible for the revolutionary and political activity of every member; and each member will be responsible for the revolutionary and political activity of the Union."

And following this, which is the absolute negation of any individual independence and freedom of initiative and action, the proponents, remembering that they are anarchists, call themselves federalists and thunder against centralisation, "the inevitable results of which," they say, "are the enslavement and mechanisation of the life of society and of the parties."

But if the Union is responsible for what each member does, how can it leave to its individual members and to the various groups the freedom to apply the common programme in the way they think best? How can one be responsible for an action if one does not have the means to prevent it? Therefore, the Union and in its name the Executive Committee, would need to monitor the action of the individual members and order them what to do and what not to do; and since disapproval after the event cannot put right a previously accepted responsibility, no-one would be able to do anything at all before having obtained the go-ahead, the permission of the committee. And on the other hand, can an individual accept responsibility for the actions of a collectivity before knowing what it will do and if he cannot prevent it doing what he disapproves of?

Moreover, the authors of the Project say that it is the "Union" which proposes and disposes. But when they refer to the wishes of the Union do they perhaps also refer to the wishes of all the members? If so, for the Union to function it would need everyone always to have the same opinion on all questions. Now, while it is normal that everyone should be in agreement on the general and fundamental principles, because otherwise they would not be and remain united, it cannot be assumed that thinking beings will all and always be of the same opinion on what needs to be done in the different circumstance and on the choice of persons to whom to entrust executive and directional responsibilities.

In reality—as it emerges from the text of the Project itself—the will of the Union can only mean the will of the majority, expressed through congresses which nominate and control the *Executive Committee* and decide on all the important questions. Naturally, the congresses would consist of representatives elected by the majority of member groups, and these representatives would decide on what to do, as ever by a majority of votes. So, in the best of cases, the decisions would be taken by the majority of a majority, and this could easily, especially when the opposing opinions are more than two, represent only a minority.

Furthermore it should be pointed out that, given the conditions in which anarchists live and struggle, their congresses are even less truly representative than the bourgeois parliaments. And their control over the executive bodies, if these have authoritarian powers, is rarely opportune and effective. In practice anarchist congresses are attended by whoever wishes and can, whoever has enough money and who has not been prevented by police measures. There are as many present who represent only themselves or a small number of friends as there are those truly representing the opinions and desires of a large collectivity. And unless precautions are taken against possible traitors and spies—indeed, because of the need for those very precautions—it is impossible to make a serious check on the representatives and the value of their mandate.

In any case this all comes down to a pure majority system, to pure parliamentarianism.

It is well known that anarchists do not accept majority government (*democracy*), any more than they accept government by the few (*aristocracy, oligarchy*, or dictatorship by one class or party) nor that of one individual (*autocracy, monarchy* or personal dictatorship).

Thousands of times anarchists have criticised so-called majority government, which anyway in practise always leads to domination by a small minority.

Do we need to repeat all this yet again for our Russian comrades?

Certainly anarchists recognise that where life is lived in common it is often necessary for the minority to come to accept the opinion of the majority. When there is an obvious need or usefulness in doing something and, to do it requires the agreement of all, the few should feel the need to adapt to the wishes of the many. And usually, in the interests of living peacefully together and under conditions of equality, it is necessary for everyone to be motivated by a spirit of concord, tolerance and compromise. But such adaptation on the one hand by one group must on the other be reciprocal, voluntary and must stem from an awareness of need and from goodwill to prevent the running of social affairs from being paralysed by obstinacy. It cannot be imposed as a principle and statutory norm. This is an ideal which, perhaps, in daily life in general, is difficult to attain in entirety, but it is a fact that in every human grouping anarchy is that much nearer where agreement between majority and minority is free and spontaneous and exempt from any imposition that does not derive from the natural order of things.

So if anarchists deny the right of the majority to govern human society in general—in which individuals are nonetheless constrained to accept certain restrictions, since they cannot isolate themselves without renouncing the conditions of human life—and if they want everything to be done by the free agreement of all, how is it possible for them to adopt the idea of government by majority in their essentially free and voluntary associations and begin to declare that anarchists should submit to the decisions of the majority before they have even heard what those might be?

It is understandable that non-anarchists would find Anarchy, defined as a free organisation without the rule of the majority over the minority, or vice versa, an unrealisable utopia, or one realisable only in a distant future; but it is inconceivable that anyone who professes to anarchist ideas and wants to make Anarchy, or at least seriously approach its realisation—today rather than tomorrow—should disown the basic principles of anarchism in the very act of proposing to fight for its victory.

***

In my view, an anarchist organisation must be founded on a very different basis from the one proposed by those Russian comrades.

Full autonomy, full independence and therefore full responsibility of individuals and groups; free accord between those who believe it useful to unite in cooperating for a common aim; moral duty to see through commitments undertaken and to do nothing that would contradict the accepted programme. It is on these bases that the practical structures, and the right tools to give life to the organisation should be built and designed. Then the groups, the federations of groups, the federations of federations, the meetings, the congresses, the correspondence committees and so forth. But all this must be done freely, in such a way that the thought and initiative of individuals is not obstructed, and with the sole view of giving greater effect to efforts which, in isolation, would be either impossible or ineffective.

Thus congresses of an anarchist organisation, though suffering as representative bodies from all the above-mentioned imperfections, are free from any kind of authoritarianism, because they do not lay down the law; they do not impose their own resolutions on others. They serve to maintain and increase personal relationships among the most active comrades, to coordinate and encourage programmatic studies on the ways and means of taking action, to acquaint all on the situation in the various regions and the action most urgently needed in each; to formulate the various opinions current among the anarchists and draw up some kind of statistics from them—and their decisions are not obligatory rules but suggestions, recommendations, proposals to be submitted to all involved, and do not become binding and enforceable except on those who accept them, and for as long as they accept them.

The administrative bodies which they nominate—Correspondence Commission, etc.—have no executive powers, have no directive powers, unless on behalf of those who ask for and approve such initiatives, and have no authority to impose their own views—which they can certainly maintain and propagate as groups of comrades, but cannot present as the official opinion of the organisation. They publish the resolutions of the congresses and the opinions and proposals which groups and individuals communicate to them; and they serve—for those who require such a service—to facilitate relations between the groups and cooperation between those who agree on the various initiatives. Whoever wants to is free to correspond with whomsoever he wishes, or to use the services of other committees nominated by special groups.

In an anarchist organisation the individual members can express any opinion and use any tactic which is not in contradiction with accepted principles and which does not harm the activities of others. In any case a given organisation lasts for as long as the reasons for union remain greater than the reasons for dissent. When they are no longer so, then the organisation is dissolved and makes way for other, more homogeneous groups.

Clearly, the duration, the permanence of an organisation depends on how successful it has been in the long struggle we must wage, and it is natural that any institution instinctively seeks to last indefinitely. But the duration of a libertarian organisation must be the consequence of the spiritual affinity of its members and of the adaptability of its constitution to the continual changes of circumstances. When it is no longer able to accomplish a useful task it is better that it should die.

***

Those Russian comrades will perhaps find that an organisation like the one I propose and similar to the ones that have existed, more or less satisfactorily at various times, is not very efficient.

I understand. Those comrades are obsessed with the success of the Bolsheviks in their country and, like the Bolsheviks, would like to gather the anarchists together in a sort of disciplined army which, under the ideological and practical direction of a few leaders, would march solidly to the attack of the existing regimes, and after having won a material victory would direct the constitution of a new society. And perhaps it is true that under such a system, were it possible that anarchists would involve themselves in it, and if the leaders were men of imagination, our material effectiveness would be greater. But with what results? Would what happened to socialism and communism in Russia not happen to anarchism?

Those comrades are anxious for success as we are too. But to live and to succeed we don't have to repudiate the reasons for living and alter the character of the victory to come.

We want to fight and win, but as anarchists—for Anarchy.

74. SOME THOUGHTS ON THE POST-REVOLUTIONARY PROPERTY SYSTEM[1]

Our opponents, the beneficiaries and defenders of the current social system, are in the habit of justifying the right to private property by stating that property is the condition and guarantee of liberty.

And we agree with them. Do we not say repeatedly that poverty is slavery?

But then, why do we oppose them?

The reason is clear: in reality the property that they defend is capitalist property, namely property that allows its owners to live from the work of others and which therefore depends on the existence of a class of the disinherited and dispossessed, forced to sell their labour to the property owners for a wage below its real value.

Indeed, in all countries of the modern world the majority of the population must live by seeking work from those with a monopoly of the land and means of labour and when they obtain it they receive a wage that is always below its value and often barely sufficient to ward off starvation. This means that workers are subjected to a kind of slavery which, though it may vary in degree of harshness, always means social inferiority, material penury and moral degradation, and is the primary cause of all the ills that beset today's social order.

To bring freedom to all, to allow everyone, in full freedom, to gain the maximum degree of moral and material development, and enjoy all the benefits that nature and labour can bestow, everyone must have their own property; everyone, that is, must have the right to that piece of land and those raw materials and tools and equipment that are needed to work and produce without exploitation and oppression. And since we cannot expect the propertied classes to spontaneously surrender the privileges they have usurped, the workers will have to expropriate that property and it must become the property of all.

1 In *The Anarchist Revolution: Polemical Articles 1924–1931*, edited and introduced by Vernon Richards (London: Freedom Press, 1995), p. 113–9. Originally published as "Qualche considerazione sul regime della proprietà dopo la rivoluzione," *Il Risveglio Anarchico* (Geneva), no. 784 (30 November 1929).

This has to be the task of the next revolution and to it we must lend our best efforts. But since social life cannot allow for interruption, we must at the same time give consideration to the practical means of using the assets we would by then hold in common, and the ways of ensuring that all members of society enjoy equal rights.

The property system will therefore be the problem that arises at the very same moment that we proceed with expropriation.

Naturally we cannot claim or hope to pass at one fell swoop from the current system to other perfect and definitive systems. During the moment of revolution, when the first priority is to act quickly and to immediately fulfill the most urgent needs, everything possible will be done, depending on the will of those involved and the actual conditions which are determined and circumscribed by them. But it is essential that from the very beginning there is an idea of what needs to be done to propel things as far as possible towards that end.

Should property be individually or collectively owned? And should the collective owner of undivided assets be the local group, the operational group, the ideological affinity group, the family group—or shall it involve all the members of the whole nation, and beyond that, of all mankind?

What will the forms of production and exchange be? Will the victorious system be *communism* (producers' associations and free consumption for all) or *collectivism* (production in common and distribution of goods according to the labour of the individual) or *individualism* (to each the individual means of production and possession of the product of their own labour), or some other compound form which individual interests and social instincts, illuminated by experience, might suggest?

Probably all possible forms of ownership, use of the means of production and all forms of distribution will be experimented with simultaneously, in the same or other locations, and they will be merged together and adapted in various ways until practical experience identifies the best form or forms.

In the meantime, as I have already mentioned above, the need not to interrupt production and the impossibility of suspending consumption of basic necessities will ensure that little by little, as expropriation takes place, agreement will be reached on the way to continue running social life. Whatever is possible will be done, and so long as everything is done to prevent the establishment and consolidation of new privileges there will be time to find better solutions.

***

But what is the solution that seems best to me and which is the one to aim for?

I call myself a communist because communism seems to me the ideal target for humanity, as people's love for one another grows and large-scale production frees them from fear of hunger, and thereby destroys the main obstacle to solidarity. But, really, more than the practical forms of economic organisation, which must necessarily be adapted to circumstance and will be under continual development, the important thing is the spirit which moves these organisations and the methods with which they are set up. What is important, in my opinion, is that they are guided by the spirit of justice and a desire for the good of all, and that they are always created freely and on a voluntary basis.

All forms of organisation, if there really is freedom and a spirit of solidarity, aim at the same goal—human emancipation and progress—and will end by agreeing with one another and merging. But if, on the other hand, there is lack of freedom and goodwill to all, then there is no form of organisation that will not breed injustice, exploitation and despotism.

***

Let us briefly look at the main systems which have been proposed as a solution to the problem.

As regards anarchist aspirations, the two basic systems in contention are *individualism* (by which I mean individualism as a means of distribution of wealth and I will not struggle with abstruse philosophical concepts which, in this context, are irrelevant) and *communism.*

Collectivism, about which little is said nowadays, is an intermediate system which brings together the merits and the defects of the two above-mentioned systems, and, perhaps, precisely because it is a halfway house, will be widely applied, at least during the transition between the old and new society. But I will not deal specifically with this because the same objections can be made of it as are made of individualism and communism.

Complete individualism would seem to consist in dividing between all individuals all land and all other wealth in proportions that are virtually equal and equivalent, in such a way that all persons, from the outset of their lives, are supplied with equal means, and each individual can rise to the heights that their faculties and activities permit. In order to preserve this equality from the outset the concept of heredity would be abolished and periodically there would be fresh divisions of land and wealth to keep pace with changes in the population figures.

This system would clearly not be economically viable; that is, it would not be conducive to the best use of wealth. Even if it could be applied in small and primitive agrarian communities it would certainly be impossible in an extensive collective and advanced agrarian-industrial civilisation, in which a considerable portion of the population would not be in direct touch with the land and equipment for producing material goods, but would be carrying out useful and essential services for all. Moreover, how can the land be divided with at least relative justice, given that the value of various different areas of land differs so much according to productivity, health of the soil and position? And how can one divide up the great industrial enterprises which, to operate, depend on the labour of a great number of workers, working simultaneously? And how to fix the value of things and trade without at the same time falling back on the evils of competition and hoarding?

It is quite true that advances in chemistry and engineering tend towards an equalling out of productivity and fertility of different areas of land; that the development of means of transport—the motor car and the aeroplane—will tend to spread benefits far more widely; that the electric motor is a decentralising factor in industry and enables isolated individuals and small groups to do machine work; that science may, in all countries, discover or synthesise the raw materials needed for production. And then, when these and other advances come about, ease and abundance of production will cease to be the overriding economic problem it is today and growth in human solidarity will render useless and repugnant any minute and hair-splitting calculations as to what one or the other person is entitled to.

But these are things that will happen in a more or less distant future, while here I have been dealing with today and the near future. And today a social organisation based on individual ownership of the means of production, maintaining and creating antagonisms and rivalries between producers and a conflict of interests between producers and consumers, would always be under threat from the possible advent of authority, a government that would re-establish the privileges that had been overthrown. In any case it could not exist, not even provisionally, unless it were moderated and strenghtened by all kinds of voluntary associations and cooperatives.

The primary dilemma for the revolution always remains: whether to organise voluntarily to the advantage of all, or to be organised under the power of a government to the advantage of the ruling class.

***

Let us now turn to communism.

Theoretically, so far as human relations are concerned, communism seems the ideal system to replace struggle by solidarity, to make the best possible use of natural energy and human labour and of humanity one great family of brothers and sisters whose purpose is to help and love one another.

But is this practicable in the moral and material condition in which humanity now finds itself? And what are its boundaries?

Universal communism—a single community of all human beings—is an aspiration, an ideal goal towards which to move, but certainly it could not now take on a concrete form of economic organisation; nor probably could it do so for a long time to come; the longer term will be the concern of our descendants.

At present one can think only of a multiplicity of communities made up of neighbouring and kindred populations, who would have a number of different relationships between one another, whether communist or commercial; and even within these limits there is always the problem of a possible conflict between communism and liberty. Because, without prejudice to the sentiment which propels people towards a conscious and desired solidarity and which will induce us to fight for and put into practice the greatest possible degree of communism, I believe that total communism—especially if extended over a vast area of territory—would be as impossible and antilibertarian today as complete individualism would be economically unviable and impossible.

To organise a communist society on the grand scale, the whole of economic life—means of production, exchange and consumption—would have to be radically transformed. And this could only be done gradually, as objective circumstances permit, and to the extent that the majority of the population understand the advantages and know how to provide for themselves. If, on the other hand, this could be done at one stroke, at the wishes and through the excessive power of one party, the masses, used to obeying and serving, would accept the new form of life as a new law, imposed by a new government, and would wait for a supreme power to impose on all how to produce and to control consumption. And the new power, not knowing and not able to satisfy immensely varied and often contradictory needs and desires, and not wanting to declare itself a useless bystander by leaving to the interested parties the freedom to do as they wanted and could, would reconstitute a State, founded, like all States, on military and police power; and this, if it managed to last, would only substitute new and more fanatical bosses for the old ones. On the pretext (and indeed with the honest and sincere intention) of regenerating the world with a new Gospel, a single rule would be imposed on all, all liberties suppressed and all free initiative made impossible. In consequence, discouragement and paralysis of production would set in; clandestine and fraudulent commercial practices would take over; there would be an arrogant and corrupt bureaucracy, general misery and, finally, a more or less complete return to the same conditions of oppression and exploitation that the revolution was meant to abolish.

The Russian experience must not have taken place in vain.

***

To conclude, it seems to me that no system can be viable and truly liberate humanity from atavistic bondage, if it is not the result of free development.

If there is to be a society in which people live together on a free and cooperative basis for the greater good of all and no longer convents and despotisms, held together by religious superstition or brute force, human societies cannot be the artificial creation of one person or sect. They must be the result of the concurring or conflicting needs and desires of all members of society who, through repeated trial and error, find the institutions which, at a given moment, are the best ones possible, and develop and change them according to changing circumstances and desires.

Communism, individualism, collectivism or any other imaginable system may be preferred and its triumph worked for through propaganda and example. But, at the risk of sure disaster, what one must always guard against is the claim that one's own system is the only and infallible system, good for all, and in all places and for all time; and that victory can be won in other ways than by persuasion, based on the evidence of the facts.

What is important, and indispensable, indeed the essential departure point, is to ensure that every person has the means to be free.

When the government, which defends the proprietors and the landowners, is defeated, or at any rate rendered powerless, it will be up to everybody, and especially those among the populance who have the spirit of initiative and organisational ability, to provide for the satisfaction of immediate needs and to prepare for the future, destroying privileges and harmful institutions and at the same time making the useful institutions, which today exclusively or mainly serve the ruling classes, work for the benefit of all.

The special mission for the anarchists is to be on guard for liberty against the aspirants to power and against the possible despotism of the majority.

75. THE ANARCHISTS IN THE PRESENT TIME[1]

A section of our movement is eagerly discussing the practical problems that the revolution will have to solve.

This is good news and a good omen, even if the solutions proposed so far are neither abundant nor satisfactory.

The days are gone when people used to believe that an insurrection would suffice for everything, that defeating the army and the police and knocking down the powers that be would be enough to bring about all the rest, i.e. the most essential part.

It used to be claimed that providing sufficient food, adequate accommodations, and good clothes to everyone immediately after the victorious uprising would be enough for the revolution to be founded on unshakable ground and be able to readily proceed towards higher and higher ideals. Nobody took the trouble to check whether there would actually be enough goods for everyone and whether the existing goods were in the places where they were most needed. The display of stores overflowing with goods deceptively influenced the hungry and ragged crowds. The agitators, whether conscious or not of the error, found that illusion an effective means of propaganda. However, if on the one hand it is well known today that the production done by everyone for the benefit of everyone else with the aid of mechanics and chemistry can indefinitely grow, on the other hand it is also true that the current system's rule is that capitalists get the workers to produce only as much as they can profitably sell, stopping the production at the point where their profit stops growing. If by mistake or by competition among capitalists an overproduction occurs, a crisis comes and drives the marketplace back to that condition of relative scarcity, which is most advantageous for manufacturers and dealers. Hence it is clear how dangerous it is to spread the belief that goods abound and that there is no urge to set to work.

1 Translated from "Gli anarchici nel momento attuale," *Vogliamo!* (Biasca, Switzerland) 2, no. 6 (June, 1930).

Gone are also the days when we could say that demolishing is our task, and that our descendants will see to reconstructing. That was a cheap statement that could only be accepted back when an imminent revolution was unlikely. It only aimed at arousing aversion and hate against the present situation, to sharpen the desire of change. However, the European situation is now full of revolutionary potential; at any time we might have to pass from theory to practice, from propaganda to action. Now it is time to remember that the social and individual lives allow no interruption: we have to live and to feed our children and ourselves everyday, until our children can start seeing to it.

So, we are agreed in thinking that apart from the problem of assuring victory against the material forces of the adversary there is also the problem of giving life to the revolution after victory. We are in agreement that a revolution that resulted in chaos would not be a vital revolution.

But one must not exaggerate; it should not be thought that we must, and can, find, here and now, a perfect solution for every possible problem. One should not want to foresee and determine too much, because instead of preparing for anarchy we might find ourselves indulging in unattainable dreams or even becoming authoritarians, and consciously or otherwise, proposing to act like a government, which in the name of freedom and the popular will, will subject people to its domination.

I happen to read the strangest things: strange if one considers that they were written by anarchists.

For instance, a comrade says that "the crowd would rightly rail against us if we had first urged them to the painful sacrifices of a revolution and then we told them: do what your will suggests you do: get together, produce, and live together as it best suits you."

What! Did not we always tell the crowd that they can expect their good neither from us nor from others? That they have to win their good for themselves? That they will get only what they can take and they will keep only what they can defend? It is just and natural for us, initiators, animators and part ourselves of the mass, to try and push the movement in the direction that seems best to us, and be as ready as possible for anything that needs to be done. However, the fundamental principle is still that making decisions is up to the free will of those concerned.

I also read: "We will create a regime that, though not fully libertarian, will have our mark and above all will pave the way to the progressive realization of our principles."

What is this? A little tiny government, a model of goodness, which will kill itself as soon as possible to give way to anarchy!!!

Were not we already in agreement that governments do not tend to kill themselves, but rather to perpetuate themselves and become more and more despotic? Were not we agreed that the mission of the anarchists is to fight, while enduring it, any regime not based on a complete freedom? Did not we also use to claim that anarchists in power would not fare better than the others?

Another comrade, who is among those who most care about the necessity of having a "plan," and basically puts all his hope in the workers' unions, says:

"After the triumph of the revolution, let the management of all the means of production, transportation, exchange, etc. be given to the working class, previously educated by us to this great social function."

Previously educated by us to this great social function! How many centuries should go by before the revolution wished by that comrade? If only centuries were sufficient! The fact is that one cannot educate the masses if they are not in a position, or obliged by necessity, to act for themselves; the revolutionary organization of the workers, useful and necessary as it is, cannot be stretched indefinitely: at a certain point if it does not erupt in revolutionary action, either the government strangles it or the organization itself degenerates and breaks up—and one has to start all over again from the beginning.

How true that the most "practical" people are often the most naive utopians!

Would not all this discussion sound quite academic if, in the concrete, it was about a country where the free workers' organization is destroyed and prohibited, the freedoms of press, assembly, and association are abolished, and the agitators, be they anarchist, socialist, communist, or republican are either abroad as refugees, or on forced residence on an island, or locked in prison, or put in the condition of being unable to speak, to move about, and almost even to breath?

Can one reasonably hope that the next upheaval, in a country in such conditions, will be a social revolution, in the broad and utter sense that we attribute to this word? Does not it look like winning back the necessary conditions for propaganda and organization is rather the one possible and urgent task nowadays?

It seems to me that all these difficulties, uncertainties, and contradictions crop up when one wants to make anarchy without anarchists, or believes that propaganda is enough to convert the whole of the population, or its vast majority, before the surrounding conditions have radically changed.

Some people claim that "the revolution will be anarchist or will not be at all." This is yet another of those pretentious phrases that a thorough analysis proves to be either meaningless or greatly mistaken. In fact, if one means that the revolution, as we intend it, must be anarchist, such claim is just a tautology, i.e. a roundabout that explains nothing, as if one claimed, for instance, that white paper must be white. If it is meant, instead, that there cannot be any other revolution but an anarchist one, then the claim is a great mistake, as the life of human societies has already seen and will certainly see again movements that radically change the existing conditions and give a new direction to the history to come, thus deserving the name of revolutions. I would be unable to accept the view that all past revolutions though they were not anarchist revolutions were useless, nor that future ones, which will still not be anarchist, will be useless. Indeed, I incline to the view that the complete triumph of anarchy will come by evolution, gradually, rather than by violent revolution: when an earlier or several earlier revolutions will have destroyed the major military and economic obstacles which are opposed to the spiritual development of the people, to increasing production to the level of needs and desires, and to the harmonizing of contrasting interests.

In any case, if we take into account our sparse numbers and the prevalent attitudes among the masses, and if we do not wish to confuse our wishes with the reality, we must expect that the next revolution will not be an anarchist one, and therefore what is more pressing, is to think of what we can and must do in a revolution in which we will be a relatively small and badly armed minority.

***

Some comrades, perhaps still under the spell of the socialist brags and illusions born by the Russian revolution, believe that the authoritarians have an easier task than ourselves, because they have a "plan": get hold of the power and forcibly impose their system.

Such belief is wrong. Communists and socialists certainly wish to grab the power, and in certain circumstances they may succeed. However, the most intelligent among them know too well that, once in power, they could well tyrannize the people and submit it to whimsical and dangerous experiments, they could well replace the bourgeoisie with a new privileged class, but they could not realize socialism, they could not apply their "plan." How can a millenary society be destroyed and a new and better society be established by the decrees made by few people and imposed by bayonets! This is the one honest reason (I do not want to deal with others that can be less easily confessed) why, in Italy, socialists and communists withheld their co-operation and blocked the revolution when it was possible to make one. They felt they would not be able to keep control of the situation and would have to either give way to the anarchists or become an instrument of reaction. As for the countries where they actually got the power... what they did is well known.

If only we had the material force to get rid of the material force that oppresses us, our task would be much easier, because we require nothing of the masses but what the masses can and want to do; we only do all that we can to develop their capability and will.

But we must, however, beware of ourselves becoming less anarchist because the masses are not ready for anarchy. If they want a government, it is unlikely that we will be able to prevent a new government being formed, but this is no reason for our not trying to persuade the people that government is useless and harmful or of preventing the government from also imposing on us and others like us who do not want it. We will have to exert ourselves to ensure that social life and especially economic standards improve without the intervention of government, and thus we must be as ready as possible to deal with the practical problems of production and distribution, remembering, incidentally, that those most suited to organize work are those who now do it, each in his own trade.

***

We must seek to play an active, and if possible a preponderant role in the insurrectionary act. But with the defeat of the forces of repression which serve to keep the people in slavery; with the demobilization of the army, the dissolution of the police and the magistrature, etc.; having armed the people so that it can resist any armed attempt by reaction to reestablish itself; having called on willing hands to undertake the organization of public services and to provide, with concepts of just distribution, for the most urgent needs, using with care the existing stocks in the various localities—having done all this, we shall have to see to it that there must be no wasted effort and that those institutions, those traditions and habits, those methods of production, exchange and aid should be respected and utilized, if they perform, even insufficiently or badly, necessary services, seeking by all means to destroy every trace of privilege, but being wary of destroying anything that cannot be replaced by something that serves the general good more effectively. We must push the workers to take possession of the factories, to federate among themselves and work for the community, and similarly the peasants should take over the land and the produce usurped by the landlords, and come to an agreement with the industrial workers on the necessary exchange of goods.

If we are unable to prevent the constitution of a new government, if we are unable to destroy it immediately, we should in either case refuse to support it in any shape or form. We should reject military conscription, and refuse to pay taxes. Disobedience on principle, resistance to the bitter end against every imposition by the authorities, and an absolute refusal to accept any position of command.

If we are unable to overthrow capitalism, we shall have to demand for ourselves and for all who want it, the right of free access to the necessary means of production to maintain an independent existence.

Advise when we have suggestions to offer; teach if we know more than others; set the example for a life based on free agreement between individuals; defend even with force if necessary and possible, our autonomy against any government provocation... but command—never.

In this way we shall not achieve anarchy, which cannot be imposed against the wishes of the people, but at least we shall be preparing the way for it.

76. AGAINST THE CONSTITUENT ASSEMBLY AS AGAINST THE DICTATORSHIP[1]

Everyone has the right to state and defend their ideas, but nobody has the right to misrepresent someone else's ideas to strengthen their own.

After years without seeing the *Martello*, the issue of June 21 fell into my hands. I found in it an article signed X., which talks, in a more or less imaginary way, about an insurrectionary project, which was allegedly promoted by myself, Giulietti, and... D'Annunzio. From the article it appears that someone else who writes under the name of Ursus had previously written about such events, but I could not manage to find his article.[2]

Never mind. I cannot tell now how the events referred to by X. and Ursus actually happened, because this is not the right time to let the public, and thus the police, know what one may have done or attempted to do. Also, I could not betray the trust that may have been put in me by persons who would not like to be named now. I can be surprised, though, that these X. and Ursus, moved by the desire to find support to their tactical thesis, have not realized how tactless it is to involve someone who usually does not receive newspapers, and thus does not know what is said about him and cannot reply—in addition to their feeling no duty, in a personal matter, to take at least responsibility for what they say and sign with their real names.

What I care about—and what makes me take the trouble of pointing out said articles—is protesting the completely false statement that, at any moment whatsoever of my political activity, I may

1 Translated from "Contro la Costituente come contro la dittatura," *L'Adunata dei Refrattari* (New York) 9, no. 36 (4 October 1930).

2 *Il Martello* was the periodical published in New York by Carlo Tresca. Malatesta had very limited access to the anarchist press, due to the tight control by Mussolini's police on his mail. "Ursus" was the pen name of the Italian anarchist Antonio Cavalazzi. In a letter of 25 June 1930 to Luigi Fabbri, Malatesta wrote: "There is some truth in what Ursus says, but it is somehow distorted." The project in question was conceived in early 1920. A couple of meetings were held in Rome, but since D'Annunzio required the socialists' support, the project aborted after the socialists rejected the idea.

have been a supporter of the Constituent Assembly. The issue bears such a theoretical and practical relevance, that it could become topical any moment, and it cannot leave cold anyone who calls himself anarchist and wants to act like an anarchist in any given situation.

To be precise, at the time when the events badly recollected by X. and Ursus occurred, I was striving, with my words and writings, to fight the faith and hope put by many subversives (obviously non-anarchist) in the possibility of a Constituent Assembly.

At that time I claimed, as I have always done before and after, that a Constituent Assembly is the means used by the privileged classes, when a dictatorship is not possible, either to prevent a revolution, or, when a revolution has already broken out, to stop its progress with the excuse of legalizing it, and to take back as much as possible of the gains that the people had made during the insurrectional period.

The Constituent Assembly, which dulls and stifles people, and the dictatorship, which crushes and kills them, are the two dangers that threaten any revolution. Anarchists must aim their efforts against them.

Of course, since we are a relatively small minority, it is quite possible, and even likely, that the next upheaval will end up in the convocation of a Constituent Assembly. However, this would not happen with our participation and co-operation. It would happen against our will, despite our efforts, simply because we will not have been strong enough to prevent it. In this case, we will have to be as distrustful and inflexibly opposed to a Constituent Assembly as we have always been to ordinary parliaments and any other legislative body.

***

Let this be quite clear. I am not an advocate of the "all or nothing" theory. I believe that nobody actually behaves in such a way as implied by that theory: it would be impossible.

This is just a slogan used by many to warn about the illusion of petty reforms and alleged concessions from government and masters, and to always remind of the necessity and urgency of the revolutionary act: it is a phrase that can serve, if loosely interpreted, as an incentive to a fight without quarter against every kind of oppressors and exploiters. However, if taken literally, it is plain nonsense.

The "all" is the ideal that gets farther and wider as progresses are made, and therefore it can never be reached. The "nothing" would be some abysmally uncivilized state, or at least a supine submission to the present oppression.

I believe that one must take all that can be taken, whether much or little: do whatever is possible today, while always fighting to make possible what today seems impossible.

For instance, if today we cannot get rid of every kind of government, this is not a good reason for taking no interest in defending the few acquired liberties and fighting to gain more of those. If now we cannot completely abolish the capitalist system and the resulting exploitation of the workers, this is no good reason to quit fighting to obtain higher salaries and better working conditions. If we cannot abolish commerce and replace it with the direct exchange among producers, this is no good reason for not seeking the means to escape the exploitation of traders and profiteers as much as possible. If the oppressors' power and the state of the public opinion prevent now from abolishing the prisons and providing to any defence against wrongdoers with more humane means, not for this we would lose interest in an action for abolishing death penalty, life imprisonment, close confinement, and, in general, the most ferocious means of repression by which what is called social justice, but actually amounts to a barbarian revenge, is exercised. If we cannot abolish the police, we would not allow, without protesting and resisting, the policemen to beat the prisoners and allow themselves all sorts of excesses, overstepping the limit prescribed to them by the laws in force themselves...

I am breaking off here, as there are thousands and thousands of cases, both in individual and social life, in which, being unable to obtain "all," one has to try and get as much as possible.

At this point, the question of fundamental importance arises about the best way of defending what one has got and fighting to obtain more; for there is one way that weakens and kills the spirit of independence and the consciousness of one's own right, thus compromising the future and the present itself, while there is another way that uses every tiny victory to make greater demands, thus preparing the minds and the environment to the longed complete emancipation.

What constitutes the characteristic, the raison d'etre of anarchism is the conviction that the governments—dictatorships, parliaments, etc.—are always instruments of conservation, reaction, oppression;

and freedom, justice, well-being for everyone must come from the fight against authority, from free enterprise and free agreement among individuals and groups.

***

One problem worries many anarchists nowadays, and rightly so.

As they find it insufficient to work on abstract propaganda and revolutionary technical preparation, which is not always possible and is done without knowing when it will be fruitful, they look for something practical to do here and now, in order to accomplish as much as possible of our ideas, despite the adverse conditions; something that morally and materially helps the anarchists themselves and at the same time serves as an example, a school, an experimental field.

Practical proposals are coming from various sides. They are all good to me, if they appeal to free initiative and to a spirit of solidarity and justice, and tend to take individuals away from the domination of the government and the master. And to avoid wasting time in continuously recurring discussions that never bring new facts or arguments, I would encourage those who have a project to try to immediately accomplish it, as soon as they find support from the minimal necessary number of participants, without waiting, usually in vain, for the support of all or many—experience will show whether those projects were workable, and it will let the vital ones survive and thrive.

Let everyone try the paths they deem best and fittest to their temperament, both today with respect to the little things that can be done in the present environment, and tomorrow in the vast ground that the revolution will offer to our activity. In any case, what is logically mandatory for us all, if we do not want to stop being truly anarchist, is to never surrender our freedom in the hands of an individual or class dictatorship, a despot or a Constituent Assembly; for what depends on us, our freedom must find its foundation in the equal freedom of all.

77. PETER KROPOTKIN: RECOLLECTIONS AND CRITICISMS BY ONE OF HIS OLD FRIENDS[1]

Peter Kropotkin is undoubtedly one of those who contributed most—more even, perhaps, than Bakunin and Elisée Reclus—to the elaboration and propagation of the Anarchist idea, and for this he has well merited the admiration and gratitude which all Anarchists feel for him.

But respect for truth and the supreme interest of the cause make it necessary to declare that his work has not been wholly and exclusively beneficent. This was not his fault; on the contrary, it was just the eminence of his merits which caused the evils which I propose to indicate.

It was only natural that Kropotkin could not, nor could any other man, avoid mistakes and comprehend the whole truth. Under these circumstances it would have been right to profit by his precious contributions, and to continue to search for new progress.

But Kropotkin's literary talents, the value and extent of his work, his prestige due to his fame as a man of great learning, the fact that he had sacrificed a highly privileged position to defend, at the price of danger and suffering, the cause of the people, and with all that the charm of his personality, which laid under a spell all who had the good fortune to come near to him, all this gave him such a reputation and influence that he appeared to be, and to a great extent really was, the recognized teacher of the great majority of Anarchists.

It happened thus that criticism was discouraged, and the development of the idea was arrested. For many years, in spite of the iconoclastic and progressive spirit of Anarchists, most of them on the field of theory and practice did nothing but study and repeat Kropotkin. To say something differing from him was to many comrades almost an act of heresy.

1 *Freedom Bulletin* (Stroud, Gloucestershire), no. 12 (July 1931), translated by Max Nettlau. The translation is from Malatesta's French original, published as "Pierre Kropotkine: Souvenirs et critiques d'un de ses vieux amis," *Le Réveil Anarchiste* (Geneva) 31, no. 820 (18 April 1931). However, the article first appeared in Russian translation, in the Kropotkin memorial issue of the review *Probuzhdenie* (Detroit) in February 1931, on the tenth anniversary of Kropotkin's death.

Hence it would be right to submit Kropotkin's teachings to severe and unprejudiced criticism, to distinguish between what is always true and alive and that which later thought and experience may have demonstrated to be erroneous. This would, by the way, not concern Kropotkin alone, for the errors which can be placed to his charge were professed by Anarchists before Kropotkin had acquired an eminent position in the movement. He has confirmed and continued them by giving them the support of his talent and prestige; but we, the old militants, we have all, or nearly all, our share of responsibility in this.

***

In writing this time on Kropotkin, I do not propose to examine throughly all his doctrine. I will only record some impressions and recollections which might help, I believe, toward a better understanding of his moral and intellectual personality and of his merits and faults.

Before all, however, I will say a few words which come from my heart, for I cannot think of Kropotkin without being moved by the recollection of his great kindness. I remember what he did in Geneva in the winter of 1879 or 1880 to help a group of Italian refugees in distress, to which I belonged; I remember the care, which I might call maternal, which he took of me in London one night when I had been the victim of an accident and had knocked at his door; I remember a thousand traits of his gentle behaviour with everyone; I remember the atmosphere of cordiality which one felt in his society. For he was really a good man, of that almost unconscious kindness which feels the urge to relieve all suffering and to spread around him smiles and joy. One might, indeed, have said that he was kind without knowing it: in any case, he did not like to be told so. He felt offended because in an article written on the occasion of his seventieth birthday, I had said that kindness was the first of his qualities.[2]

2 The article appeared in the Parisian *Les Temps Nouveaux* of 14 December 1912. Malatesta stated that he preferred to talk about the man than about the thinker. "He loves human beings," he wrote. "Everything he thinks and everything he does is motivated by that goodness, by that great love for human beings, for all human beings, that seems to be the essential trait of his character." He portrayed Kropotkin as a "systematic mind": "he set anarchist ideas in a philosophical framework that may or may not be agreed with. But, all theory aside, he is an anarchist..."

He rather preferred to show his energy and fierceness, perhaps because these latter qualities had been developed in the struggle and for the struggle, whilst kindness was the spontaneous expression of his intimate nature.

***

I had the honour and the good fortune to be attached to Kropotkin for many years by most fraternal friendship. We liked each other because the same passion, the same hopes, animated us, and also the same illusions.

Being both of an optimistic temperament (I believe, however, that Kropotkin's optimism by far surpassed mine and sprang perhaps from a different source), we saw things rose-coloured, alas! too much rose-coloured; we hoped—this happened more than fifty years ago—for an early revolution which would realize our ideals. During this long period there were many moments of doubt and discouragement. I remember, for instance, Kropotkin, on one occasion saying to me: "My dear Henry, I am afraid that only you and I believe in an early revolution." But such moments passed quickly, and confidence soon returned; we explained in one way or the other the difficulties of the hour and the scepticism of comrades, and we continued to work and hope.

Nevertheless, one must not believe that we were of the same opinion on everything. On the contrary, we were far from agreeing upon many fundamental ideas, and we seldom met without some point of difference causing angry discussions between us. But as Kropotkin was always sure he was right and could not endure contradiction calmly, and as I, for my part, had much respect for his knowledge, and much thought for his indifferent health, we always ended by changing the subject to prevent our becoming too much irritated.

But this did not impair the intimate character of our relations, for we liked each other and we cooperated for sentimental rather than for intellectual reasons. However differently we explained facts or justified our conduct by arguments, in practice we wanted the same things and were impelled by the same ardent desire for freedom, justice, and well being for everyone, hence we could march together in agreement.

And, in fact, there was never a serious disagreement between us until the day when, in 1914, a question of practical conduct of capital importance for me and for him presented itself: of the attitude which

Anarchists ought to take with regard to the War. On this disastrous occasion his old preference for all that was Russian or French were rekindled and strengthened, and he declared himself passionately a partisan of the Entente. He seemed to have forgotten that he was an Internationalist, a Socialist, and an Anarchist; he forgot what he had said himself not long ago on the war which the capitalists prepared;[3] he expressed admiration for the worst statesmen and generals of the Entente; he treated Anarchists who refused to enter the Sacred Union as cowards, deploring that age and health did not permit him to take a rifle and to march against the Germans. No means of coming to an understanding. For me this was a real pathological case. In every way this was one of the most painful, the most tragical moments of my life (and I dare to say, also, of his life), that moment when, after the most painful of discussions, we separated as adversaries, nearly as enemies.

My pain for the loss of a friend was great, and also for the damage resulting to the cause by the dismay which such a defection would spread among Anarchists. But, in spite of all, my love and esteem for the man remained intact, and also the hope that when the frenzy of the hour had passed and he would have seen the consequences of the war which could have been foretold, he would recognize his error and become again the Kropotkin of old.

***

Kropotkin was at one and the same time a scientist and a social reformer. He was possessed by two passions: the desire to know and the desire to bring about the well-being of humanity. Two noble passions these, which can be useful one to the other, and which one would like to see in every man, without there being by this one and the same thing. But Kropotkin had an eminently systematic mind. He wanted to explain everything according to the same principle, he wanted to reduce all to a unity—and he did so, often even, in my opinion, in the teeth of logic. Thus he based his social aspirations upon science, as they were, in his opinion, only rigorously scientific deductions.

I have no specific competence to be able to pass judgment on Kropotkin as a scientist. I know that in his young days he had

3 As Nettlau notes, "this refers to the pamphlet *War*, published in French, by *Les Temps Nouveaux*, Paris, 1912, 22 pp., and in Italian, by *Il Risveglio*, Geneva, March, 1912, 22 pp."

rendered remarkable services to geography and to geology; I appreciate the great value of his book, *Mutual Aid*, and I am convinced that with his great culture and his highly developed intelligence he could have given greater contributions to the progress of science if his attention and activities had not been absorbed by the social struggle. It seems, however, to me that he lacked something to make him a real man of science; the capacity to forget his desires and preconceptions in order to observe the facts with an impassive objectivity. He seemed to me to be rather what I should really call a poet of science. He might have been able to arrive at new truths by intuitive genius, but others would have had to verify these truths, men with less genius or no genius at all, but better gifted with what is called the scientific spirit. Kropotkin was too passionate to be an exact observer.

It was his habit to conceive a hypothesis and then to search for the facts which ought to justify it; this might be a good method for discoveries, but it happened to him without this being his wish, that he could not see the facts which contradicted the hypothesis.

He could not make up his mind to admit a fact and often not even to take it into consideration, if he did not first succeed in explaining it, that is, to make it enter into his system.

As an example, I will relate an episode occasioned by myself.

Being in the Argentine Pampa some time between 1885 and 1889, I happened to read something on the experiments in hypnotism of the Nancy school. The subject interested me greatly, but I had not then the means to get further information. Returning to Europe, I met Kropotkin in London and asked him if he could give me information on hypnotism. He replied right away that nothing of this must be believed, that it was all fraud or hallucination. Some time later, when we met again, conversation drifted once more to the subject of hypnotism, and with surprise I noticed that his opinion had completely changed; the hypnotic phenomena had become an interesting subject worthy of study. What then had happened? Had he become acquainted with new facts? Or had he found convincing proofs of the facts which he denied at first? Nothing of the kind. He had simply read in a book of I know not what German physiologist a theory on the relations between the two hemispheres of the brain which could, by hook or by crook, explain the said phenomena.

With such a disposition of mind, which made him arrange facts in his own way in questions of pure science where there was no reason that passion should trouble the intellect, one could foresee what would happen in questions concerning closely his greatest desires and most cherished hopes.

***

Kropotkin professed the materialist philosophy which dominated the scientists of the second half of the nineteenth century, the philosophy of Moleschott, Büchner, Vogt, etc., consequently his conception of the universe was rigorously mechanical.

According to this system, will (a creative power, the source and nature of which we cannot understand, as, by the way, we do not understand the source and nature of "matter" and of other "first principles"), will, I say, which contributed more or less to the determination of the conduct of individuals and of societies, does not exist, is an illusion. All that was, is, and shall be, from the orbits of the stars to the birth and decay of a civilization, from an earthquake to the thought of a Newton, from the perfume of a rose to the smile of a mother, from the cruelty of a tyrant to the kindness of a saint, all did, does, and will happen by the fatal consecutive series of causes and effects of a mechanical character, leaving no room for any possibility of variation. The illusion of the existence of a will would be itself only a mechanical fact.

Naturally, logically, if will has no power, if it does not exist, if everything is necessary and cannot happen in another way, then the ideas of freedom, of justice, of responsibility, have no meaning, do not correspond to anything real.

By logic, in that case, one may only contemplate the things that happen with indifference, pleasure or pain, according to everybody's sensibility, but with no hope and without any possibility of changing anything.

***

So Kropotkin, who was very severe on the historical fatalism of the Marxist, fell into the mechanical fatalism which is much more paralysing.

But philosophy could not kill the powerful will that lived in Kropotkin. He was too much convinced of the truth of his system to renounce it, or even to agree calmly when doubts were expressed about it. But he was too passionate, too great a lover of freedom and justice, to be stopped by the difficulties of a logical contradiction and to give up the struggle. He found a way out by inserting Anarchy into his system and by making of it a scientifically established truth.

He affirmed himself in his conviction by maintaining that recent discoveries in all sciences, from astronomy to biology and sociology, concurred in demonstraning more and more that Anarchy is the mode of social organization exacted by Nature's laws. One might have objected to him that, whatever conclusions might be drawn from contemporary science, it was certain that if new discoveries would destroy the present scientific belief, he, Kropotkin, would have remained an Anarchist in the teeth of logic. But Kropotkin could not have brought himself to admit the possibility of a conflict between science and his social aspirations, and he would always have imagined some means, no matter whether logical or not, of conciliating his mechanistic philosophy with his Anarchism.

Thus, after having said[4] that "Anarchism is a conception of the universe based upon the mechanical interpretation of phenomena, comprehending the whole of Nature, including the life of societies" (I confess that I have never succeeded in understanding what this means), Kropotkin forgot his mechanical conception as if it were a mere nothing, and threw himself into the struggle with the impulse, the enthusiasm, and the confidence of one who believes in the efficacy of his will, and hopes by his action to obtain, or to help to obtain, what he desired.

***

In reality, Kropotkin's Anarchism and Communism, before being a question of reasoning, were the result of his sensibility. The heart in him spoke first, and then came the reasoning to justify and to strengthen the impulses of the heart.

The basis of his character was constituted by love of man, sympathy for the poor and the oppressed. He really suffered by the sufferings of others, and injustice, even if in his favour, was insupportable to his spirit.

At the time when I frequently met him in London,[5] he made his living by contributing to magazines and other scientific publications, and he was in a situation of comparative ease. But he felt

---

4 In *Modern Science and Anarchism*, notes Nettlau.

5 This refers mainly to the years 1881–1882, notes Nettlau.

it as a reproach to be better off than most of the manual workers, and he seemed always to wish to excuse his little comforts. He often said of himself and those in a similar situation: "If we have obtained instruction and developed our faculties, if we have access to intellectual pleasures, if we live in material conditions which are not too bad, this is because we benefited by the chance of our birth from the exploitation which weighs upon the workers; to struggle for their emancipation is for us a duty, a sacred debt which we must pay."

By love of justice, as if to expiate the privileges which he had enjoyed, he had given up his position and neglected his beloved studies in order to devote himself to the education of the workers of St. Petersburg, and to the struggle against the despotism of the Tsars. Impelled by the same sentiments, he had later joined the International and accepted Anarchist ideas. Finally, among the different Anarchist conceptions he had chosen the Communist-Anarchist programme which, being based upon solidarity and love, goes beyond justice itself.[6]

But naturally, as might be foreseen, his philosophy was not without influence upon his manner of conceiving the future and the struggle which had to be waged to arrive at it.

Since by his philosophy all that happens had to happen, Communist-Anarchism, which he desired, had necessarily to triumph as by a natural law. And this took all incertitude away from him and hid every difficulty. The bourgeois world was fated to fall; it was already in dissolution, and revolutionary action only helped to accelerate the fall.

His great influence as a propagandist, besides his talent, was owing to the fact that he showed these happenings to be so simple, so easy, so inevitable that those who heard or read him were seized by enthusiasm.

The moral difficulties vanished, because he attributed to the "people," to the mass of the workers, all virtues and all capacities. He exalted, with good reason, the moralising influence of work, but he

6 In a letter of 18 May 1931 to Luigi Fabbri, Malatesta wrote: "Strictly speaking, justice means giving to the others the equivalent of what they give to you; it means Proudhon's *échange égal* ... Instead love gives all it can and wishes it could give ever more, without counting, without calculating ... It seems to me that there are two contrasting feelings in the human mind: the feeling of sympathy, or love, for one's fellow human beings, which is always beneficial; and the feeling of justice, which gives rise to unending strife, because everyone finds it fair what suits him best."

did not sufficiently recognize the depressing and corrupting effects of misery and subjection, and he thought that the abolition of capitalist privileges and governmental power were sufficient to make all men begin immediately to love one another as brothers and to care for the interests of others as much as for their own.

In the same way he saw no material difficulties or he easily got rid of them. He had accepted the idea then current among anarchists that the accumulated products of the land and of industry were so abundant that for quite a long time it would not be necessary to give a thought to production, and he always said that the immediate problem was that of consumption;[7] that to ensure the victory of the revolution it was essential to satisfy at once and amply the needs of all: production would naturally follow the rhythm of consumption. Hence that idea of the *prise au tas* (taking from the heap) which he made a fashion, and which is certainly the simplest manner of conceiving Communism and the most apt to please the masses, but also the most primitive and the most really Utopian.

And when one remarked to him that this mass of products could not exist, because the owners of the means of production normally have only produced what they can sell with profit, and that perhaps during the first stages of the revolution rationing might have to be organized, and an impulse given to intensive production rather than encouragement to the taking from the heap, which after all does not exist, he began to study the question directly[8] and arrived at the conclusion that in fact abundance does not exist, and that in certain countries one was always under the menace of famine. But he became reassured when thinking of the great possibilities of agriculture aided by science. He took as examples the results obtained by some agriculturists and some agricultural scientists on a limited area, and from this he drew the most encouraging conclusions, not thinking of the obstacles which the ignorance and the spirit of routine of the peasants would have put in the way, nor of the time which, in any case, would be required for the universal spread of the new methods of cultivation and of distribution.

As always, Kropotkin saw things as he would have wished them to be, and as we all hope that some day they will be: he assumed as

7 On this subject, see the article "The Products of Soil and Industry."

8 Nettlau notes: "His article 'The Capital of the Revolution' in *La Révolte*, early in 1891, contains Kropotkin's first consideration of this subject, and his studies were caused by Malatesta's criticism expressed to him during the year 1890."

existing, or as immediately realisable that which can only be gained by long and hard-working effort.

***

Kropotkin conceived Nature as a kind of Providence thanks to which harmony must reign in everything, human societies included. This has made many Anarchists repeat this phrase, of a perfectly Kropotkinian flavour: "Anarchy is natural order."

One might ask how it comes that if Nature's law is really harmony, Nature has waited for Anarchists to come into existence, and still waits until they are victorious, before destrying the terrible and murderous disharmonies which at all times men have suffered.

Would it not be nearer to truth to say that Anarchy is the struggle within human societies against the disharmonies of Nature?

***

I have dwelt on the two errors into which, in my opinion, Kropotkin has fallen, his theoretic fatalism and his excessive optimism, because I believe I have seen the evil effects which they had upon our movement.

There were comrades who took seriously the fatalistic theory (euphemistically called determinist), and who, in consequence, lost all their revolutionary spirit. Revolution is never made, they would say, it will perhaps arrive in its time; but it is useless, unscientific, and even ridicolous to want to make it—and with these good reasons they withdrew, and thought of their own affairs. However, it would be a mistake to think that this was for all a cheap excuse for retiring. I knew several comrades of ardent temperament, ready to face every danger, who have sacrificed their position, their liberty, and even their life in the name of Anarchy, being convinced all the time of the uselessness of their action. They have been prompted by disgust of present society, by revenge, by despair, by love of the beautiful deed, but without believing that by this they have helped the cause of the revolution, and consequently without selecting the goal and the right moment, and without any thought of co-ordinating their action with that of others.

In another direction, some who, without giving a thought to philosophy, wished to work to hasten the revolution, believed their task to be much easier than it really is, did not foresee the difficulties, , were not properly prepared, and thus they were powerless on the day when perhaps a possibility of doing something practical did exist.

May the errors of the past serve as a lesson to do better in the future.

***

I have finished. I do not think that my criticisms can belittle Kropotkin, who remains one of the purest glories of our movement. If they are correct, they will serve to show that no man is exempt from error, not even if he possesses the high intelligence and the heroic heart of a Kropotkin. In every way, Anarchists will always find in his writings a treasury of fruitful ideas, and in his life an example and an incentive in the struggle for what is good.

78. APROPOS OF "REVISIONISM"[1]

I have been passed a clipping from *Il Martello* containing a sort of open letter addressed to me by a comrade signing himself Pardaillan by way of a response to my recent article "Authoritarian Rehashes," in which I targeted certain authoritarian tendencies evident within our camp.[2]

I am always happy when I can find someone to contradict me because I am far from believing that I am always right and I hope that I can always learn something from the opposing case, so I am grateful to Pardaillan for having been so kind as to take my poor little piece under his notice. But I would have preferred greater clarity because, to be honest, I cannot quite fathom what motives prompted this comrade to answer me.

He says that in the past—and more specifically within movements in the immediate post-war years—better and more could be achieved. And who has any doubts about that? The same could always be said without fear of error, of any movement, even if one knows nothing about it and maybe especially if one knows nothing about it. But there is no point unless one identifies what those mistakes were, how they might have been avoided and, above all, what needs doing if there is to be no repetition. I readily confess that countless errors of action and omission have been made, albeit that, in specific instances, it might be the case that I regard as a merit that which others may see as a mistake and vice versa. But that was not the subject matter of the article in question.

Pardaillan insists on the necessity of *drafting a practical programme of short-term things to be done* in order to adapt anarchism to the real situation today and tomorrow, and I whole-heartedly agree. Of course, even on this score, and especially on this score, a distinction needs to be made between practical proposals that might actually lead towards the achievement of anarchy and those that, in order to

---

1 Translated from "A proposito di 'revisionismo,'" *L'Adunata dei Refrattari* (New York) 10, no. 28 (1 August 1931).

2 Malatesta's earlier article "Rimasticature autoritarie" had first appeared in *Il Risveglio Anarchico* (Geneva) of 1 May and had been reprinted in *L'Adunata dei Refrattari* of 23 May. *Il Martello* was the anarchist periodical edited in New York by Carlo Tresca. Pardaillan was the pseudonym of R. Tavani.

secure a few real or imagined short term benefits might lead us to renege upon the libertarian nature of our programme and place us on a course leading to a goal opposed to our own goal. But that was not the subject matter of my article either.

In that article I confined myself to countering the notion articulated by some comrades that in the coming revolution we should force people to do as we want until such time as they are persuaded that we are right and will do unsolicited that which we will initially have forced them into doing. Tantamount to setting ourselves up as a government and working a genuine miracle, that is, a government in a hurry to leave the scene and hell bent on making itself redundant.

Pardaillan says that this is not what the "revisionists" are after, or at any rate, not what he wants. Instead, he wants to *bring about a situation where it is not feasible for some to compel the rest*; which, let it be said, is anarchism summed up.

And after that?

If that is how things stand, we are in agreement and Pardaillan could have spared himself the chore of answering me. All I could say to him would be that he should carry on with his critique and his investigations, specify the mistakes he deplores and the cures he proposes and assist in the drafting of the practical program close to his heart. And do so without fear of being "excommunicated." We have no pontiffs in our ranks to usher people into or ban them from entering what he terms the anarchist church; and there is no need for any. Anybody who no longer feels himself to be an anarchist withdraws voluntarily, with greater or lesser bluntness and elegance; and anybody who feels like an anarchist remains such even if he is alone in his opinion about the tactical interpretation of anarchism.

***

Yet do we really see eye to eye?

Despite every appearance, the tone of the letter, and the very fact that he felt impelled to reply to me make me suspect that there is no agreement, deep down. And so I should like to ask him to explain himself plainly on the matter of "government."

It is not a matter of quibbling over the various meanings of the term government and of including either the rules according to which a home or an enterprise is run, or the agreement between the members of an association, or the modalities of social coexistence thrust upon us by necessity and voluntarily accepted, or the technical management of some task or social function, etc.

When anarchists say they want to abolish government, they are plainly talking about government in the historical and political sense of the word, as generally understood and accepted, to wit, a person or group of persons holding a monopoly and command over an armed force and who use it to impose its will upon the people; its will, naturally, mirrors ideas and interests of their own as well as those of a party or class.

Does Pardaillan reject such a government, regardless of its derivation and the persons who make it up?

Does he think that a government (in the aforementioned sense of the word) naturally tends—by virtue of the demands of its existence and the corruptive impact that power being more or less unaccountable, has upon men—tends, as I say, to curtail and suppress the freedom of all and to support or conjure up a privileged class with a common interest in shoring up the established order? Does he think that the difference between one government and another, that is, between the greater or lesser measure of freedom that it leaves the people, depends not so much on the kindness or criminality, cleverness or stupidity of those who govern as on the consciousness and resistance of the governed?

Or does he think, rather, that a government made up of "anarchists" would and could organise the life of society along egalitarian and libertarian lines, school the people in freedom and solidarity and set itself the target of making itself redundant as quickly as it can?

Does he think that in order to *bring about a situation where it is not feasible for some to compel the rest* we must begin by forcing folk to do what we want?

Does he think that we anarchists are that much better than everybody else and by nature so superior that we can withstand the corruptive influence of power and, forgive the vulgar comparison, get oak trees to bring forth figs? And also, is he not afraid that when there is a chance of taking up a position of command in anarchy's name, lots of politicians would call themselves "anarchists," just as they call themselves "socialists" when they have hopes of becoming deputies in socialism's name?

Does it not occur to him that we ought to act as anarchists at all times, even at the risk of being defeated, thereby renouncing a victory that might be our victory as individuals, but would be the defeat of our ideas?

I should like to have Pardaillan's answers to these and other similar questions that he himself can guess, not so much in order to establish who is right and who is wrong (in the final analysis events will decide that) but in order to see where we agree and disagree, so as to be able to debate usefully without beating about the bush.

***

And now, leaving the polemic with Pardaillan to one side, I should like to set out my opinion on the reason why some comrades, whose sincerity and ardent yearning for anarchy to succeed are beyond question, are led to expose the very foundations of anarchism to discussion.

The same sort of things befall every party in the wake of a setback and there would be nothing odd if the same thing were to hit our ranks. But it seems to me that in our case this frantic quest for new paths is not so much the consequence of newer, bolder, and truer ideas as the effect of the persistence of old illusions that these comrades, for all their long experience, still hope to immediately turn into reality, just as we hoped back when the movement was just starting out.

Sixty or more years ago, we used to think that anarchy and communism could come about as the direct, immediate consequence of a successful insurrection. It is not, we used to say, a matter of achieving some day anarchy and communism, but of starting the social revolution with anarchy and communism. In our manifestoes we would repeat that on the very evening of the day on which the government forces will be routed, each can have his basic needs met and savor the benefits of the revolution without further delay.

In a nutshell, that was the notion that, after being embraced by Kropotkin later on, was popularized by him and well nigh fixed as anarchism's definitive program.

Our confidence, our all too juvenile cocksureness, were based on a number of mistakes.

For a start, bedazzled like most people by full grain stores and warehouses filled to overflowing with unsold goods, it was our belief that everything necessary for living was available in superabundance and that one had only to stretch out a hand and one would find anything he needed.

Besides, we were convinced that the people, eager for freedom and justice, also had the ability to self-organize spontaneously and to look to their own interests by themselves.

In our opinion, it would be enough to knock down the material obstacles, to wit, the armed forces that defended the property-owners, and everything else would take care of itself.

We were out, above all else, to perfect our ideal, deluding ourselves that the masses would fall in behind us, and actually believing that we were merely spokesmen for the deep-seated instincts of those masses.

We were few in number but had boundless confidence in the efficacy of propaganda. Our rationale for this was as naïve as could be: if, we reckoned, the propaganda made by ten of us has made our numbers increase to twenty within a month, now that there are twenty of us, give us another month and there will be forty and from forty up to eighty and so on and so on. Our numbers doubling on a monthly basis, it would not be long before we had strength enough to make the revolution.

The rapid organisation of trades bodies and the spirit of solidarity between the oppressed in their struggle for emancipation would iron out every difficulty. The International Working Men's Association (the First International), which was then thriving better than ever, seemed to be ready to replace the bourgeois organisation of society with its own.

Given that outlook, we were clearly bound to believe that anarchy would arise at once, spontaneously, through the determination and capabilities of the entire population or at any rate of the conscious, active segment of the population, once released from the brute force that held it in subjection.

But with the passage of time, study and, more so, harsh experience, showed us that many of our beliefs were wishful thinking generated by our hopes rather than corresponding to hard facts.

Indeed, we registered the fact that the goods available were, on account of the capitalist system of production, normally in short supply and were in any case so unequally distributed around the various agricultural and urban regions and localities that even a short-lived disruption of transportation and commerce would bring shortage and hunger to the most populous places.

And, what is worse, we were forced to take it on board that the masses were not possessed of the virtues with which we had been crediting them. One section of them, and in some areas the vast majority of them, stultified by poverty and religion, was a blind, unwitting instrument in the hands of the oppressors, for deployment against themselves and against any who dared rebel against oppression. The other section, which, being more evolved and blessed by environmental factors, was most accessible to our propaganda, was, as a rule, possessed neither of independence of mind, nor burning desire for freedom; having been inured to obedience, even in their aspirations and revolutionary attempts they craved guidance, direction and commands; having no spirit of enterprise, they waited for leaders to tell them what it was to do, rather than brave the effort and risk involved in thinking and acting freely, and either they remained inert, or were hobbled if their leaders were lazy, inept, or treacherous.

True, there were those among the masses who had what it takes to make good anarchists and it was up to propaganda to find them and shape them; but, unfortunately, propaganda was not as powerful as we, starry eyed after our first few swift successes, had thought. Facts showed us that in a given economic, political, and moral setting, a given number of individuals predisposed by special conditions could be converted, after which it was increasingly difficult and well nigh impossible to draw in fresh recruits until such time as fresh possibilities were opened up by the economic or political events that came along. After a certain point, numbers could only be expanded by whittling away at and tinkering with our programme; as witness the case of the democratic socialists who managed to rally impressive followings, but who had, in order to do so, been obliged to stop being genuinely socialists.

***

That being how things were, what were we to do? Withdraw from the struggle, become sceptic and apathetic, or give up on anarchy and join an authoritarian party?

Some did just that; but most of us, those whose minds harbored the "sacred fire," were more than ever seized with the nobility and grandeur of the mission that anarchists had taken upon themselves. Such folk remained convinced that the aspiration to comprehensive freedom (what we might term the anarchist spirit) has always been behind all personal and social progress, whereas political and economic privileges (which are, after all, merely different facets of the same oppression), unless sufficiently harried by anarchism, tend to drive humanity backwards towards darkest barbarism. They realized that anarchy can only come about gradually, as the masses become able to conceive it and desire it; but will never come to pass unless driven forward by a more or less consciously anarchist minority operating in such a way as to create the appropriate climate.

Remaining anarchist and acting like anarchists in every possible circumstance continued to be the duty that we were choosing and embracing.

***

I stated above that, in my view, the so-called revisionists, being still under the sway of the primitive anarchism, are kidding themselves that they can bring communism and anarchy about in a single stroke; but since even they realise that the masses are not yet ready, engage in the nonsense of expecting to prepare them using authoritarian methods. They are rather mealy-mouthed about this and I reckon that they themselves are not entirely aware of it, but it seems to us that the facts are these: they would like to conjure up communism by putting freedom on the long finger and would like to school the people in freedom by means of tyranny.

It seems to me, and I reckon that this may be the view of nearly every anarchist by now, that the revolution cannot start out with communism, unless that communism would be, as in Russia, the communism of the monastery, barracks, and prison and worse than capitalism itself. It must do immediately whatever it can, but no more than it can. It would be enough to start by attacking political authority and economic privilege by every possible means; breaking up the army and all police corps; arming every single member of the population; commandeering all foodstuffs for the good of all and ensuring uninterrupted supply lines; and driving the masses, above all driving the masses into acting without waiting for orders from on high. And stressing that nothing should be destroyed unless there is something better to be put in its place. Then we can progress towards organising a voluntary communism or whatever other arrangements (most likely many and varied) for social living the workers might prefer in the light of experience.

***

If anarchists wanted to take the functions of government upon themselves alone (something they would not be strong enough to do, by the way) or, worse still, were out to join with the authoritarian parties in order to lay down laws and binding regulations, they would be simply betraying themselves and the revolution. In which case, rather than driving for anarchism by means of their propaganda and example, they would, willy-nilly, contribute to robbing the people of any gains made during the period of insurrection: ultimately, they would be doing that which all governments have always done.

Forthcoming from Davide Turcato and AK Press:

"Whoever is Poor is a Slave":
The Internationalist Period and the South America Exile, 1871–89

"Let's Go to the People":
L'Associazione and the London Years of 1889–97

"A Long and Patient Work...":
The Anarchist Socialism of *L'Agitazione*, 1897–98

"Towards Anarchy":
Malatesta in America, 1899–1900

"The Armed Strike":
The Long London Exile of 1900–13

"Is Revolution Possible?":
Volontà, the Red Week and the War, 1913–18

"United Proletarian Front":
The Red Biennium, *Umanità Nova* and Fascism, 1919–23

"Achievable and Achieving Anarchism":
Pensiero e Volontà and Last Writings, 1924–32

"What Anarchists Want":
Pamphlets, Programmes, Manifestos and Other Miscellaneous Publications

"Yours and for Anarchy...":
Malatesta's Correspondence

Support **AK Press!**

AK Press is one of the world's largest and most productive anarchist publishing houses. We're entirely worker-run & democratically managed. We operate without a corporate structure–no boss, no managers, no bullshit. We publish close to twenty books every year, and distribute thousands of other titles published by other like-minded independent presses and projects from around the globe.

The Friends of AK program is a way that you can directly contribute to the continued existence of AK Press, and ensure that we're able to keep publishing great books just like this one! Friends pay $25 a month directly into our publishing account ($30 for Canada, $35 for international), and receive a copy of every book AK Press publishes for the duration of their membership! Friends also receive a discount on anything they order from our website or buy at a table: 50% on AK titles, and 20% on everything else. We've also added a new Friends of AK ebook program: $15 a month gets you an electronic copy of every book we publish for the duration of your membership. Combine it with a print subscription, too!

There's great stuff in the works–so sign up now to become a Friend of AK Press, and let the presses roll!

Won't you be our friend? Email friendsofak@akpress.org for more info, or visit the Friends of AK Press website: www.akpress.org/programs/friendsofak